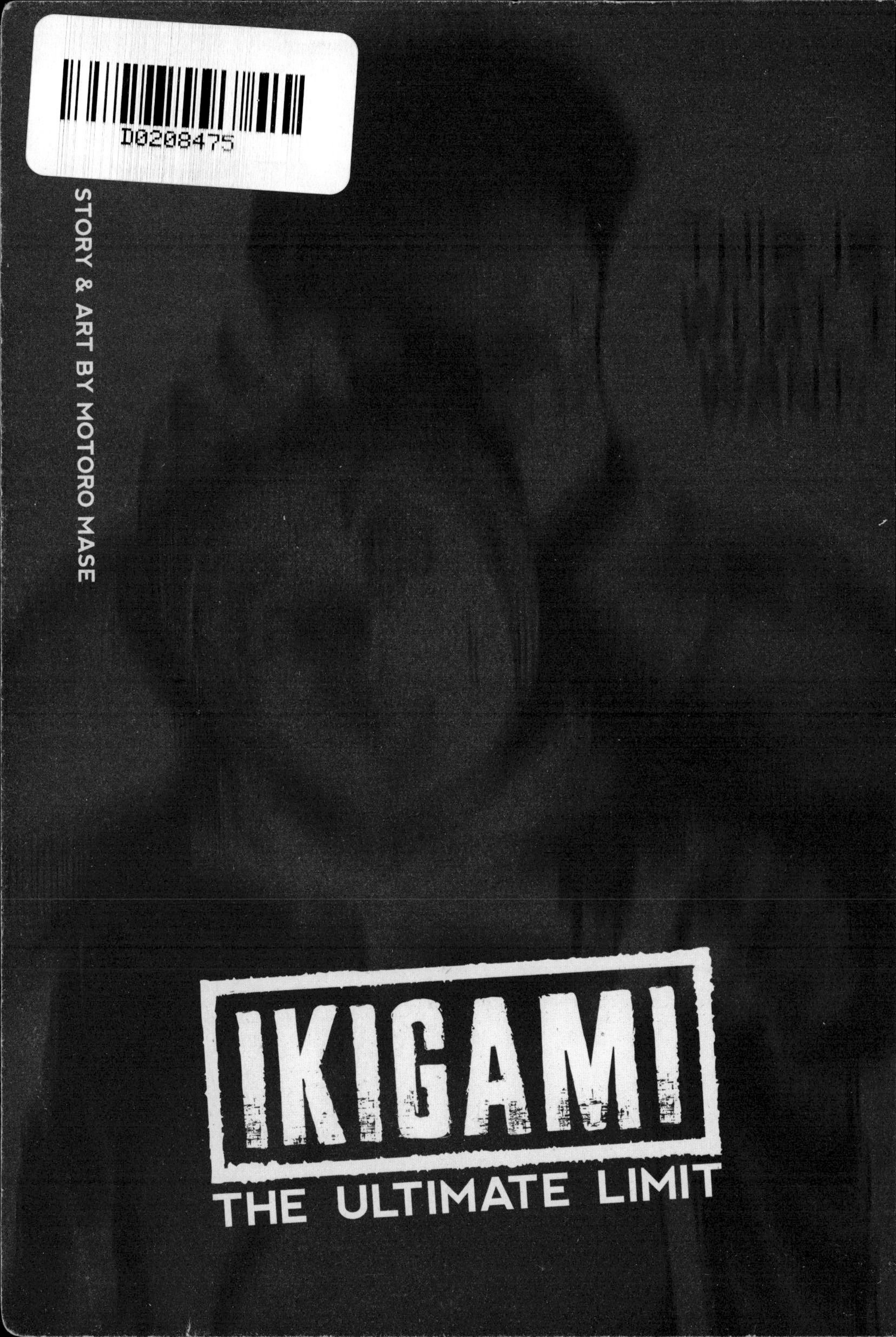

STORY & ART BY MOTORO MASE

IKIGAMI

THE ULTIMATE LIMIT

IKIGAMI
THE ULTIMATE LIMIT

The VIZ Media Edition

STORY AND ART BY Motoro Mase

Translation/John Werry
English Adaptation/Kristina Blachere
Touch-up Art & Lettering/Freeman Wong
Design/Amy Martin
Editor/Joel Enos

Editor in Chief, Books/Alvin Lu
Editor in Chief, Magazines/Marc Weidenbaum
VP, Publishing Licensing/Rika Inouye
VP, Sales & Product Marketing/Gonzalo Ferreyra
VP, Creative/Linda Espinosa
Publisher/Hyoe Narita

IKIGAMI 1 by Motoro MASE
© 2005 Motoro MASE
All rights reserved. Original Japanese edition
published in 2005 by Shogakukan Inc., Tokyo.

Printed in the U.S.A.

Published by VIZ Media, LLC
P.O. Box 77010
San Francisco, CA 94107

VIZ Media Edition
10 9 8 7 6 5 4 3 2 1
First printing, May 2009

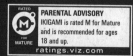

www.viz.com   store.viz.com

IKIGAMI

THE ULTIMATE LIMIT

VOL. 1   STORY & ART BY MOTORO MASE

THE ULTIMATE LIMIT

CONTENTS

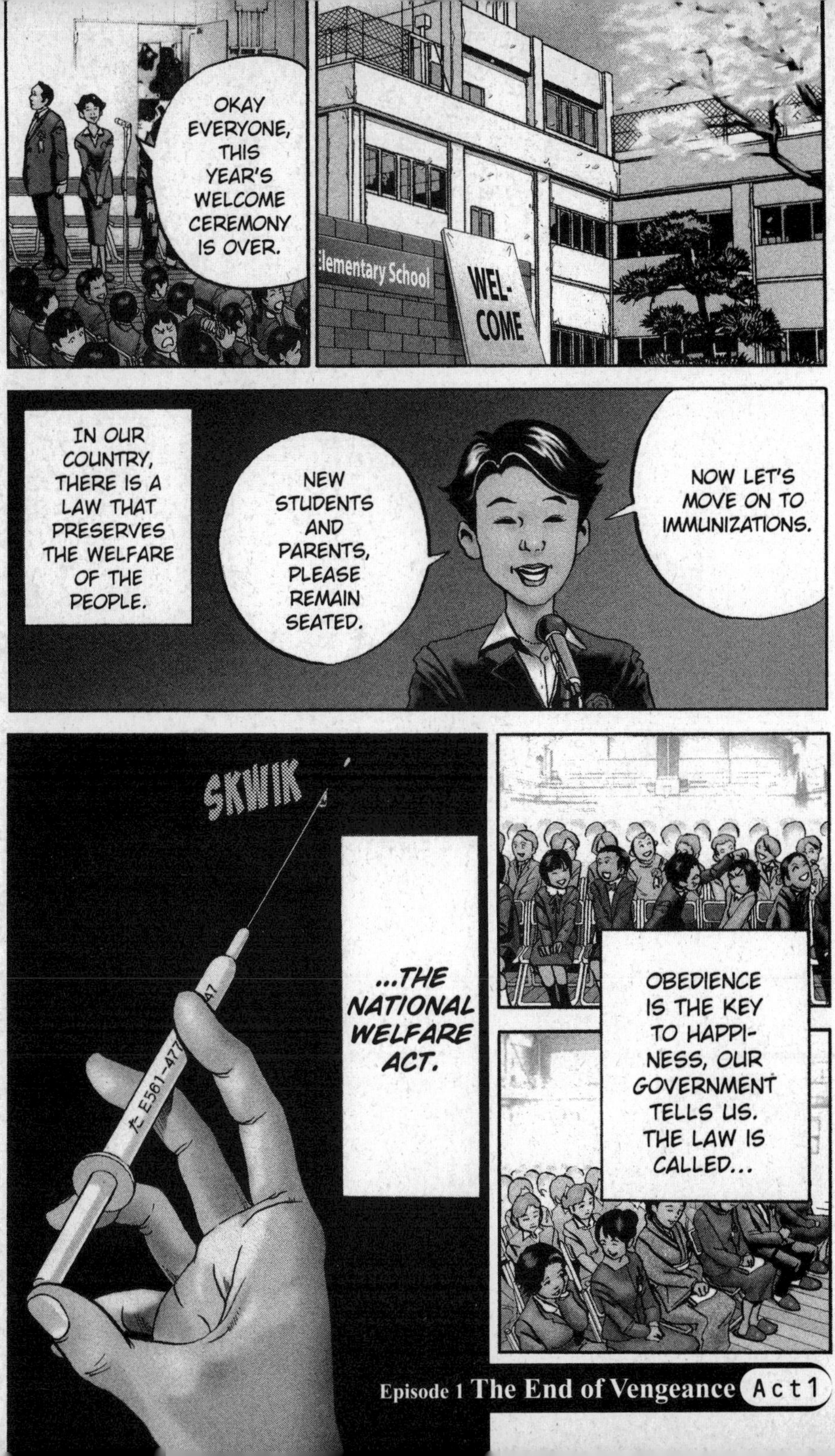
Elementary School
WEL-
COME
OKAY EVERYONE, THIS YEAR'S WELCOME CEREMONY IS OVER.
NOW LET'S MOVE ON TO IMMUNIZATIONS.
NEW STUDENTS AND PARENTS, PLEASE REMAIN SEATED.
IN OUR COUNTRY, THERE IS A LAW THAT PRESERVES THE WELFARE OF THE PEOPLE.
OBEDIENCE IS THE KEY TO HAPPI-NESS, OUR GOVERNMENT TELLS US. THE LAW IS CALLED...
SKWIK
...THE NATIONAL WELFARE ACT.
Episode 1 The End of Vengeance Act1

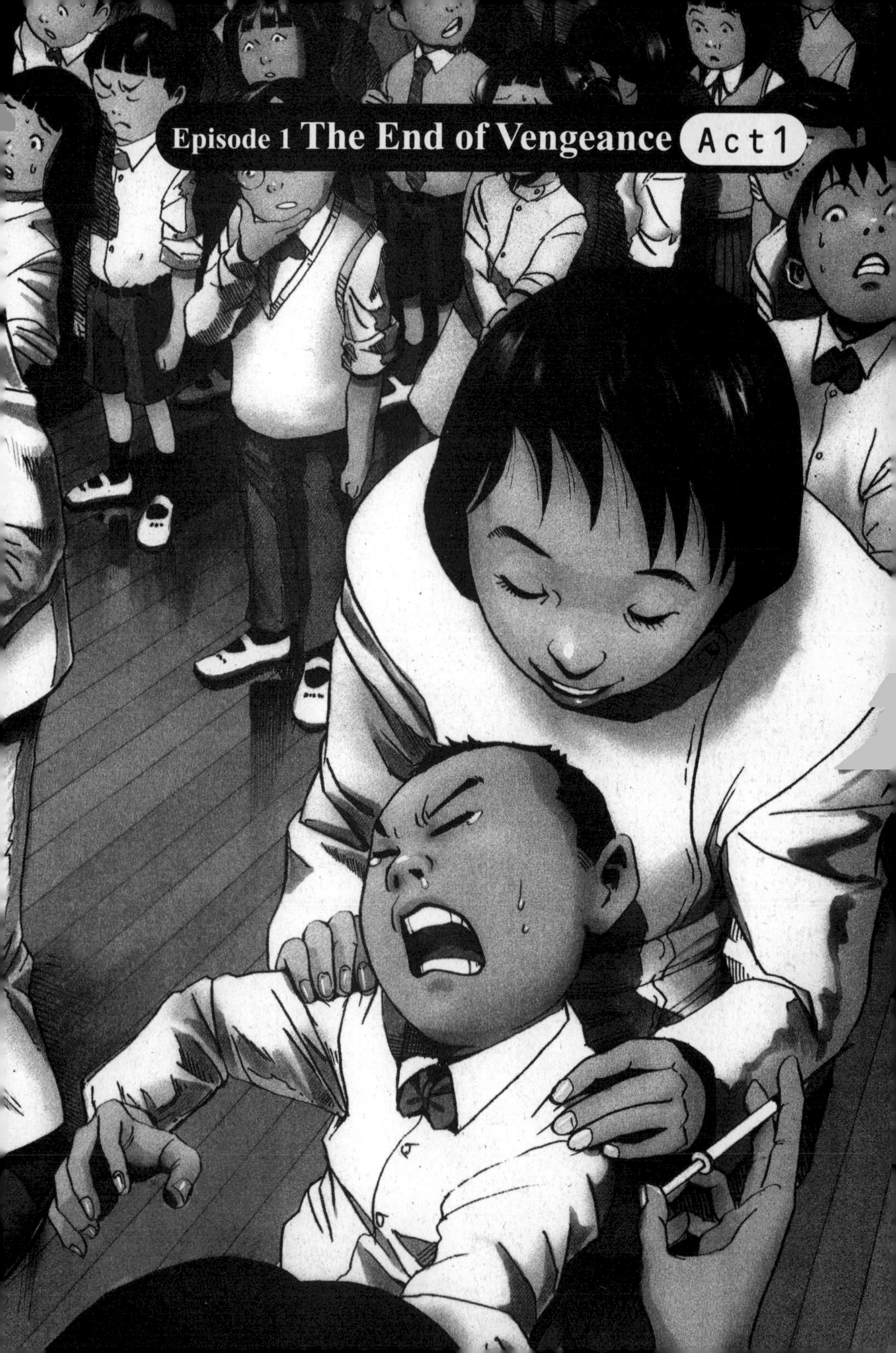
Episode 1 The End of Vengeance Act 1

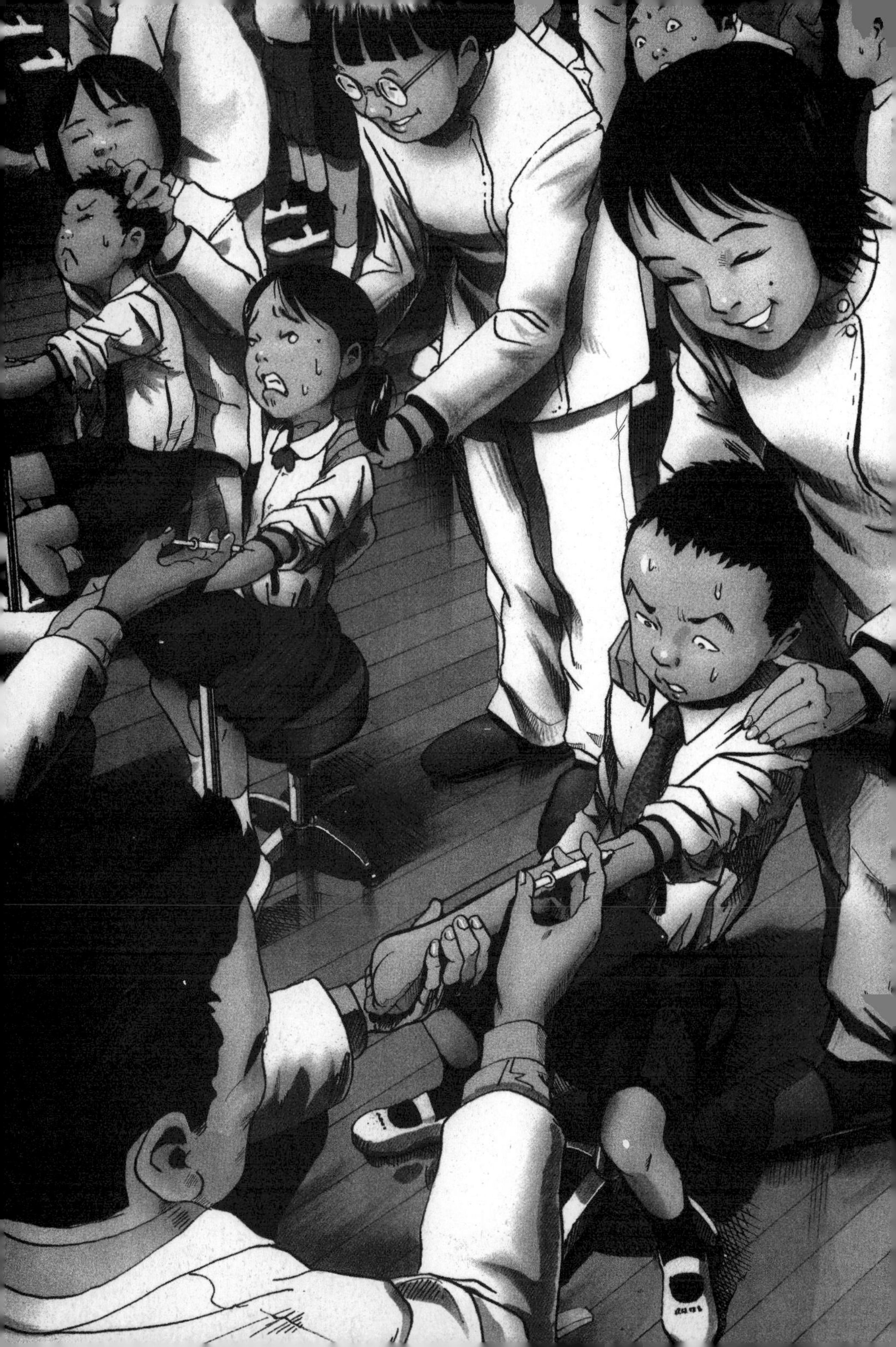

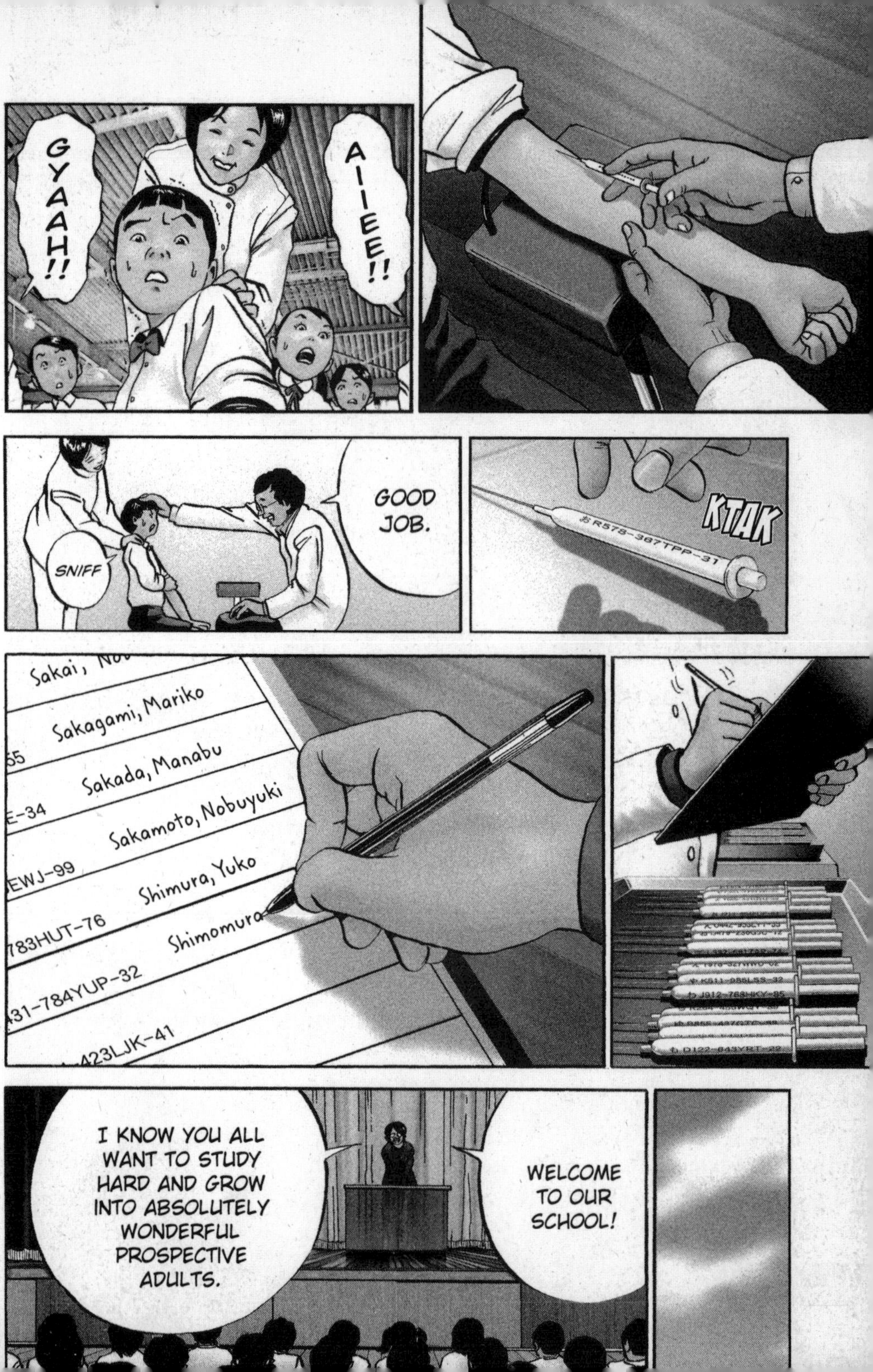
AIIEE!!
GYAAH!!
あR578-367TPP-31
KTAK
GOOD JOB.
SNIFF
Sakagami, Mariko
55
Sakada, Manabu
E-34
Sakamoto, Nobuyuki
EWJ-99
Shimura, Yuko
783HUT-76
Shimomura
431-784YUP-32
423LJK-41
WELCOME TO OUR SCHOOL!
I KNOW YOU ALL WANT TO STUDY HARD AND GROW INTO ABSOLUTELY WONDERFUL PROSPECTIVE ADULTS.

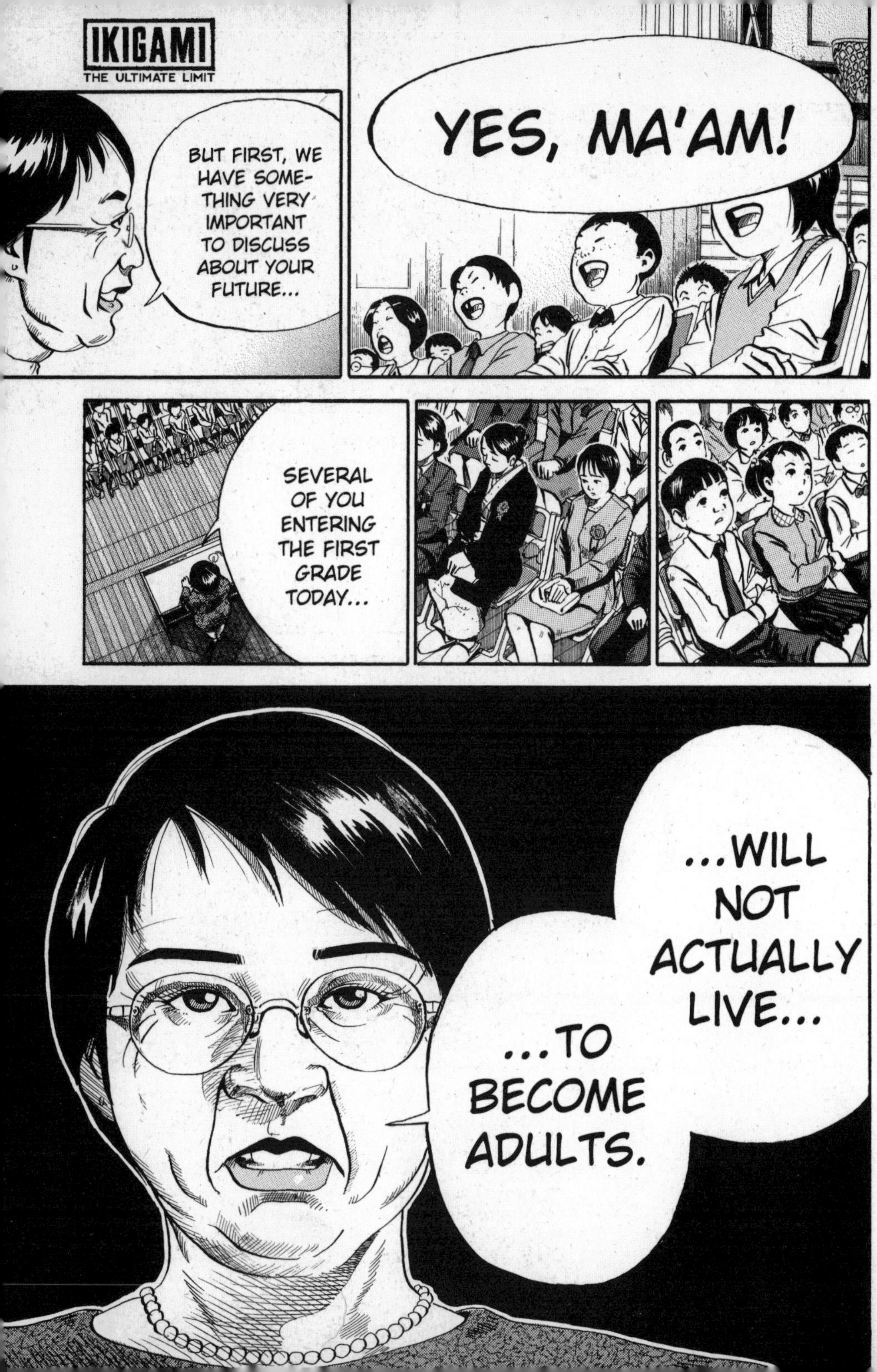
YES, MA'AM!
BUT FIRST, WE HAVE SOME-THING VERY IMPORTANT TO DISCUSS ABOUT YOUR FUTURE...
SEVERAL OF YOU ENTERING THE FIRST GRADE TODAY...
...WILL NOT ACTUALLY LIVE...
...TO BECOME ADULTS.

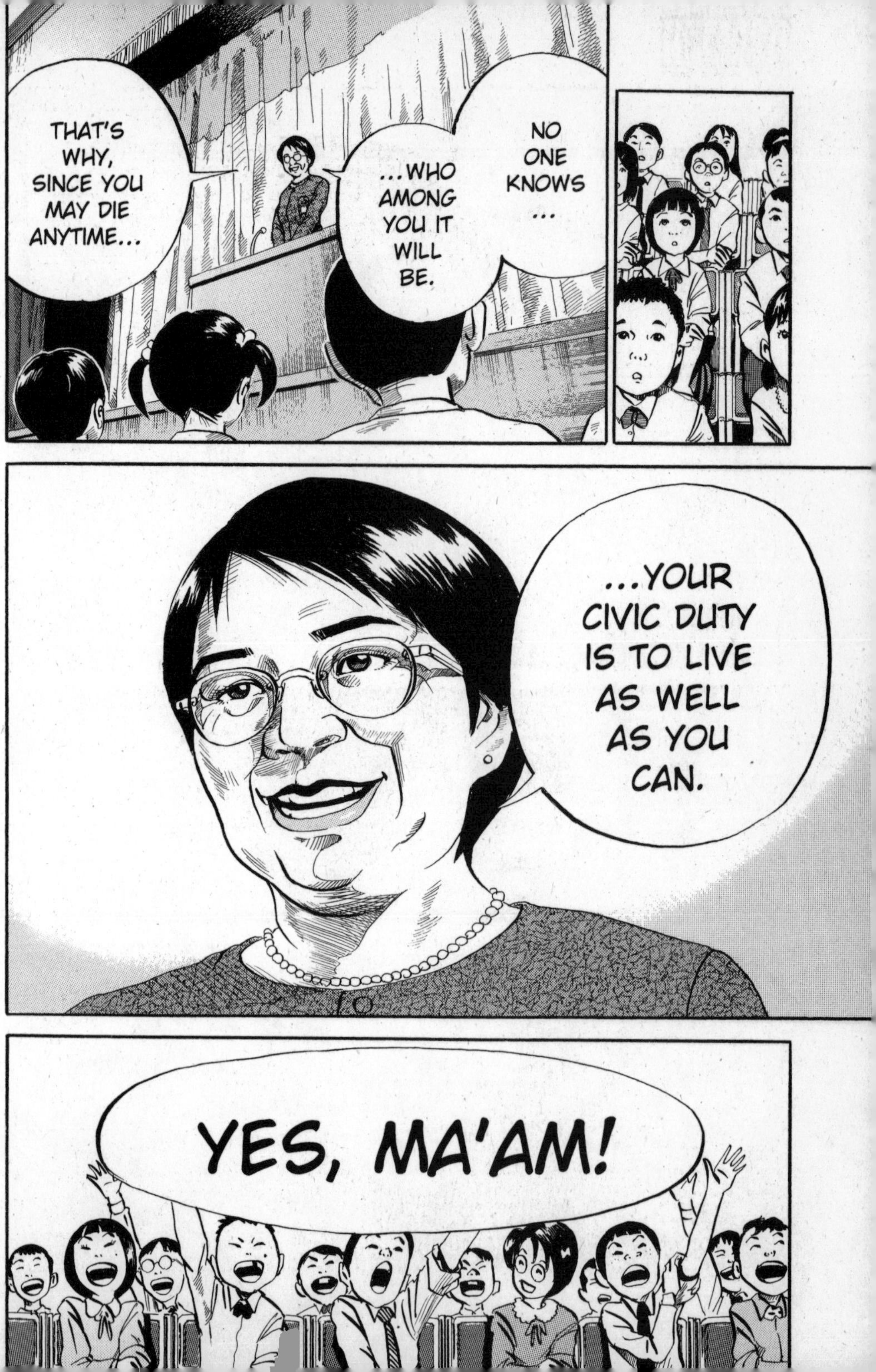
NO ONE KNOWS ...
...WHO AMONG YOU IT WILL BE.
THAT'S WHY, SINCE YOU MAY DIE ANYTIME...
...YOUR CIVIC DUTY IS TO LIVE AS WELL AS YOU CAN.
YES, MA'AM!

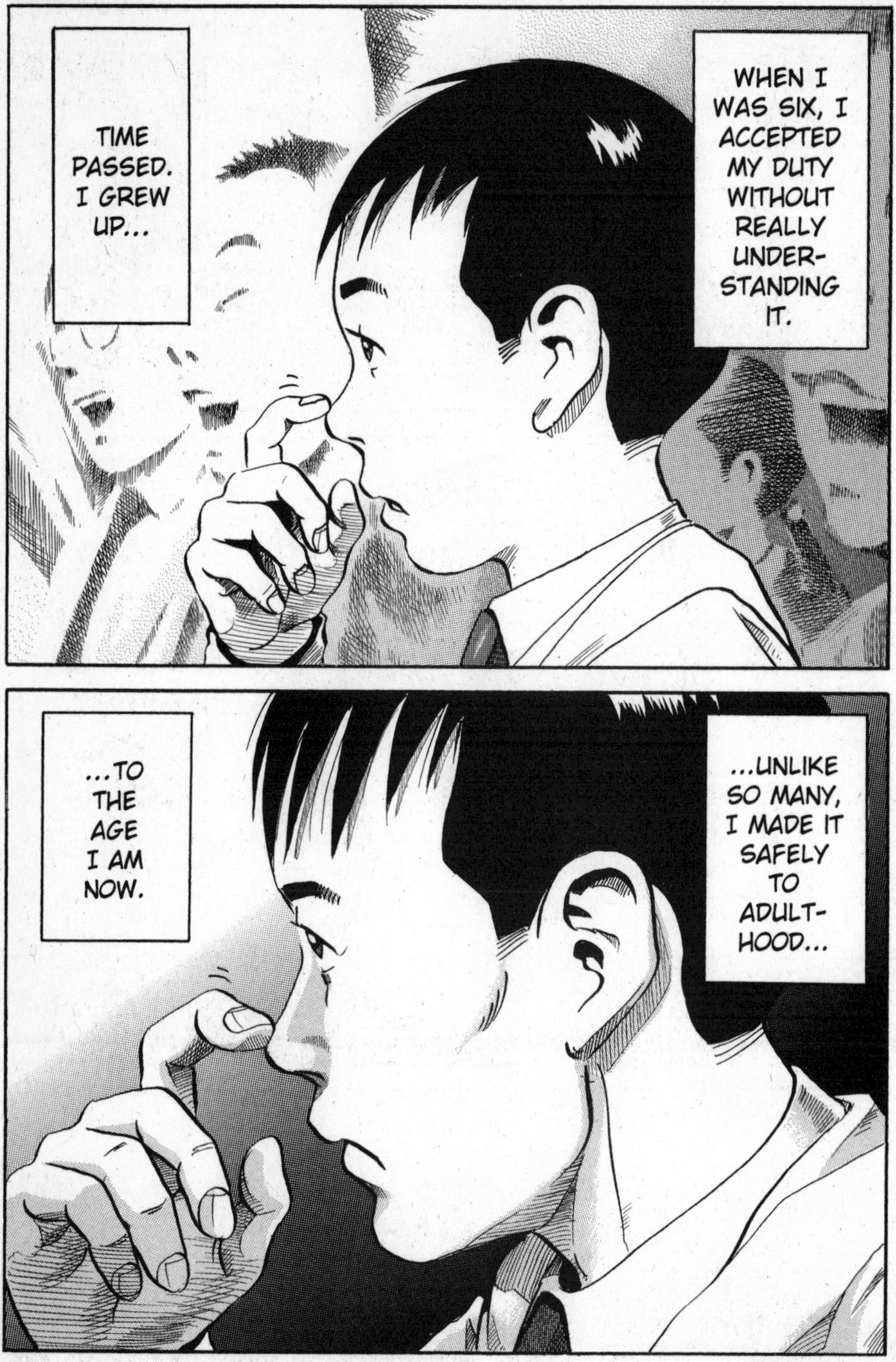
WHEN I WAS SIX, I ACCEPTED MY DUTY WITHOUT REALLY UNDER-STANDING IT.
TIME PASSED. I GREW UP...
...UNLIKE SO MANY, I MADE IT SAFELY TO ADULT-HOOD...
...TO THE AGE I AM NOW.

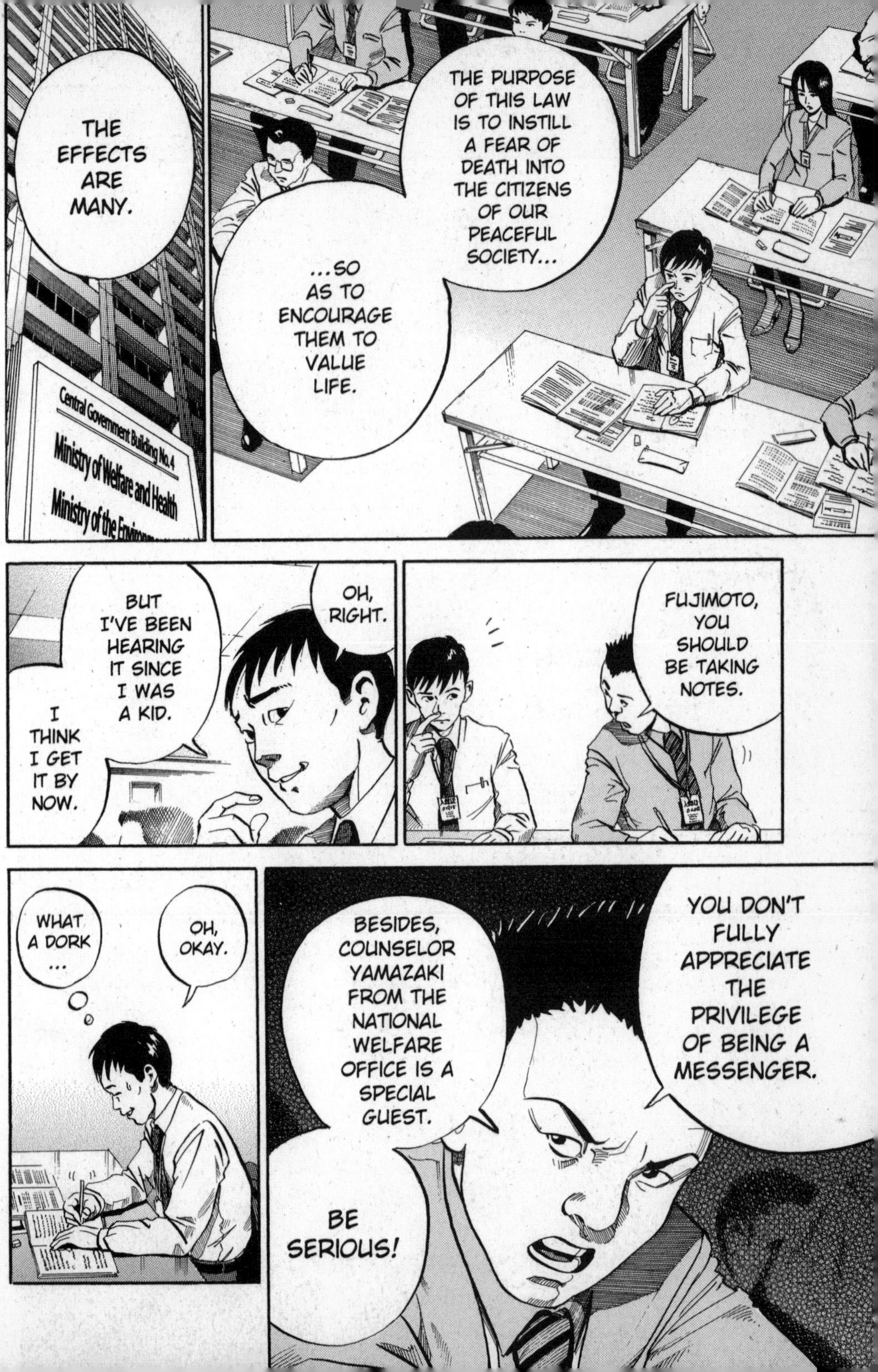
THE PURPOSE OF THIS LAW IS TO INSTILL A FEAR OF DEATH INTO THE CITIZENS OF OUR PEACEFUL SOCIETY...
...SO AS TO ENCOURAGE THEM TO VALUE LIFE.
THE EFFECTS ARE MANY.
Central Government Building No. 4
Ministry of Welfare and Health
FUJIMOTO, YOU SHOULD BE TAKING NOTES.
OH, RIGHT.
BUT I'VE BEEN HEARING IT SINCE I WAS A KID.
I THINK I GET IT BY NOW.
YOU DON'T FULLY APPRECIATE THE PRIVILEGE OF BEING A MESSENGER.
BESIDES, COUNSELOR YAMAZAKI FROM THE NATIONAL WELFARE OFFICE IS A SPECIAL GUEST.
BE SERIOUS!
OH, OKAY.
WHAT A DORK...

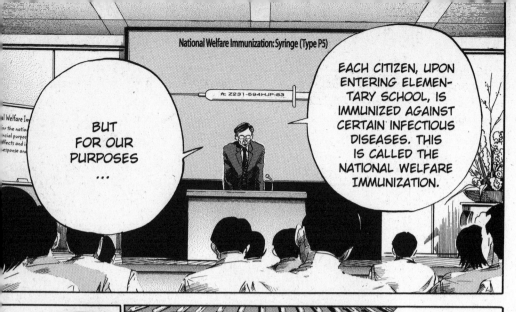

National Welfare Immunization: Syringe (Type P5)
た Z231-594HJP-83
EACH CITIZEN, UPON ENTERING ELEMENTARY SCHOOL, IS IMMUNIZED AGAINST CERTAIN INFECTIOUS DISEASES. THIS IS CALLED THE NATIONAL WELFARE IMMUNIZATION.
BUT FOR OUR PURPOSES ...
...WHAT'S IMPORTANT IS THAT 0.01 PERCENT OF THE SYRINGES CONTAIN...
...A SPECIAL NANO-CAPSULE.
ABOUT 1 IN 1,000 CITIZENS ARE INJECTED WITH THIS CAPSULE.
IT MOVES THROUGH THEIR BODY, EVENTUALLY COMING TO REST IN THE PULMONARY ARTERY.
PWAK
WHEN THE CITIZEN IS BETWEEN 18 TO 24 YEARS OLD, THE CAPSULE RUPTURES ON A PREDETERMINED DATE, KILLING THEM.

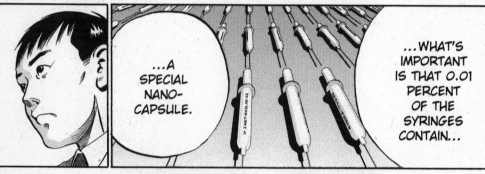

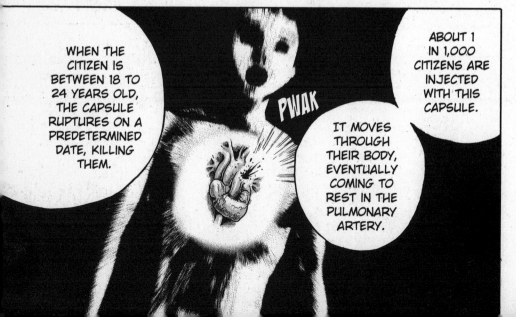

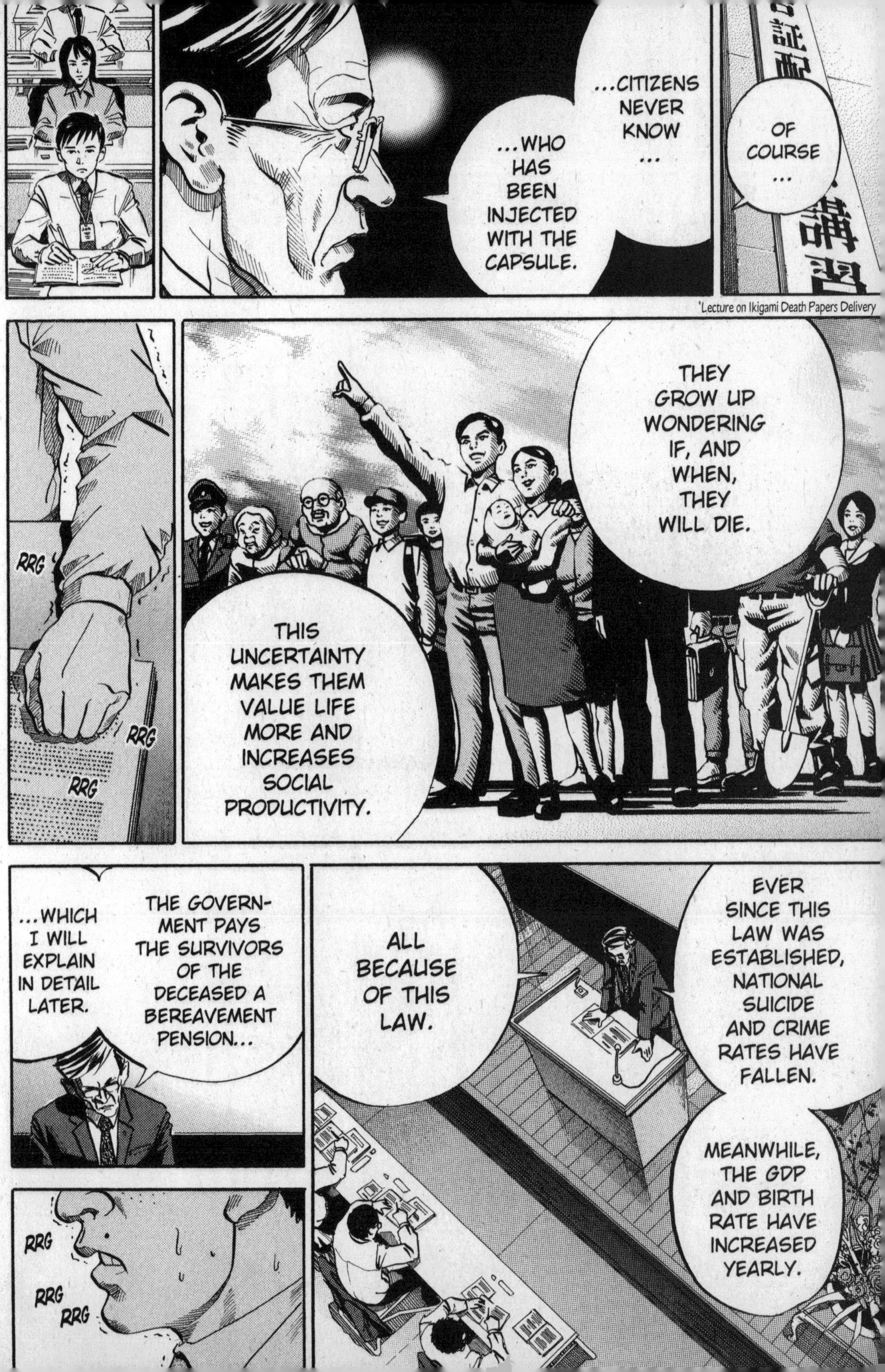
OF COURSE...
...CITIZENS NEVER KNOW...
...WHO HAS BEEN INJECTED WITH THE CAPSULE.
THEY GROW UP WONDERING IF, AND WHEN, THEY WILL DIE.
THIS UNCERTAINTY MAKES THEM VALUE LIFE MORE AND INCREASES SOCIAL PRODUCTIVITY.
RRG
RRG
RRG
EVER SINCE THIS LAW WAS ESTABLISHED, NATIONAL SUICIDE AND CRIME RATES HAVE FALLEN.
MEANWHILE, THE GDP AND BIRTH RATE HAVE INCREASED YEARLY.
ALL BECAUSE OF THIS LAW.
THE GOVERN-MENT PAYS THE SURVIVORS OF THE DECEASED A BEREAVEMENT PENSION...
...WHICH I WILL EXPLAIN IN DETAIL LATER.
RRG
RRG
RRG
*Lecture on Ikigami Death Papers Delivery

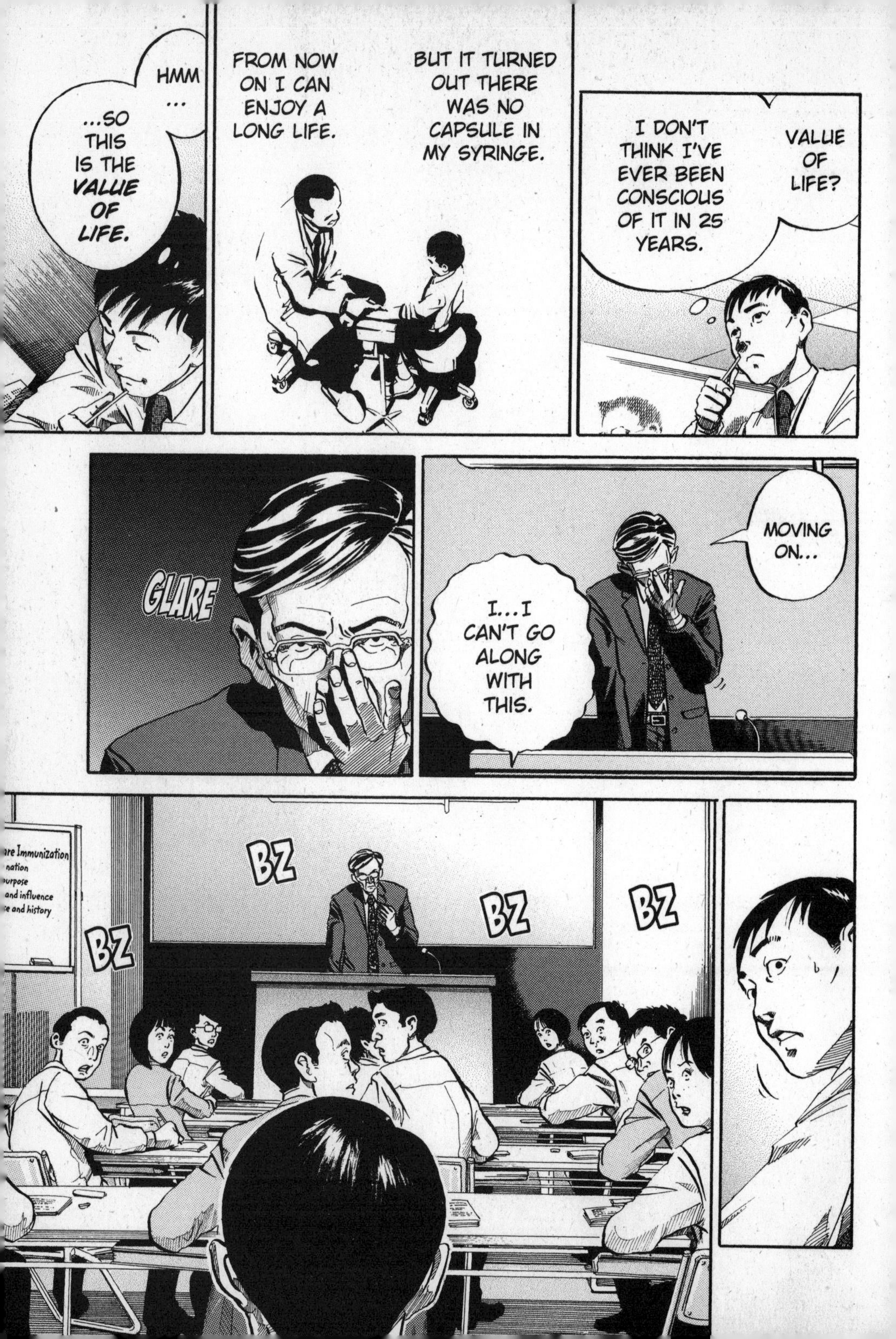
VALUE OF LIFE?
I DON'T THINK I'VE EVER BEEN CONSCIOUS OF IT IN 25 YEARS.
BUT IT TURNED OUT THERE WAS NO CAPSULE IN MY SYRINGE.
FROM NOW ON I CAN ENJOY A LONG LIFE.
HMM...
...SO THIS IS THE VALUE OF LIFE.
MOVING ON...
I...I CAN'T GO ALONG WITH THIS.
GLARE
BZ
BZ
BZ
are Immunization
nation
urpose
and influence
e and history
BZ

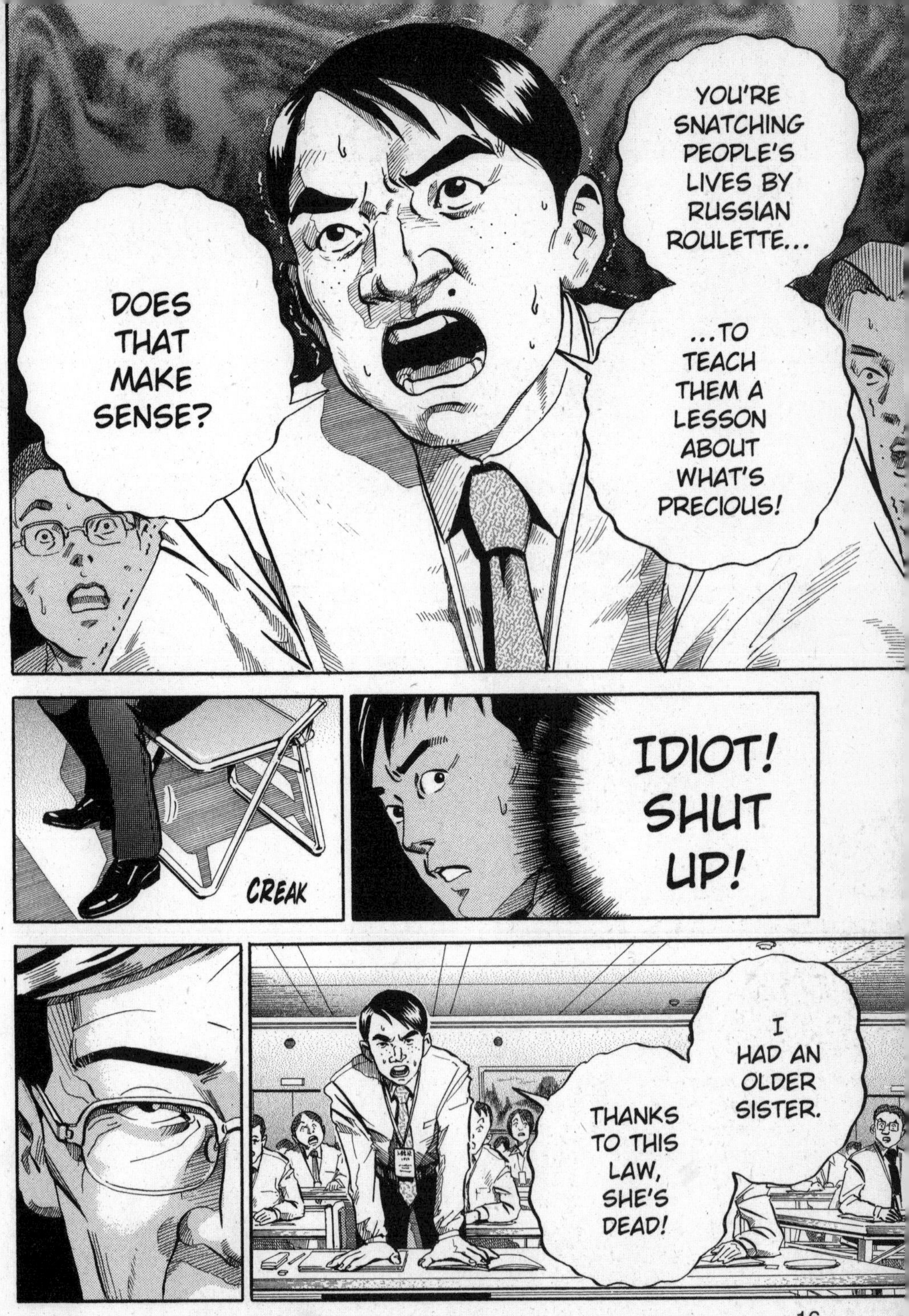
YOU'RE SNATCHING PEOPLE'S LIVES BY RUSSIAN ROULETTE...
...TO TEACH THEM A LESSON ABOUT WHAT'S PRECIOUS!
DOES THAT MAKE SENSE?
IDIOT! SHUT UP!
CREAK
...TO
I HAD AN OLDER SISTER.
THANKS TO THIS LAW, SHE'S DEAD!

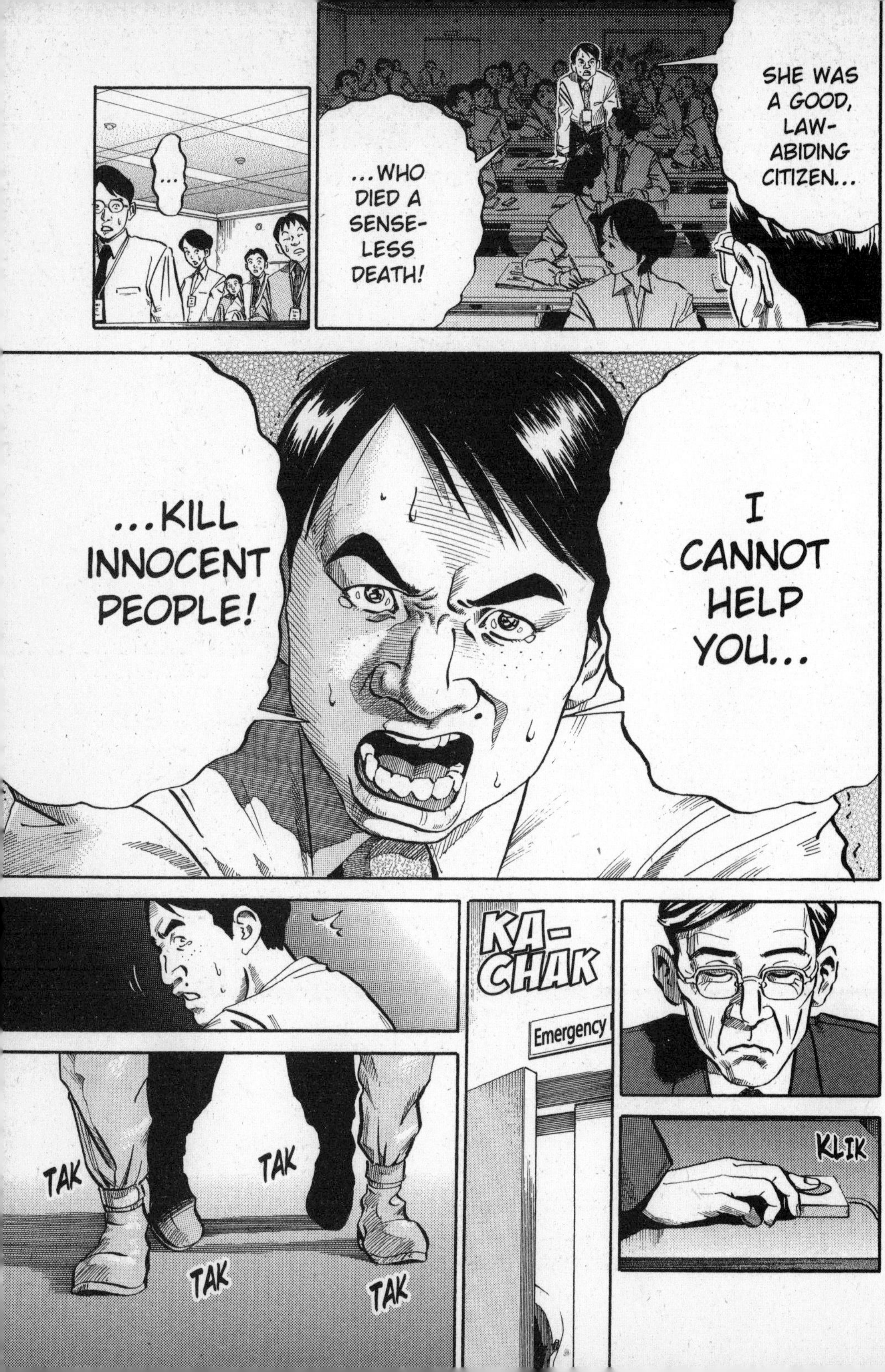
SHE WAS A GOOD, LAW-ABIDING CITIZEN...
...WHO DIED A SENSELESS DEATH!
...
I CANNOT HELP YOU...
...KILL INNOCENT PEOPLE!
KLIK
KA-CHAK
Emergency
TAK
TAK
TAK
TAK

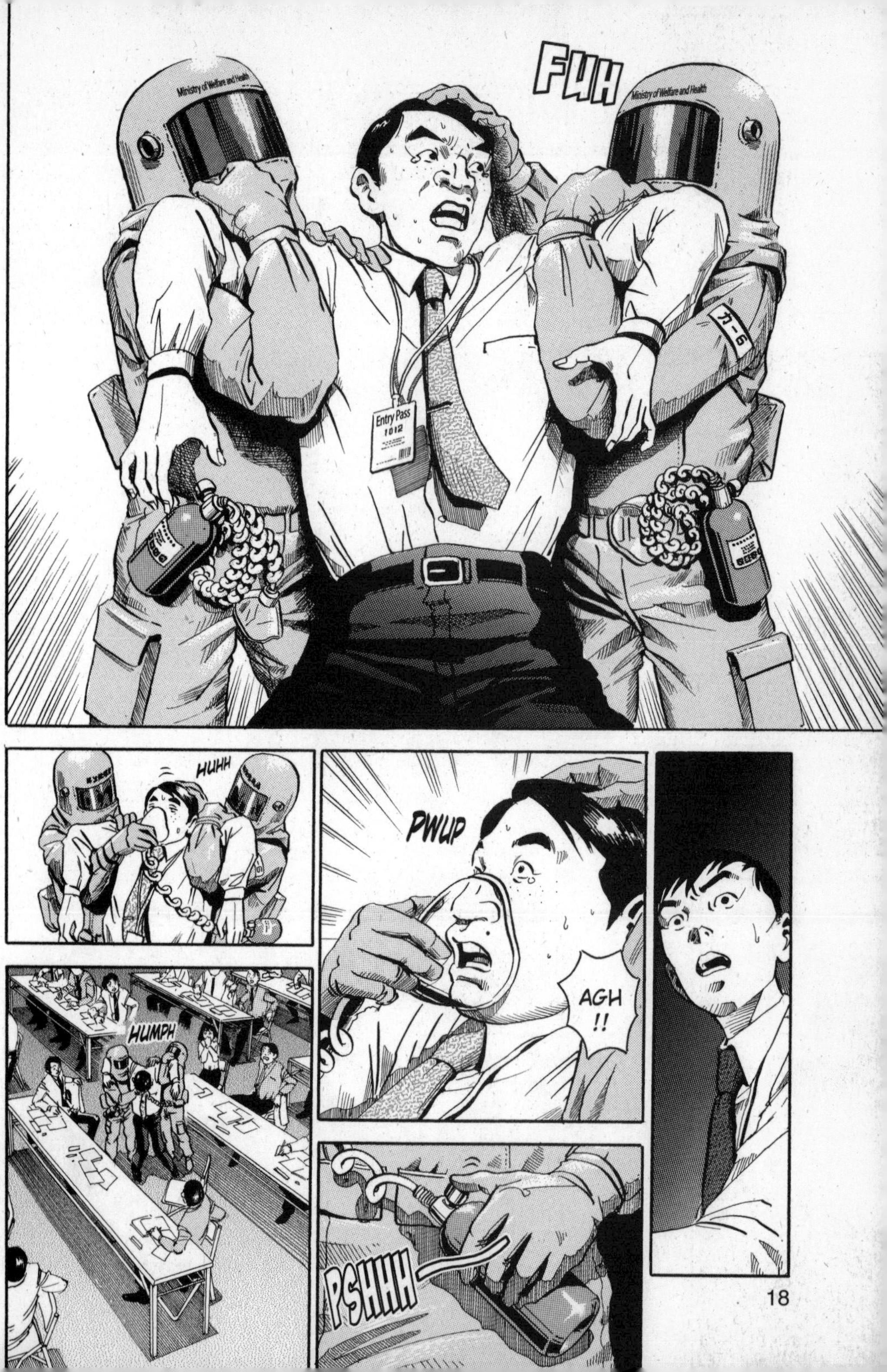
FUH
Ministry of Welfare and Health
Ministry of Welfare and Health
Entry Pass
1012
カ-6
PWUP
AGH !!
PSHHH
HUHH
HUMPH

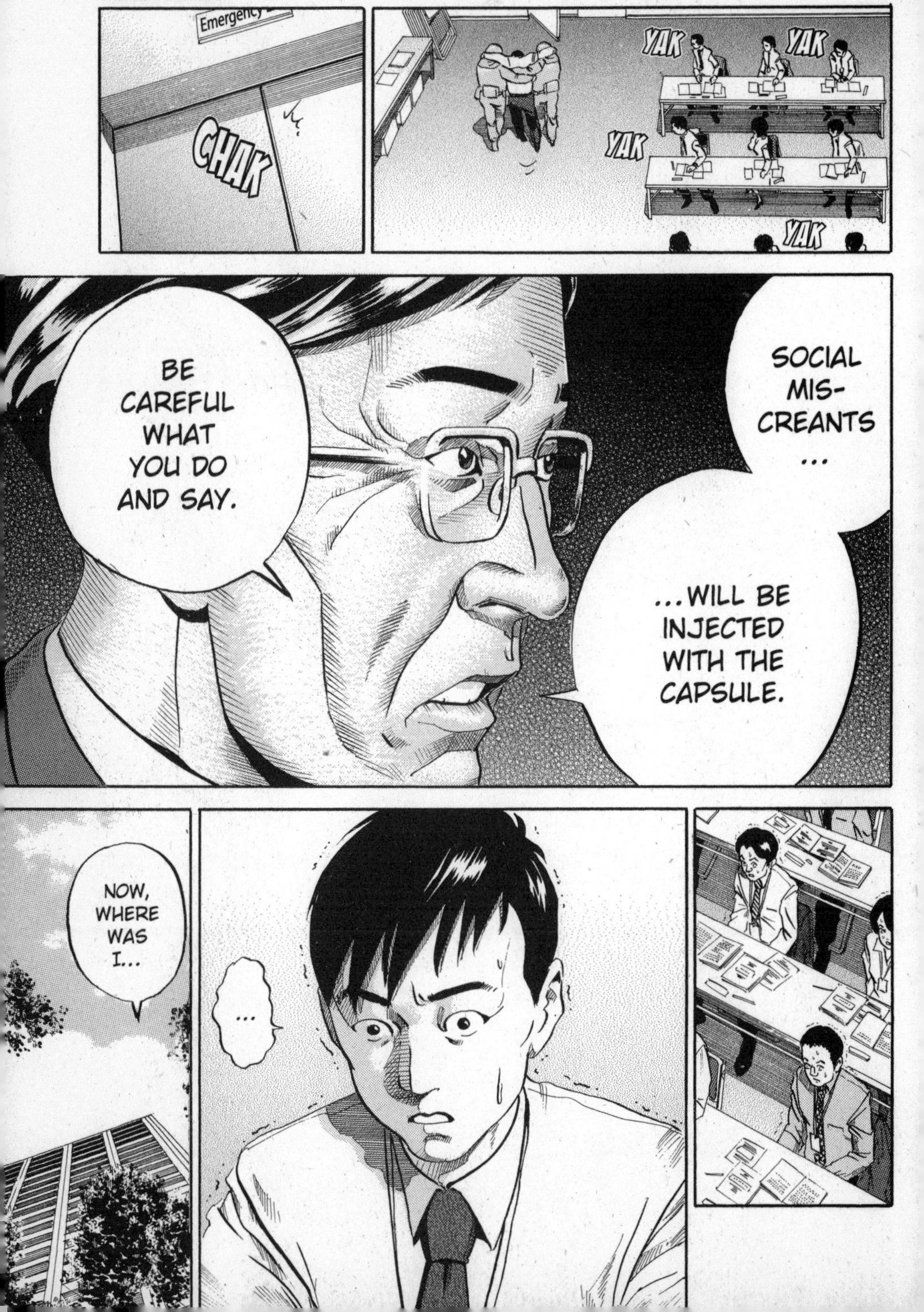
YAK
YAK
YAK
YAK
Emergency
CHAK
SOCIAL MIS-CREANTS...
...WILL BE INJECTED WITH THE CAPSULE.
BE CAREFUL WHAT YOU DO AND SAY.
...
NOW, WHERE WAS I...

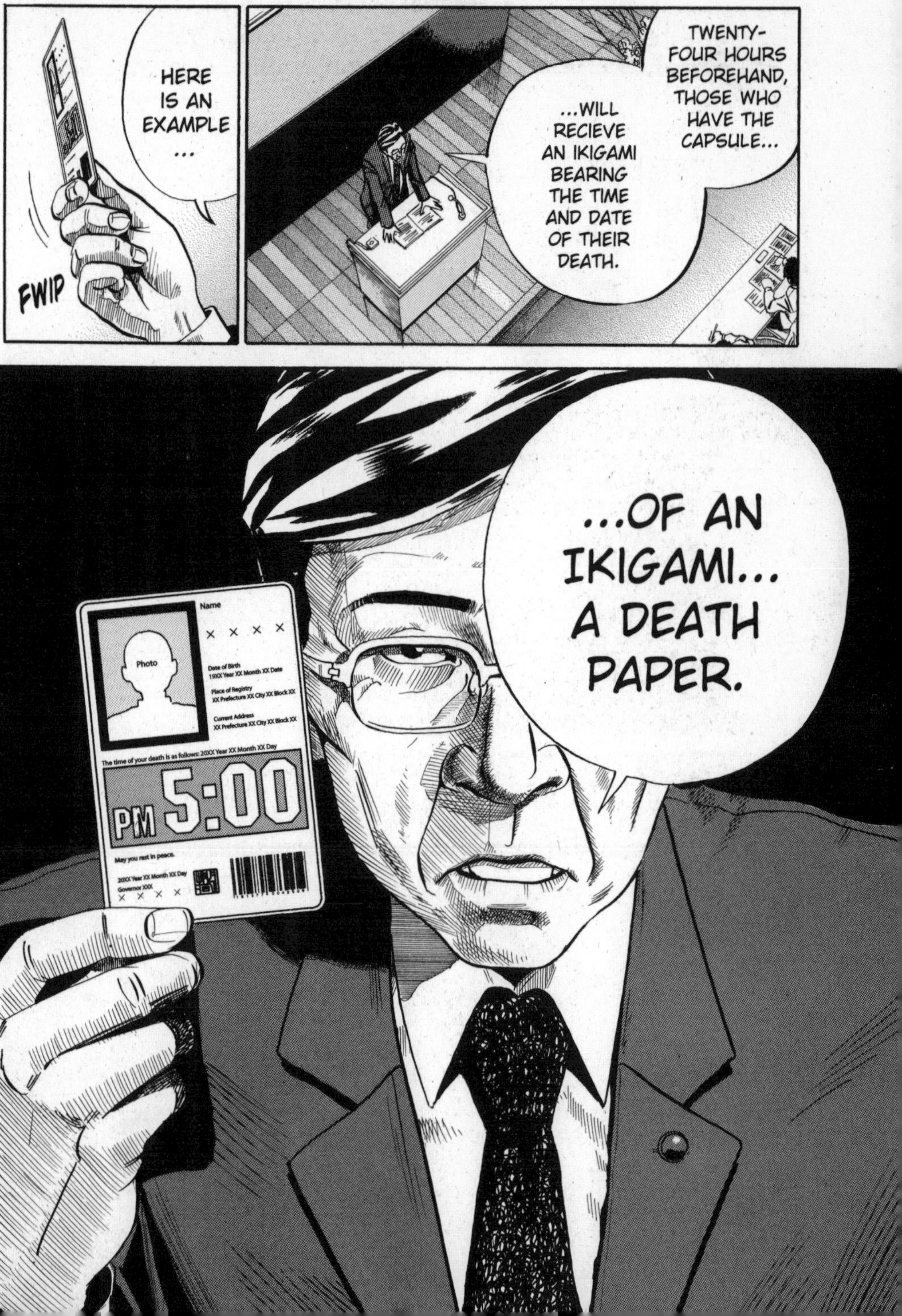
TWENTY-FOUR HOURS BEFOREHAND, THOSE WHO HAVE THE CAPSULE...
...WILL RECIEVE AN IKIGAMI BEARING THE TIME AND DATE OF THEIR DEATH.
HERE IS AN EXAMPLE ...
FWIP
...OF AN IKIGAMI... A DEATH PAPER.
Name
× × × ×
Photo
Date of Birth
19XX Year XX Month XX Date
Place of Registry
XX Prefecture XX City XX Block XX
Current Address
XX Prefecture XX City XX Block XX
The time of your death is as follows: 20XX Year XX Month XX Day
PM 5:00
May you rest in peace.
20XX Year XX Month XX Day
Governor XXX
× × × ×

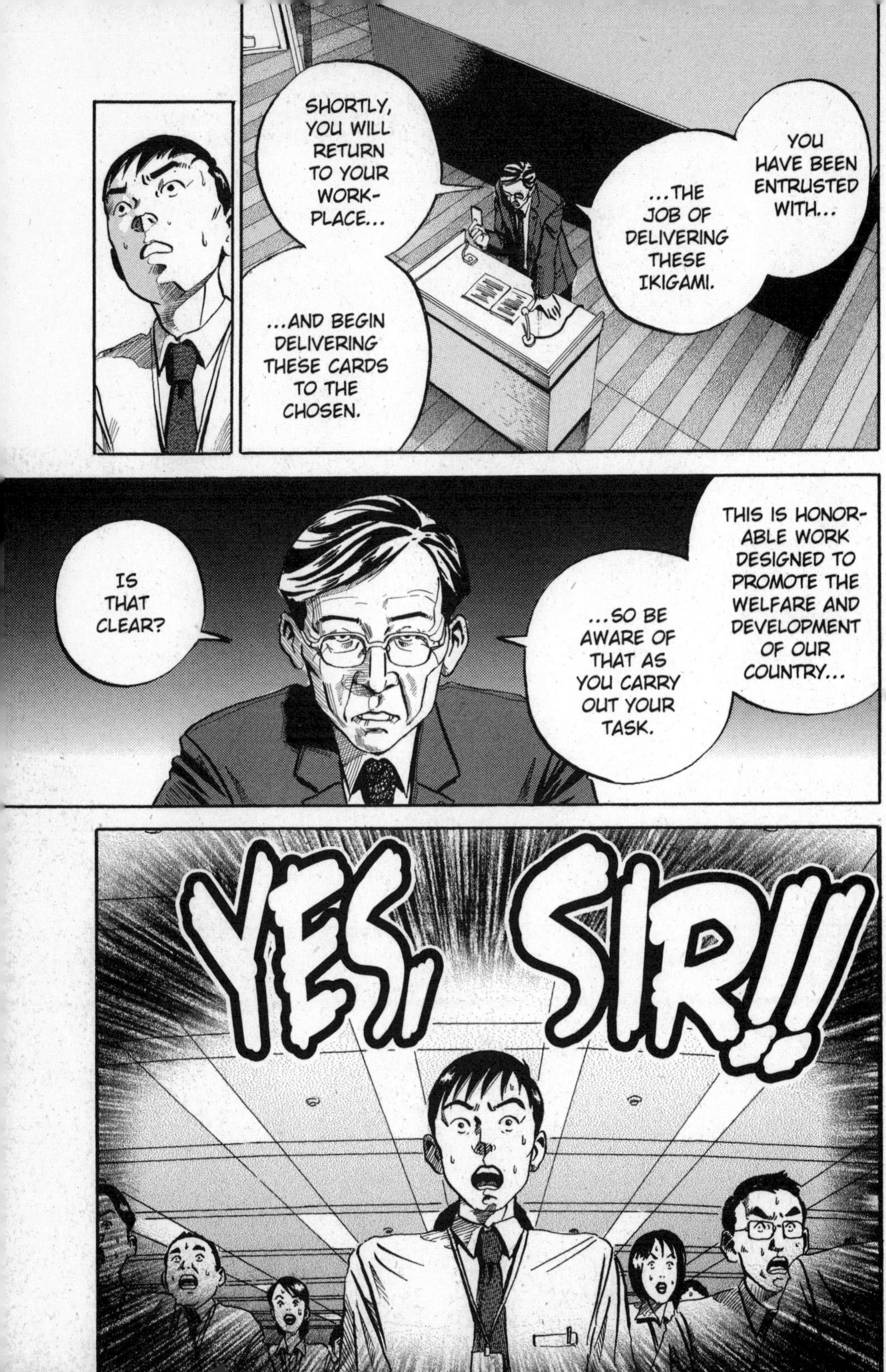
YOU HAVE BEEN ENTRUSTED WITH...
...THE JOB OF DELIVERING THESE IKIGAMI.
SHORTLY, YOU WILL RETURN TO YOUR WORK-PLACE...
...AND BEGIN DELIVERING THESE CARDS TO THE CHOSEN.
THIS IS HONOR-ABLE WORK DESIGNED TO PROMOTE THE WELFARE AND DEVELOPMENT OF OUR COUNTRY...
...SO BE AWARE OF THAT AS YOU CARRY OUT YOUR TASK.
IS THAT CLEAR?
YES, SIR!!

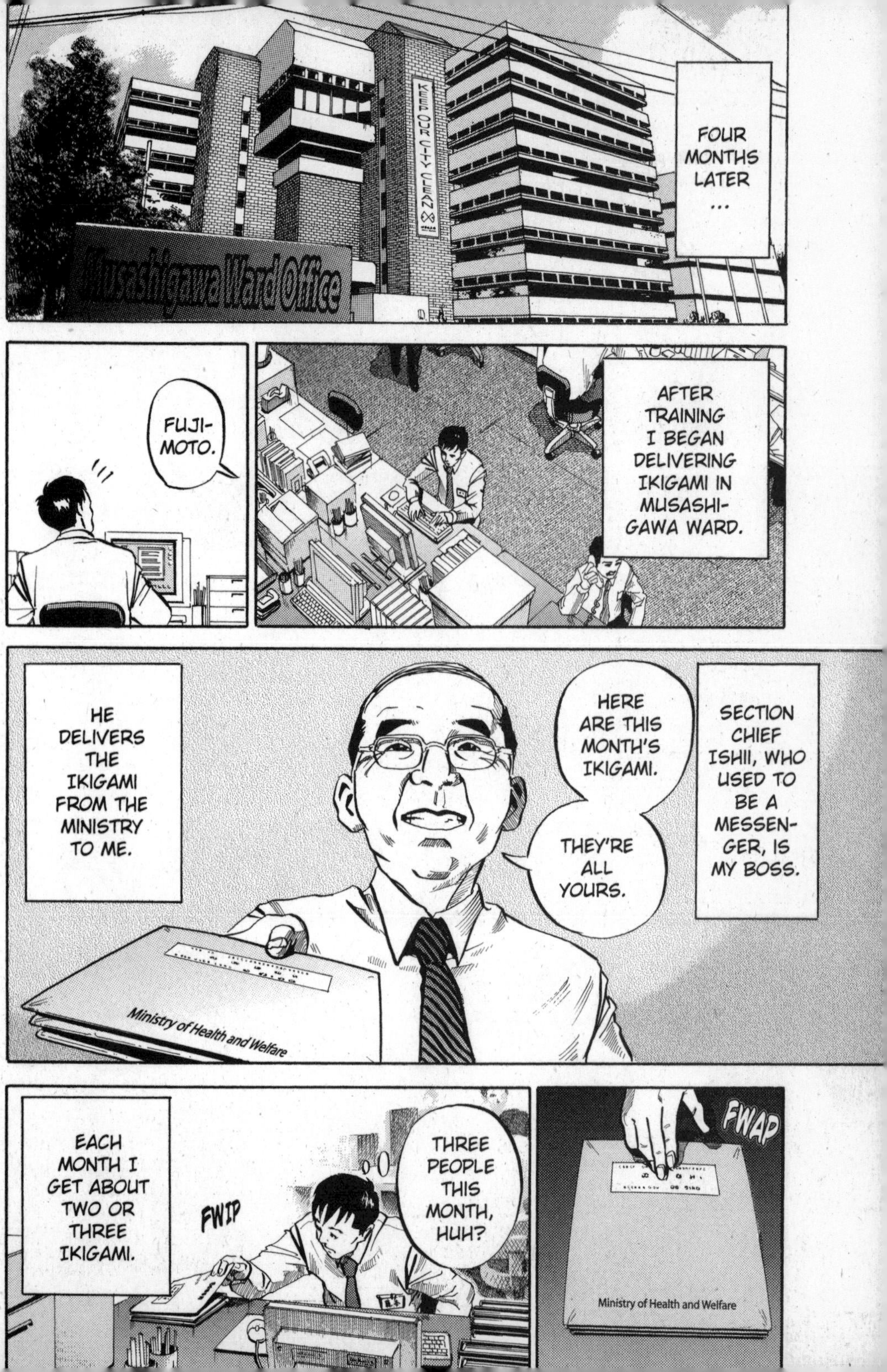
FOUR MONTHS LATER ...
KEEP OUR CITY CLEAN
Musashigawa Ward Office
AFTER TRAINING I BEGAN DELIVERING IKIGAMI IN MUSASHI-GAWA WARD.
FUJI-MOTO.
SECTION CHIEF ISHII, WHO USED TO BE A MESSEN-GER, IS MY BOSS.
HERE ARE THIS MONTH'S IKIGAMI.
THEY'RE ALL YOURS.
HE DELIVERS THE IKIGAMI FROM THE MINISTRY TO ME.
Ministry of Health and Welfare
FWAP
Ministry of Health and Welfare
THREE PEOPLE THIS MONTH, HUH?
EACH MONTH I GET ABOUT TWO OR THREE IKIGAMI.
FWIP

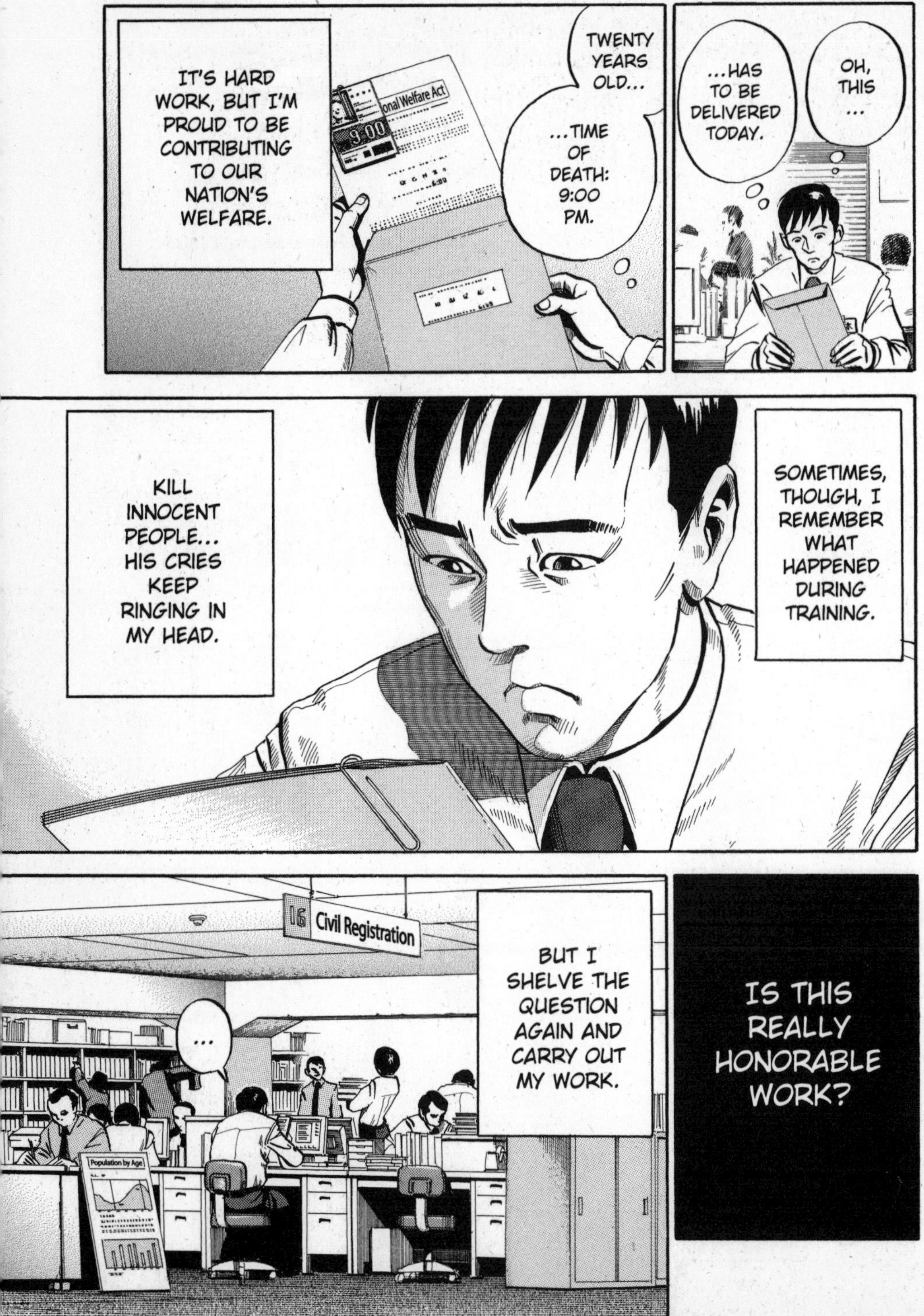
OH, THIS ...
...HAS TO BE DELIVERED TODAY.
TWENTY YEARS OLD...
...TIME OF DEATH: 9:00 PM.
onal Welfare Act
9:00
IT'S HARD WORK, BUT I'M PROUD TO BE CONTRIBUTING TO OUR NATION'S WELFARE.
SOMETIMES, THOUGH, I REMEMBER WHAT HAPPENED DURING TRAINING.
KILL INNOCENT PEOPLE... HIS CRIES KEEP RINGING IN MY HEAD.
IS THIS REALLY HONORABLE WORK?
BUT I SHELVE THE QUESTION AGAIN AND CARRY OUT MY WORK.
16 Civil Registration
Population by Age
...

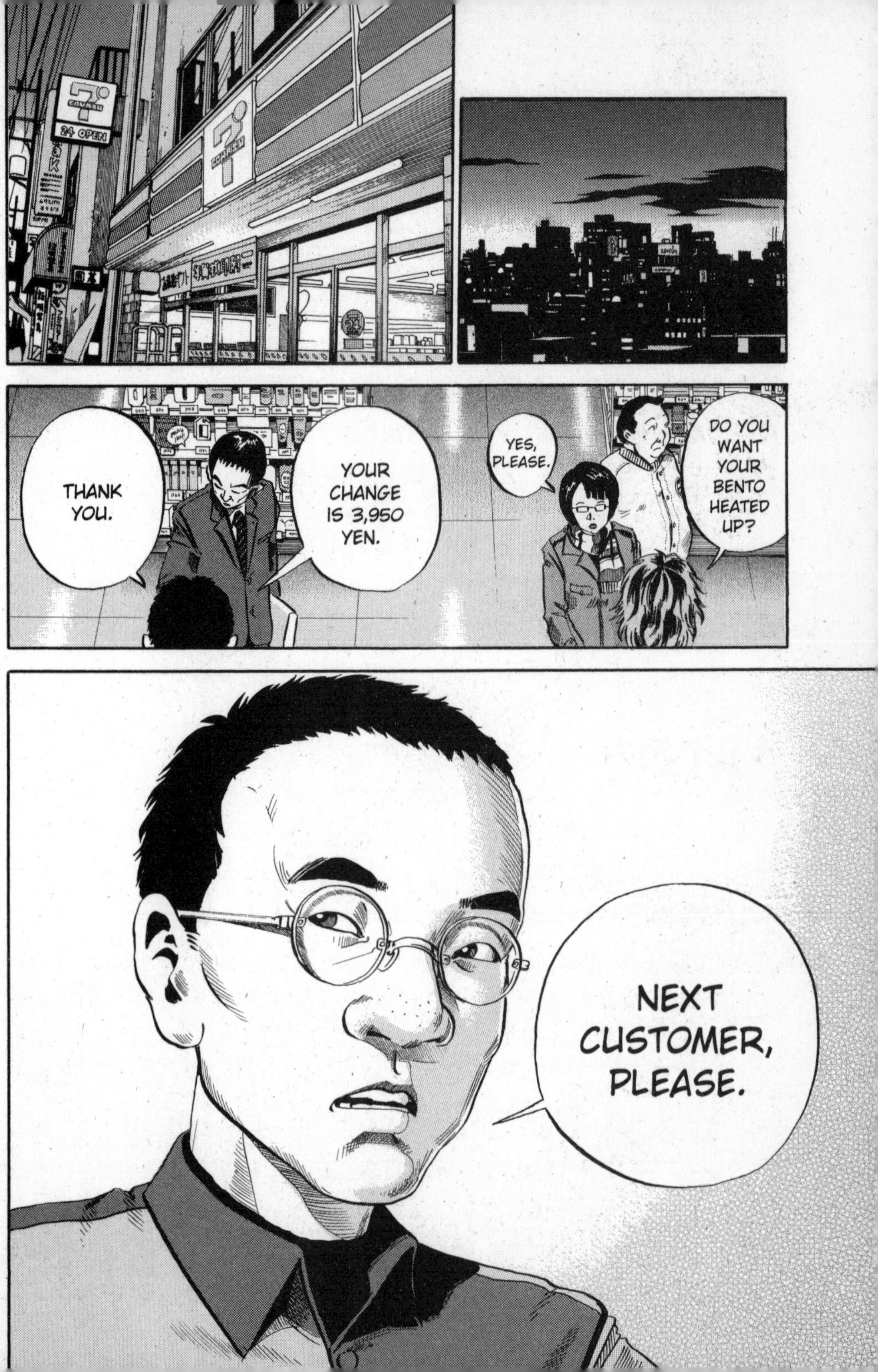
24 OPEN
DO YOU WANT YOUR BENTO HEATED UP?
YES, PLEASE.
YOUR CHANGE IS 3,950 YEN.
THANK YOU.
NEXT CUSTOMER, PLEASE.

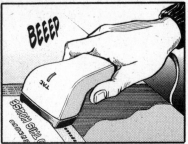

BEEEP

SLIP

THIEF!

BEEEP

......

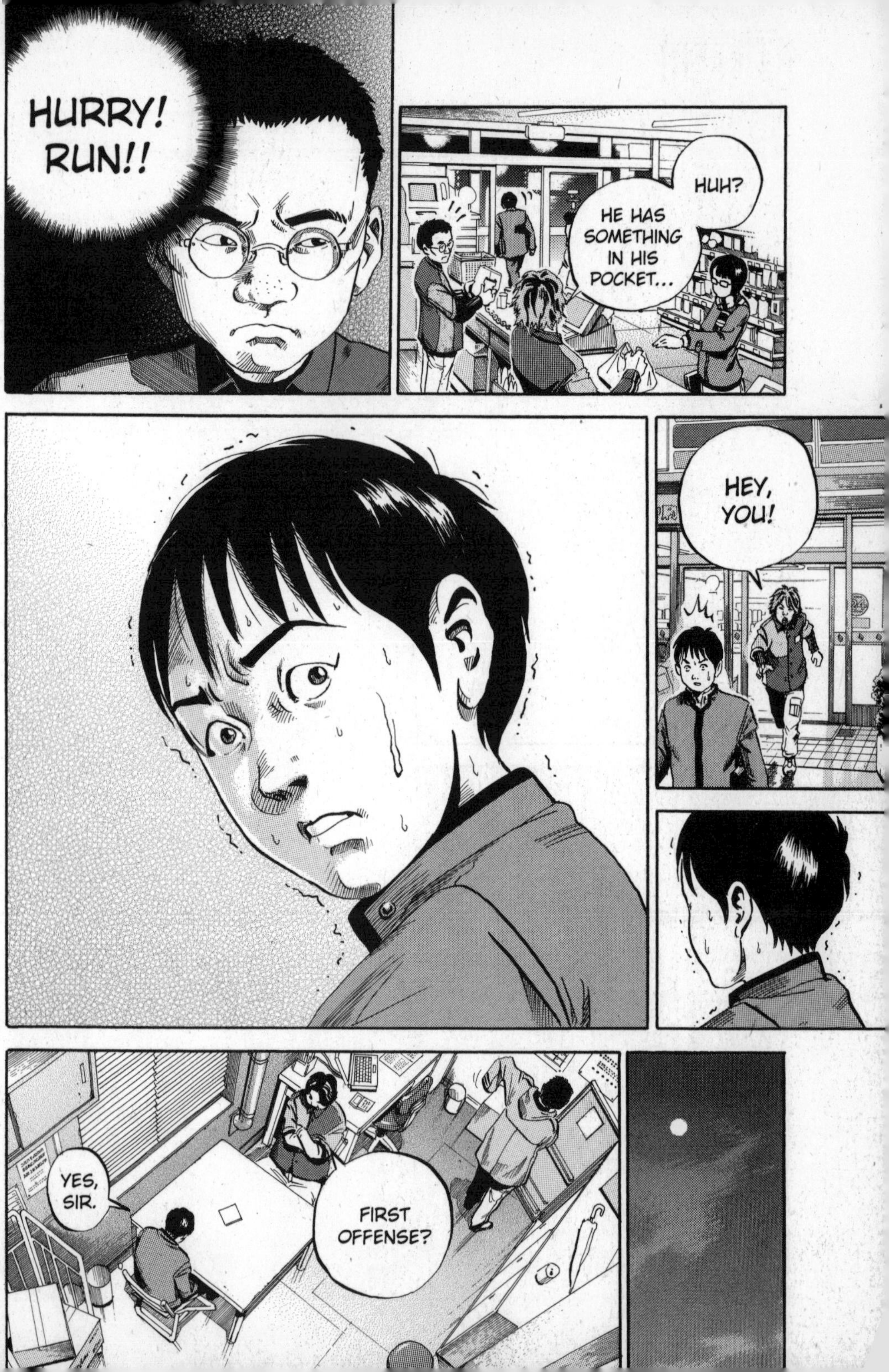
HUH?
HE HAS SOMETHING IN HIS POCKET...
HURRY! RUN!!
HEY, YOU!
FIRST OFFENSE?
YES, SIR.

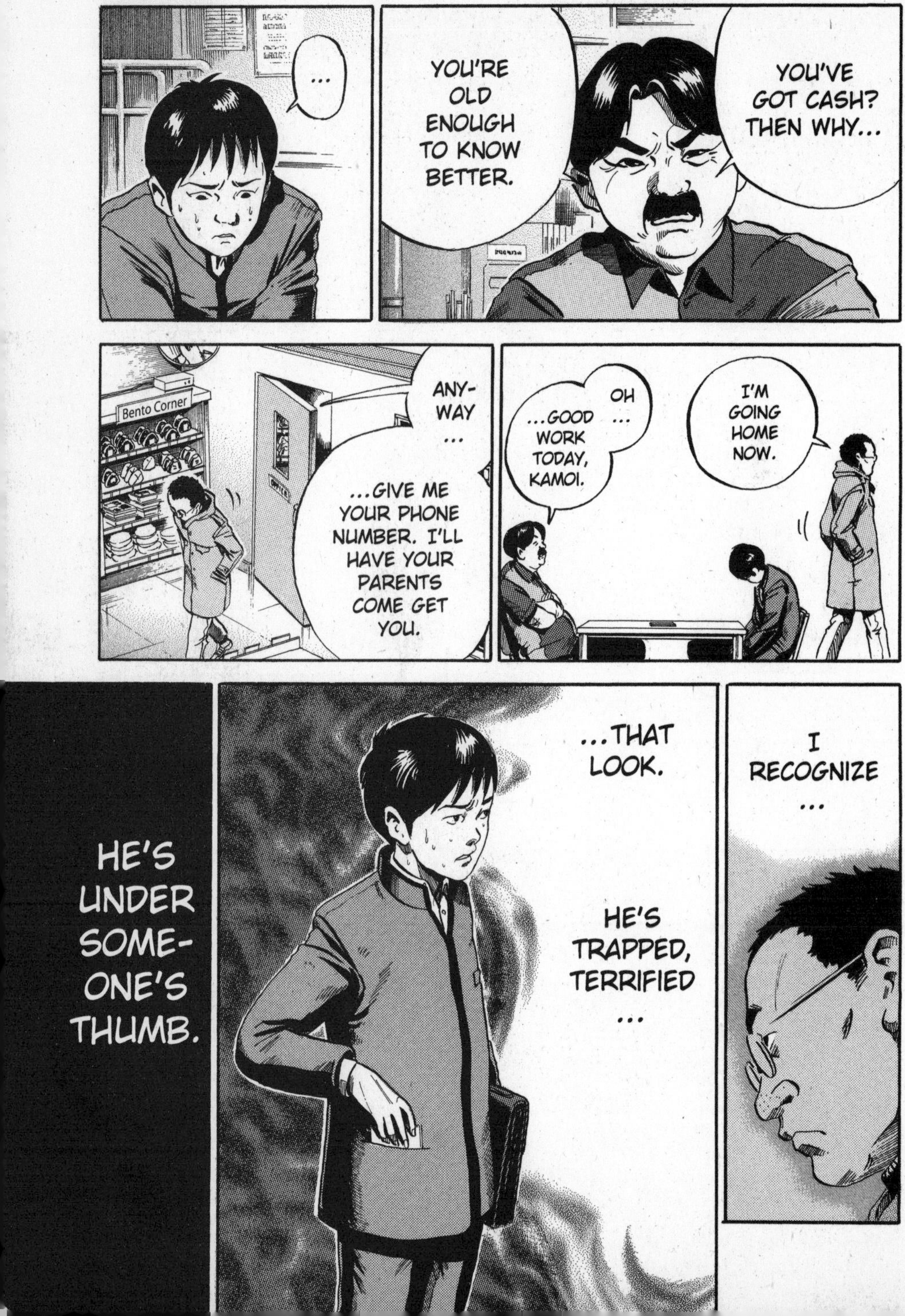
YOU'VE GOT CASH? THEN WHY...
YOU'RE OLD ENOUGH TO KNOW BETTER.
...
I'M GOING HOME NOW.
OH ... ...GOOD WORK TODAY, KAMOI.
ANY-WAY ...
...GIVE ME YOUR PHONE NUMBER. I'LL HAVE YOUR PARENTS COME GET YOU.
Bento Corner
I RECOGNIZE ...
...THAT LOOK.
HE'S TRAPPED, TERRIFIED ...
HE'S UNDER SOME-ONE'S THUMB.

IF YOU DON'T FOLLOW ORDERS, SOMETHING TERRIBLE WILL HAPPEN.

I'VE STARTED ITCHING AGAIN...

SCRATCH
SCRATCH
SCRATCH
SCRATCH
SCRATCH

UGH...

SCRATCH
SCRATCH

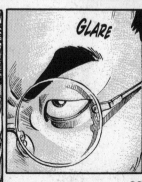

GLARE

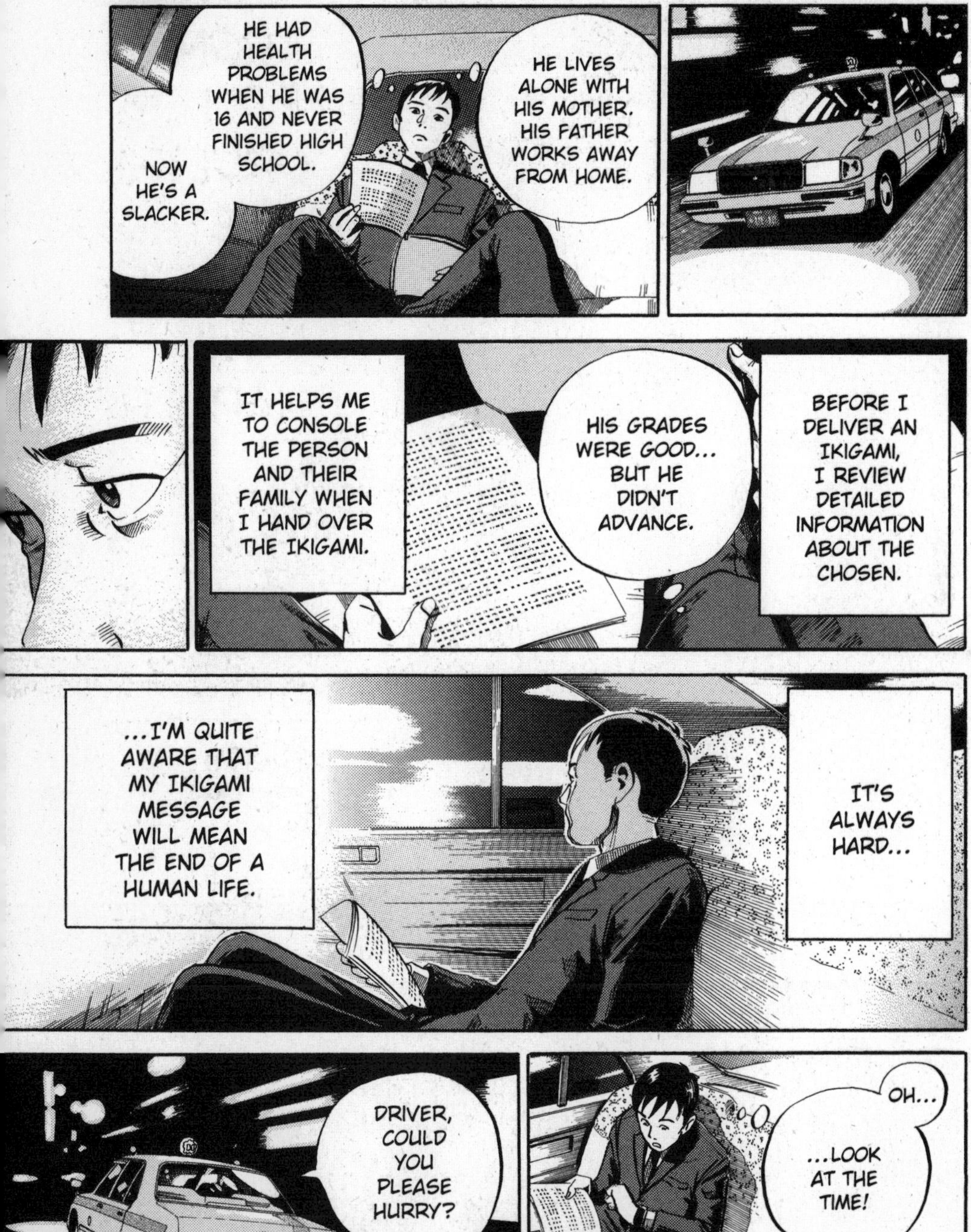
HE LIVES ALONE WITH HIS MOTHER. HIS FATHER WORKS AWAY FROM HOME.
HE HAD HEALTH PROBLEMS WHEN HE WAS 16 AND NEVER FINISHED HIGH SCHOOL.
NOW HE'S A SLACKER.
BEFORE I DELIVER AN IKIGAMI, I REVIEW DETAILED INFORMATION ABOUT THE CHOSEN.
HIS GRADES WERE GOOD... BUT HE DIDN'T ADVANCE.
IT HELPS ME TO CONSOLE THE PERSON AND THEIR FAMILY WHEN I HAND OVER THE IKIGAMI.
IT'S ALWAYS HARD...
...I'M QUITE AWARE THAT MY IKIGAMI MESSAGE WILL MEAN THE END OF A HUMAN LIFE.
OH...
...LOOK AT THE TIME!
DRIVER, COULD YOU PLEASE HURRY?

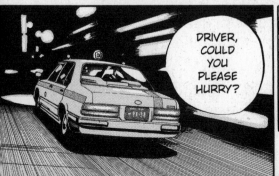

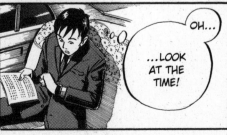

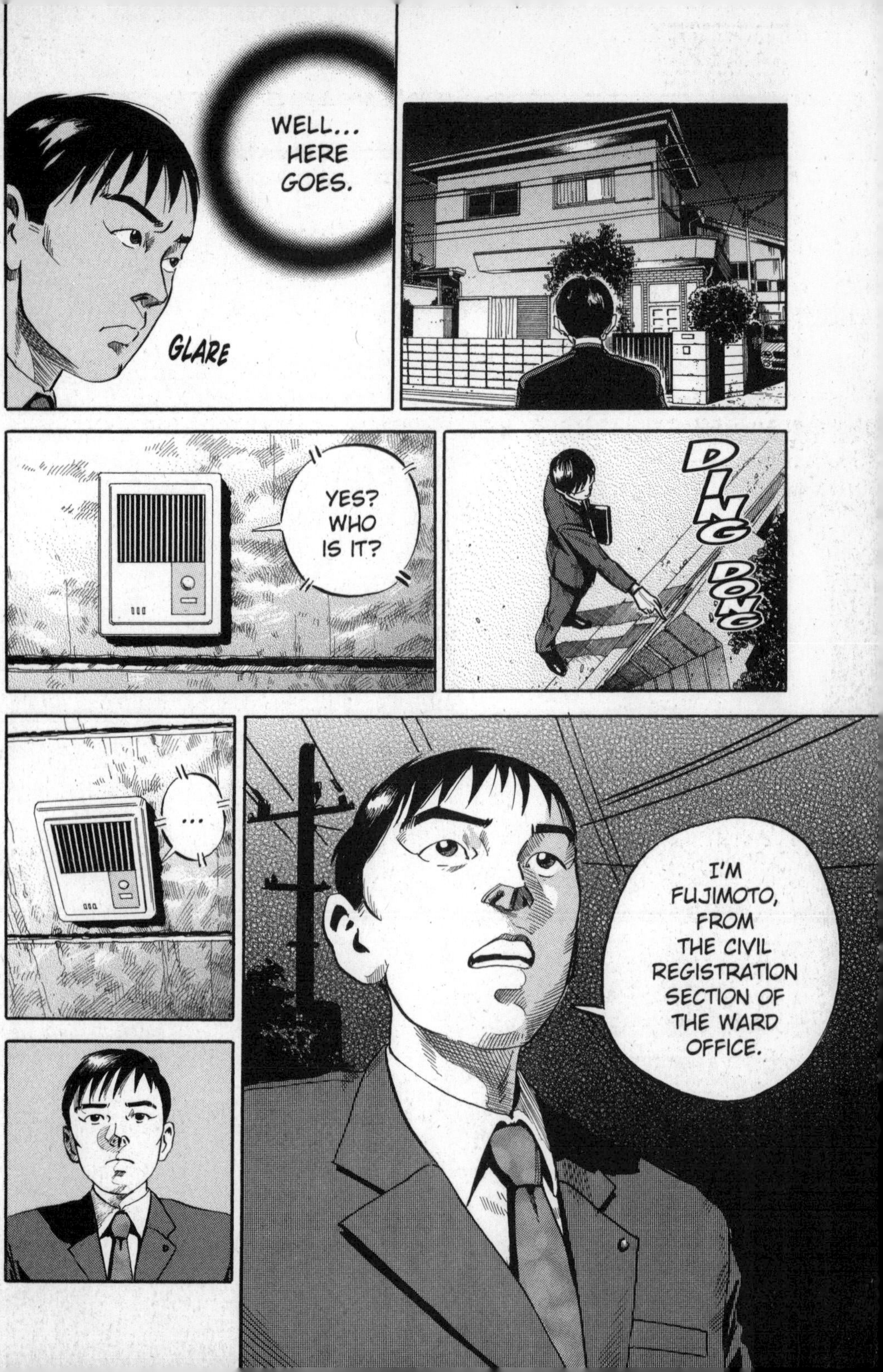
WELL... HERE GOES.
GLARE
DING DONG
YES? WHO IS IT?
I'M FUJIMOTO, FROM THE CIVIL REGISTRATION SECTION OF THE WARD OFFICE.
...

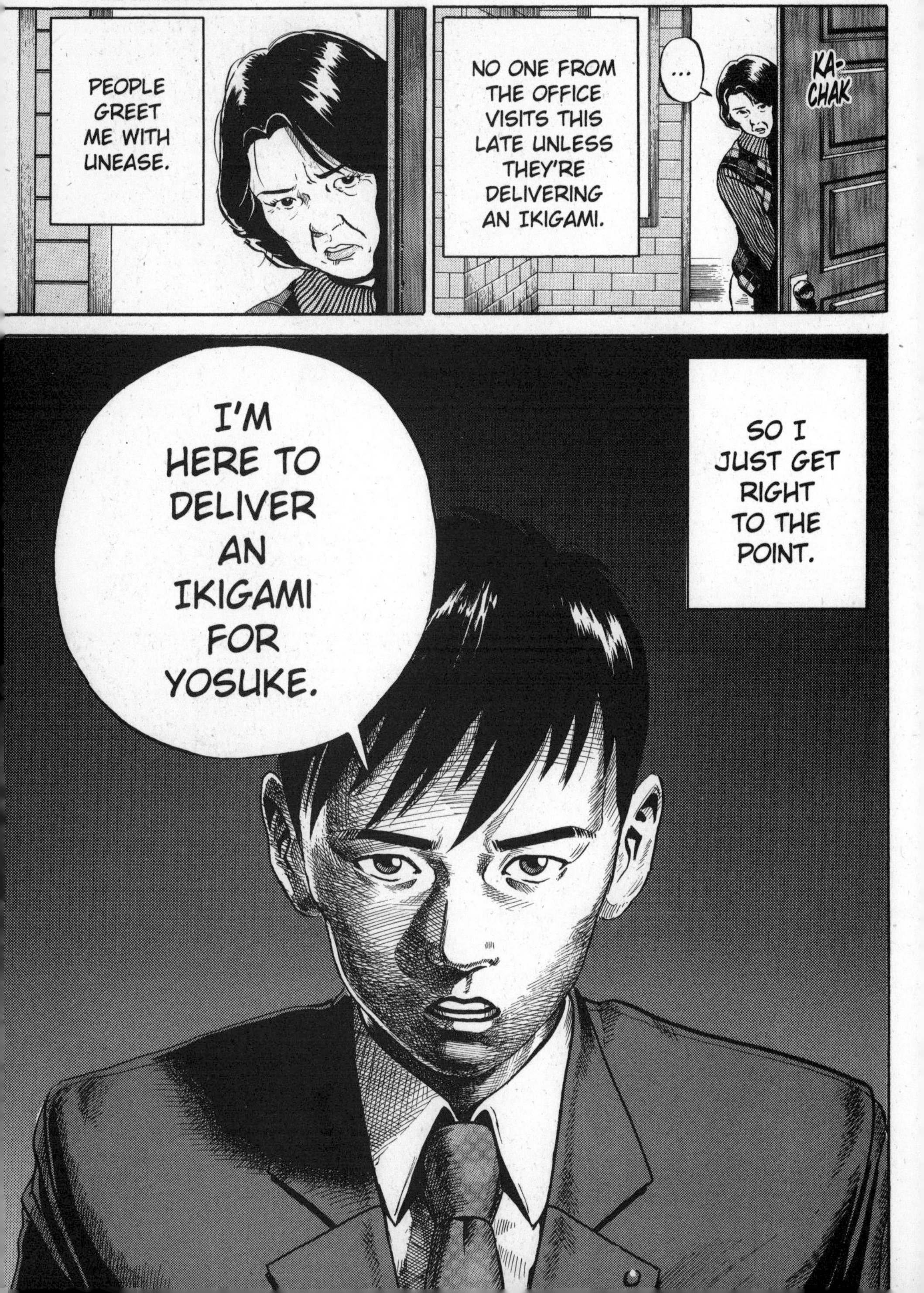
KA-CHAK
...
NO ONE FROM THE OFFICE VISITS THIS LATE UNLESS THEY'RE DELIVERING AN IKIGAMI.
PEOPLE GREET ME WITH UNEASE.
SO I JUST GET RIGHT TO THE POINT.
I'M HERE TO DELIVER AN IKIGAMI FOR YOSUKE.

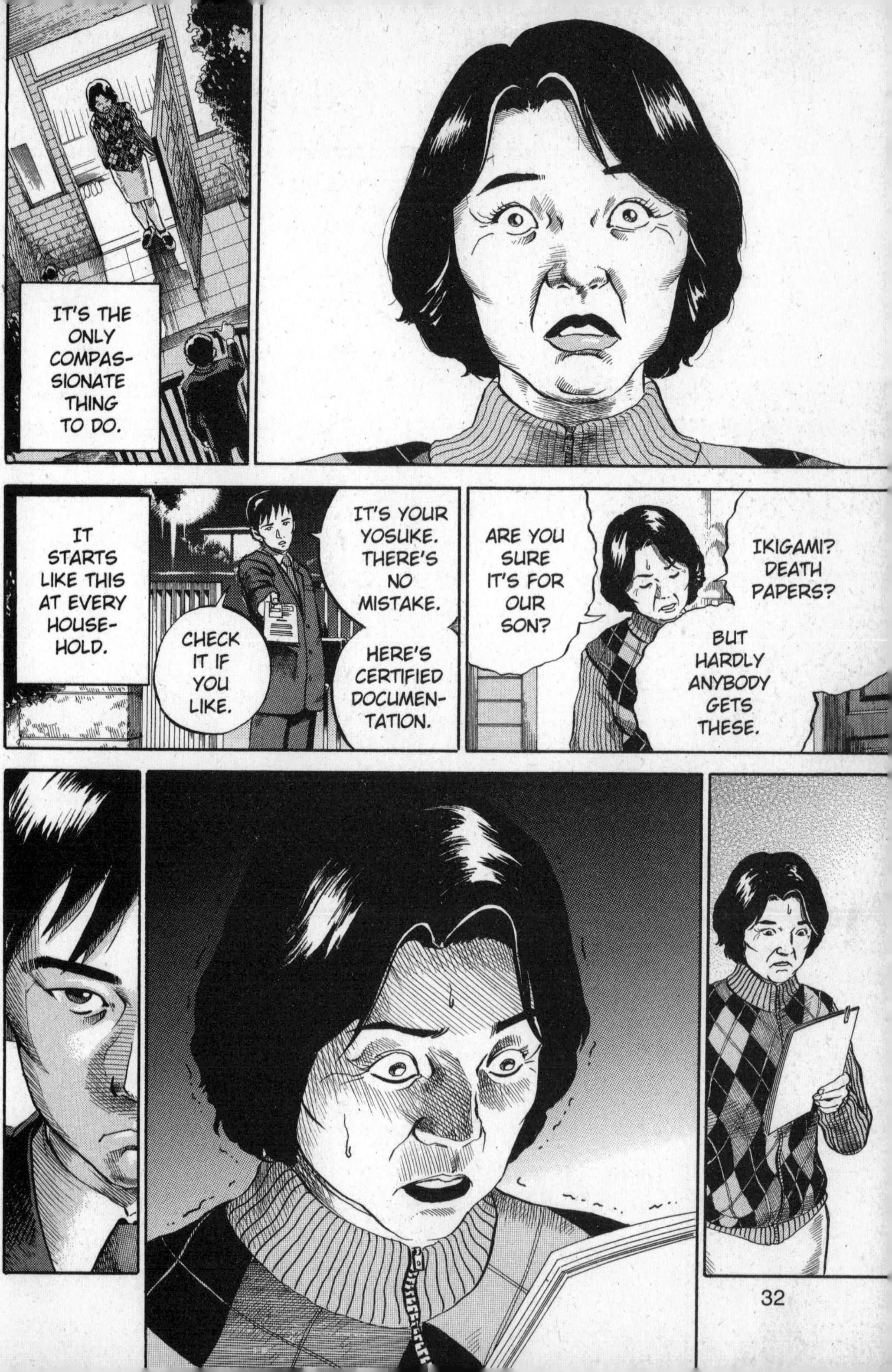
IT'S THE ONLY COMPASSIONATE THING TO DO.
IKIGAMI? DEATH PAPERS?
BUT HARDLY ANYBODY GETS THESE.
ARE YOU SURE IT'S FOR OUR SON?
IT'S YOUR YOSUKE. THERE'S NO MISTAKE.
HERE'S CERTIFIED DOCUMENTATION.
CHECK IT IF YOU LIKE.
IT STARTS LIKE THIS AT EVERY HOUSEHOLD.

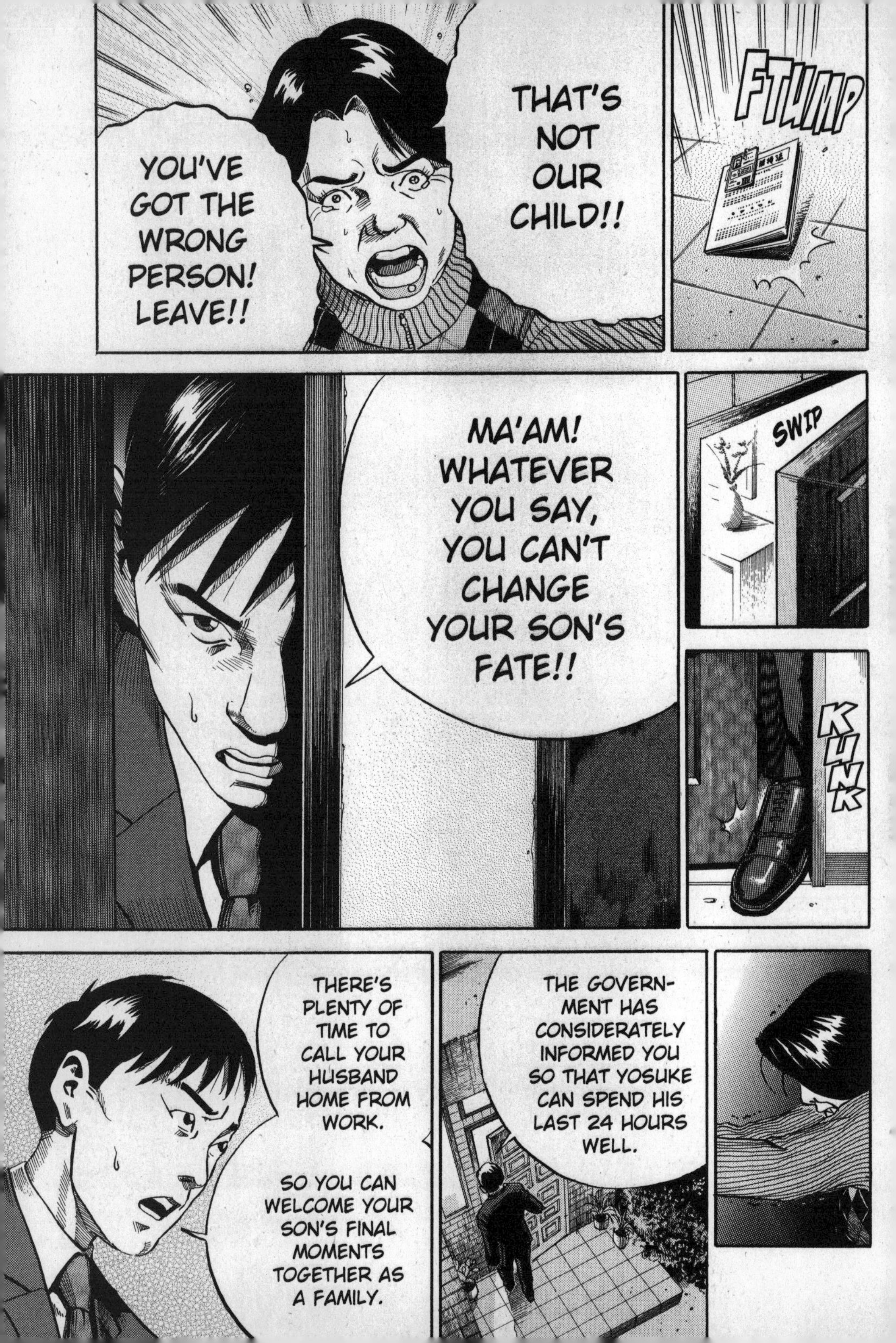
FTUMP
THAT'S NOT OUR CHILD!!
YOU'VE GOT THE WRONG PERSON! LEAVE!!
SWIP
KUNK
MA'AM! WHATEVER YOU SAY, YOU CAN'T CHANGE YOUR SON'S FATE!!
THE GOVERN-MENT HAS CONSIDERATELY INFORMED YOU SO THAT YOSUKE CAN SPEND HIS LAST 24 HOURS WELL.
THERE'S PLENTY OF TIME TO CALL YOUR HUSBAND HOME FROM WORK.
SO YOU CAN WELCOME YOUR SON'S FINAL MOMENTS TOGETHER AS A FAMILY.

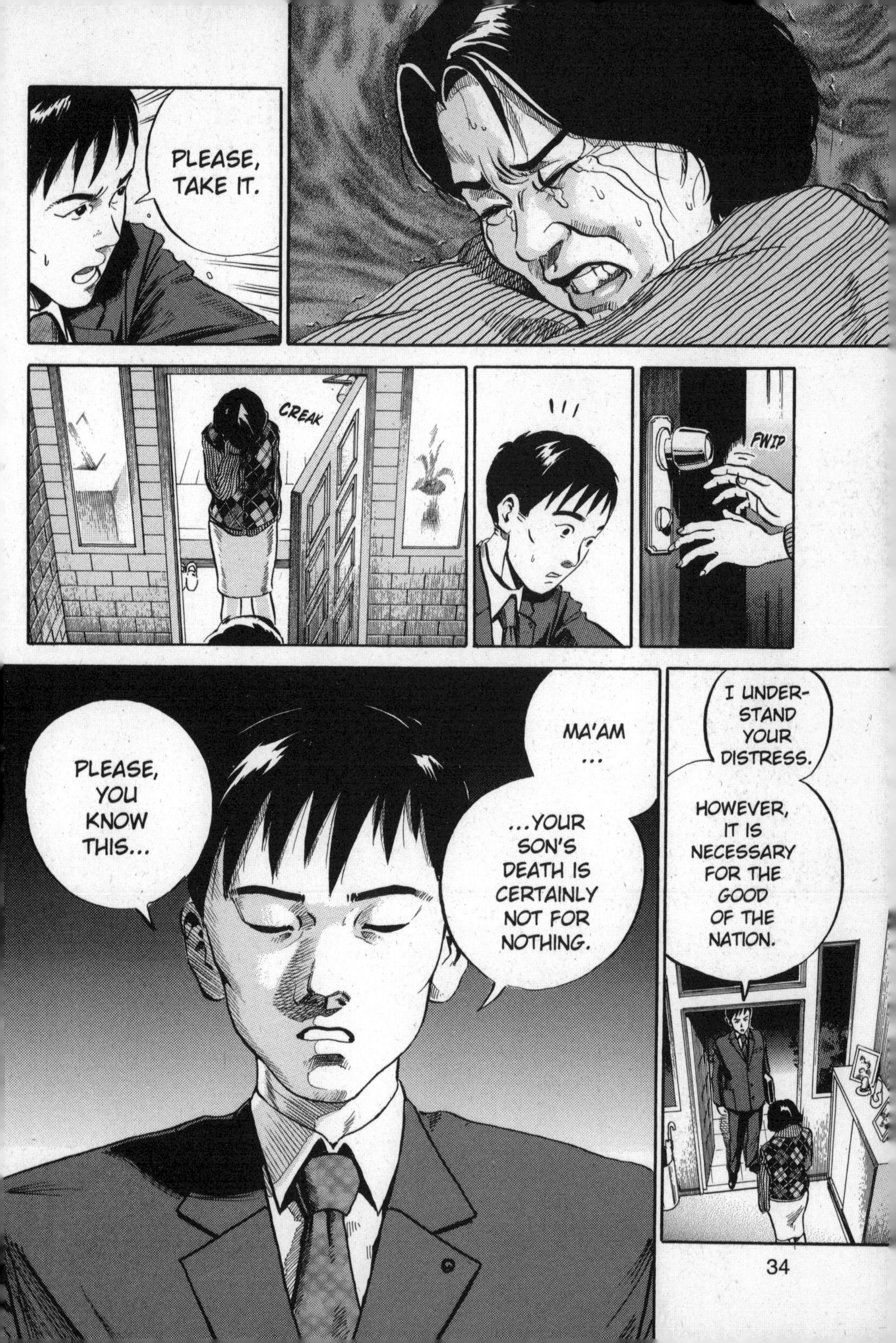
PLEASE, TAKE IT.
FWIP
CREAK
I UNDER-STAND YOUR DISTRESS.
HOWEVER, IT IS NECESSARY FOR THE GOOD OF THE NATION.
MA'AM ...
...YOUR SON'S DEATH IS CERTAINLY NOT FOR NOTHING.
PLEASE, YOU KNOW THIS...

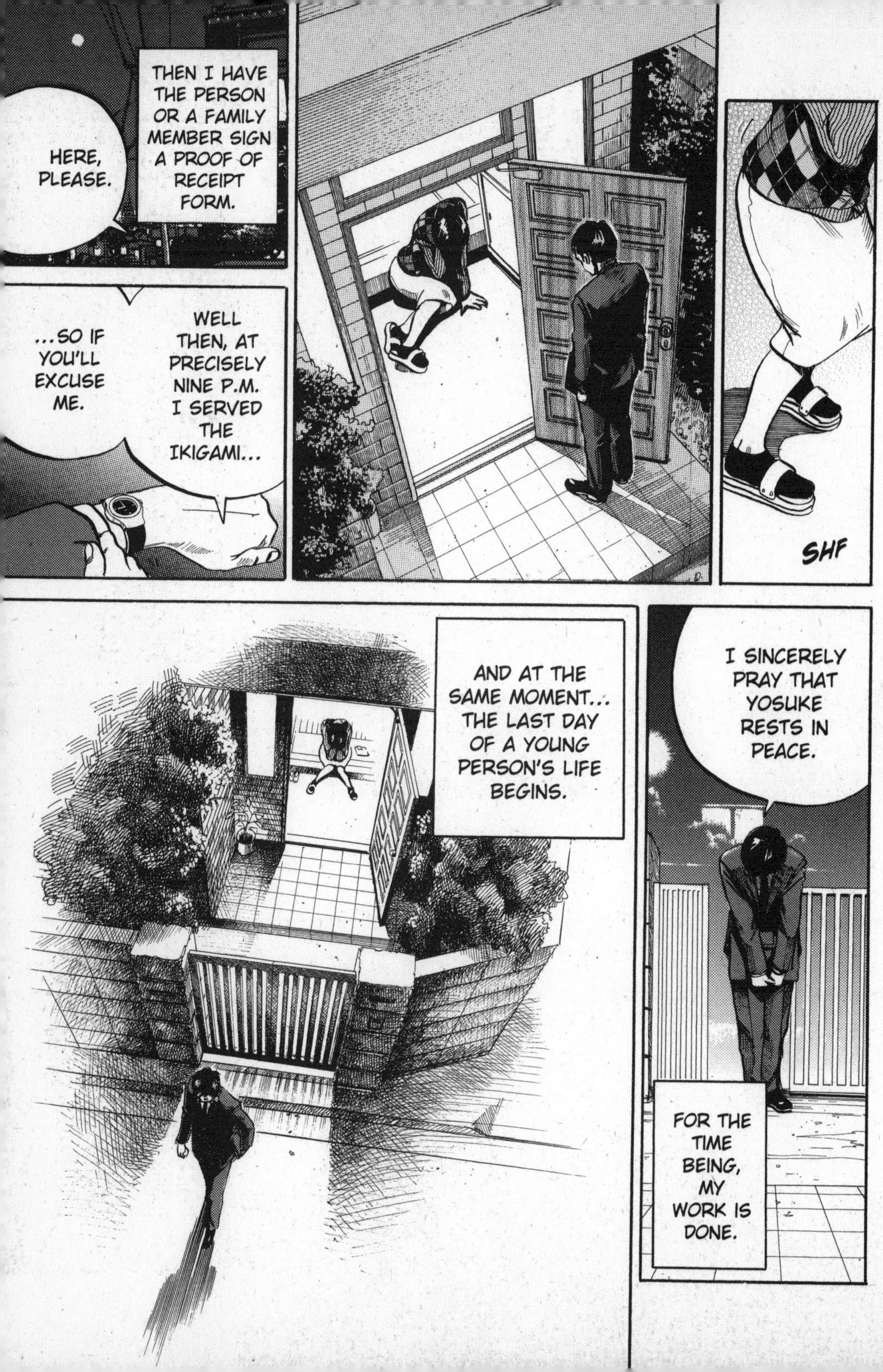
SHF
THEN I HAVE THE PERSON OR A FAMILY MEMBER SIGN A PROOF OF RECEIPT FORM.
HERE, PLEASE.
WELL THEN, AT PRECISELY NINE P.M. I SERVED THE IKIGAMI...
...SO IF YOU'LL EXCUSE ME.
I SINCERELY PRAY THAT YOSUKE RESTS IN PEACE.
FOR THE TIME BEING, MY WORK IS DONE.
AND AT THE SAME MOMENT... THE LAST DAY OF A YOUNG PERSON'S LIFE BEGINS.

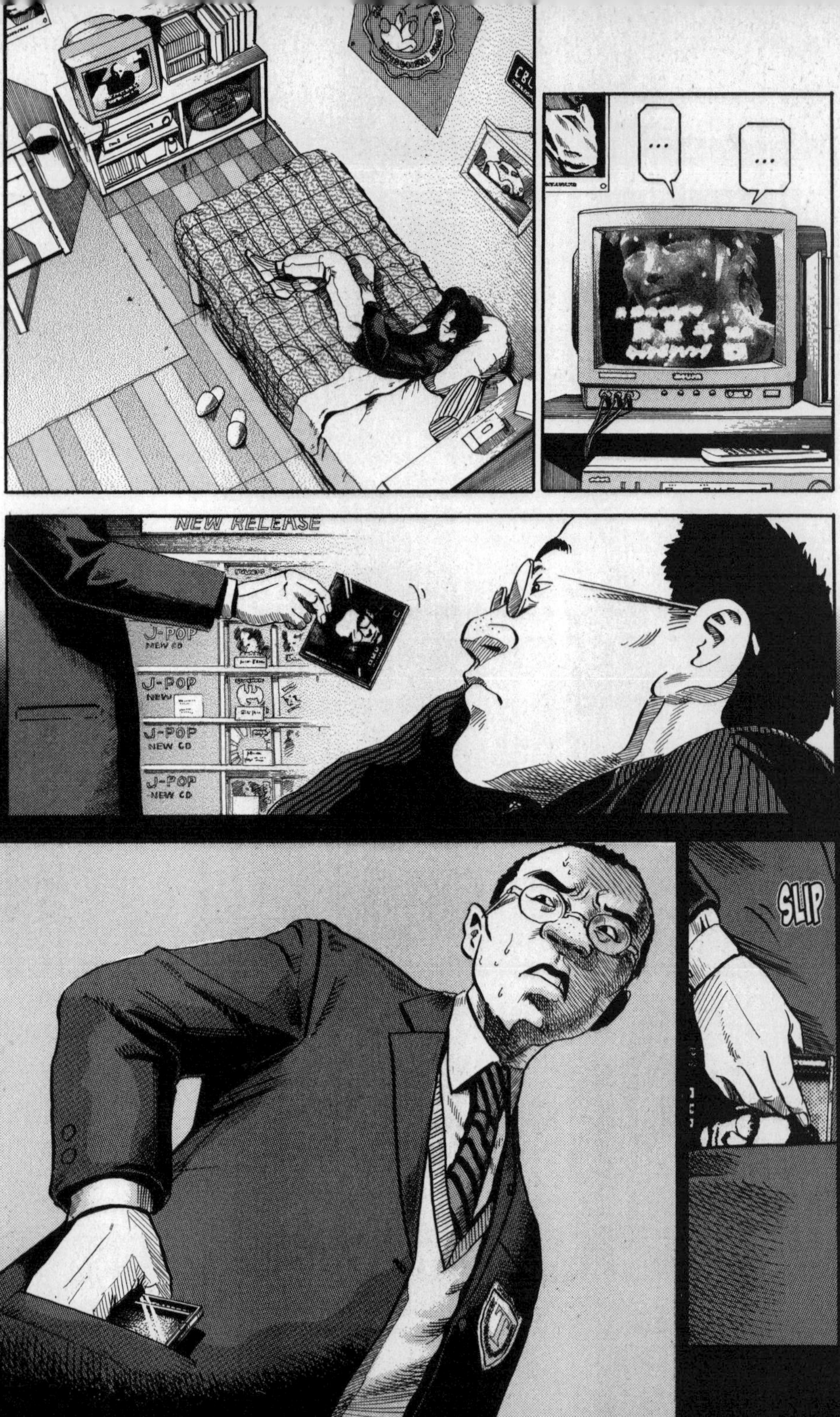
...
...
NEW RELEASE
J-POP NEW CD
J-POP NEW
J-POP NEW CD
J-POP NEW CD
SLIP

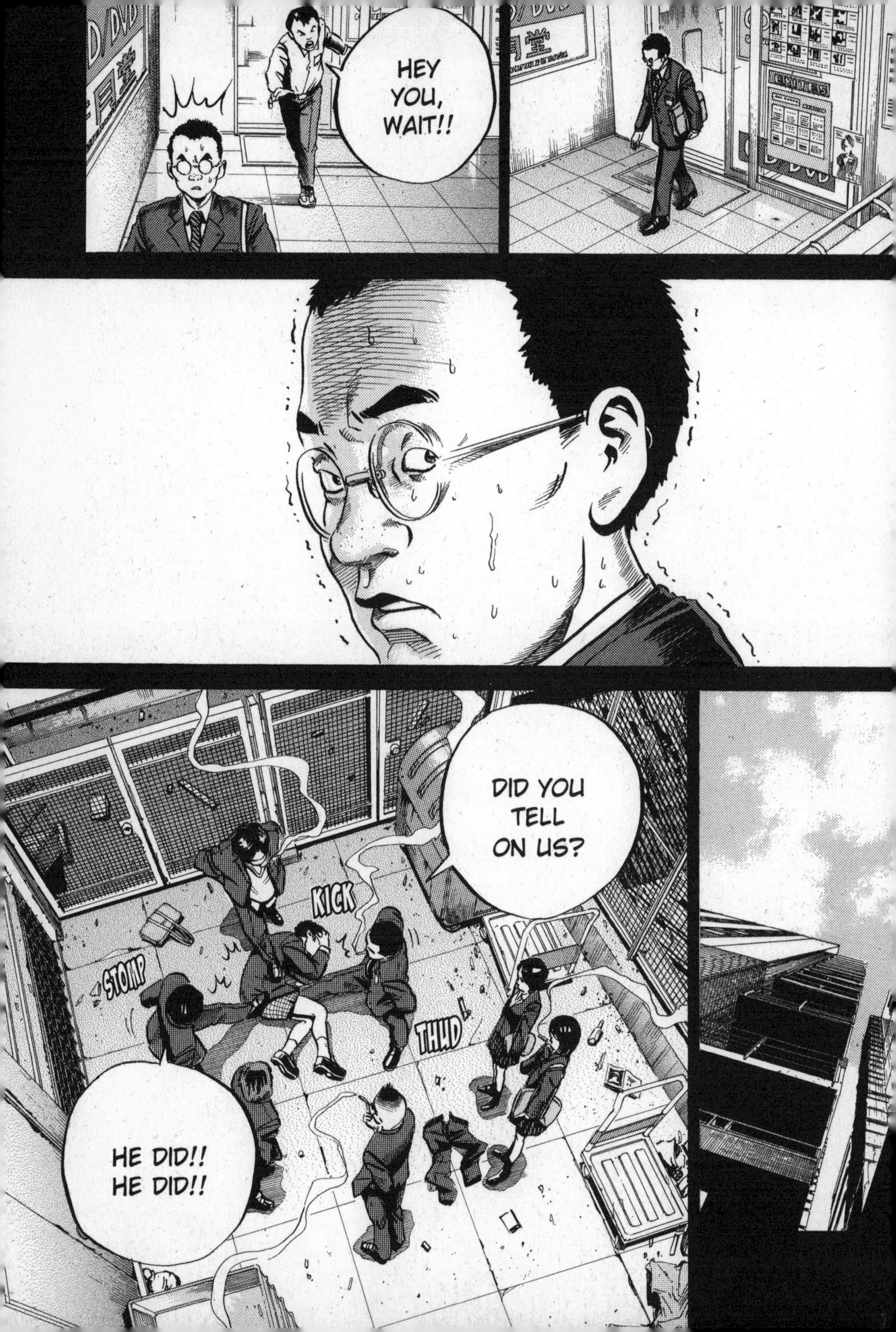

HEY YOU, WAIT!!
DID YOU TELL ON US?
KICK
STOMP
THUD
HE DID!! HE DID!!

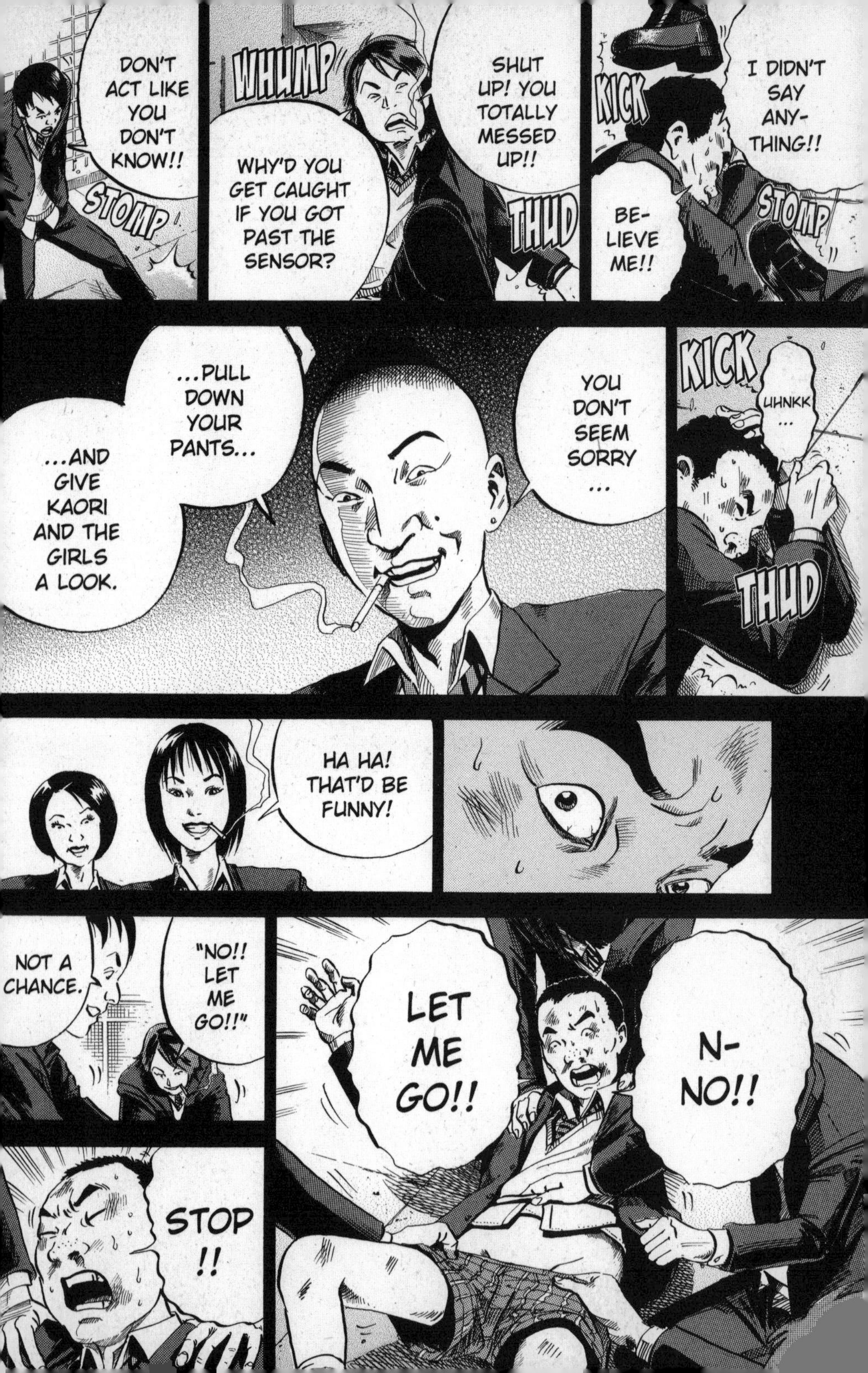
KICK
I DIDN'T SAY ANY-THING!!
BE-LIEVE ME!!
STOMP
SHUT UP! YOU TOTALLY MESSED UP!!
WHUMP
WHY'D YOU GET CAUGHT IF YOU GOT PAST THE SENSOR?
THUD
DON'T ACT LIKE YOU DON'T KNOW!!
STOMP
KICK
UHNKK...
THUD
YOU DON'T SEEM SORRY...
...PULL DOWN YOUR PANTS...
...AND GIVE KAORI AND THE GIRLS A LOOK.
HA HA! THAT'D BE FUNNY!
N-NO!!
LET ME GO!!
"NO!! LET ME GO!!"
NOT A CHANCE.
STOP!!

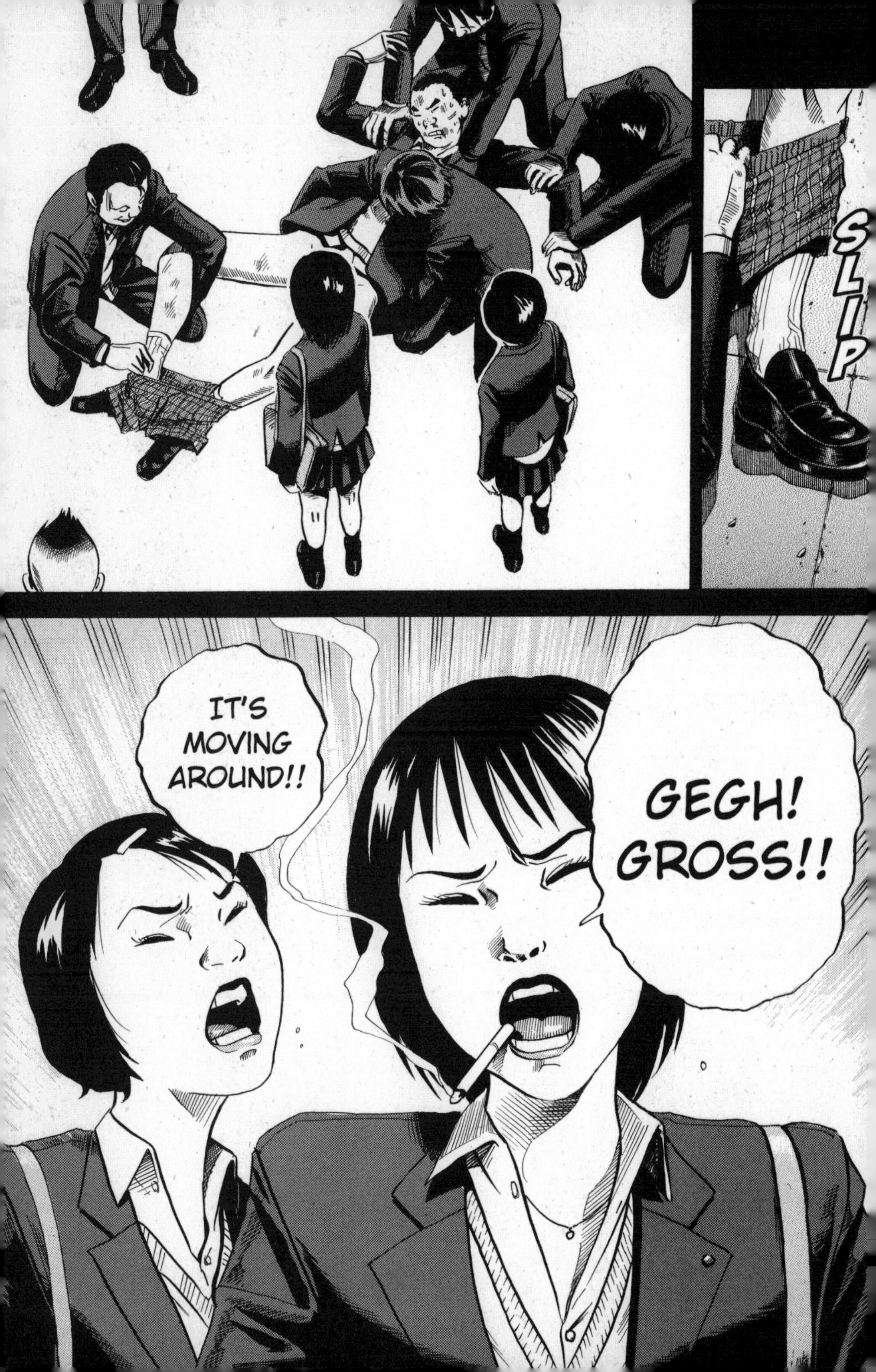
SLIP
GEGH! GROSS!!
IT'S MOVING AROUND!!

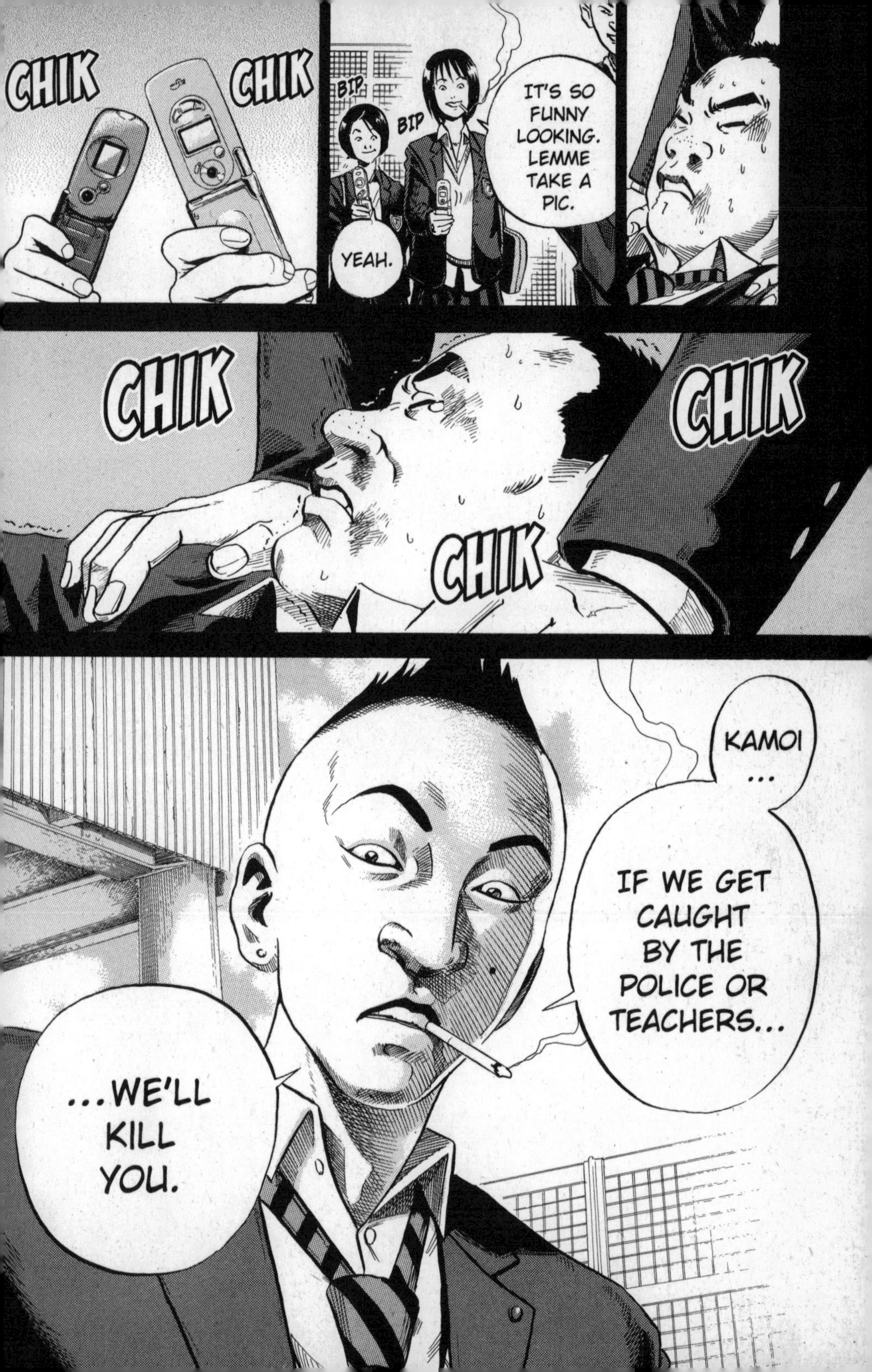
IT'S SO FUNNY LOOKING. LEMME TAKE A PIC.
BIP
BIP
YEAH.
CHIK
CHIK
CHIK
CHIK
CHIK
KAMOI ...
IF WE GET CAUGHT BY THE POLICE OR TEACHERS...
...WE'LL KILL YOU.

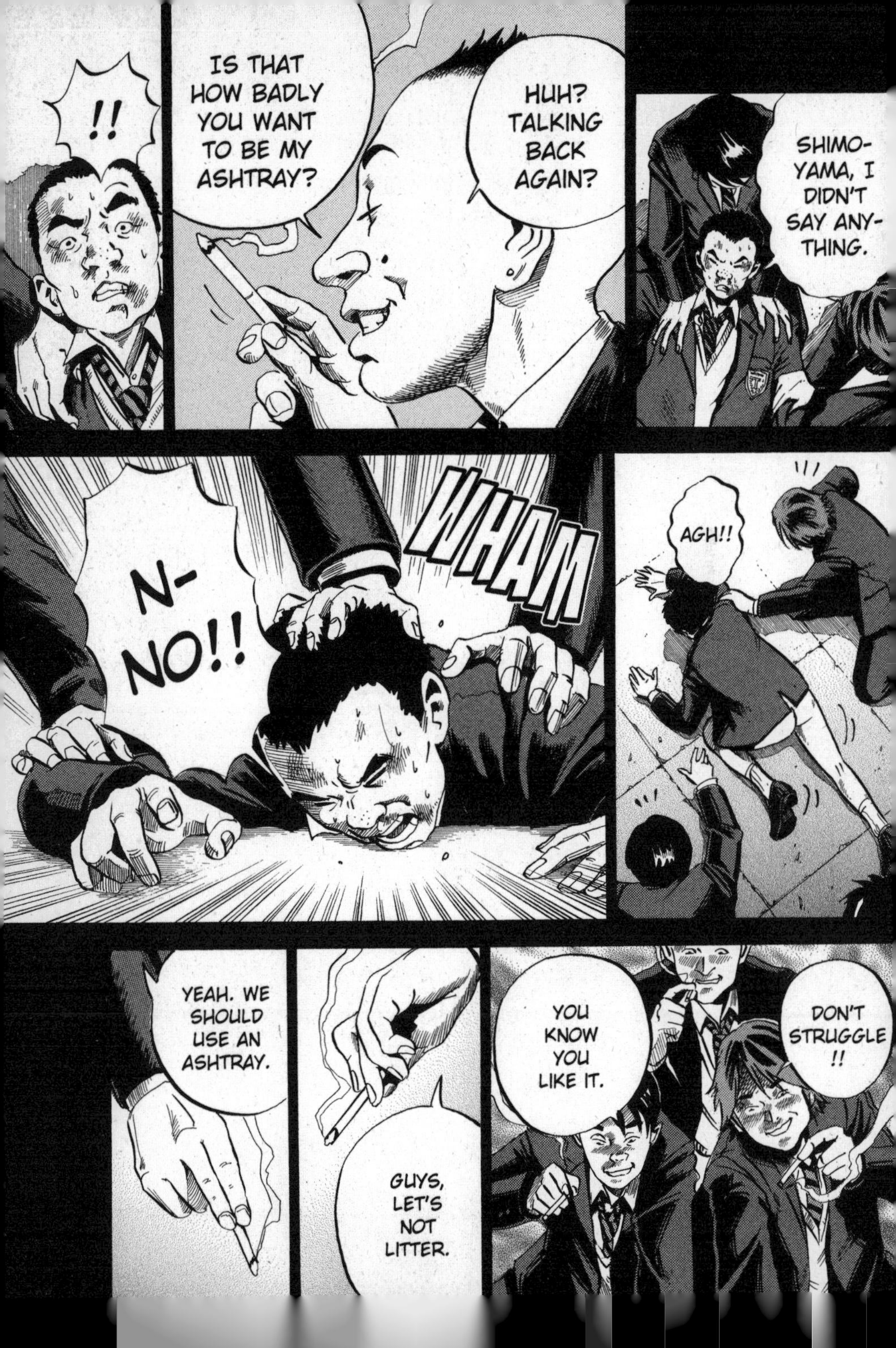
SHIMO-YAMA, I DIDN'T SAY ANY-THING.
HUH? TALKING BACK AGAIN?
IS THAT HOW BADLY YOU WANT TO BE MY ASHTRAY?
!!
AGH!!
WHAM
N-NO!!
DON'T STRUGGLE!!
YOU KNOW YOU LIKE IT.
GUYS, LET'S NOT LITTER.
YEAH. WE SHOULD USE AN ASHTRAY.

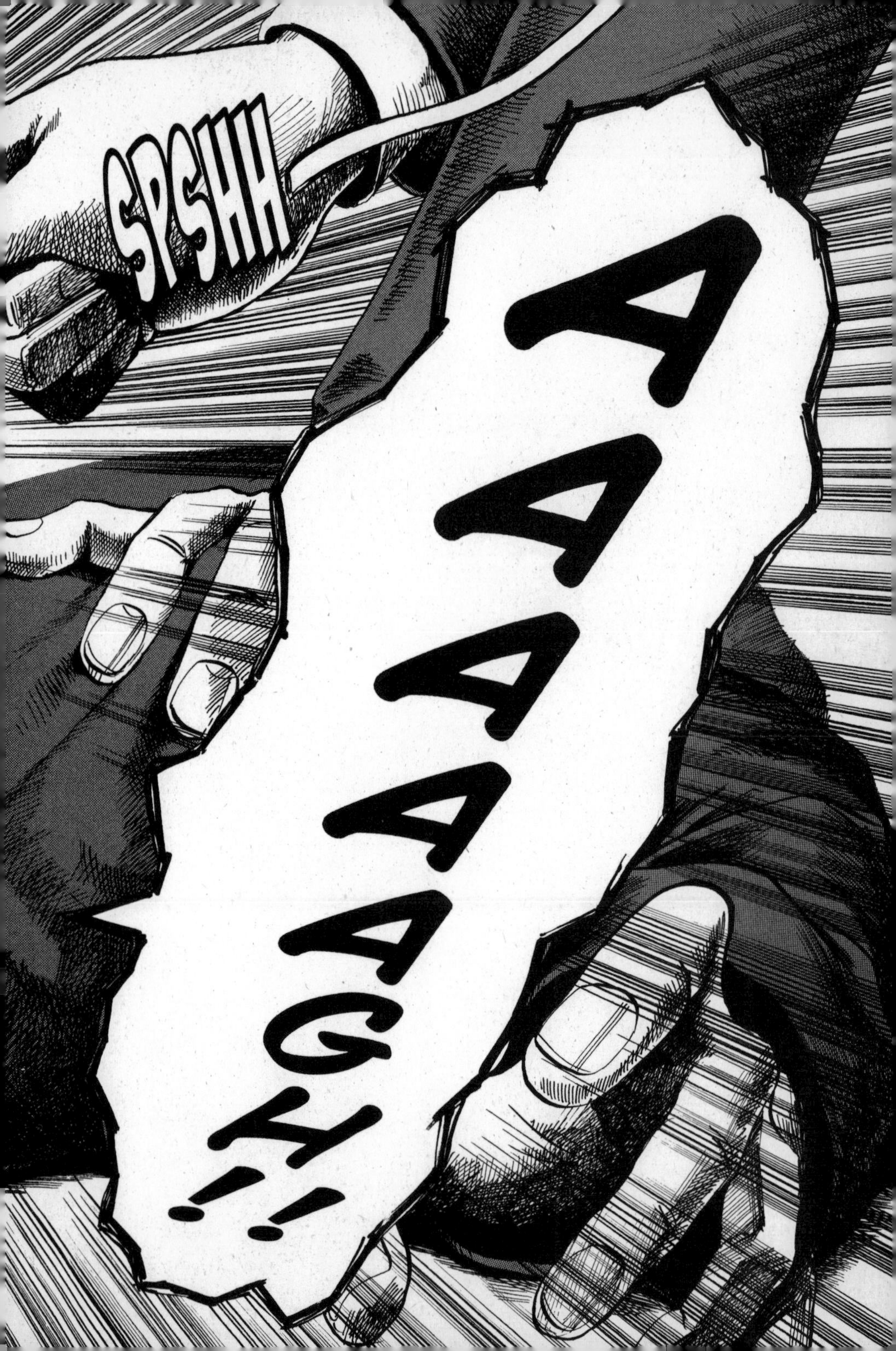
SPSHH
AAAAAAGH!!

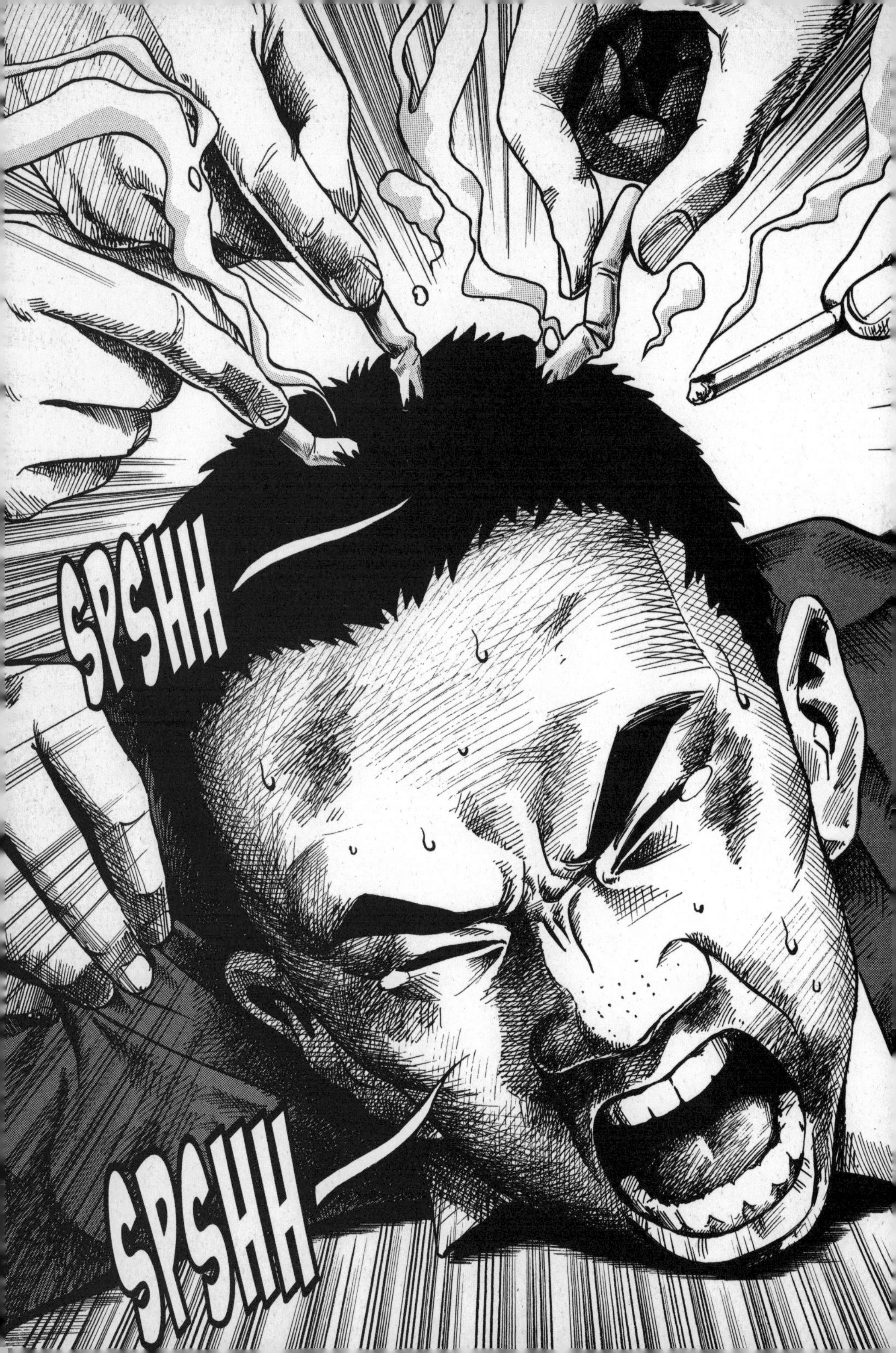
SPSHH
SPSHH

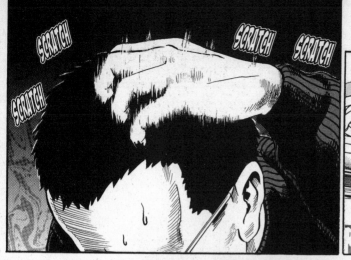

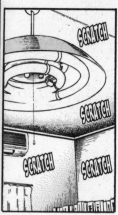

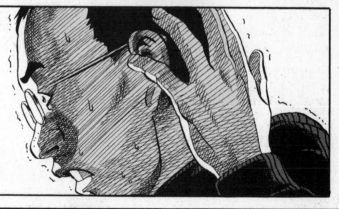

SCRATCH
SCRATCH
SCRATCH
SCRATCH
SCRATCH
SCRATCH
SCRATCH
SCRATCH
IT'S BEEN FOUR YEARS BUT...
...EVERY TIME THE BURN SCARS ITCH...
...I RELIVE THOSE MEMORIES!!

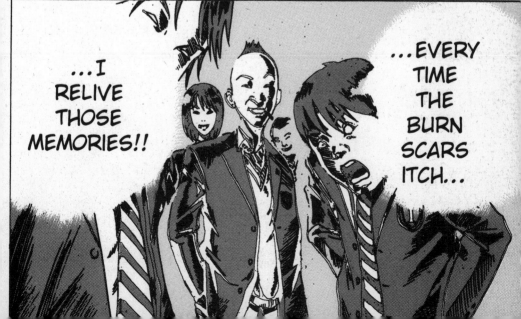

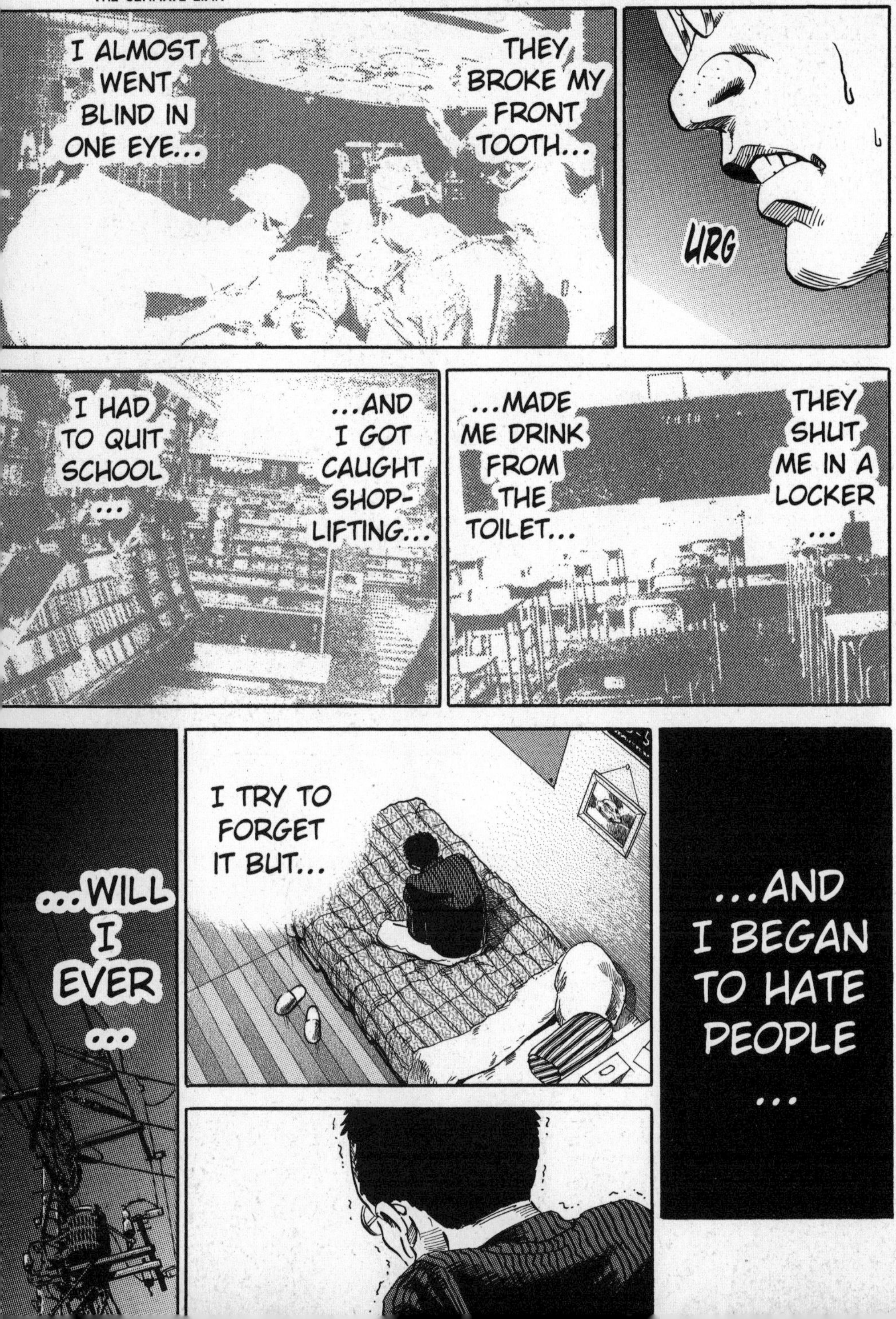
URG
THEY BROKE MY FRONT TOOTH...
I ALMOST WENT BLIND IN ONE EYE...
THEY SHUT ME IN A LOCKER ...
...MADE ME DRINK FROM THE TOILET...
...AND I GOT CAUGHT SHOP-LIFTING...
I HAD TO QUIT SCHOOL ...
...AND I BEGAN TO HATE PEOPLE ...
I TRY TO FORGET IT BUT...
...WILL I EVER ...

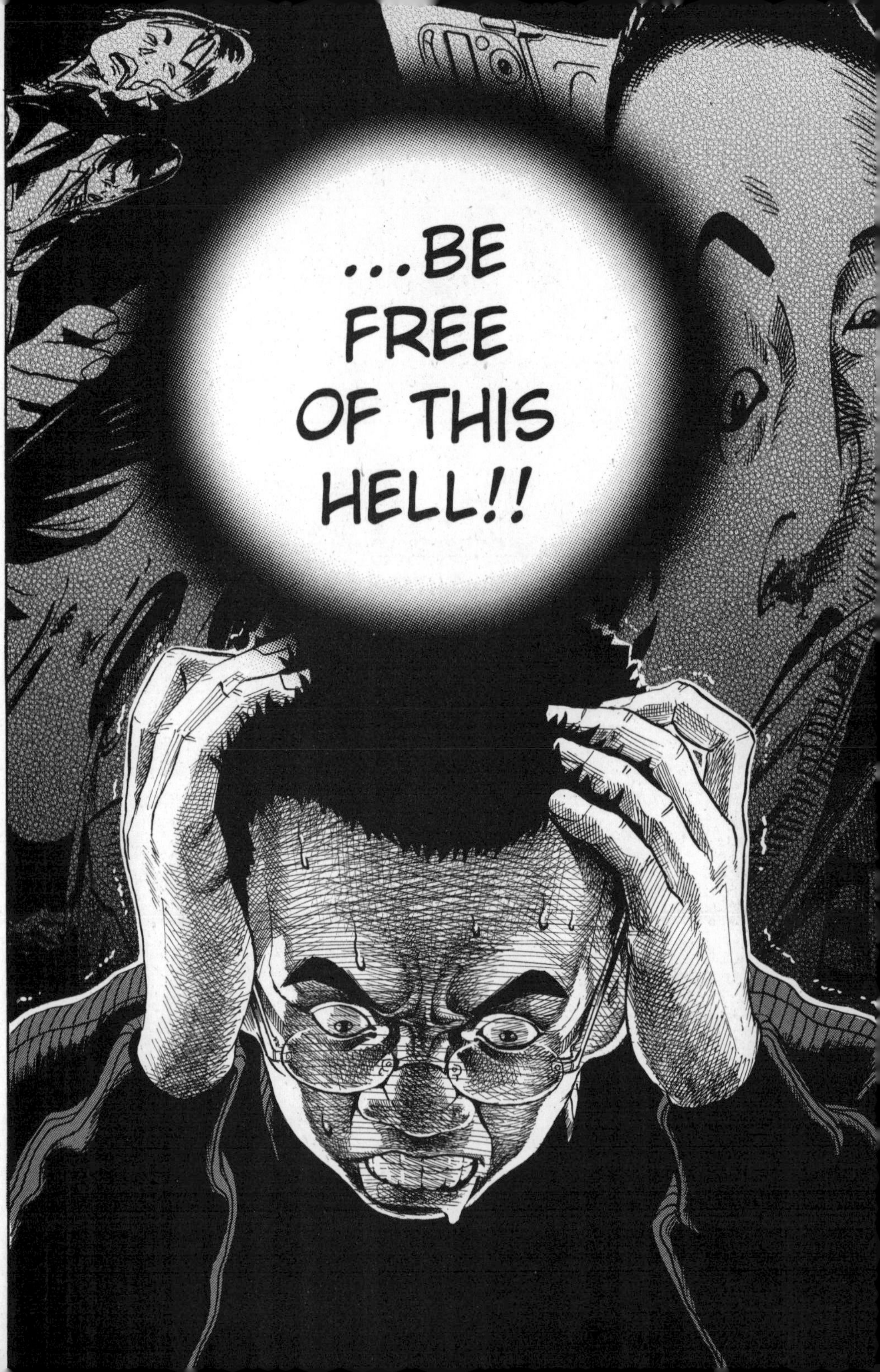
...BE FREE OF THIS HELL!!

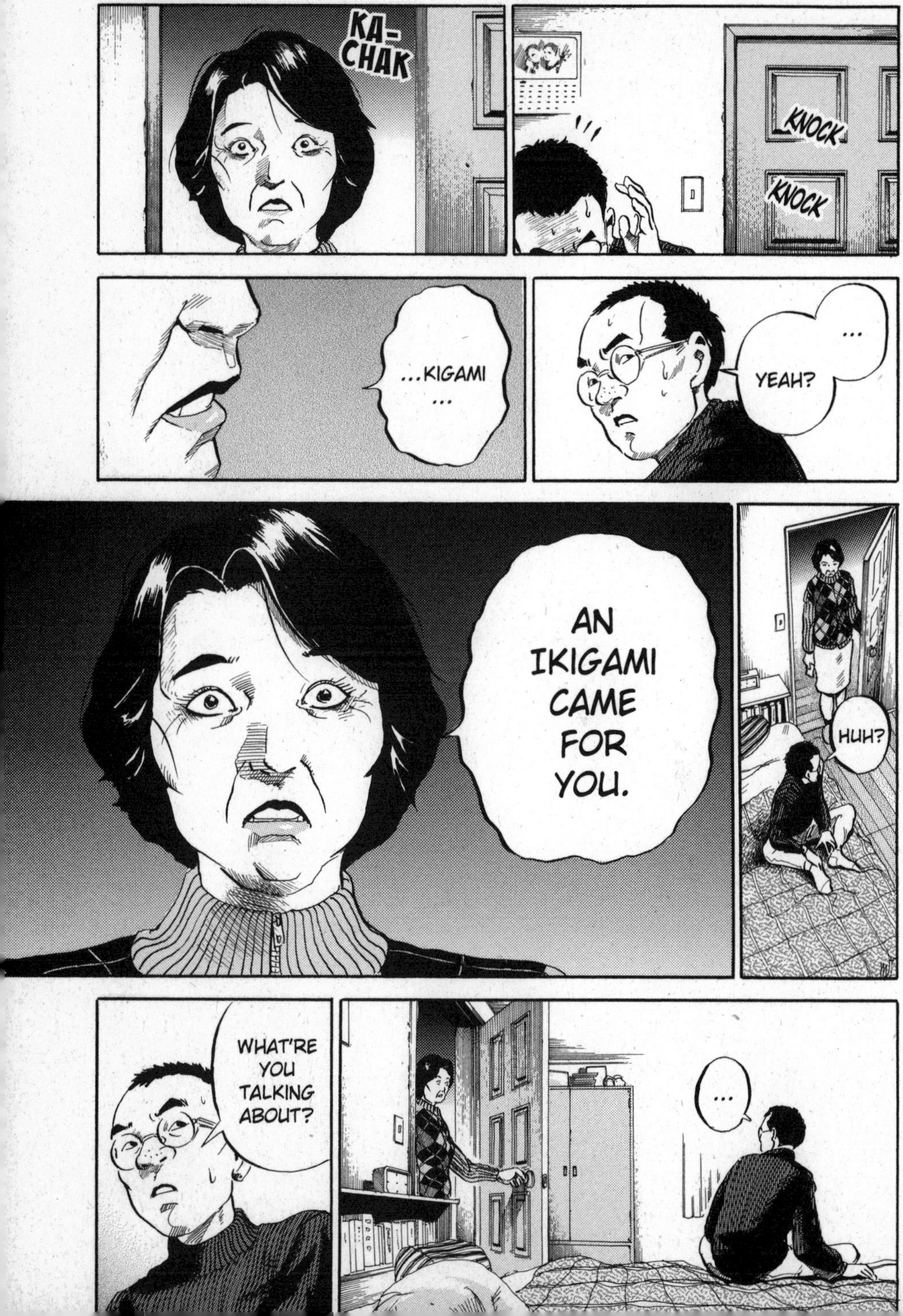
KNOCK
KNOCK
KA-CHAK
... YEAH?
...KIGAMI ...
HUH?
AN IKIGAMI CAME FOR YOU.
...
WHAT'RE YOU TALKING ABOUT?

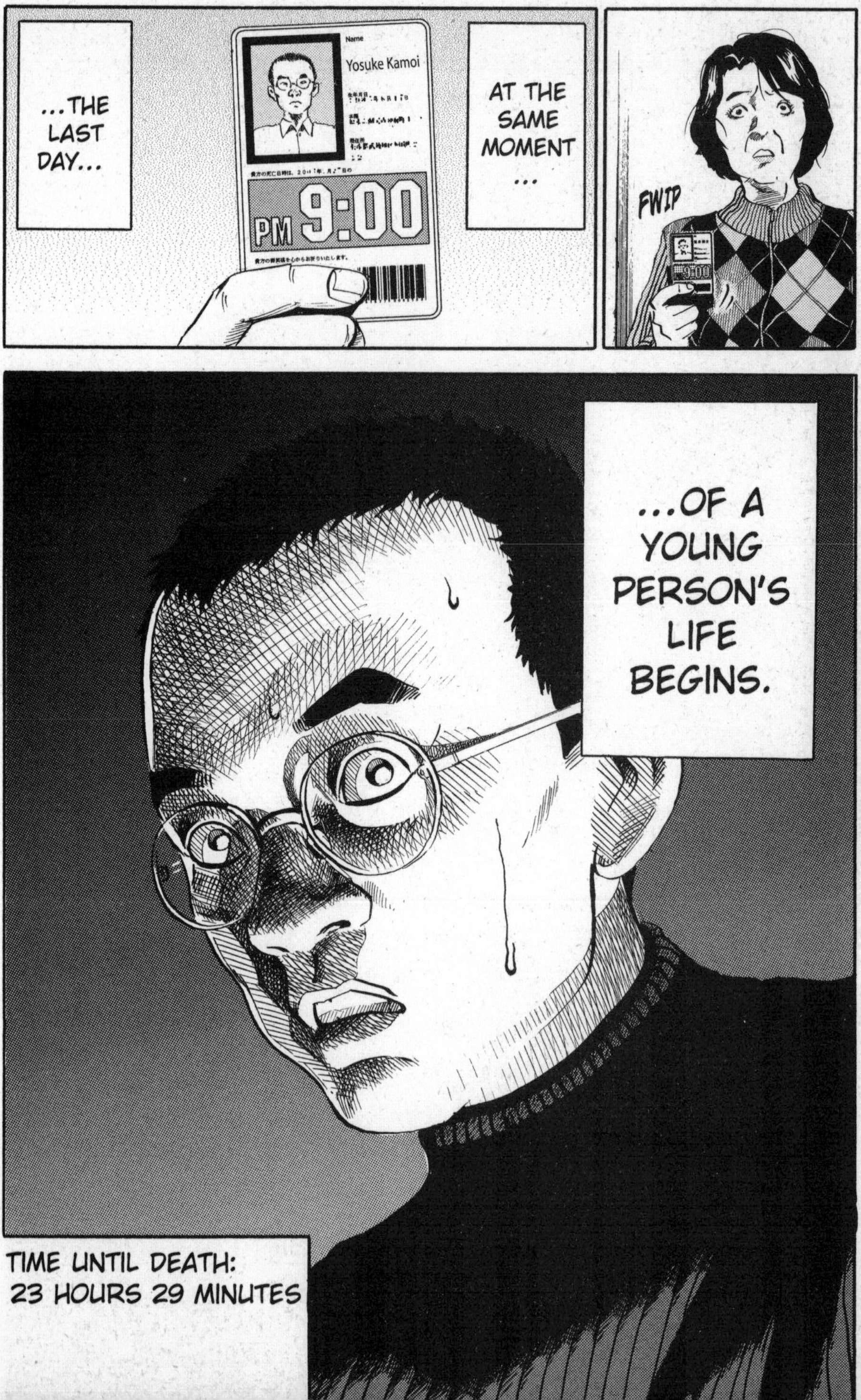
FWIP
AT THE SAME MOMENT...
Name
Yosuke Kamoi
PM 9:00
...THE LAST DAY...
...OF A YOUNG PERSON'S LIFE BEGINS.
TIME UNTIL DEATH: 23 HOURS 29 MINUTES

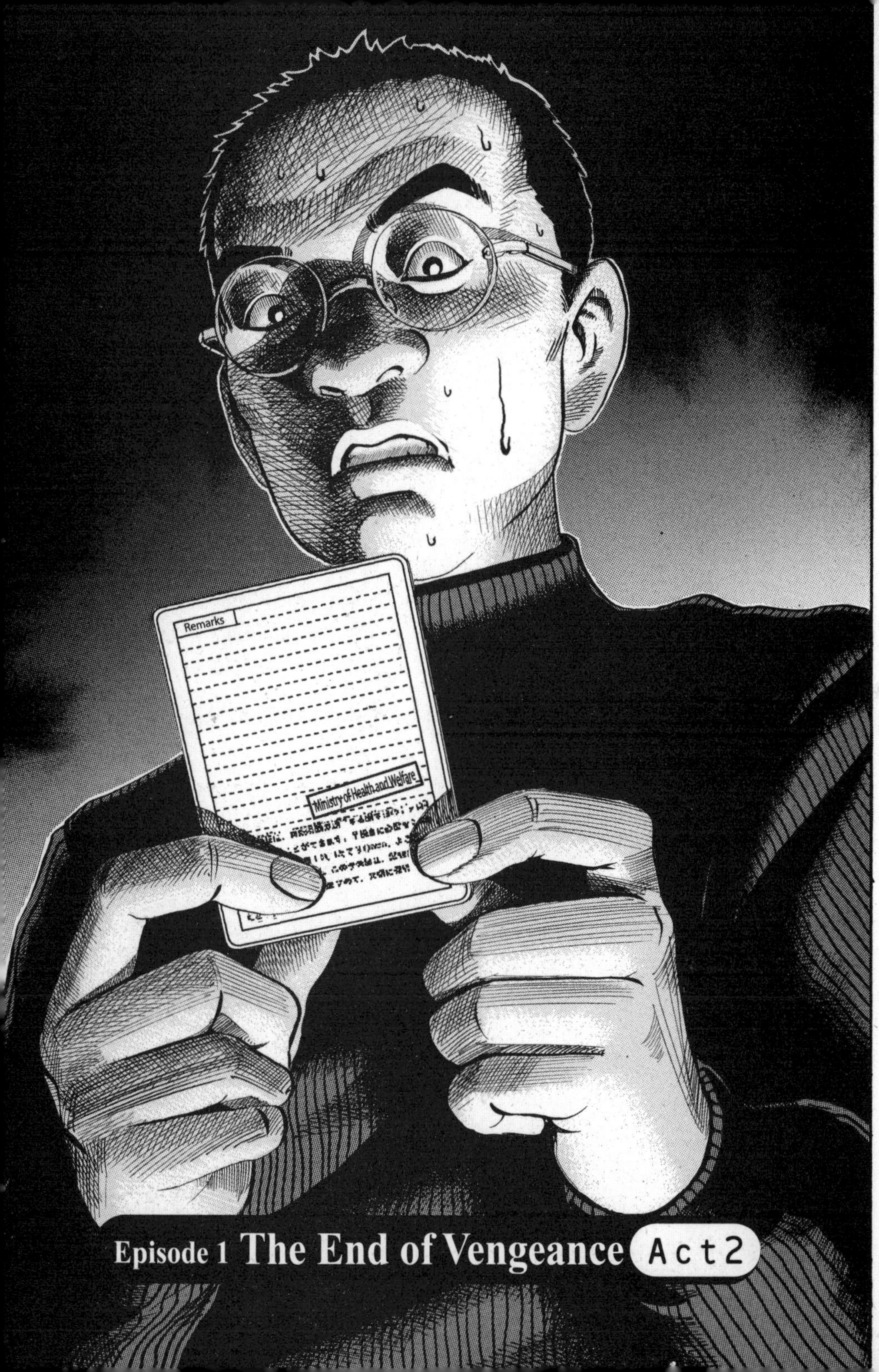
Remarks
Ministry of Health and Welfare

Episode 1 The End of Vengeance Act2

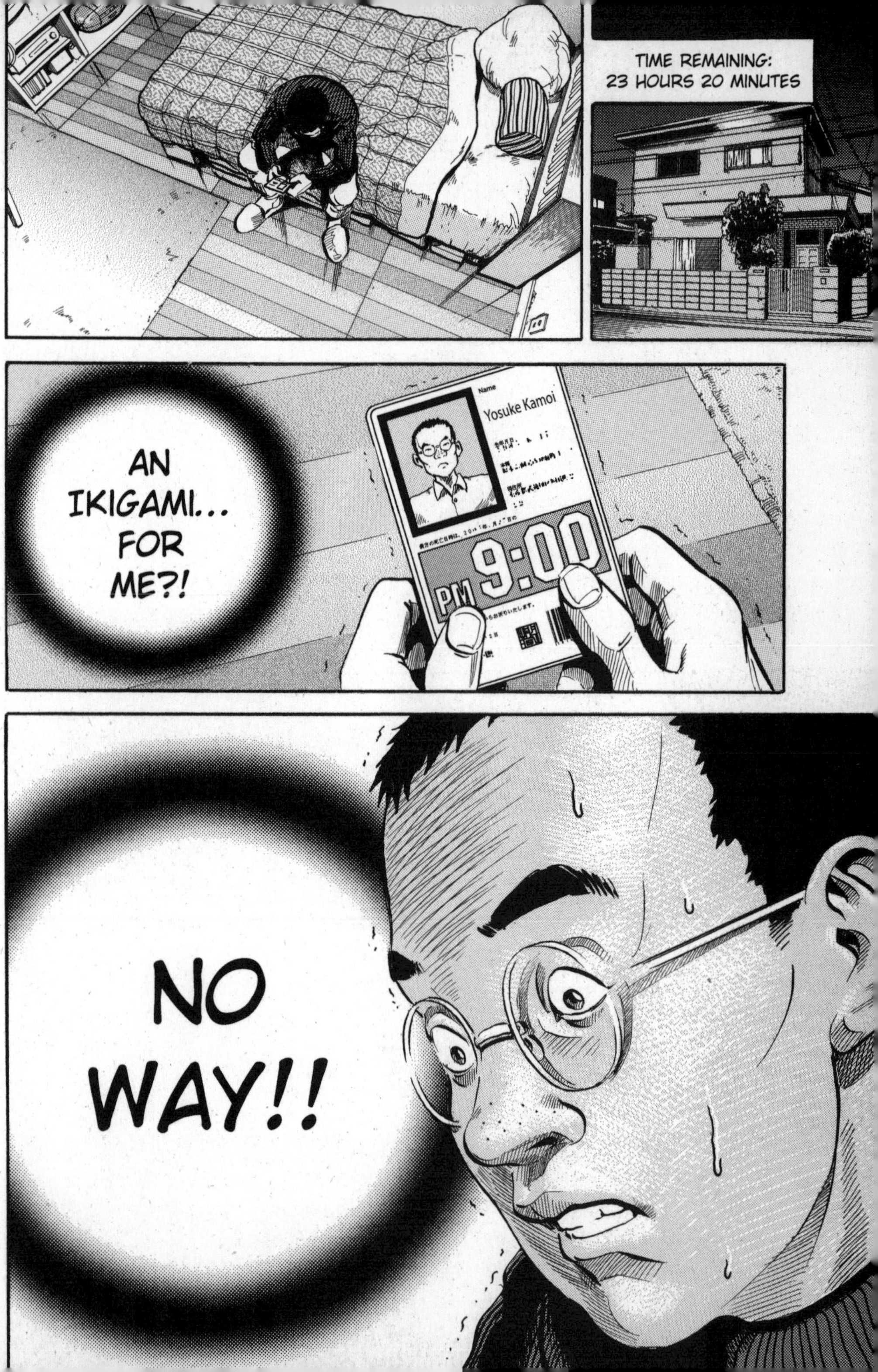
TIME REMAINING:
23 HOURS 20 MINUTES
Name
Yosuke Kamoi
PM 9:00
AN IKIGAMI... FOR ME?!
NO WAY!!

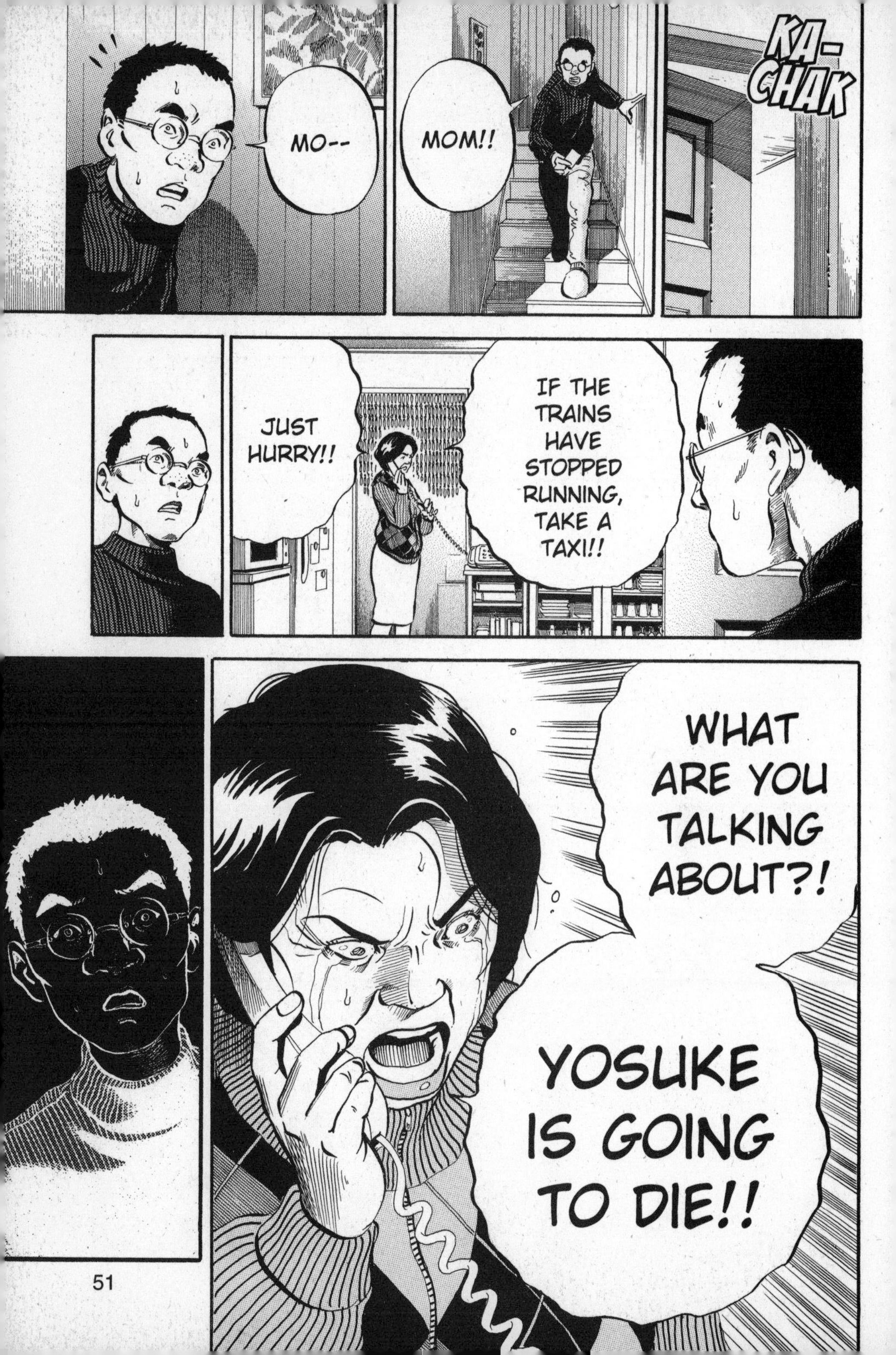
KA-CHAK
MOM!!
MO--
IF THE TRAINS HAVE STOPPED RUNNING, TAKE A TAXI!!
JUST HURRY!!
WHAT ARE YOU TALKING ABOUT?!
YOSUKE IS GOING TO DIE!!

WHAT HAPPENS WHEN YOU DIE...?

DOES EVERYTHING JUST DISAPPEAR...?

TICK
TOCK
TICK
TOCK

DOES EVERYTHING DISAPPEAR...?

YOUR DREAMS... YOUR HOPES... YOUR FUTURE... YOUR PAST...

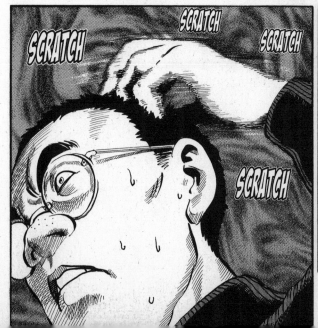

SCRATCH
SCRATCH
SCRATCH
SCRATCH

INCLUDING MY HORRIFIC PAST...

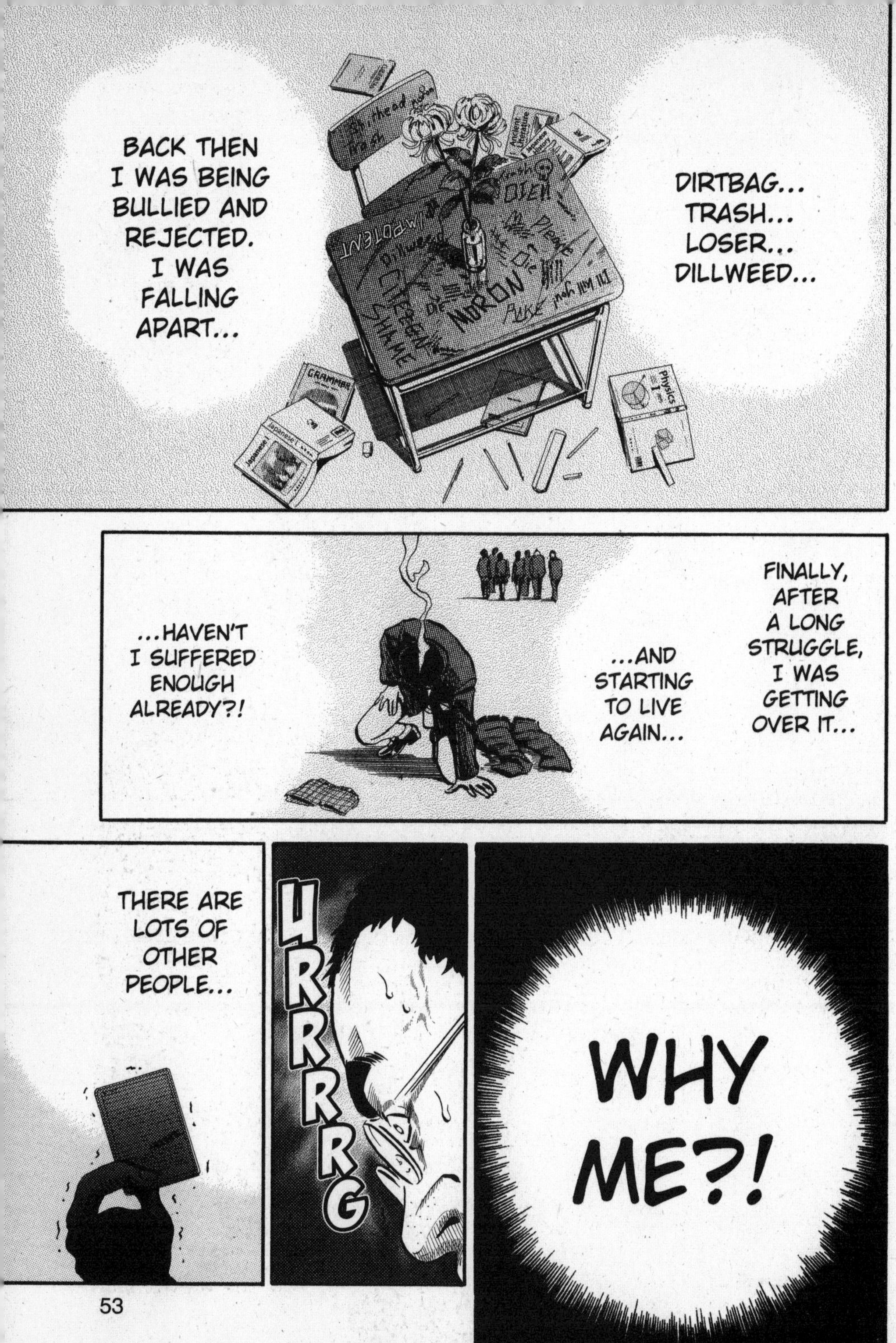
DIRTBAG... TRASH... LOSER... DILLWEED...
BACK THEN I WAS BEING BULLIED AND REJECTED. I WAS FALLING APART...
MORON
GRAMMER
Physics I
FINALLY, AFTER A LONG STRUGGLE, I WAS GETTING OVER IT...
...AND STARTING TO LIVE AGAIN...
...HAVEN'T I SUFFERED ENOUGH ALREADY?!
WHY ME?!
URRRRG
THERE ARE LOTS OF OTHER PEOPLE...

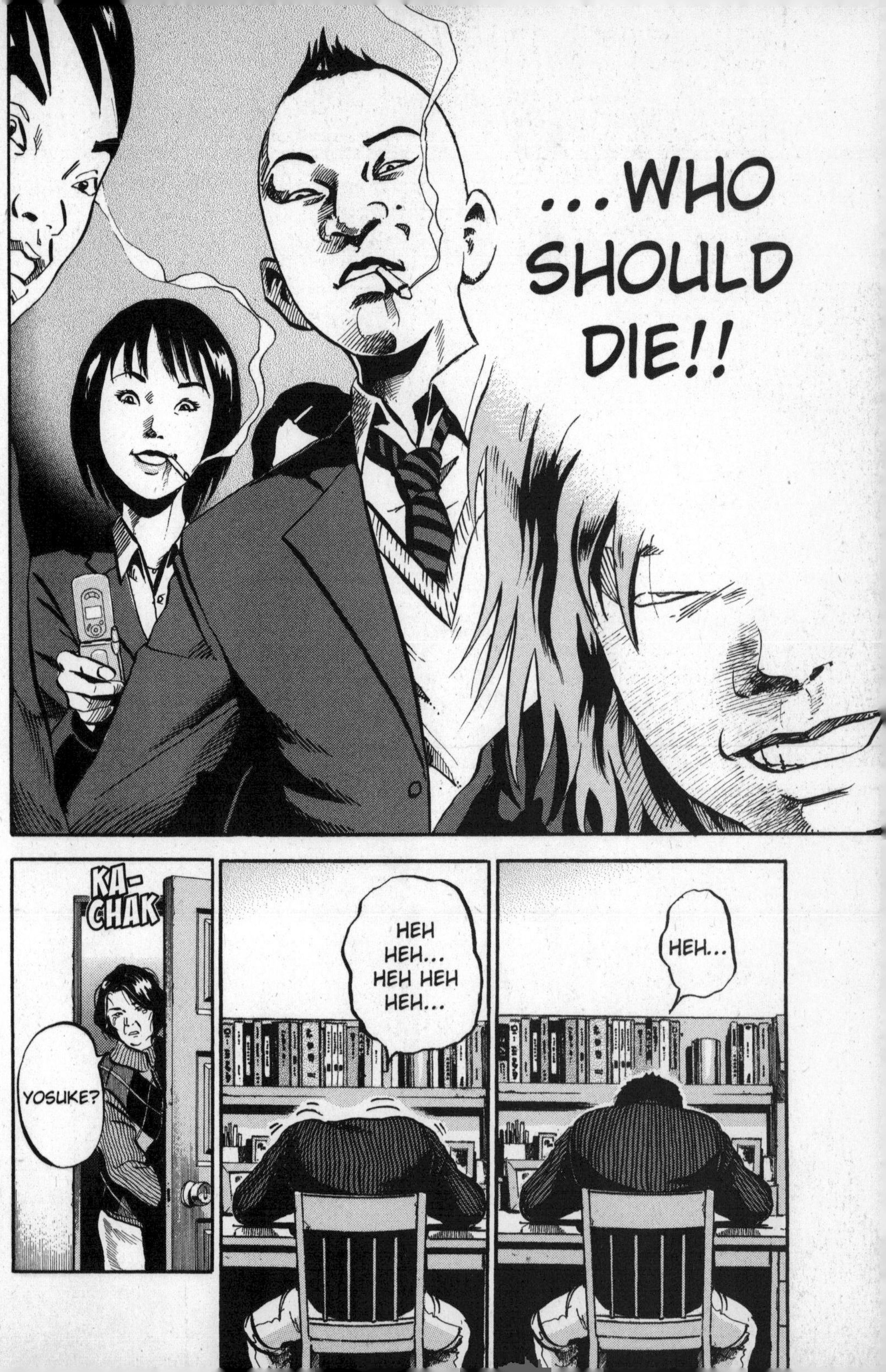
...WHO SHOULD DIE!!
HEH...
HEH HEH... HEH HEH HEH...
KA-CHAK
YOSUKE?

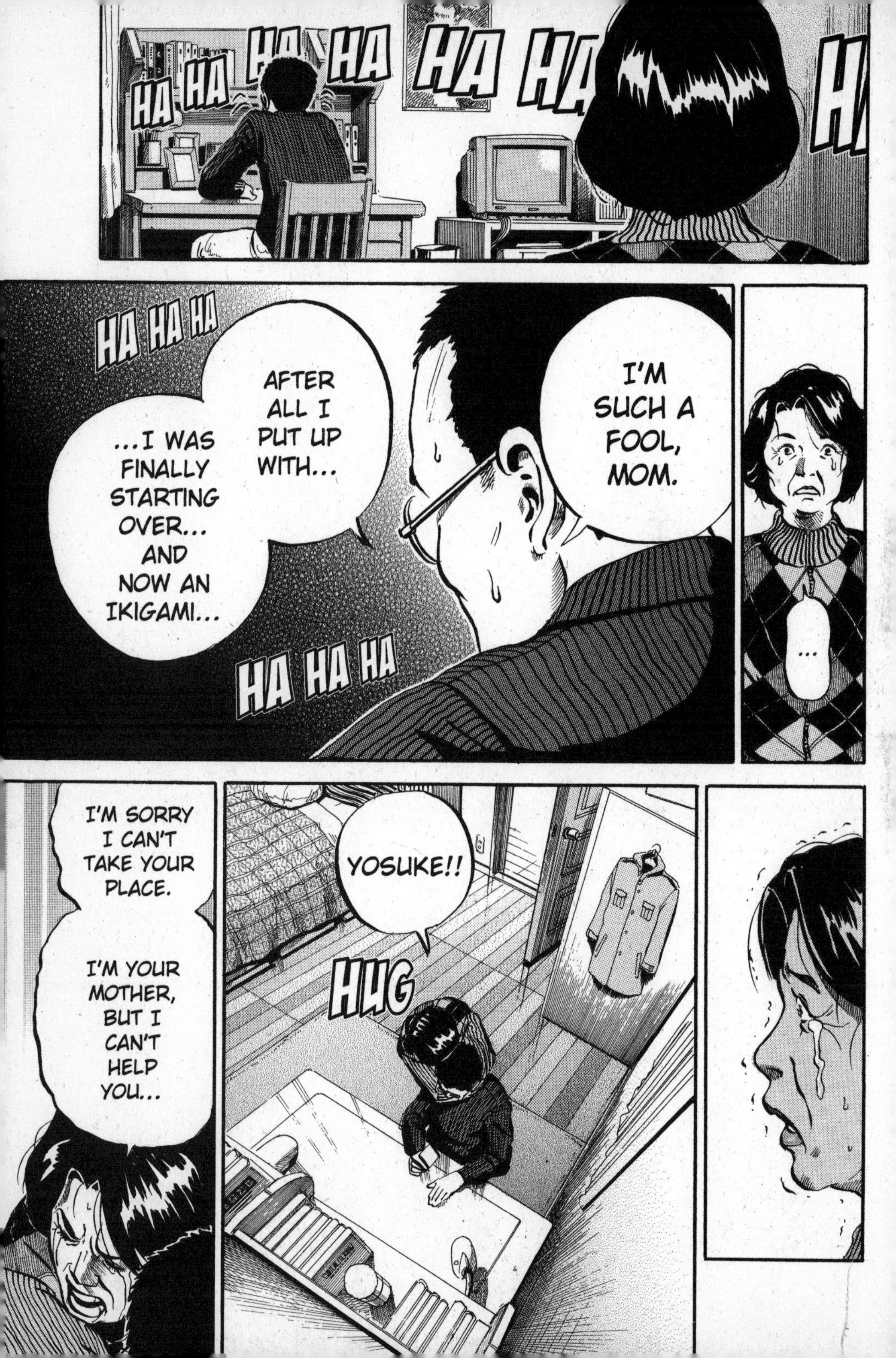
HA HA HA HA HA HA HA
...
I'M SUCH A FOOL, MOM.
AFTER ALL I PUT UP WITH...
...I WAS FINALLY STARTING OVER... AND NOW AN IKIGAMI...
HA HA HA
HA HA HA
YOSUKE!!
HUG
I'M SORRY I CAN'T TAKE YOUR PLACE.
I'M YOUR MOTHER, BUT I CAN'T HELP YOU...

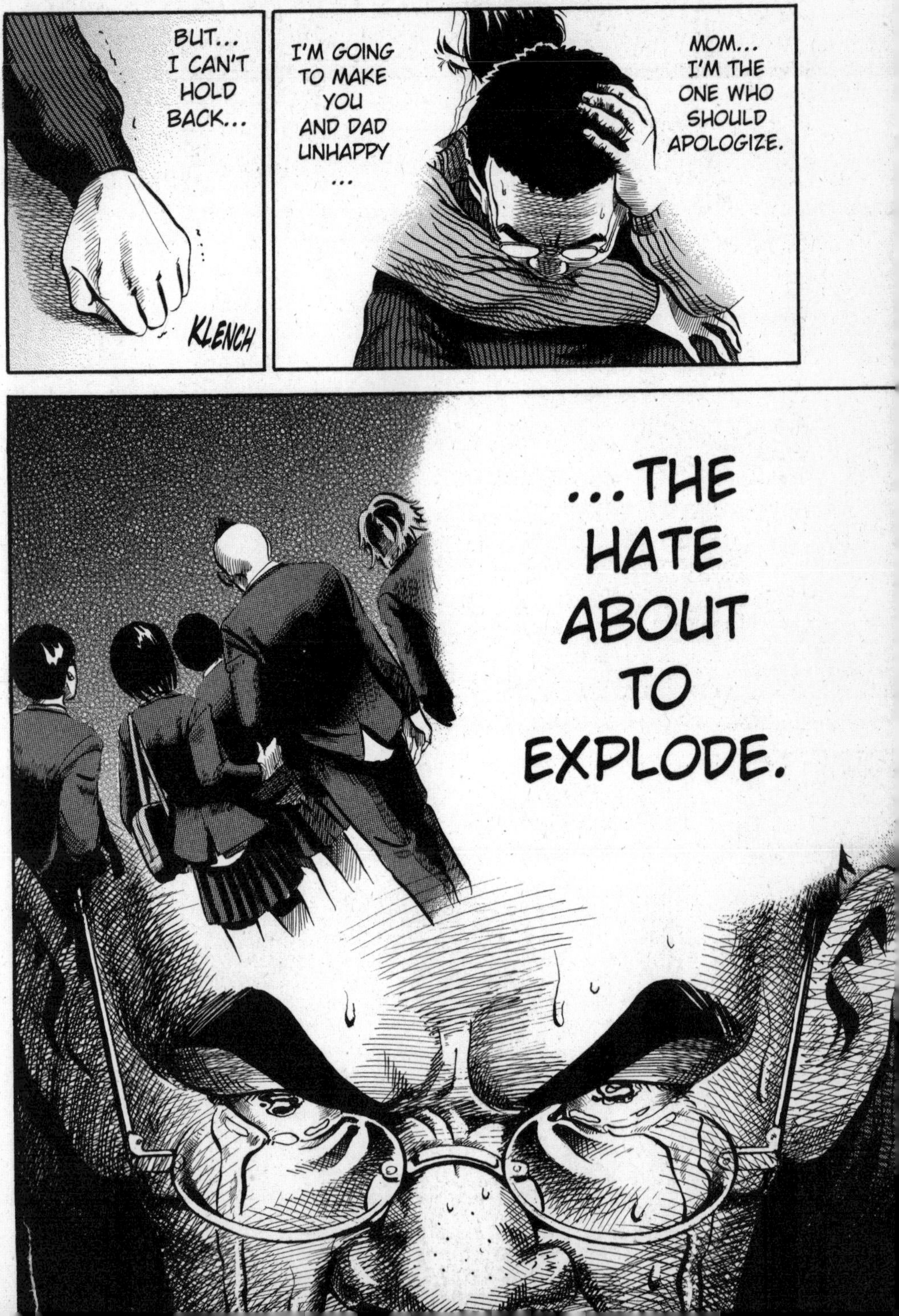
MOM... I'M THE ONE WHO SHOULD APOLOGIZE.
I'M GOING TO MAKE YOU AND DAD UNHAPPY ...
BUT... I CAN'T HOLD BACK...
KLENCH
...THE HATE ABOUT TO EXPLODE.

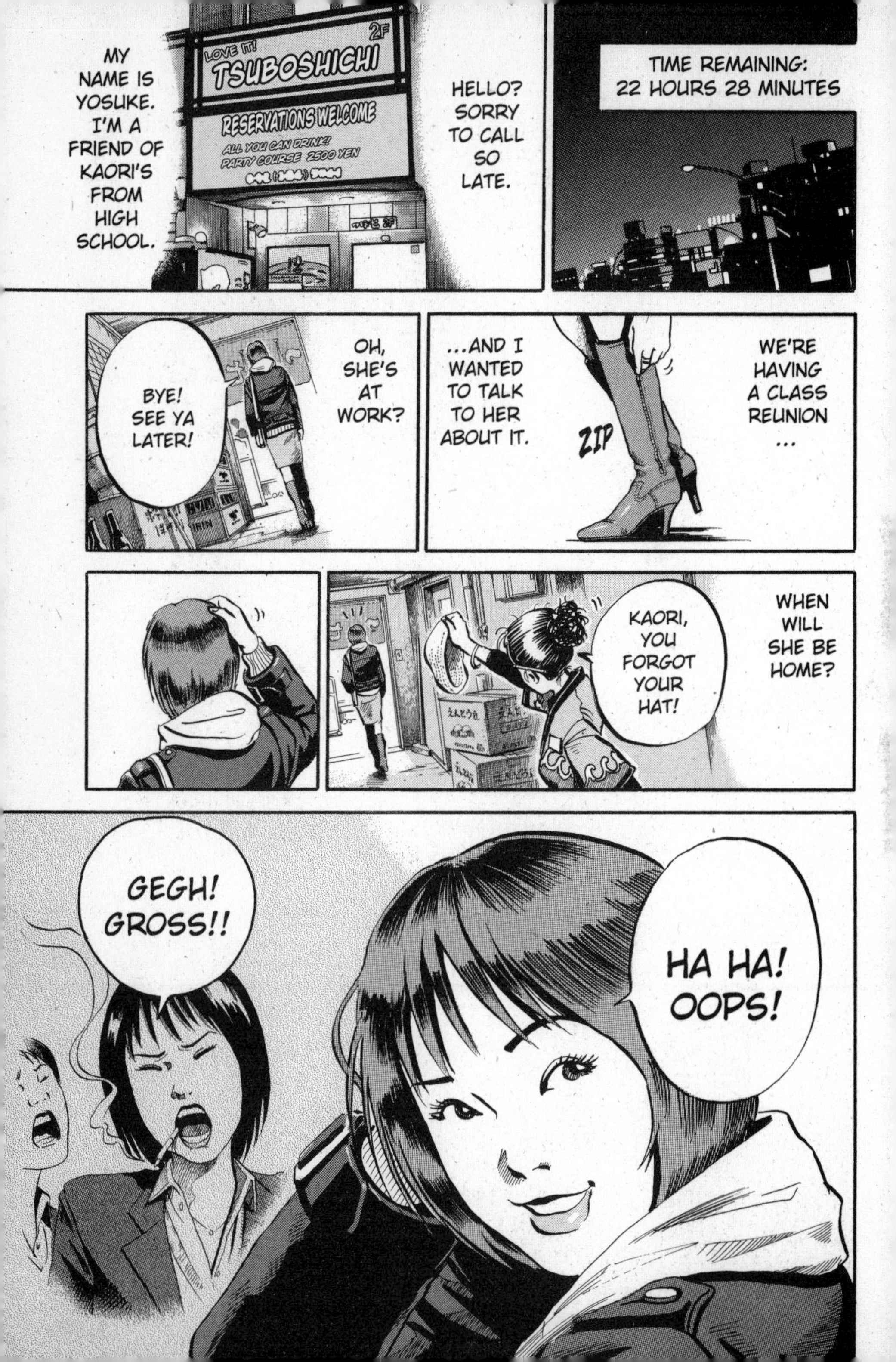
TIME REMAINING: 22 HOURS 28 MINUTES
HELLO? SORRY TO CALL SO LATE.
LOVE IT!
TSUBOSHICHI
2F
RESERVATIONS WELCOME
ALL YOU CAN DRINK!
PARTY COURSE 2500 YEN
MY NAME IS YOSUKE. I'M A FRIEND OF KAORI'S FROM HIGH SCHOOL.
WE'RE HAVING A CLASS REUNION ...
ZIP
...AND I WANTED TO TALK TO HER ABOUT IT.
OH, SHE'S AT WORK?
BYE! SEE YA LATER!
WHEN WILL SHE BE HOME?
KAORI, YOU FORGOT YOUR HAT!
HA HA! OOPS!
GEGH! GROSS!!

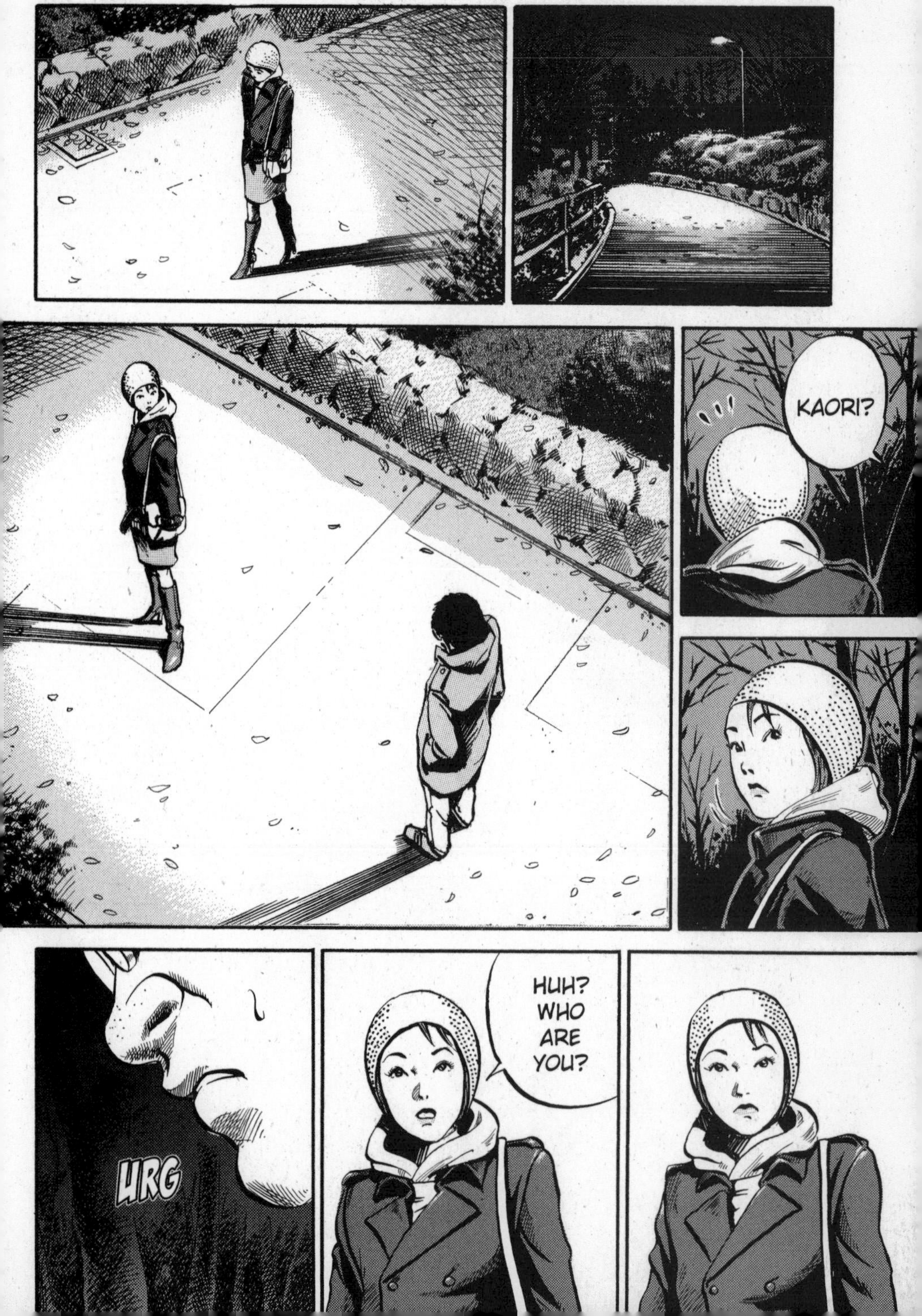
KAORI?
HUH? WHO ARE YOU?
URG

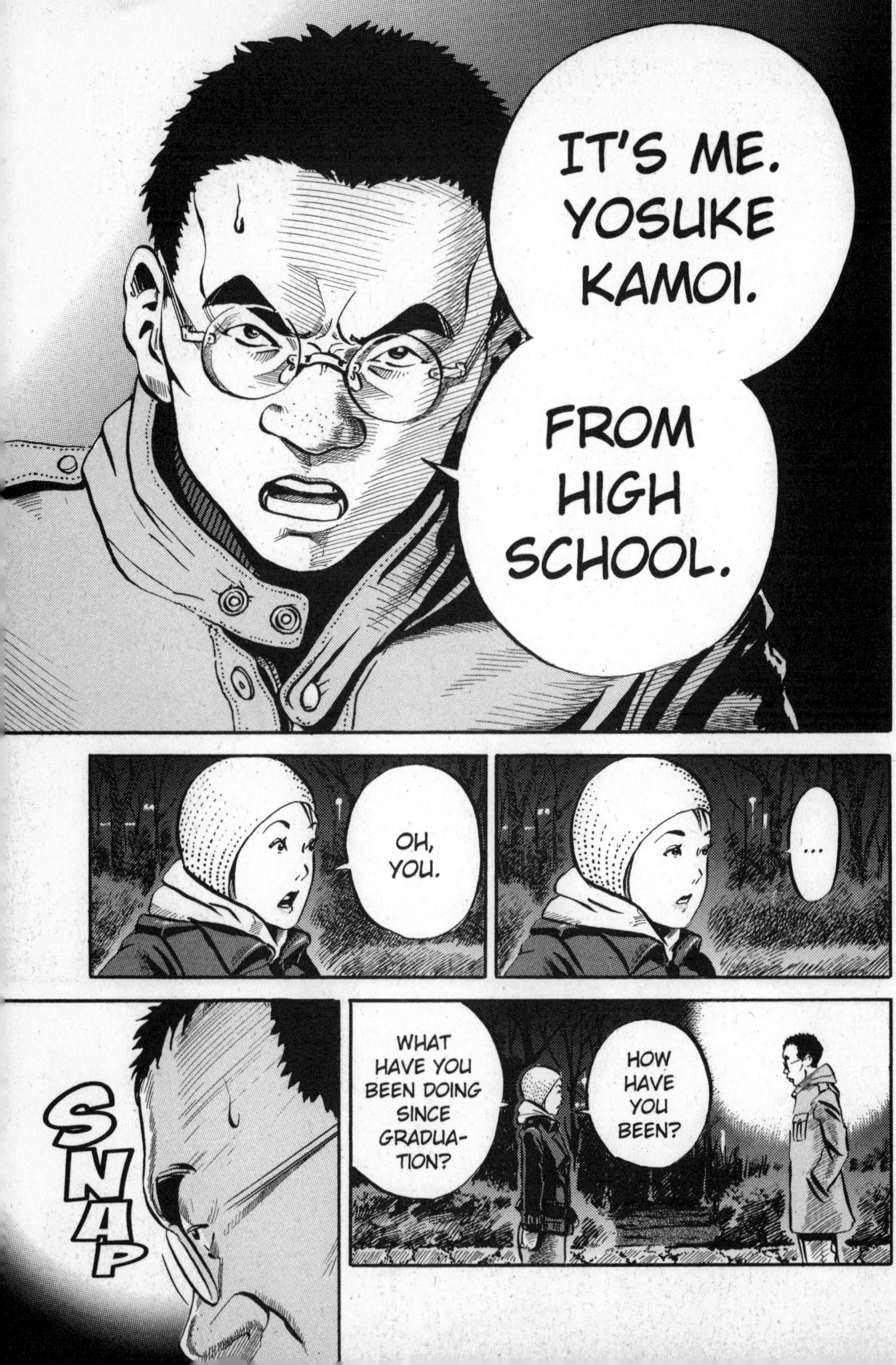
IT'S ME. YOSUKE KAMOI.
FROM HIGH SCHOOL.
...
OH, YOU.
HOW HAVE YOU BEEN?
WHAT HAVE YOU BEEN DOING SINCE GRADUA-TION?
SNAP

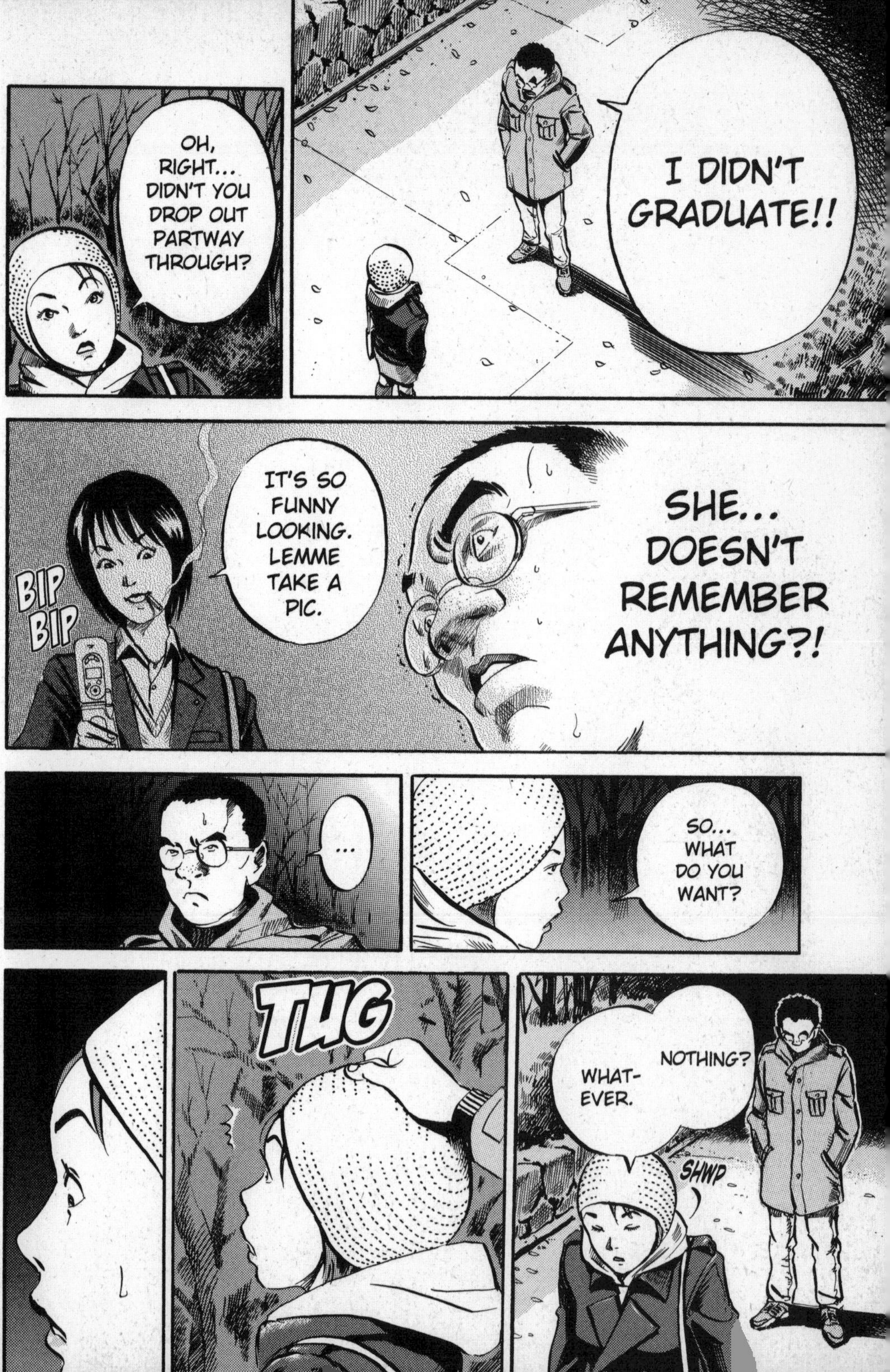
I DIDN'T GRADUATE!!
OH, RIGHT... DIDN'T YOU DROP OUT PARTWAY THROUGH?
SHE... DOESN'T REMEMBER ANYTHING?!
IT'S SO FUNNY LOOKING. LEMME TAKE A PIC.
BIP BIP
SO... WHAT DO YOU WANT?
...
NOTHING?
WHAT-EVER.
SHWP
TUG

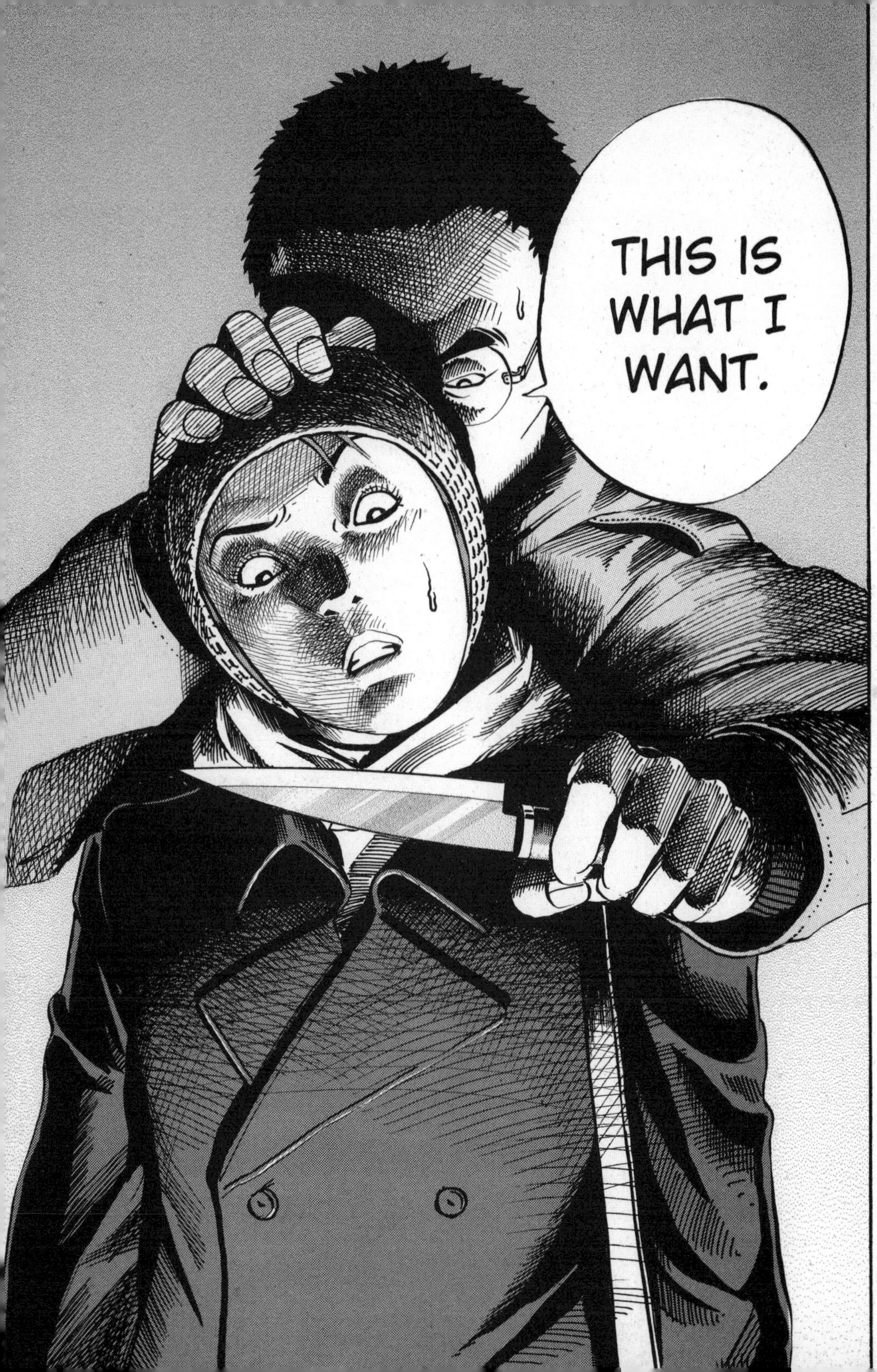
THIS IS WHAT I WANT.

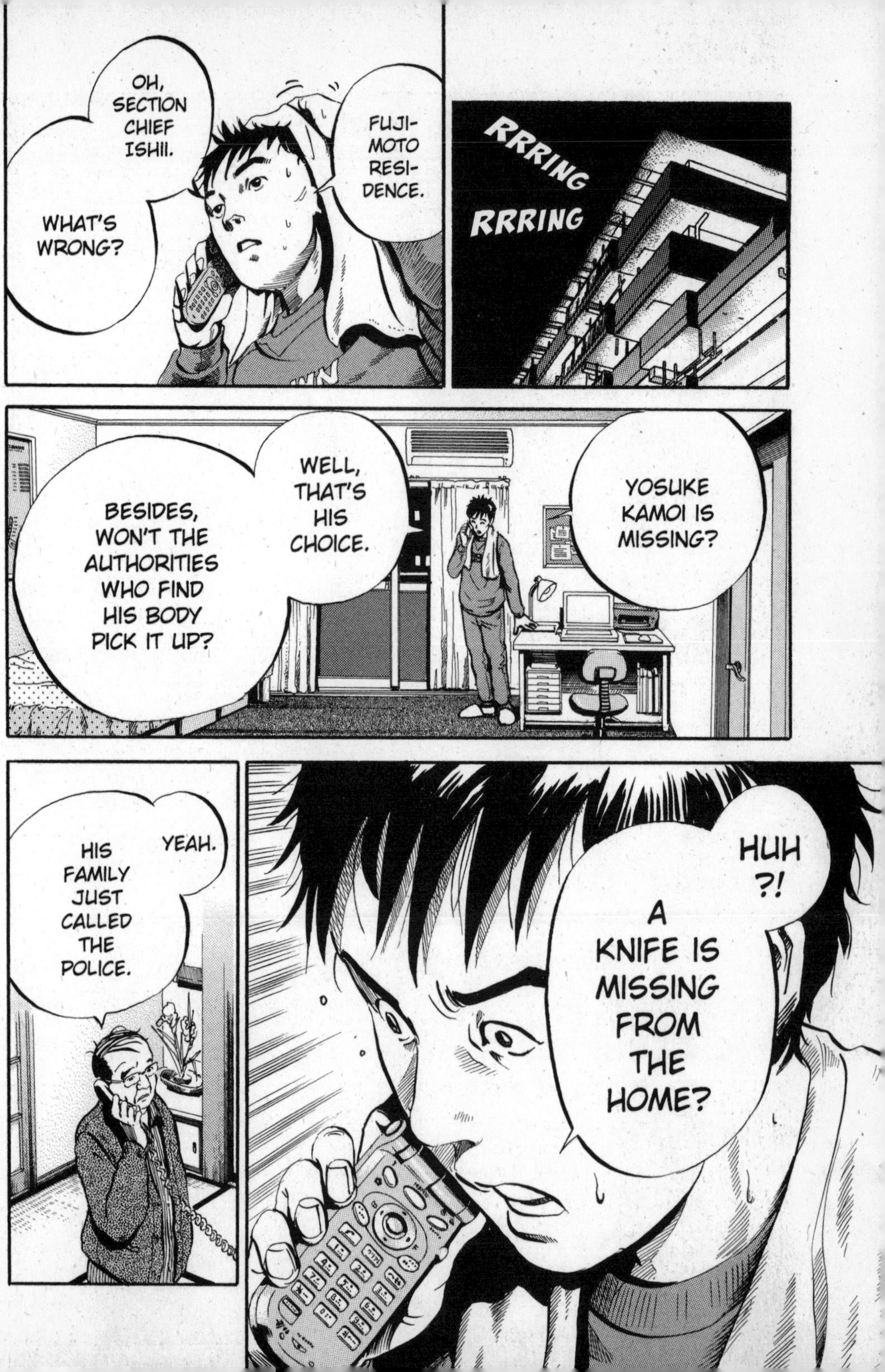
RRRING
RRRING
FUJI-MOTO RESI-DENCE.
OH, SECTION CHIEF ISHII.
WHAT'S WRONG?
YOSUKE KAMOI IS MISSING?
WELL, THAT'S HIS CHOICE.
BESIDES, WON'T THE AUTHORITIES WHO FIND HIS BODY PICK IT UP?
HUH ?!
A KNIFE IS MISSING FROM THE HOME?
YEAH.
HIS FAMILY JUST CALLED THE POLICE.

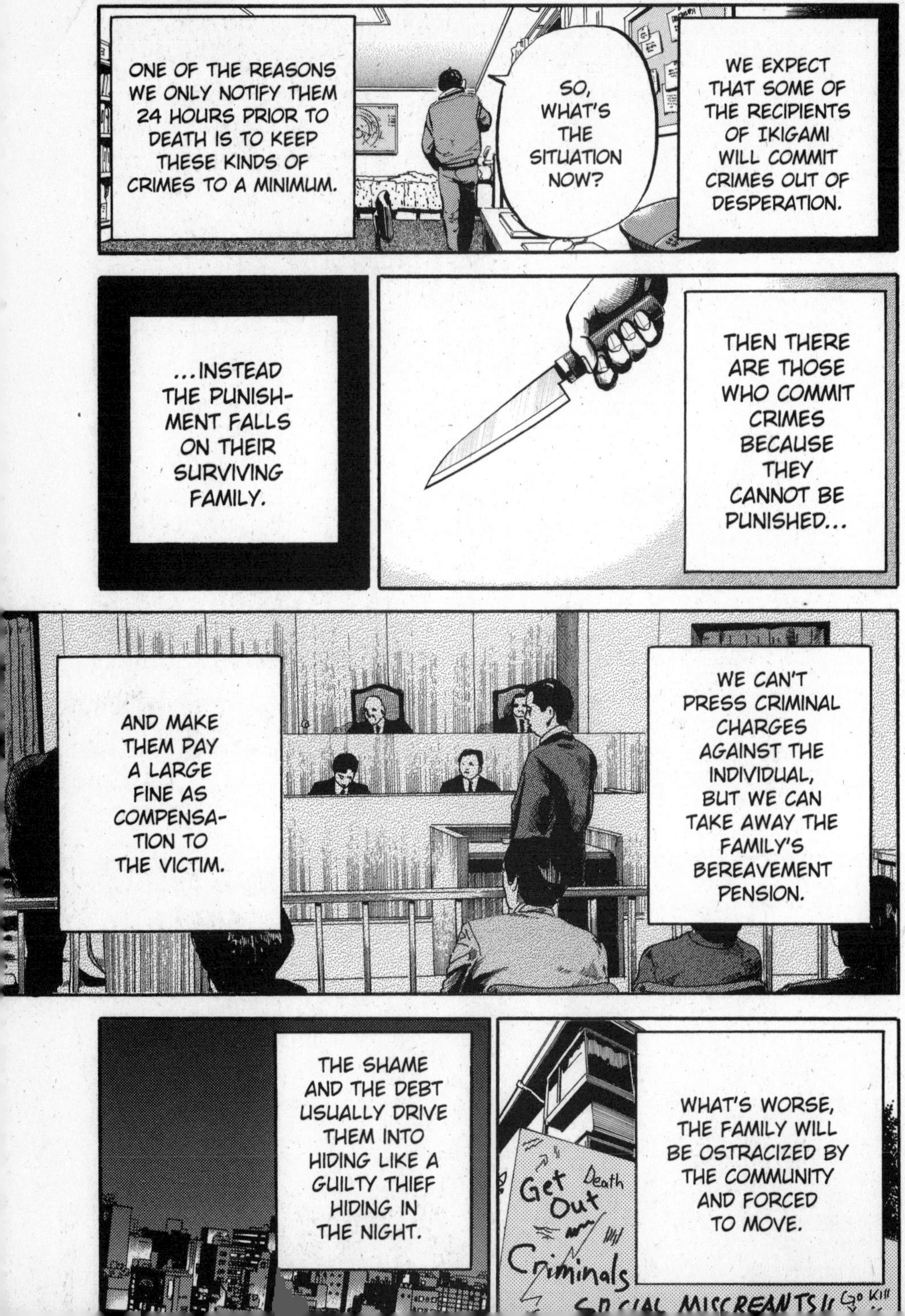
WE EXPECT THAT SOME OF THE RECIPIENTS OF IKIGAMI WILL COMMIT CRIMES OUT OF DESPERATION.
SO, WHAT'S THE SITUATION NOW?
ONE OF THE REASONS WE ONLY NOTIFY THEM 24 HOURS PRIOR TO DEATH IS TO KEEP THESE KINDS OF CRIMES TO A MINIMUM.
THEN THERE ARE THOSE WHO COMMIT CRIMES BECAUSE THEY CANNOT BE PUNISHED...
...INSTEAD THE PUNISH-MENT FALLS ON THEIR SURVIVING FAMILY.
WE CAN'T PRESS CRIMINAL CHARGES AGAINST THE INDIVIDUAL, BUT WE CAN TAKE AWAY THE FAMILY'S BEREAVEMENT PENSION.
AND MAKE THEM PAY A LARGE FINE AS COMPENSA-TION TO THE VICTIM.
WHAT'S WORSE, THE FAMILY WILL BE OSTRACIZED BY THE COMMUNITY AND FORCED TO MOVE.
Get Out
Death
Criminals
MISCREANTS!!
Go Kill
THE SHAME AND THE DEBT USUALLY DRIVE THEM INTO HIDING LIKE A GUILTY THIEF HIDING IN THE NIGHT.

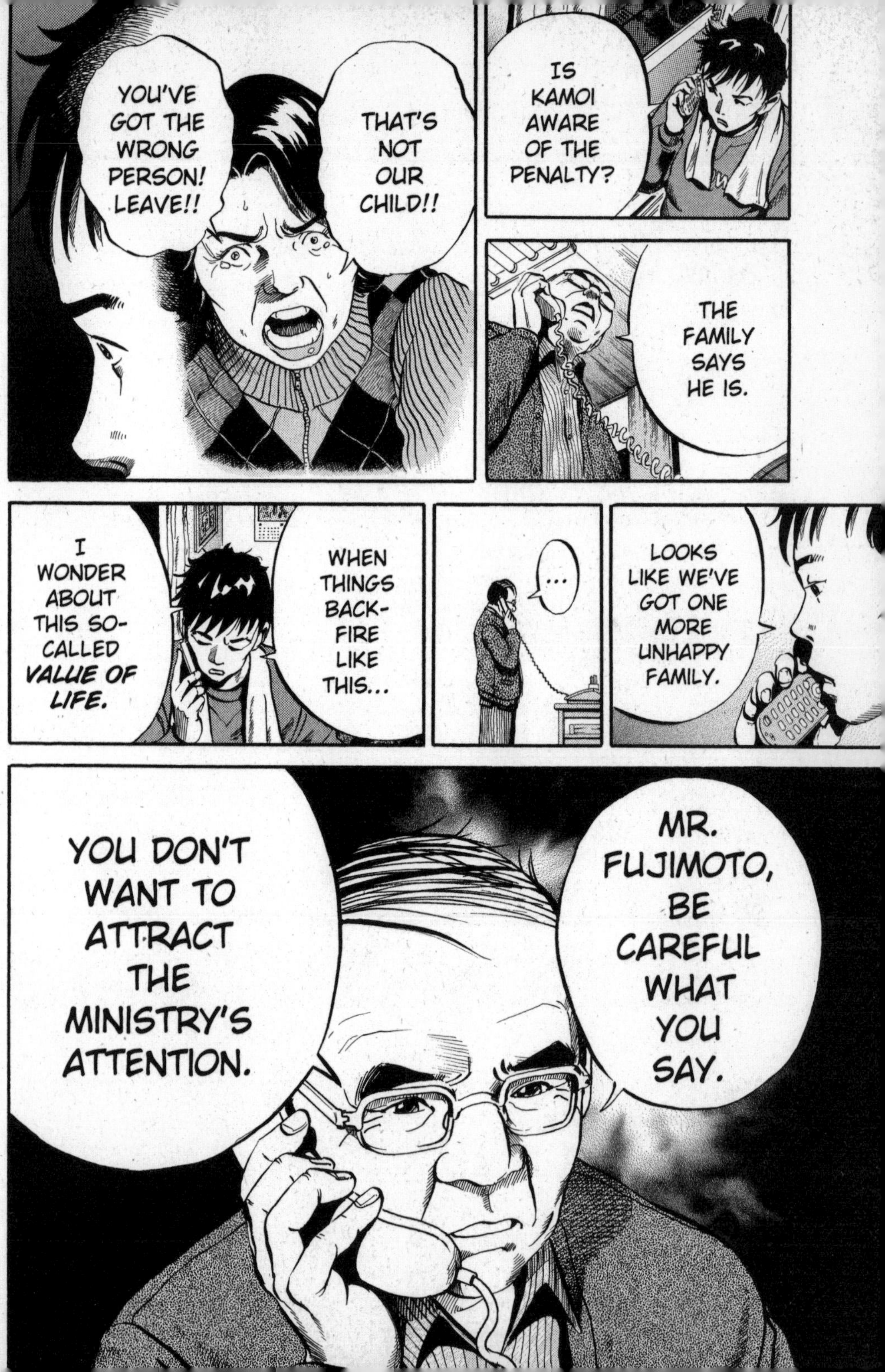
IS KAMOI AWARE OF THE PENALTY?
THE FAMILY SAYS HE IS.
THAT'S NOT OUR CHILD!!
YOU'VE GOT THE WRONG PERSON! LEAVE!!
LOOKS LIKE WE'VE GOT ONE MORE UNHAPPY FAMILY.
...
WHEN THINGS BACK-FIRE LIKE THIS...
I WONDER ABOUT THIS SO-CALLED *VALUE OF LIFE.*
MR. FUJIMOTO, BE CAREFUL WHAT YOU SAY.
YOU DON'T WANT TO ATTRACT THE MINISTRY'S ATTENTION.

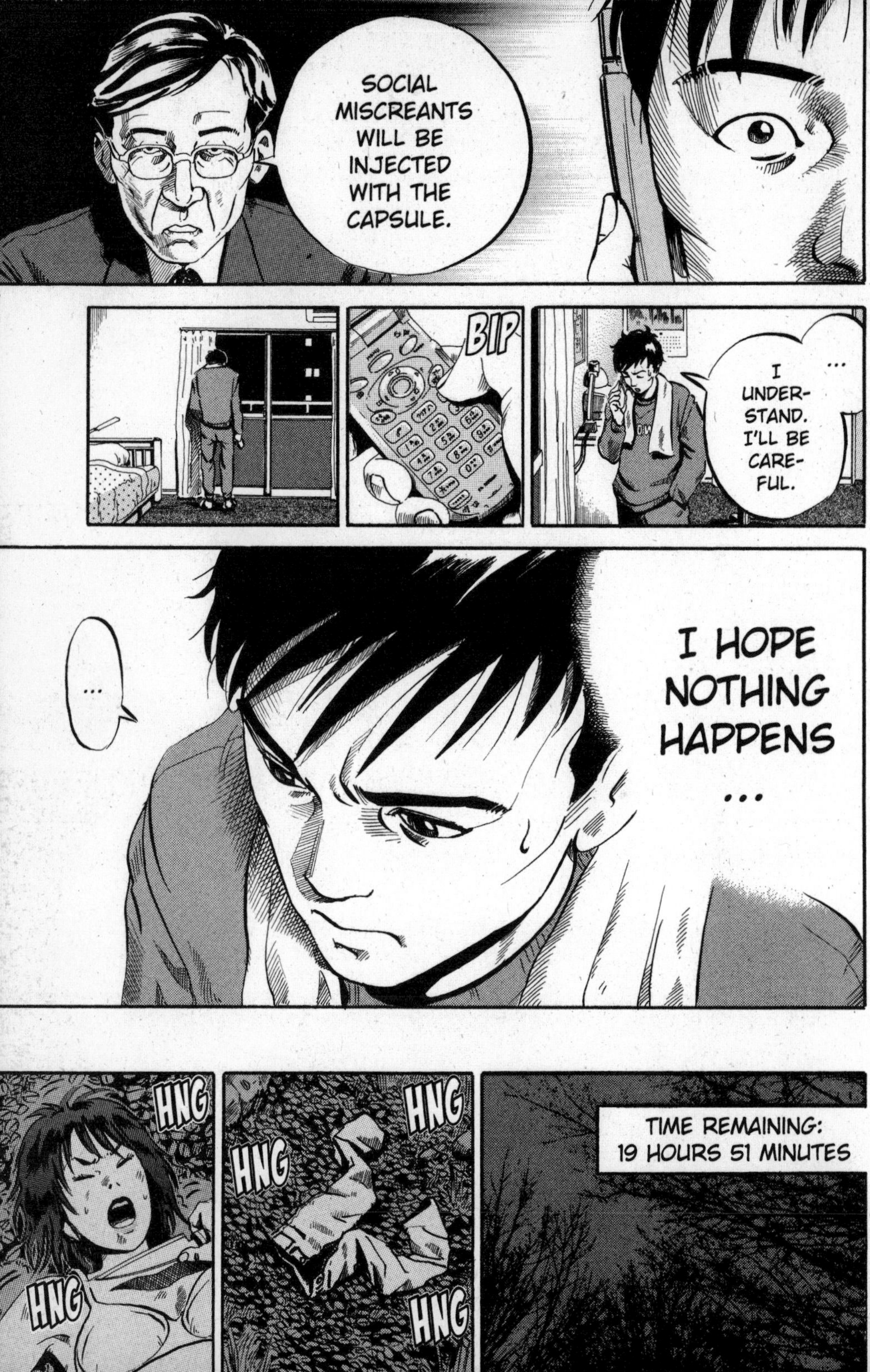
SOCIAL MISCREANTS WILL BE INJECTED WITH THE CAPSULE.
... I UNDERSTAND. I'LL BE CAREFUL.
BIP
I HOPE NOTHING HAPPENS ...
...
TIME REMAINING: 19 HOURS 51 MINUTES
HNG
HNG
HNG
HNG
HNG

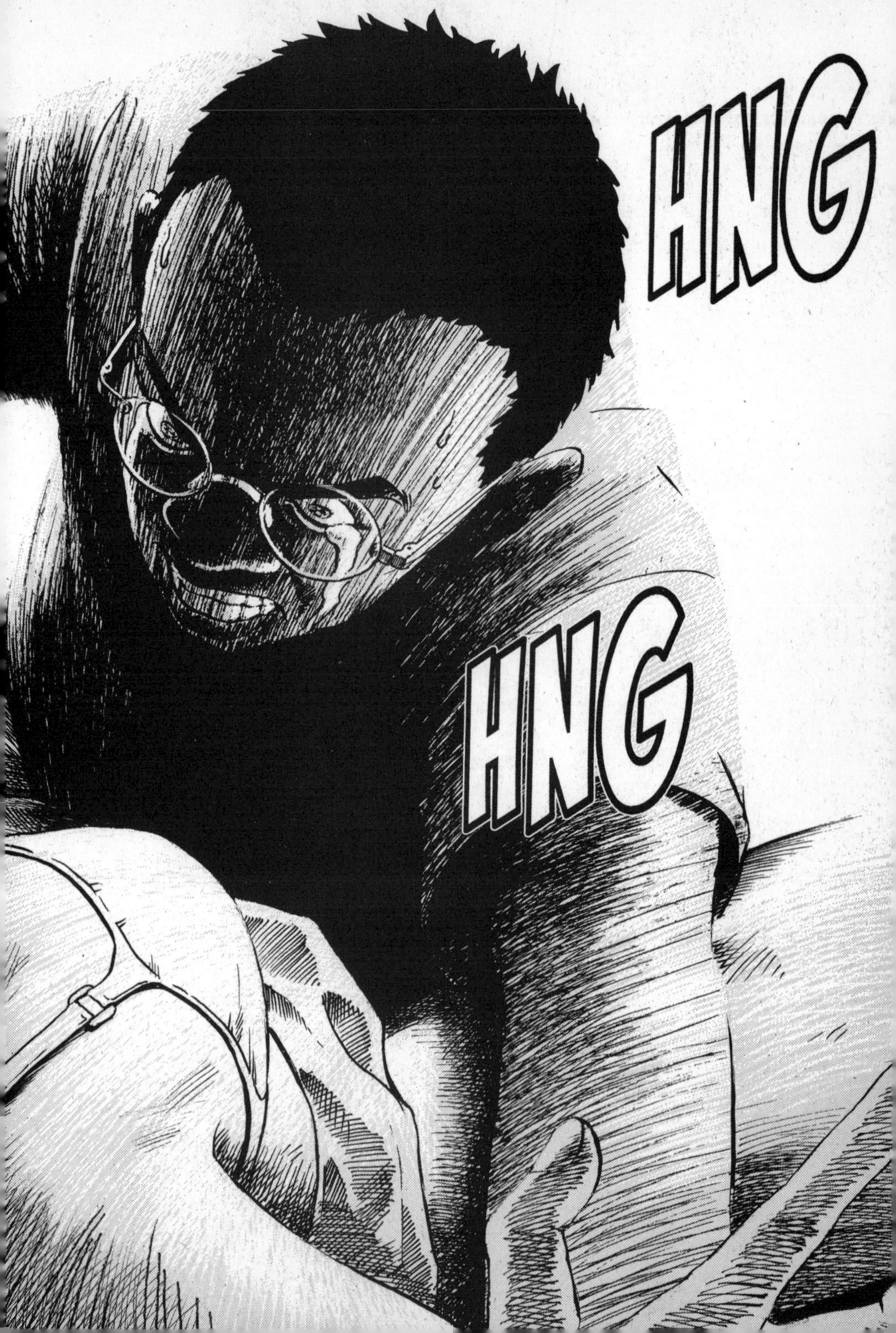
HNG
HNG

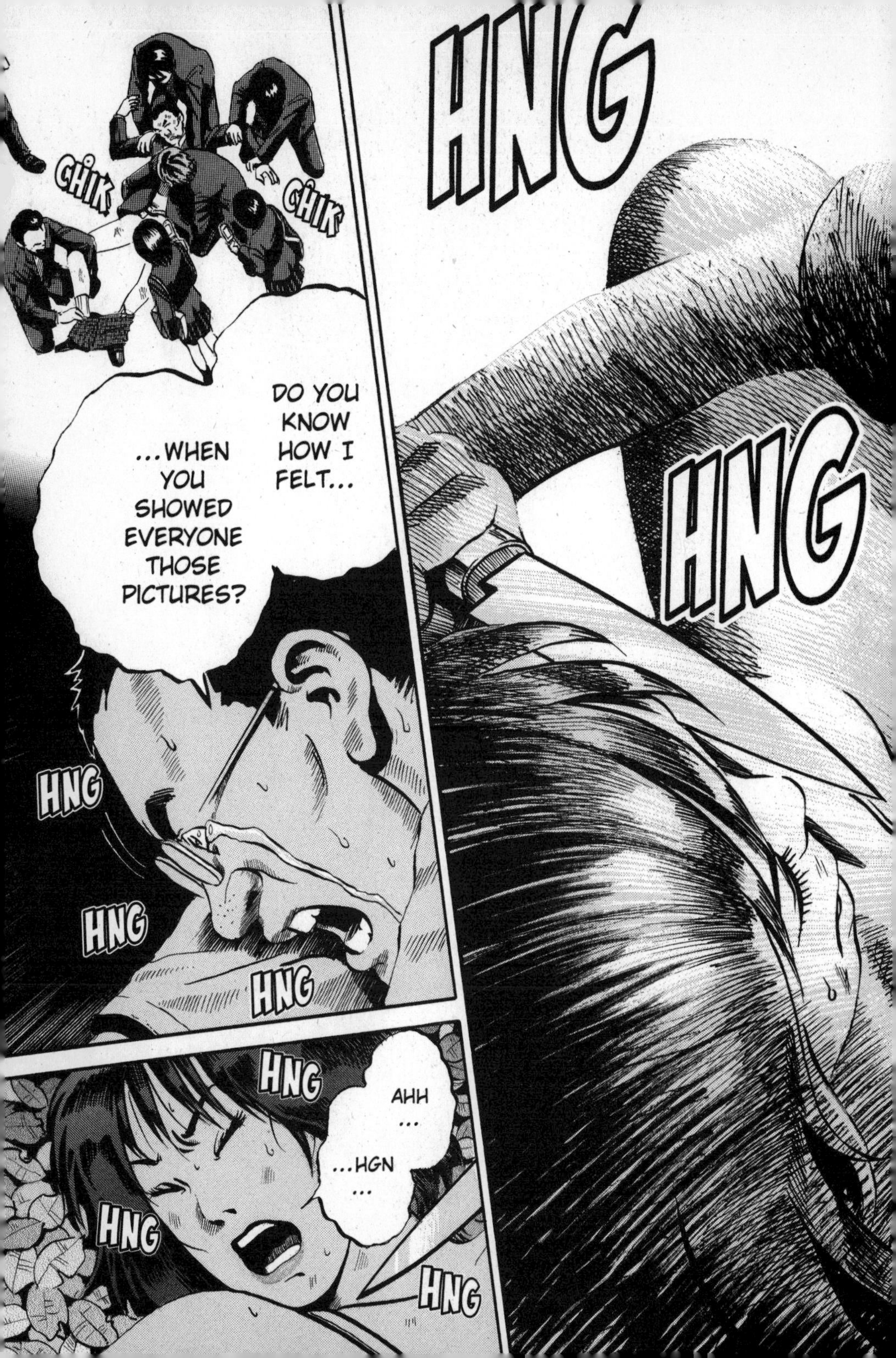
HNG
HNG
CHIK
CHIK
DO YOU KNOW HOW I FELT...
...WHEN YOU SHOWED EVERYONE THOSE PICTURES?
HNG
HNG
HNG
HNG
AHH ...
...HGN ...
HNG
HNG

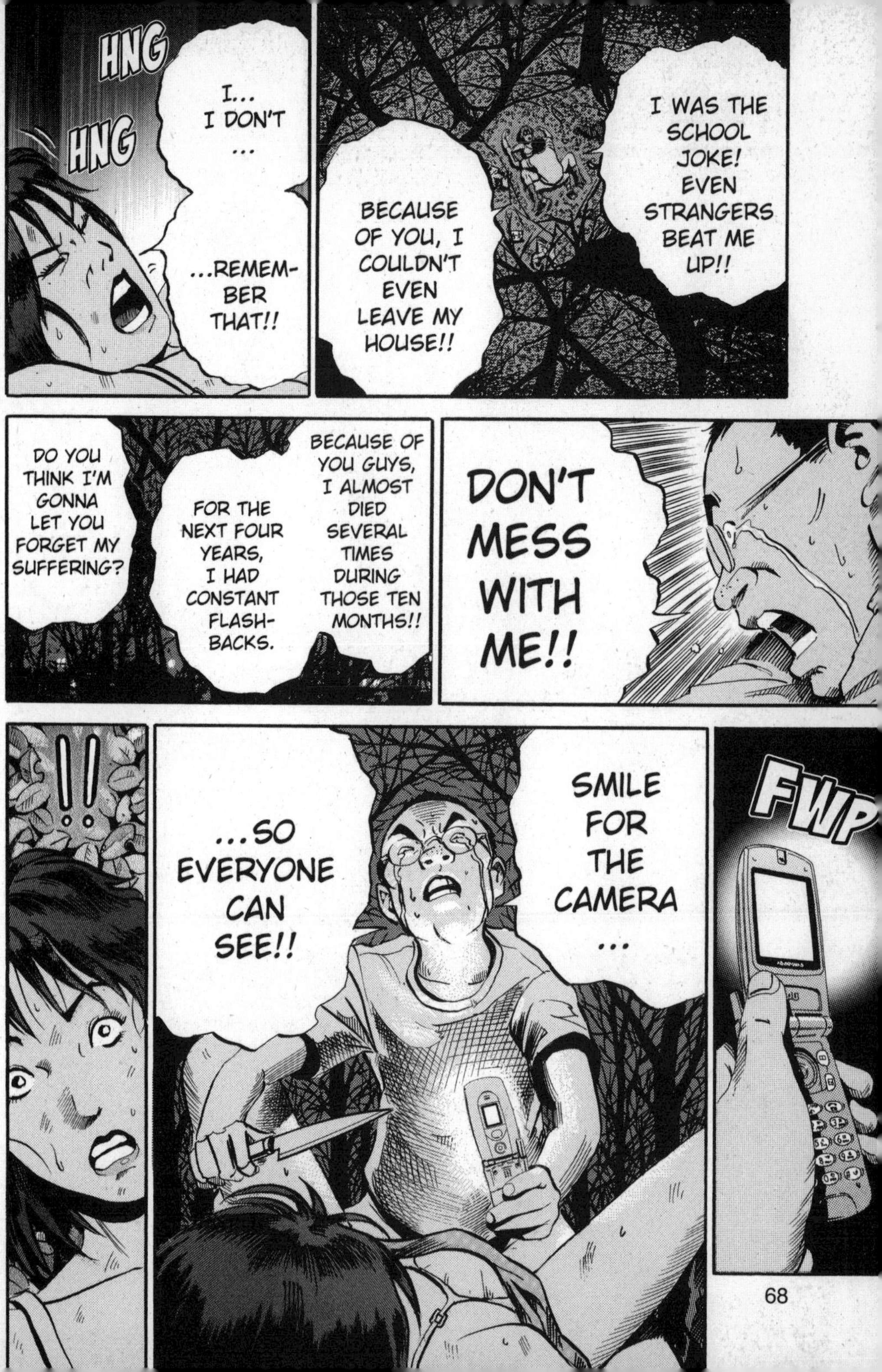

I WAS THE SCHOOL JOKE! EVEN STRANGERS BEAT ME UP!!
BECAUSE OF YOU, I COULDN'T EVEN LEAVE MY HOUSE!!
HNG
HNG
I... I DON'T ...
...REMEMBER THAT!!
DON'T MESS WITH ME!!
BECAUSE OF YOU GUYS, I ALMOST DIED SEVERAL TIMES DURING THOSE TEN MONTHS!!
FOR THE NEXT FOUR YEARS, I HAD CONSTANT FLASHBACKS.
DO YOU THINK I'M GONNA LET YOU FORGET MY SUFFERING?
FWP
SMILE FOR THE CAMERA ...
...SO EVERYONE CAN SEE!!
!!

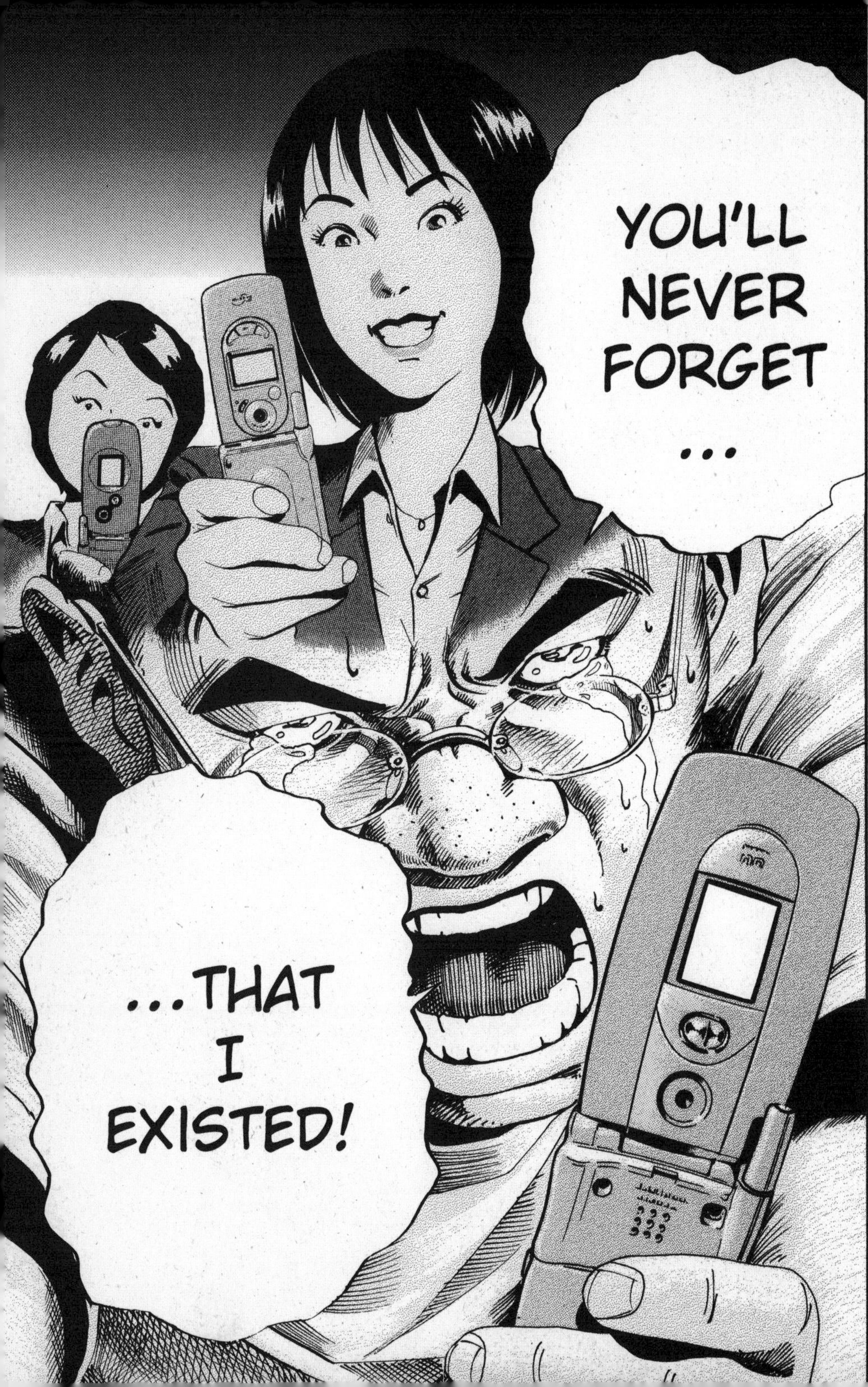
YOU'LL NEVER FORGET ...
...THAT I EXISTED!

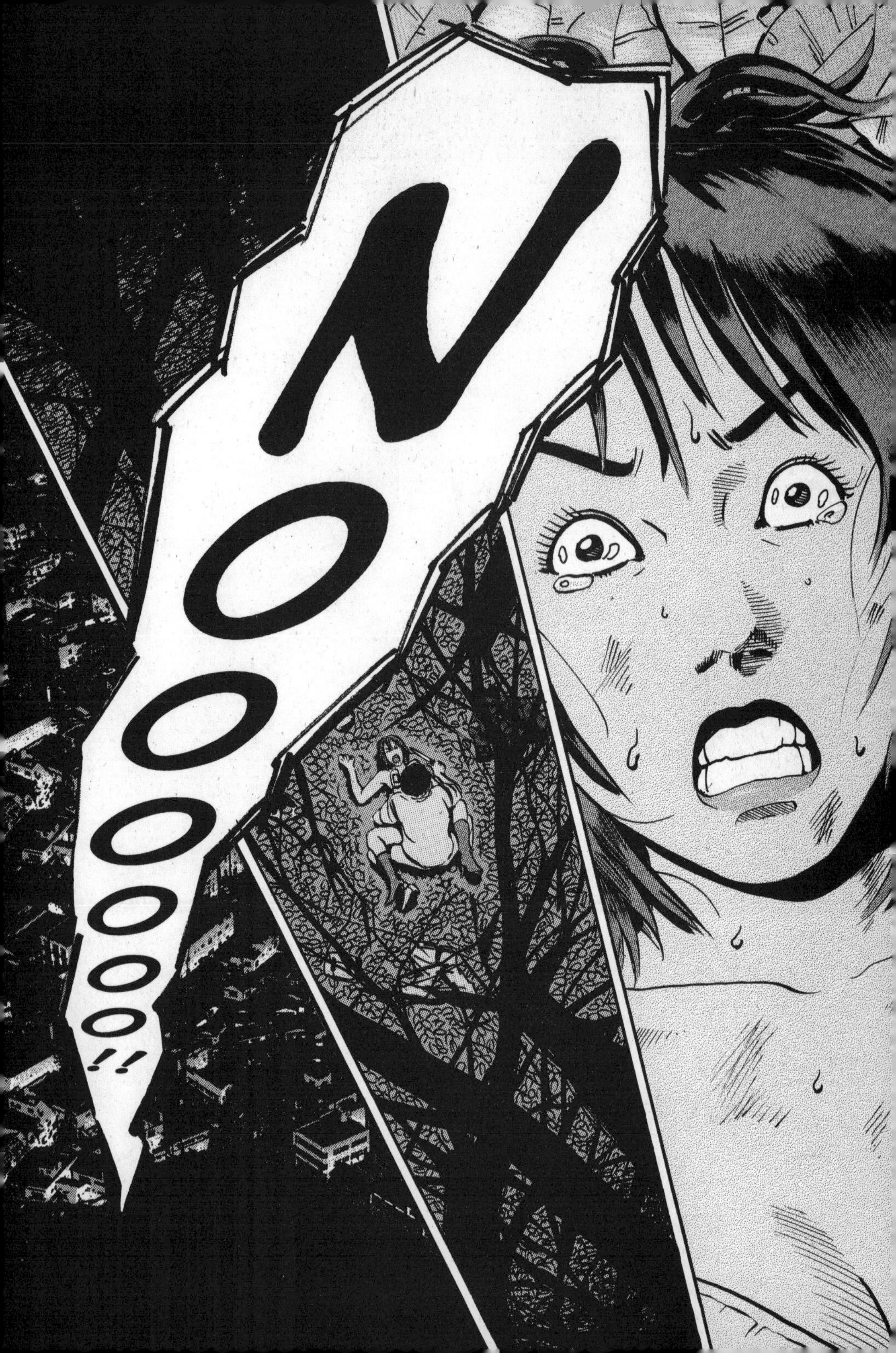
NOOOOOOOO!!

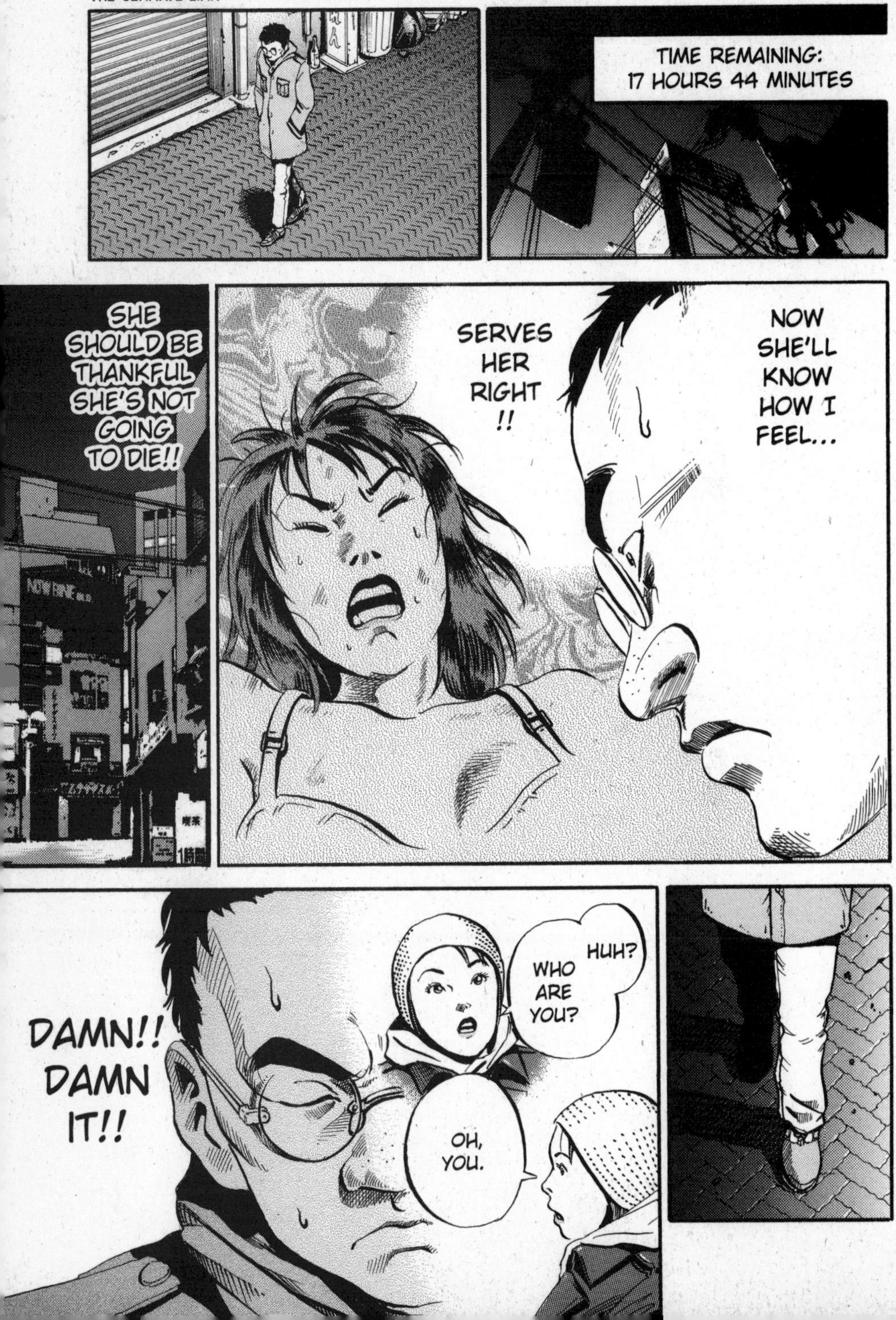
TIME REMAINING: 17 HOURS 44 MINUTES
NOW SHE'LL KNOW HOW I FEEL...
SERVES HER RIGHT!!
SHE SHOULD BE THANKFUL SHE'S NOT GOING TO DIE!!
HUH? WHO ARE YOU?
OH, YOU.
DAMN!! DAMN IT!!

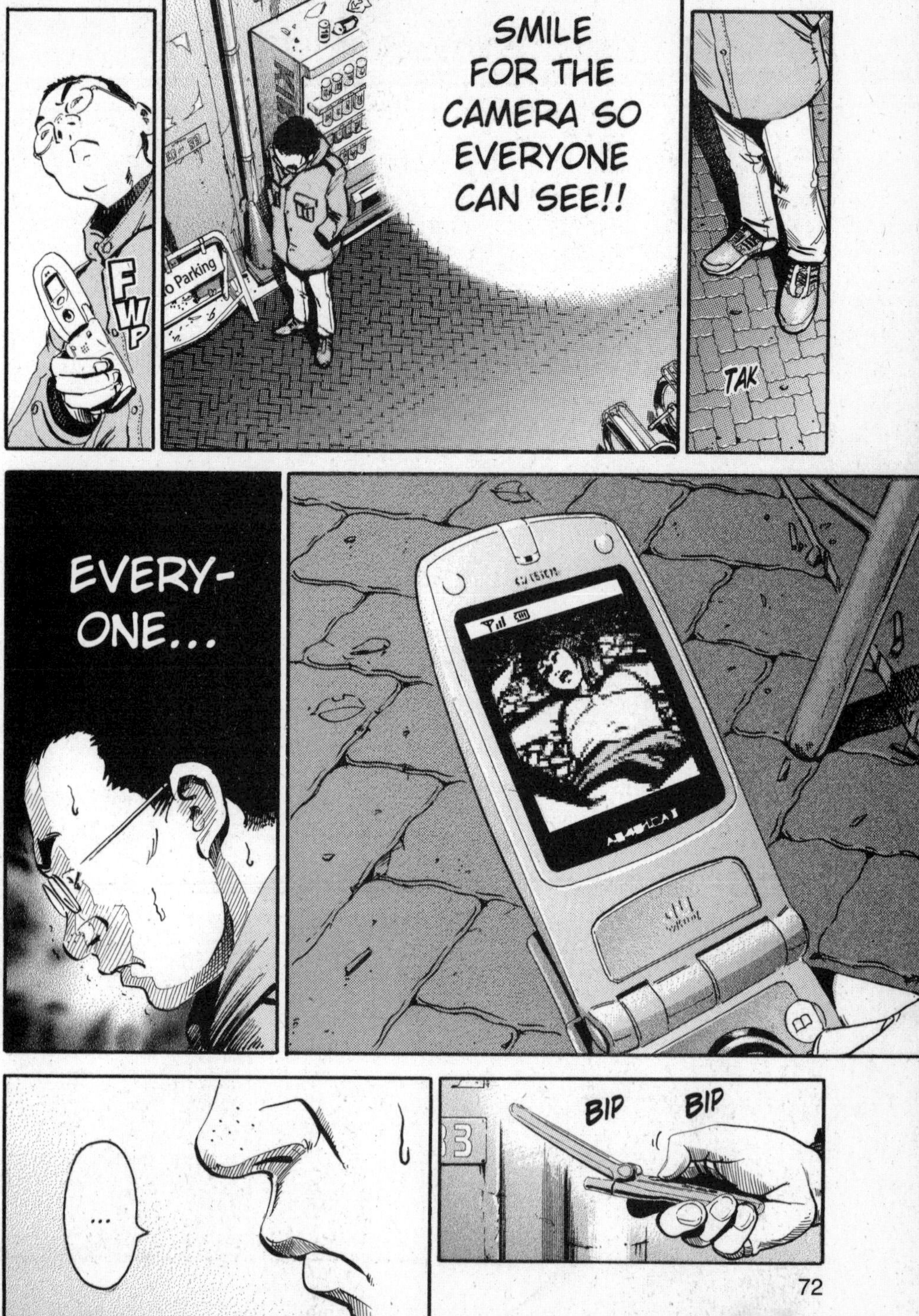
TAK
SMILE FOR THE CAMERA SO EVERYONE CAN SEE!!
FWP
EVERY-ONE...
BIP BIP
...

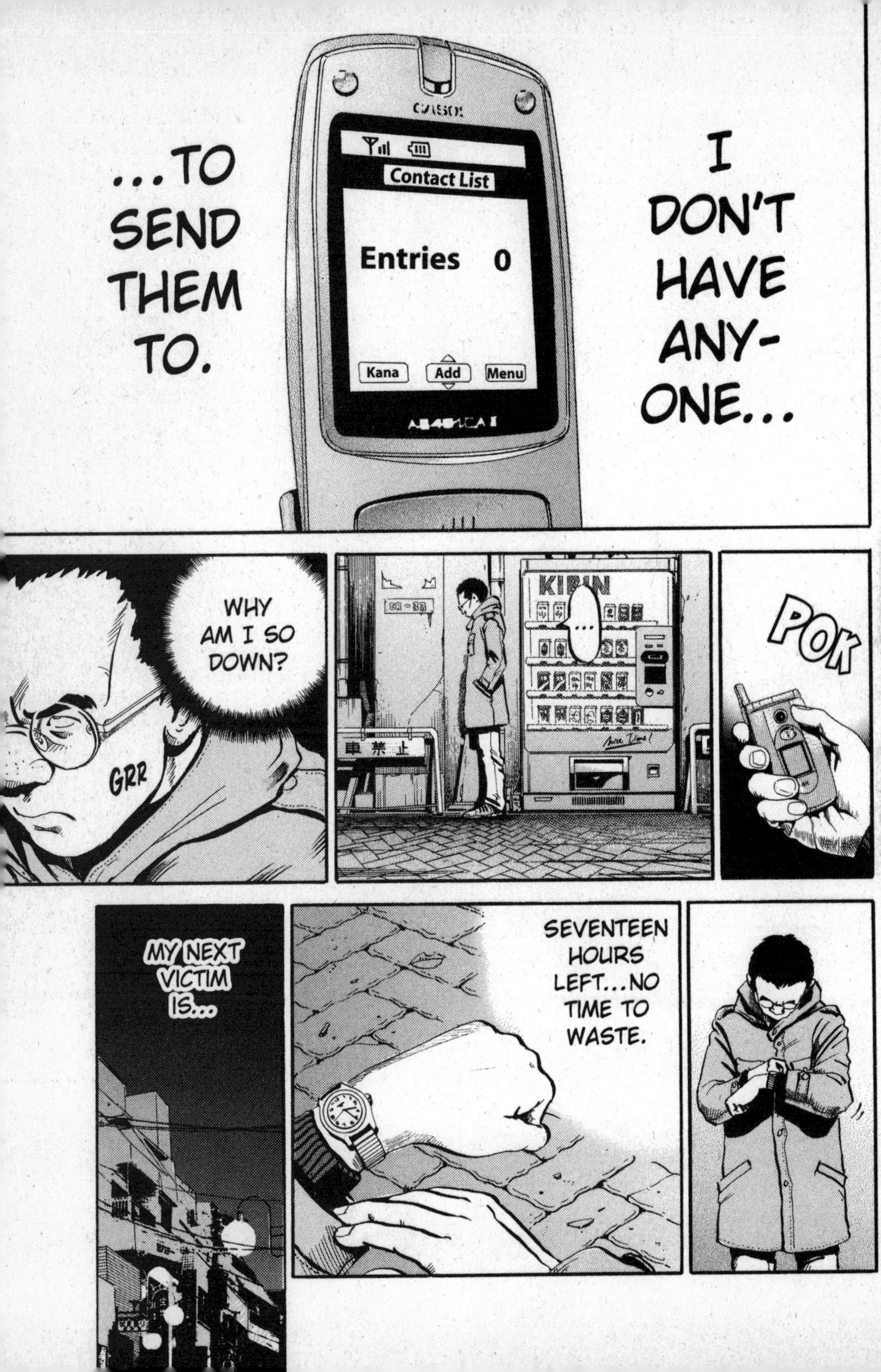
I DON'T HAVE ANYONE...
Contact List
Entries 0
Kana
Add
Menu
...TO SEND THEM TO.
POK
...
WHY AM I SO DOWN?
GRR
SEVENTEEN HOURS LEFT...NO TIME TO WASTE.
MY NEXT VICTIM IS...

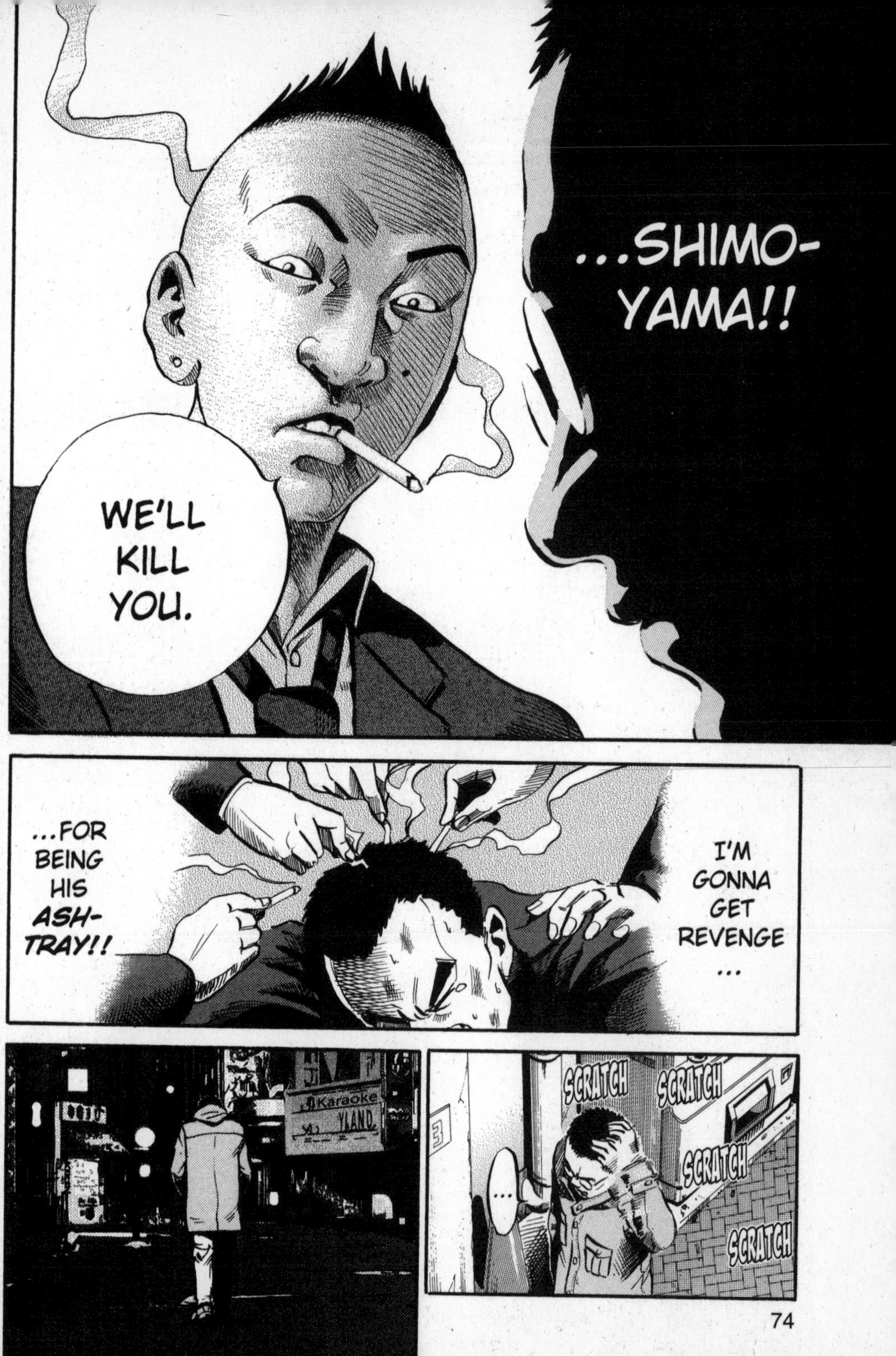
...SHIMO-YAMA!!
WE'LL KILL YOU.
I'M GONNA GET REVENGE ...
...FOR BEING HIS ASH-TRAY!!
SCRATCH
SCRATCH
SCRATCH
SCRATCH
...

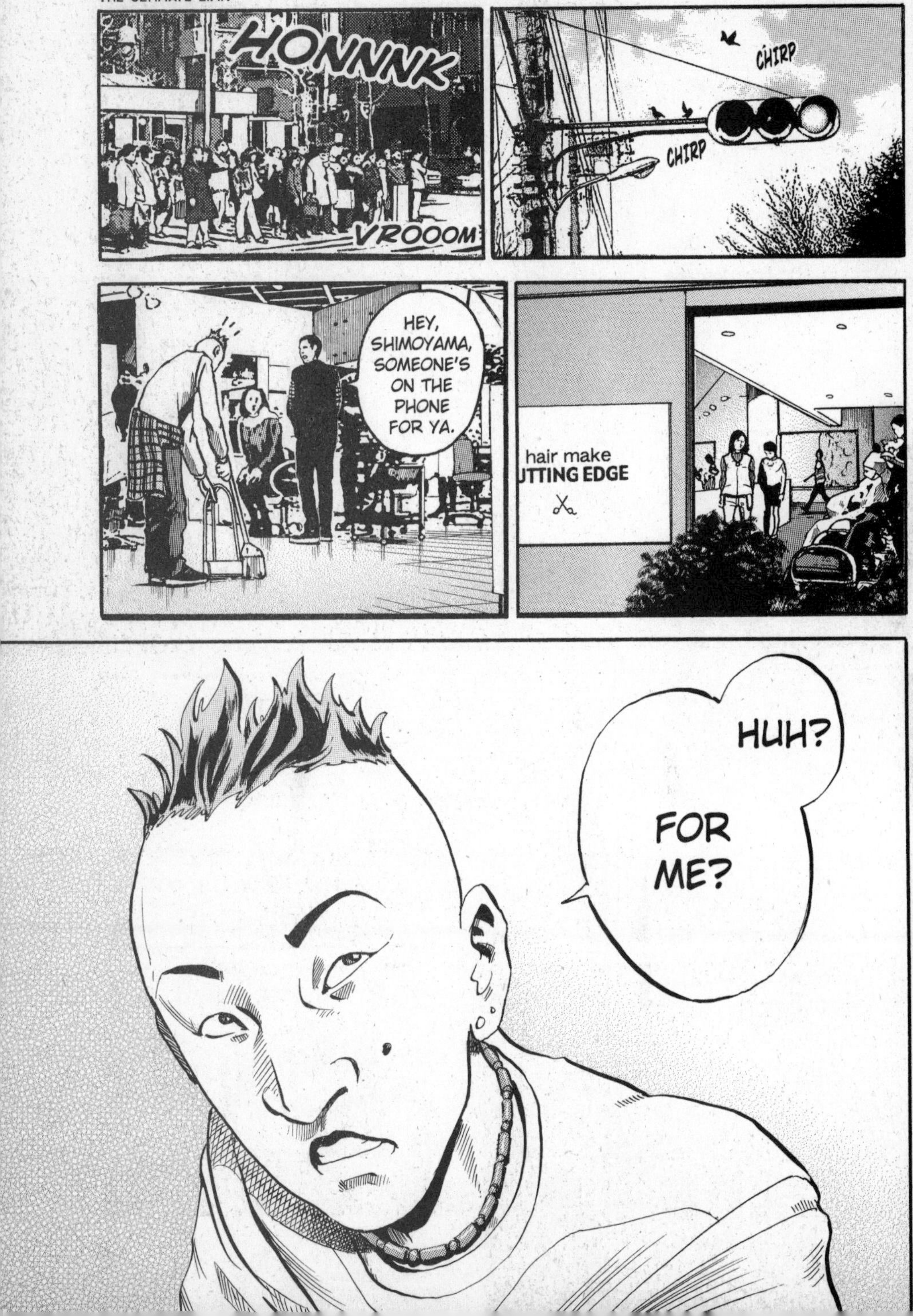
CHIRP
CHIRP
HONNNK
VROOOM
hair make
UTTING EDGE
HEY, SHIMOYAMA, SOMEONE'S ON THE PHONE FOR YA.
HUH?
FOR ME?

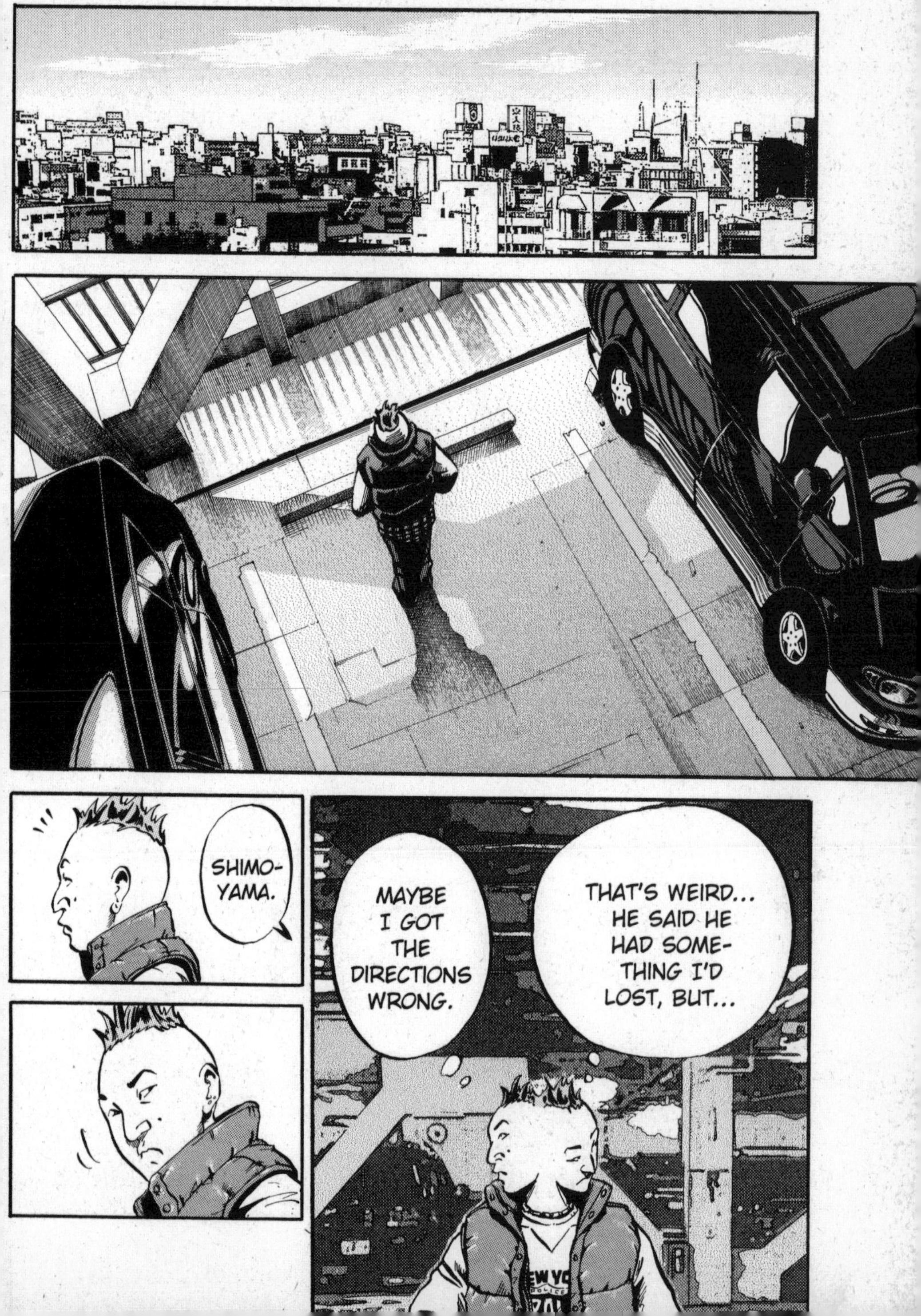
THAT'S WEIRD... HE SAID HE HAD SOME-THING I'D LOST, BUT...
MAYBE I GOT THE DIRECTIONS WRONG.
SHIMO-YAMA.

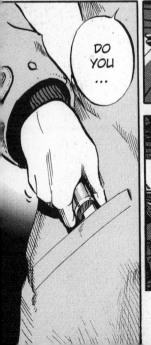

DO
YOU
...

...

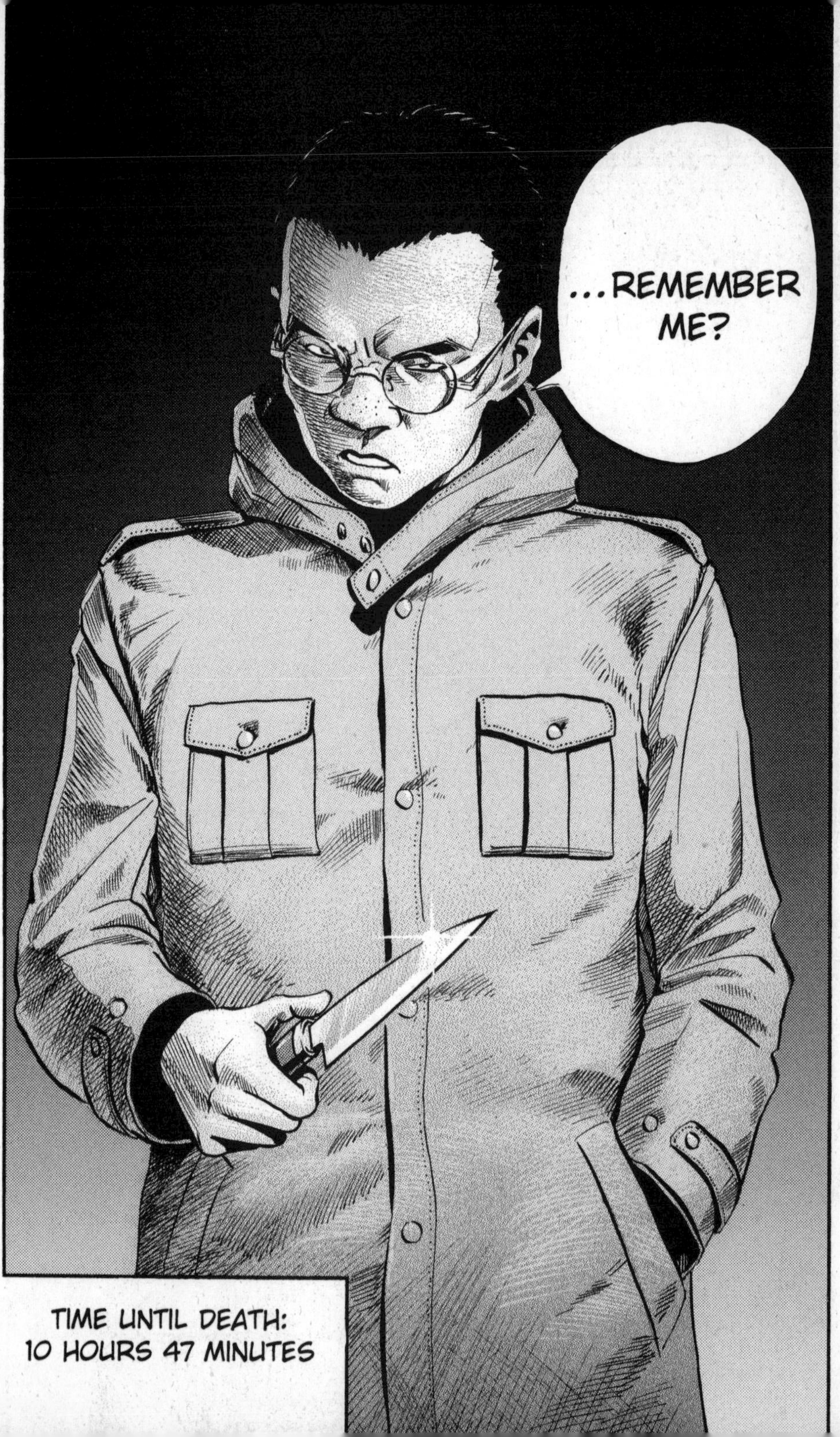
...REMEMBER ME?
TIME UNTIL DEATH: 10 HOURS 47 MINUTES

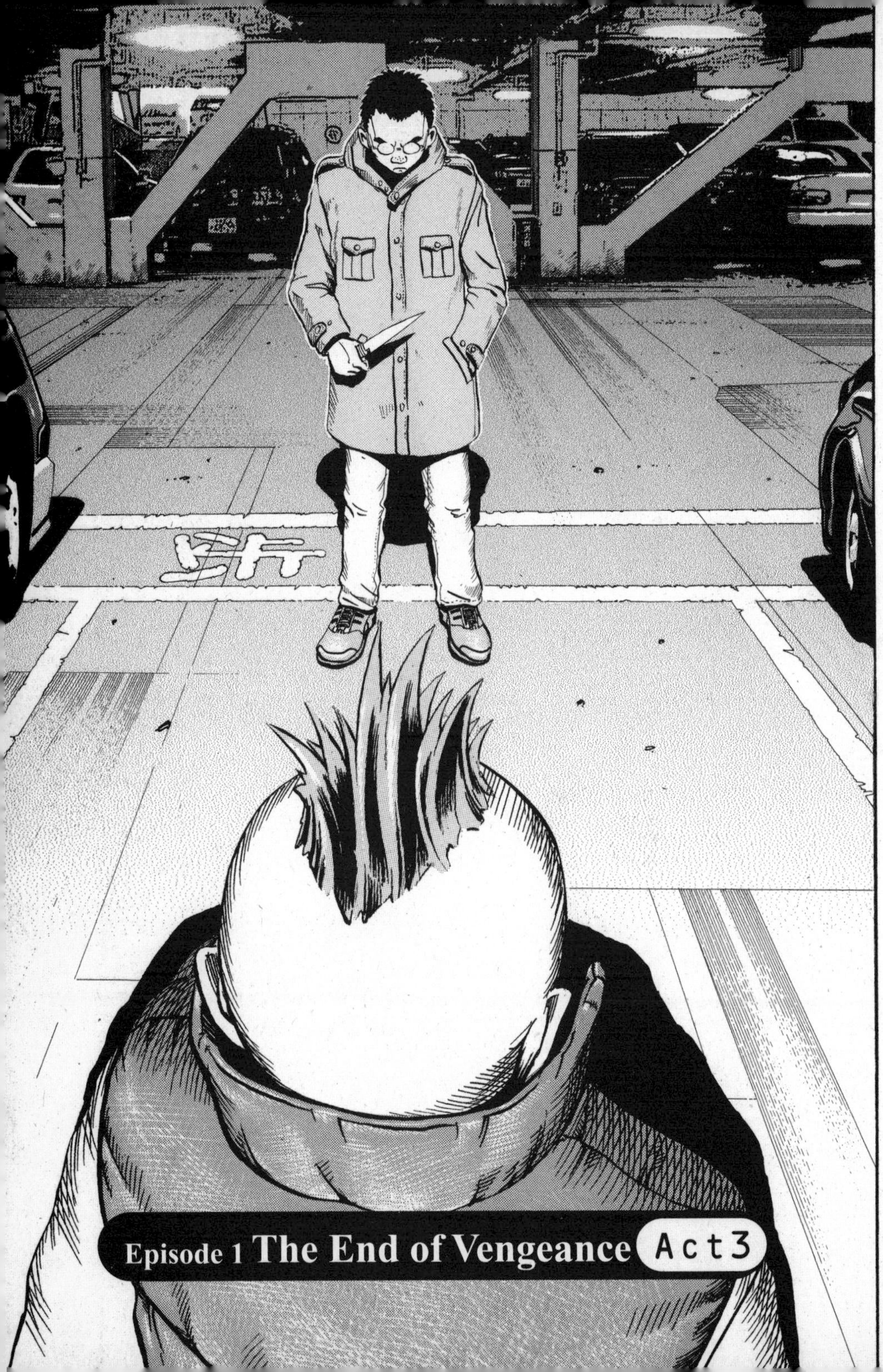
Episode 1 The End of Vengeance Act3

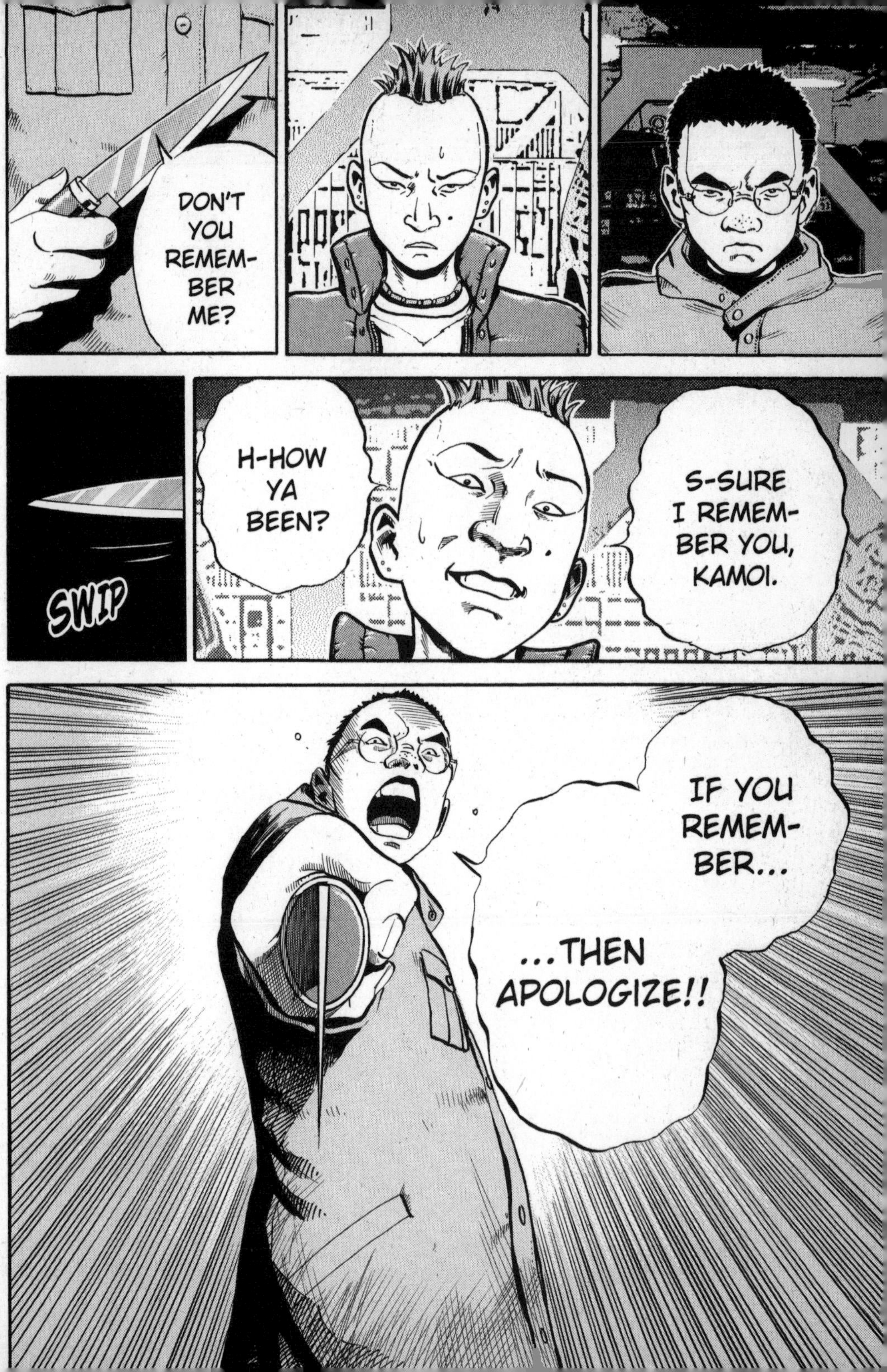
DON'T YOU REMEMBER ME?
S-SURE I REMEMBER YOU, KAMOI.
H-HOW YA BEEN?
SWIP
IF YOU REMEMBER...
...THEN APOLOGIZE!!

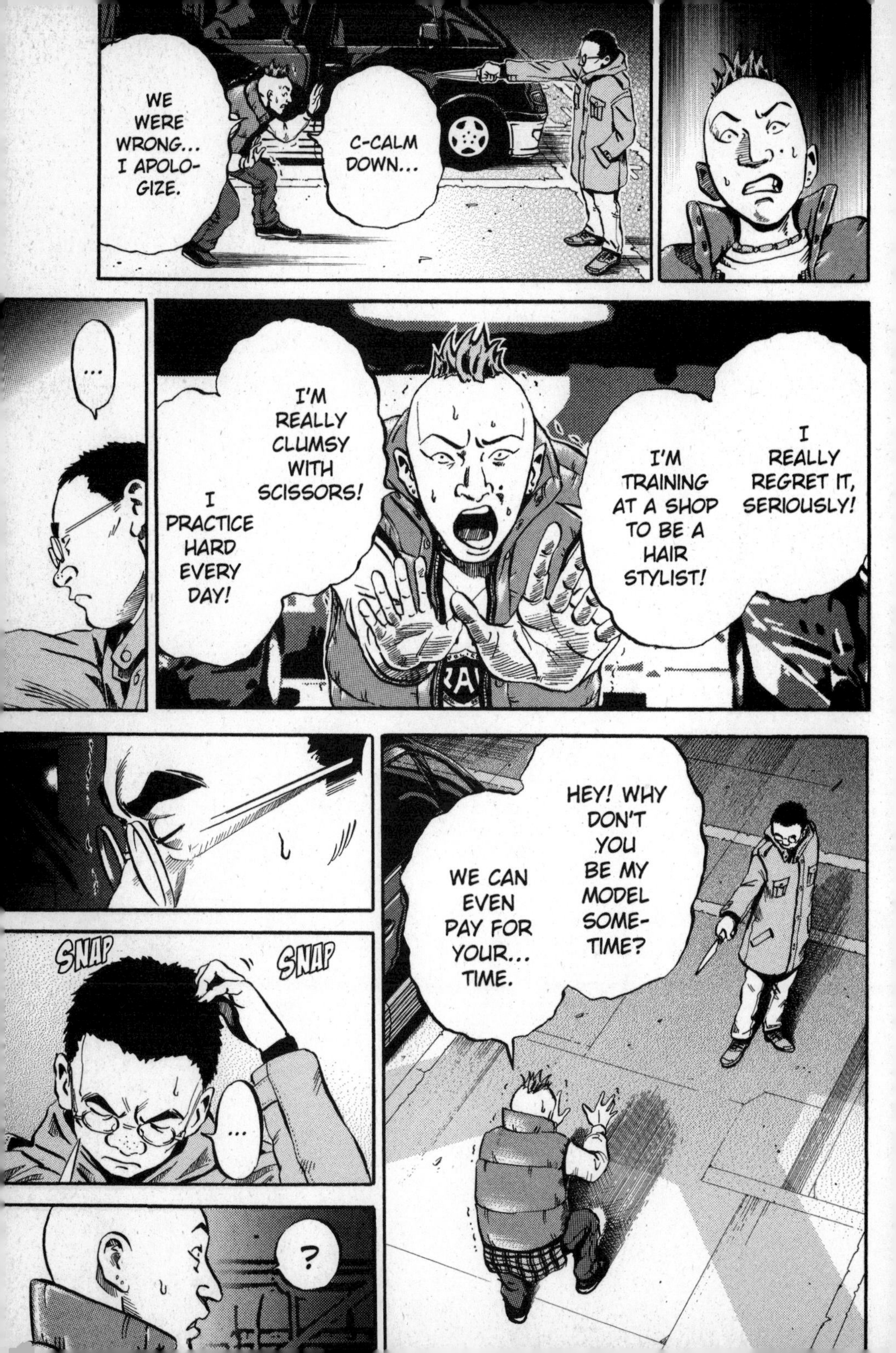
C-CALM DOWN...
WE WERE WRONG... I APOLOGIZE.
I REALLY REGRET IT, SERIOUSLY!
I'M TRAINING AT A SHOP TO BE A HAIR STYLIST!
I'M REALLY CLUMSY WITH SCISSORS!
I PRACTICE HARD EVERY DAY!
...
HEY! WHY DON'T YOU BE MY MODEL SOME-TIME?
WE CAN EVEN PAY FOR YOUR... TIME.
SNAP
SNAP
...
?

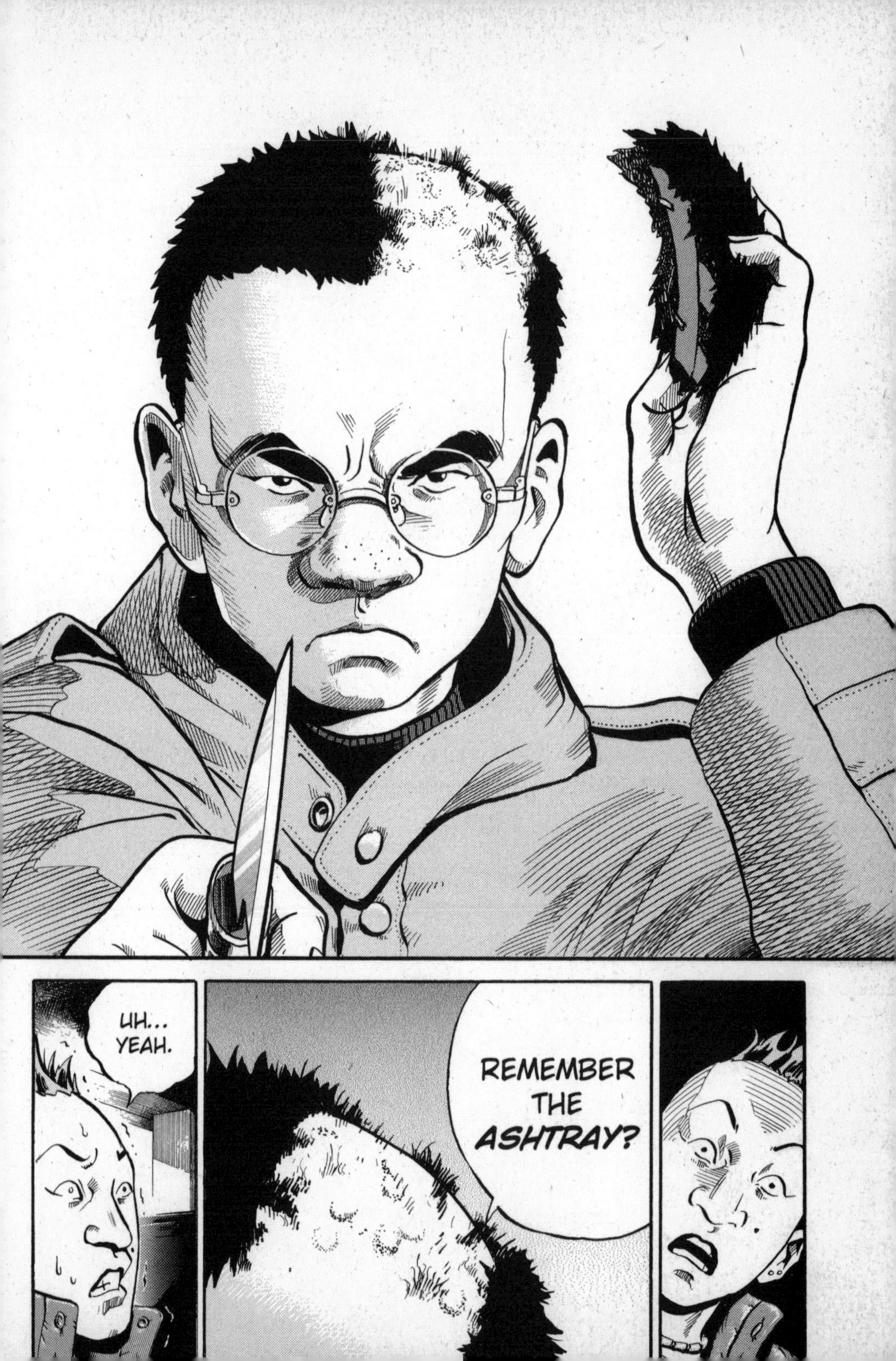
REMEMBER THE ASHTRAY?
UH... YEAH.

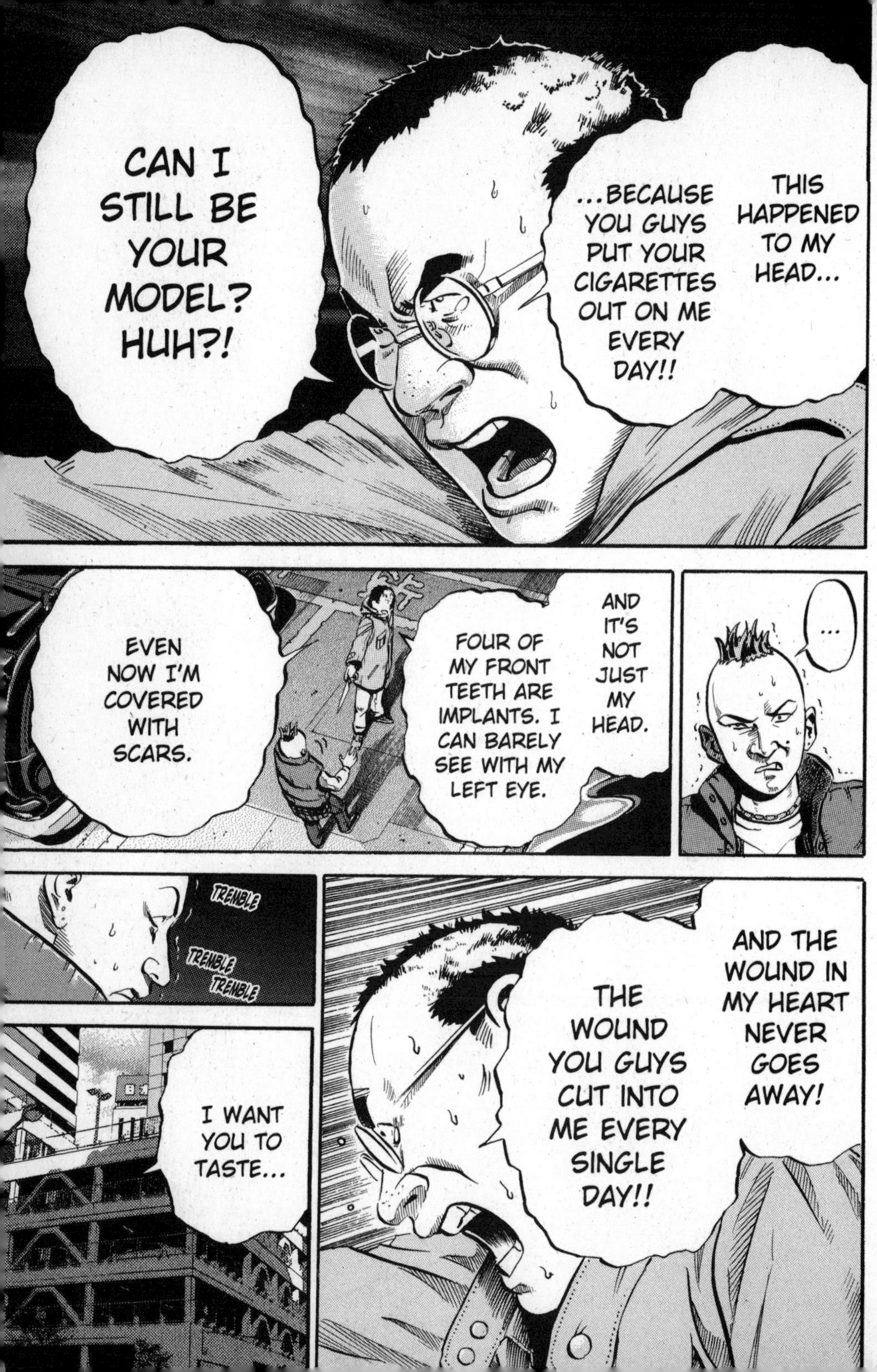
THIS HAPPENED TO MY HEAD...
...BECAUSE YOU GUYS PUT YOUR CIGARETTES OUT ON ME EVERY DAY!!
CAN I STILL BE YOUR MODEL? HUH?!
...
AND IT'S NOT JUST MY HEAD.
FOUR OF MY FRONT TEETH ARE IMPLANTS. I CAN BARELY SEE WITH MY LEFT EYE.
EVEN NOW I'M COVERED WITH SCARS.
AND THE WOUND IN MY HEART NEVER GOES AWAY!
THE WOUND YOU GUYS CUT INTO ME EVERY SINGLE DAY!!
TREMBLE
TREMBLE TREMBLE
I WANT YOU TO TASTE...

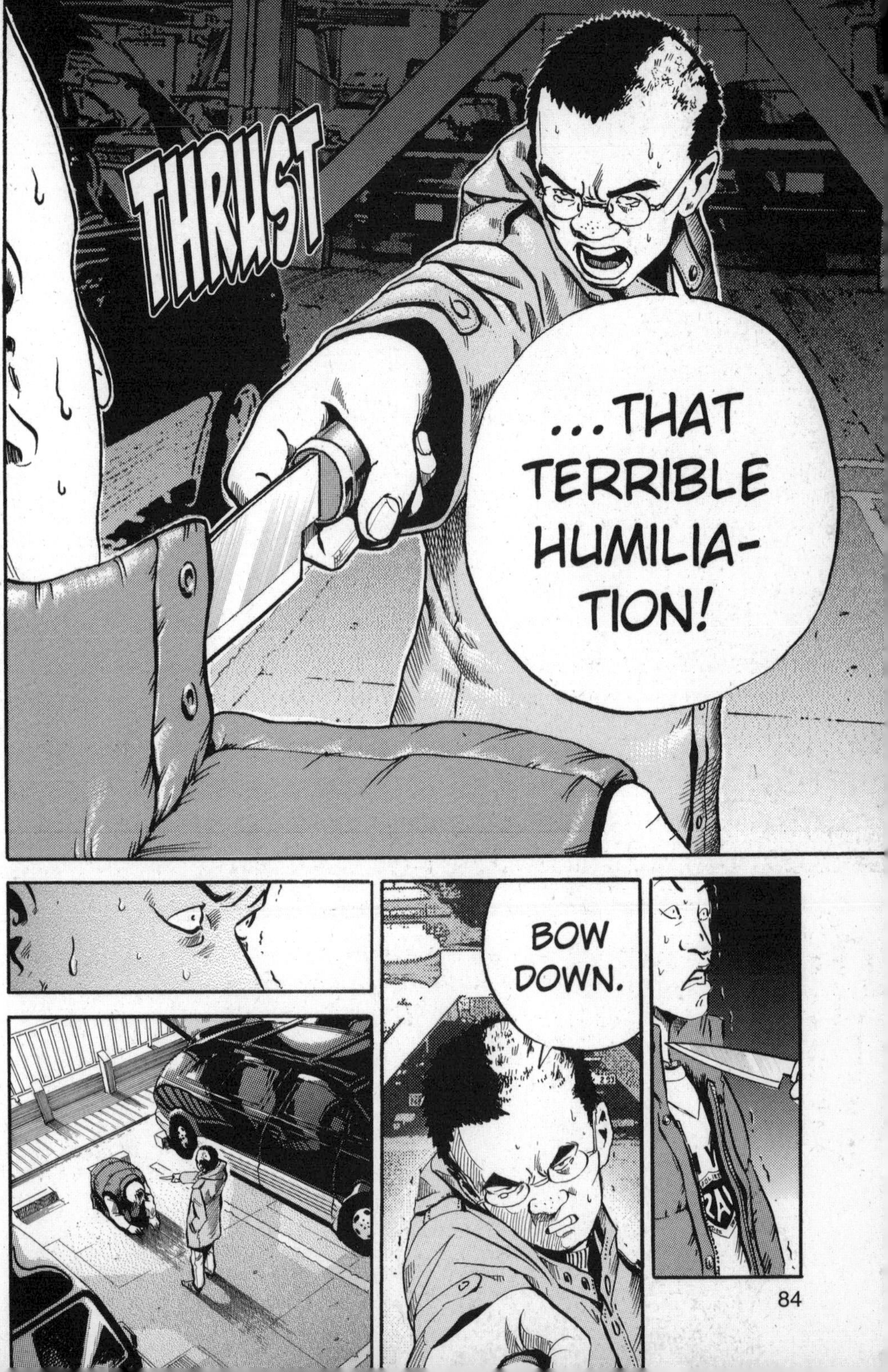
THRUST
...THAT TERRIBLE HUMILIATION!
BOW DOWN.

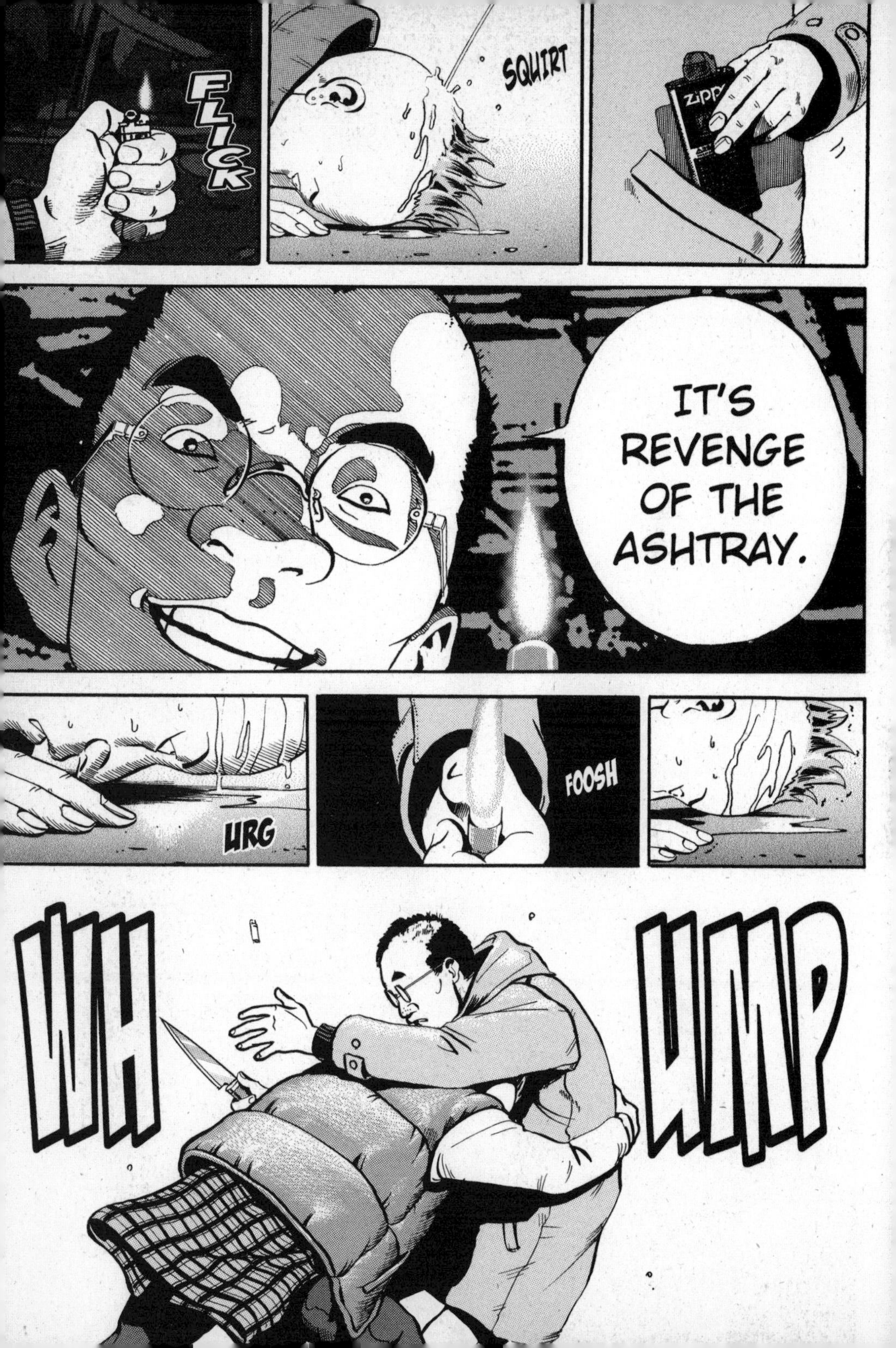
SQUIRT
FLICK
IT'S REVENGE OF THE ASHTRAY.
FOOSH
URG
WHUMP

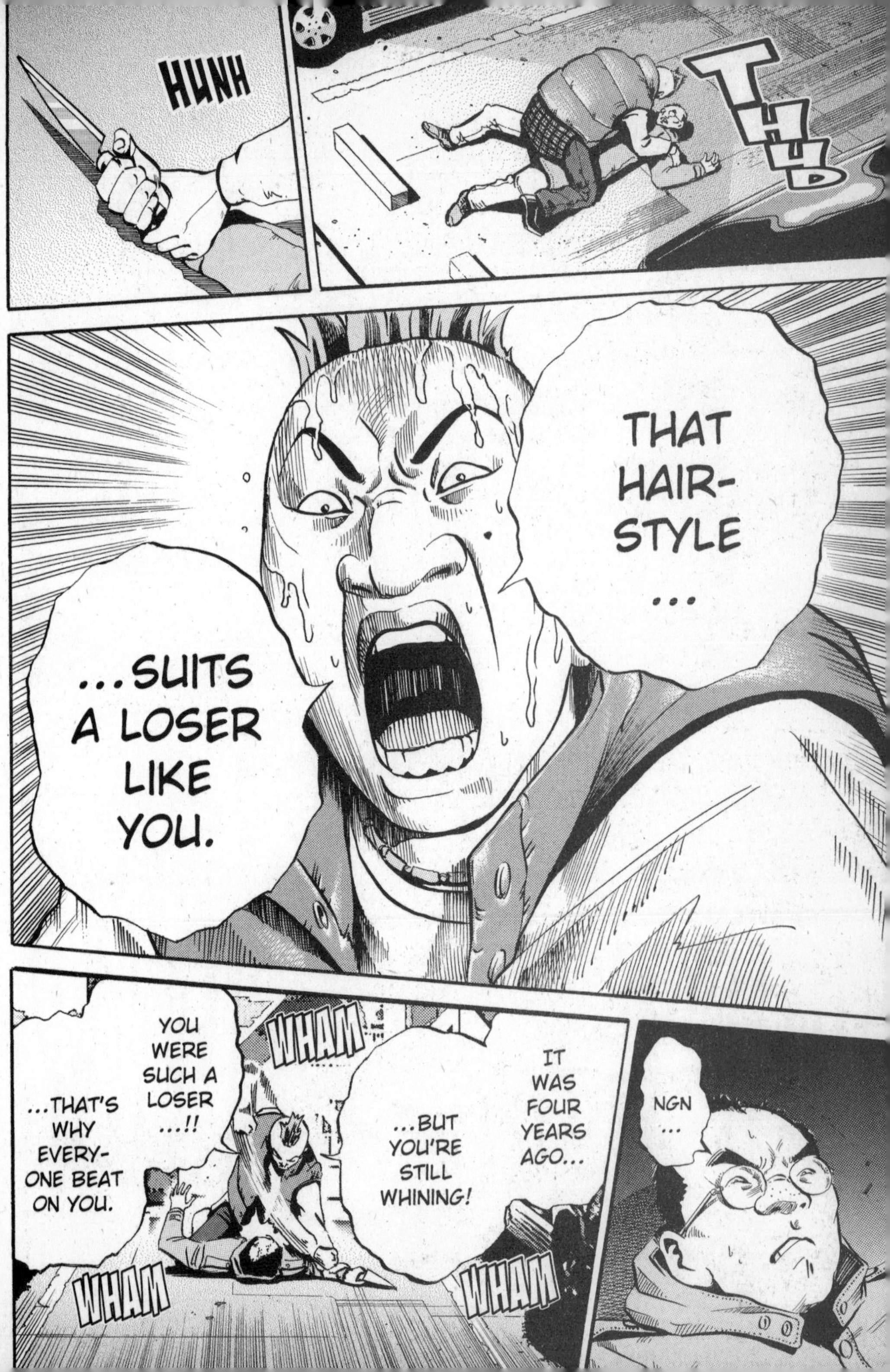
THUD
HUNH
THAT HAIR-STYLE ...
...SUITS A LOSER LIKE YOU.
NGN ...
IT WAS FOUR YEARS AGO...
...BUT YOU'RE STILL WHINING!
WHAM
YOU WERE SUCH A LOSER ...!!
...THAT'S WHY EVERY-ONE BEAT ON YOU.
WHAM
WHAM

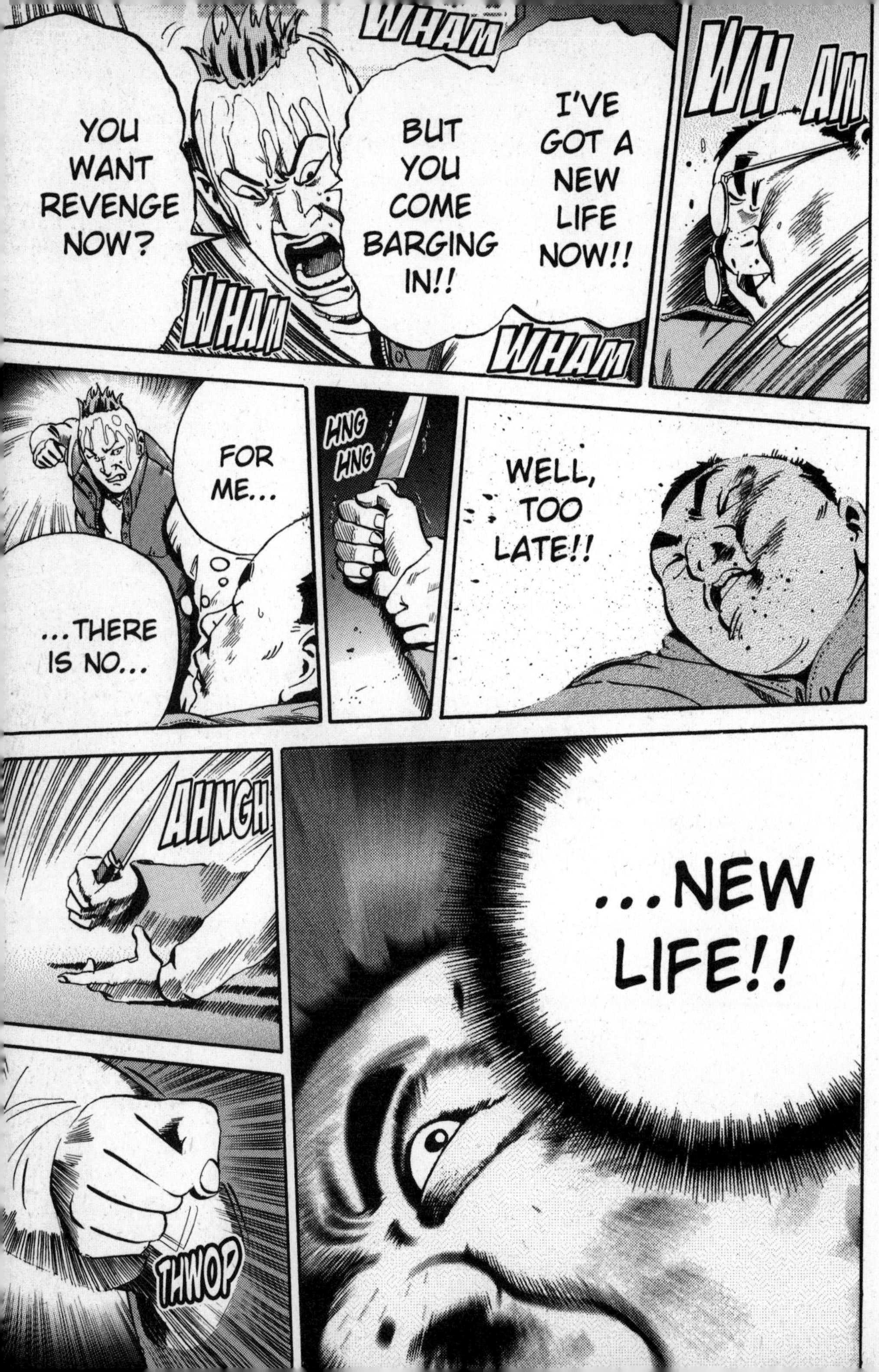
WH AM
WHAM
I'VE GOT A NEW LIFE NOW!!
BUT YOU COME BARGING IN!!
YOU WANT REVENGE NOW?
WHAM
WHAM
WELL, TOO LATE!!
HNG HNG
FOR ME...
...THERE IS NO...
...NEW LIFE!!
AHNGH
THWOP

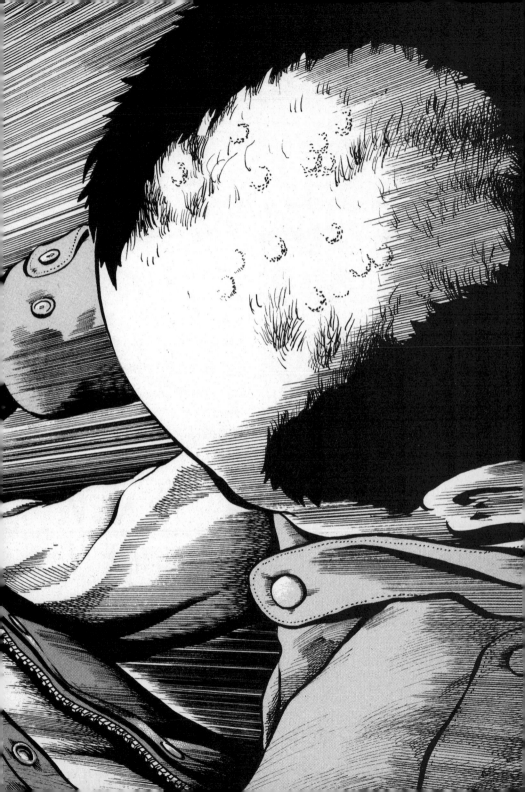

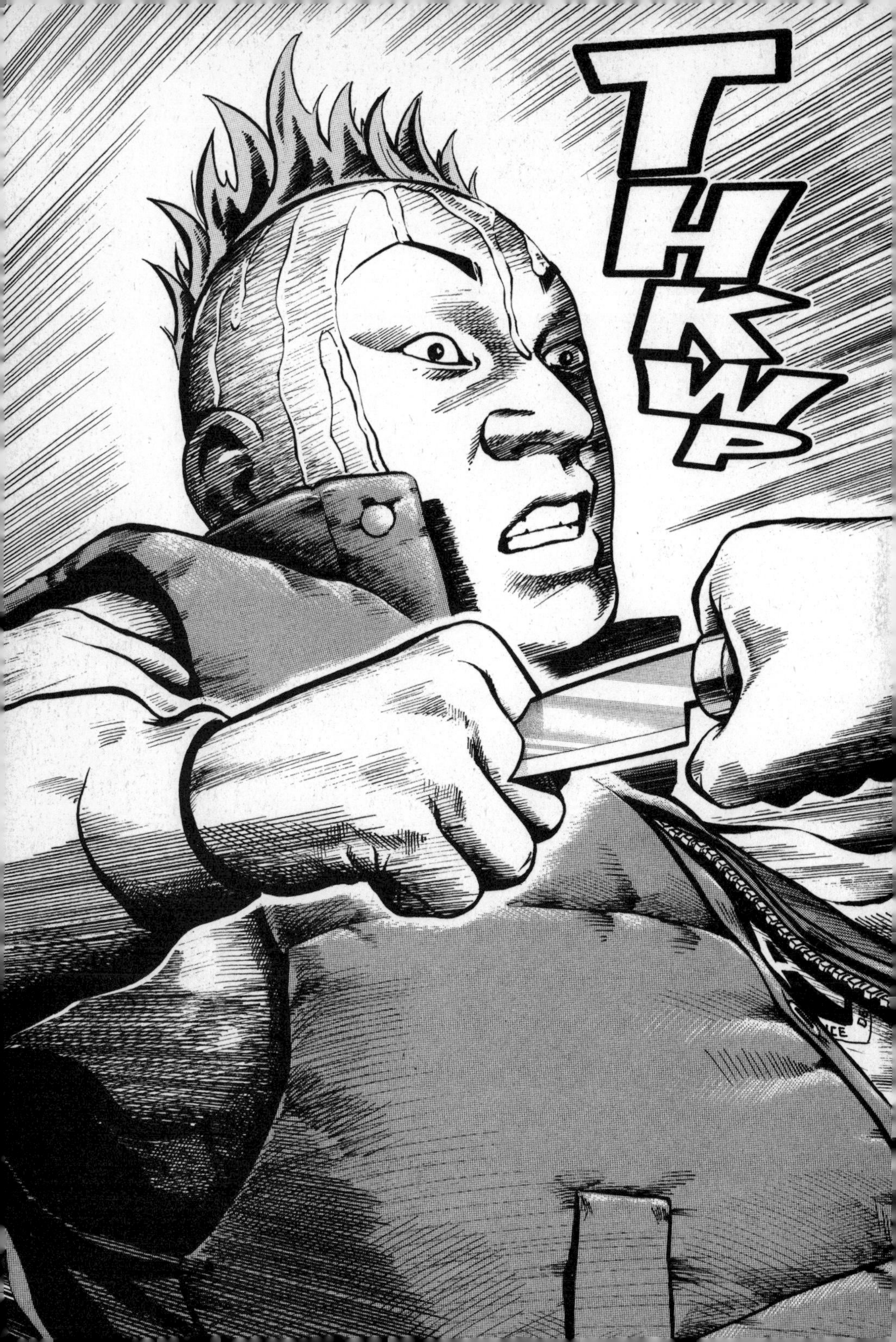
THWP

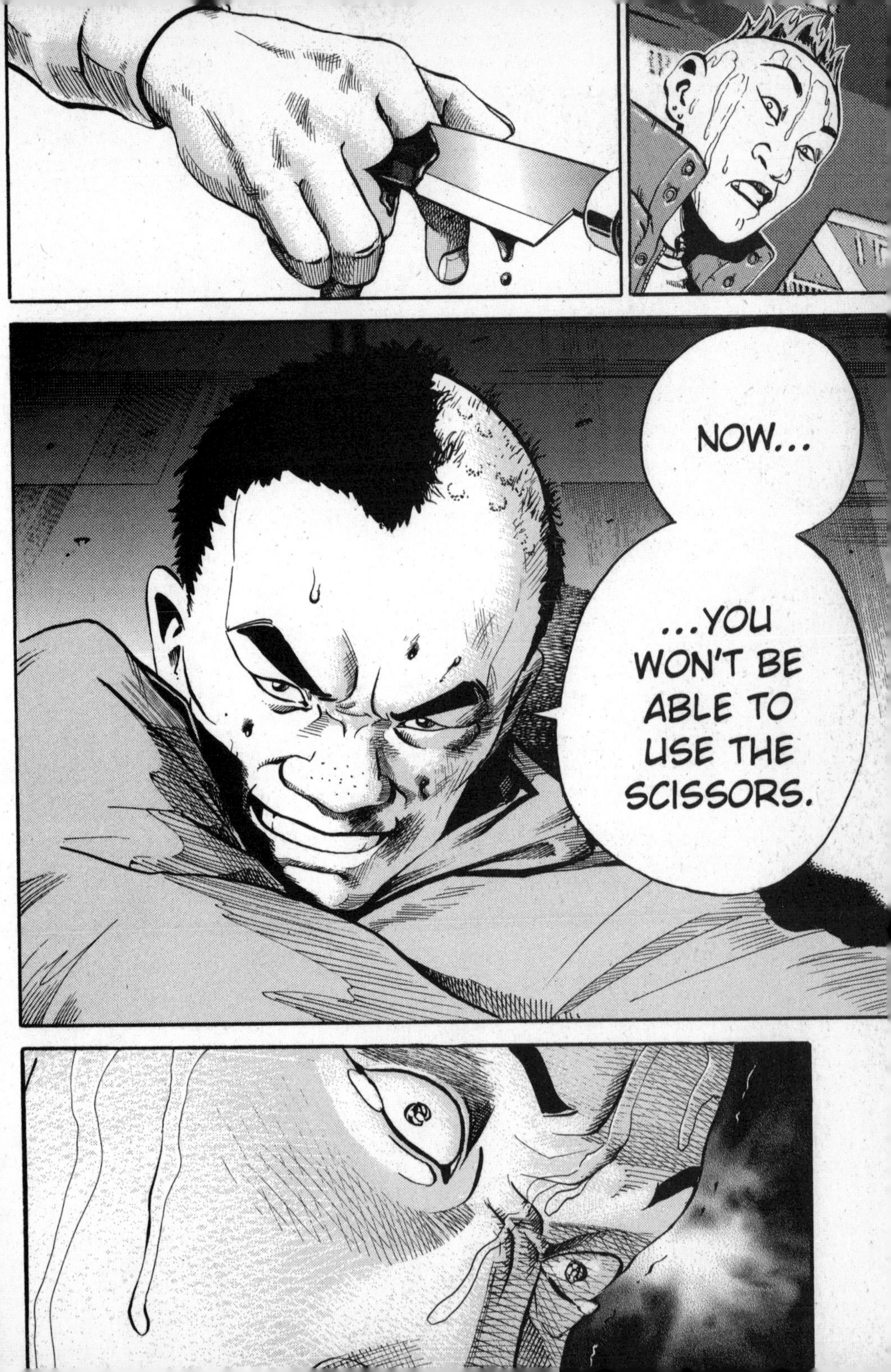
NOW...
...YOU WON'T BE ABLE TO USE THE SCISSORS.

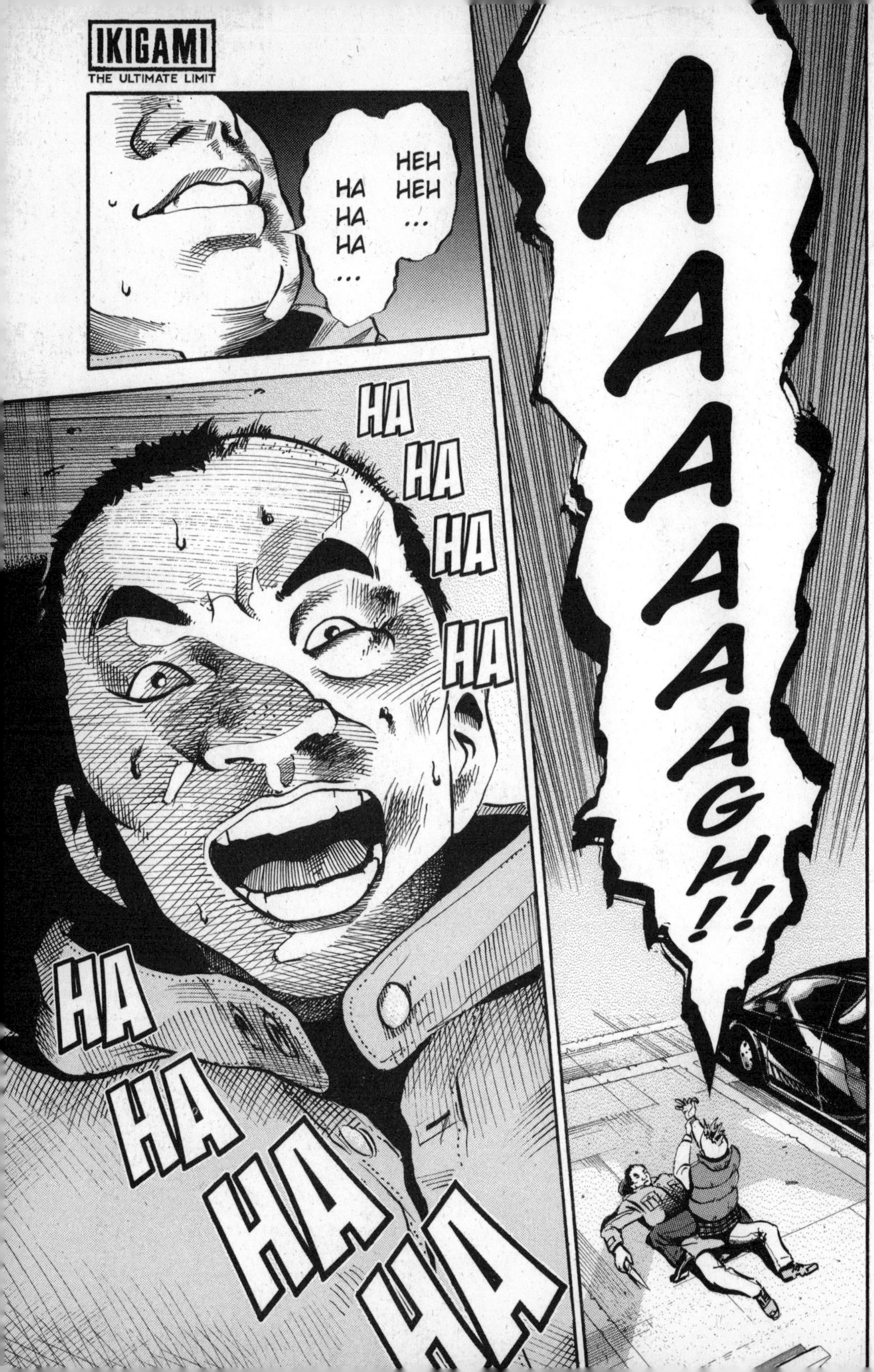
AAAAAAAGH!!
HEH HEH ...
HA HA HA ...
HA HA HA HA
HA HA HA HA

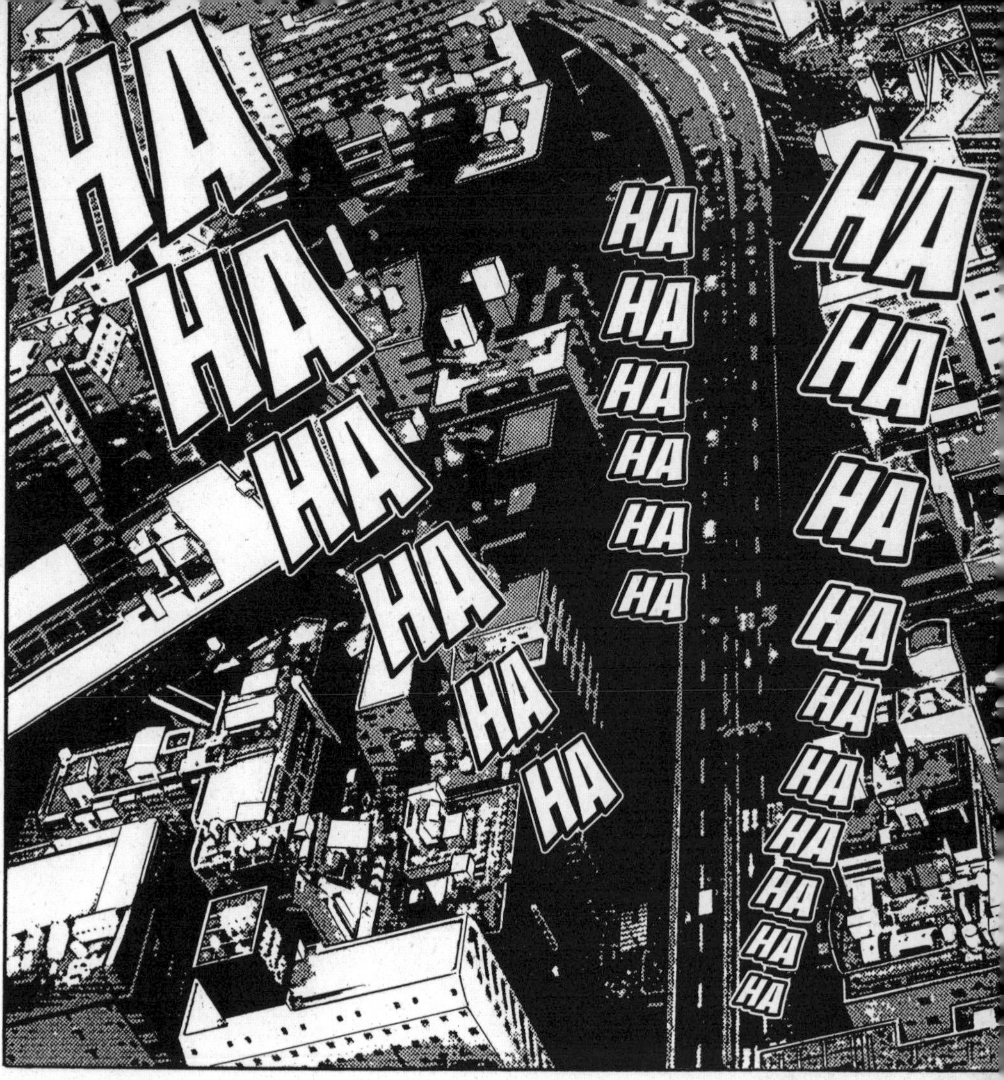

HA HA HA HA HA HA HA HA HA HA
HA HA HA HA HA HA
HA HA HA HA HA HA

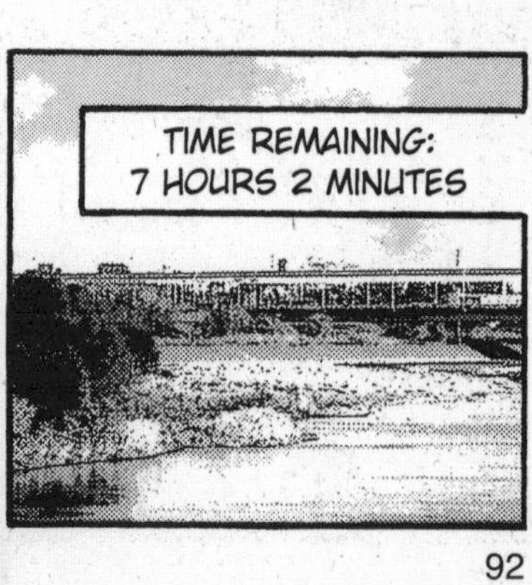

TIME REMAINING:
7 HOURS 2 MINUTES

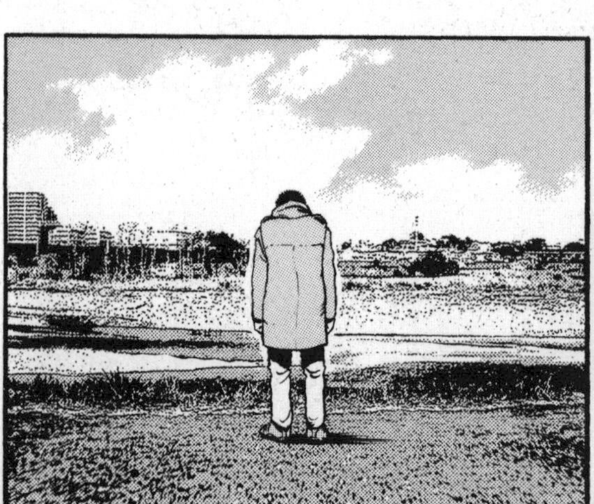

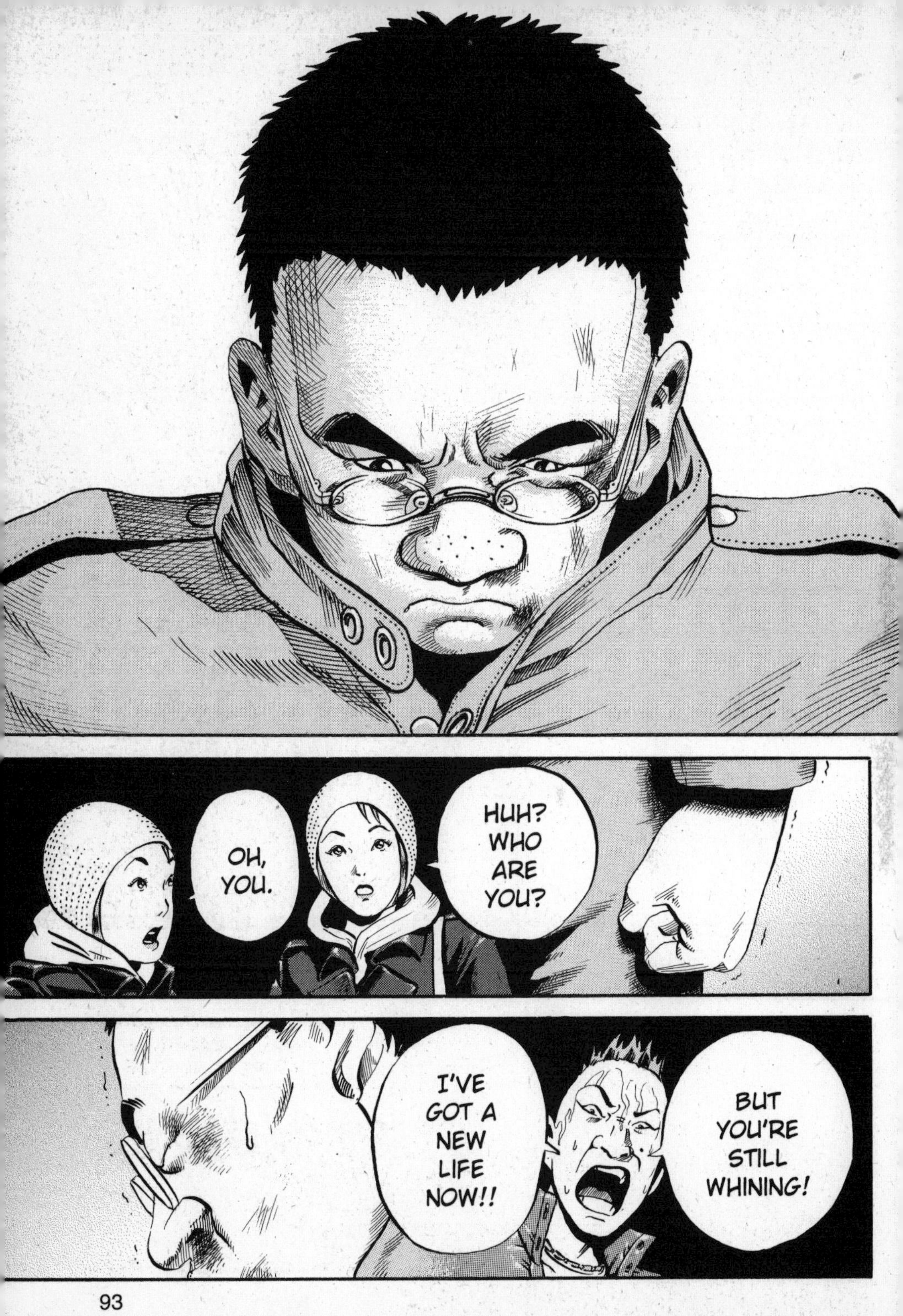
HUH? WHO ARE YOU?
OH, YOU.
BUT YOU'RE STILL WHINING!
I'VE GOT A NEW LIFE NOW!!

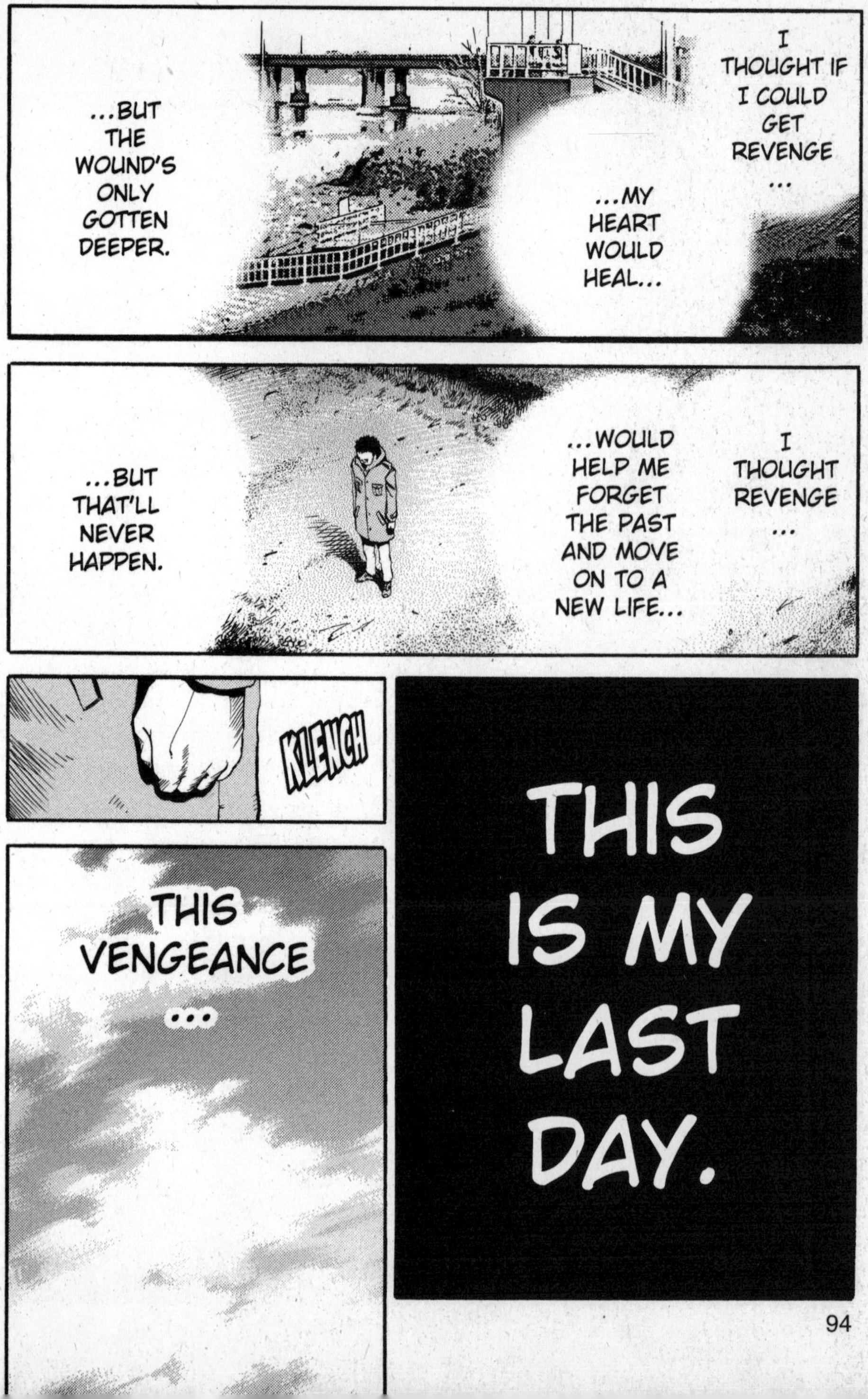
I THOUGHT IF I COULD GET REVENGE...
...MY HEART WOULD HEAL...
...BUT THE WOUND'S ONLY GOTTEN DEEPER.
I THOUGHT REVENGE...
...WOULD HELP ME FORGET THE PAST AND MOVE ON TO A NEW LIFE...
...BUT THAT'LL NEVER HAPPEN.
THIS IS MY LAST DAY.
KLENCH
THIS VENGEANCE...

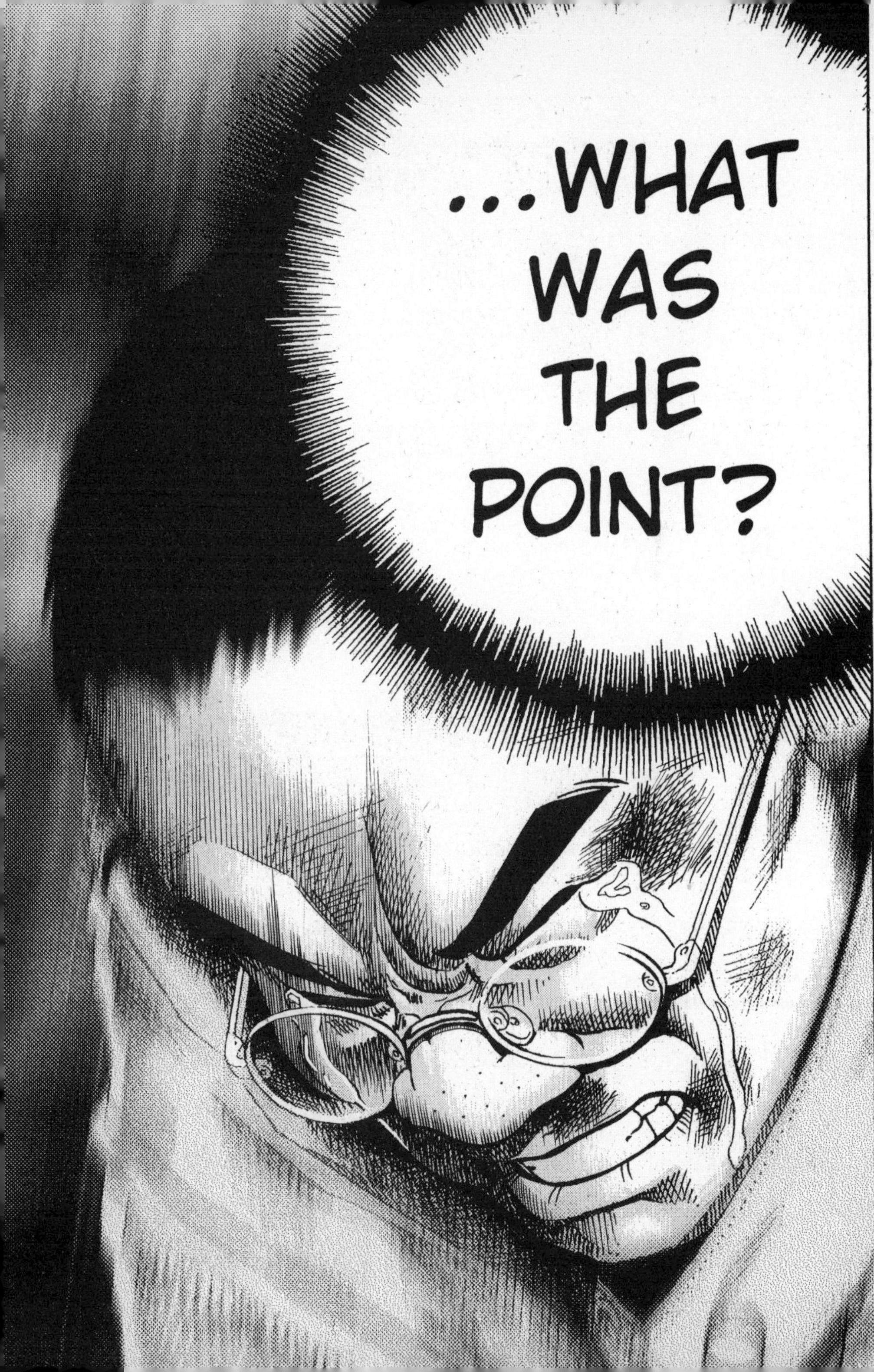
...WHAT WAS THE POINT?

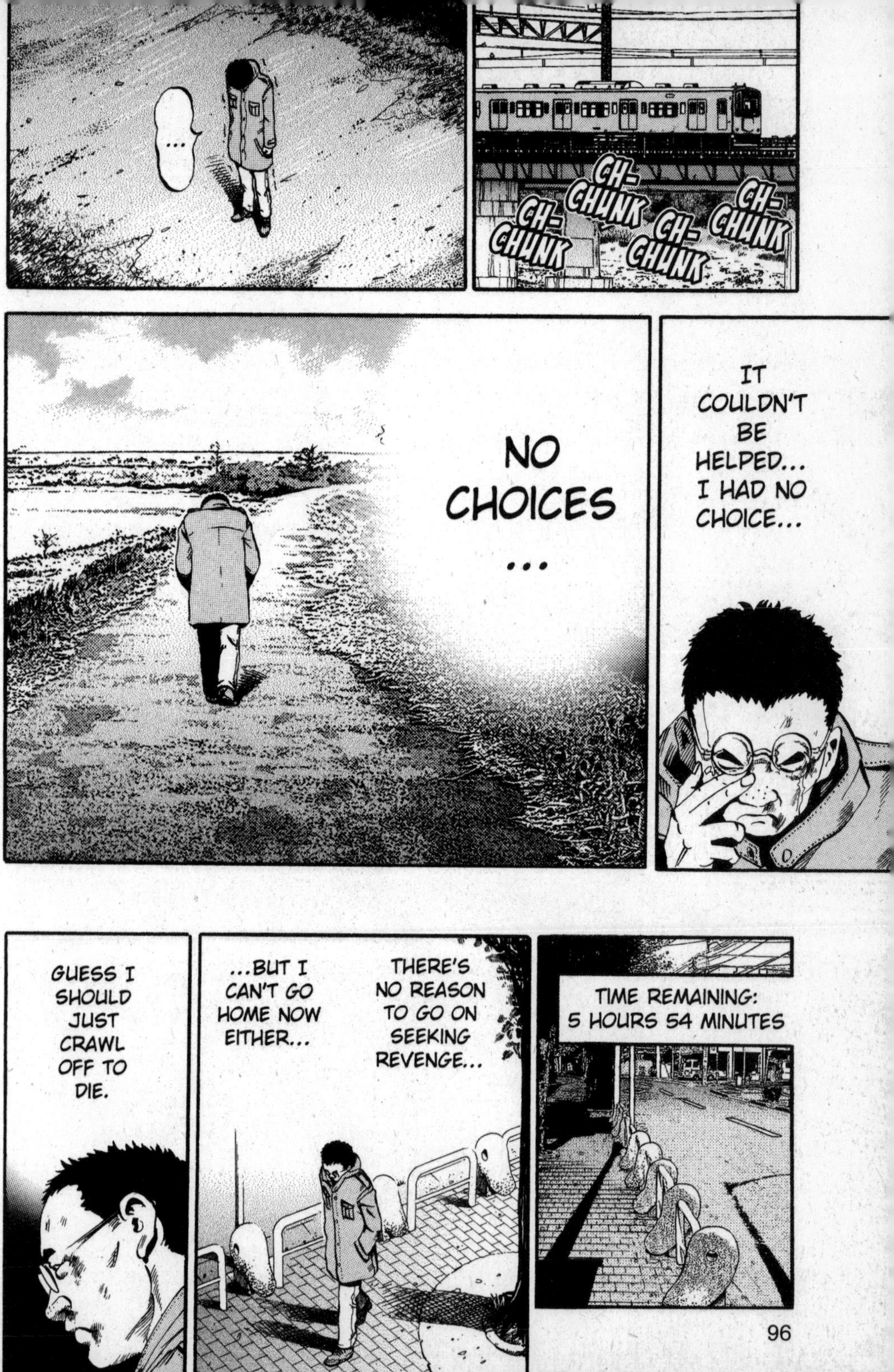

CH-CHUNK
CH-CHUNK
CH-CHUNK
CH-CHUNK
...
IT COULDN'T BE HELPED... I HAD NO CHOICE...
NO CHOICES ...
TIME REMAINING: 5 HOURS 54 MINUTES
THERE'S NO REASON TO GO ON SEEKING REVENGE...
...BUT I CAN'T GO HOME NOW EITHER...
GUESS I SHOULD JUST CRAWL OFF TO DIE.

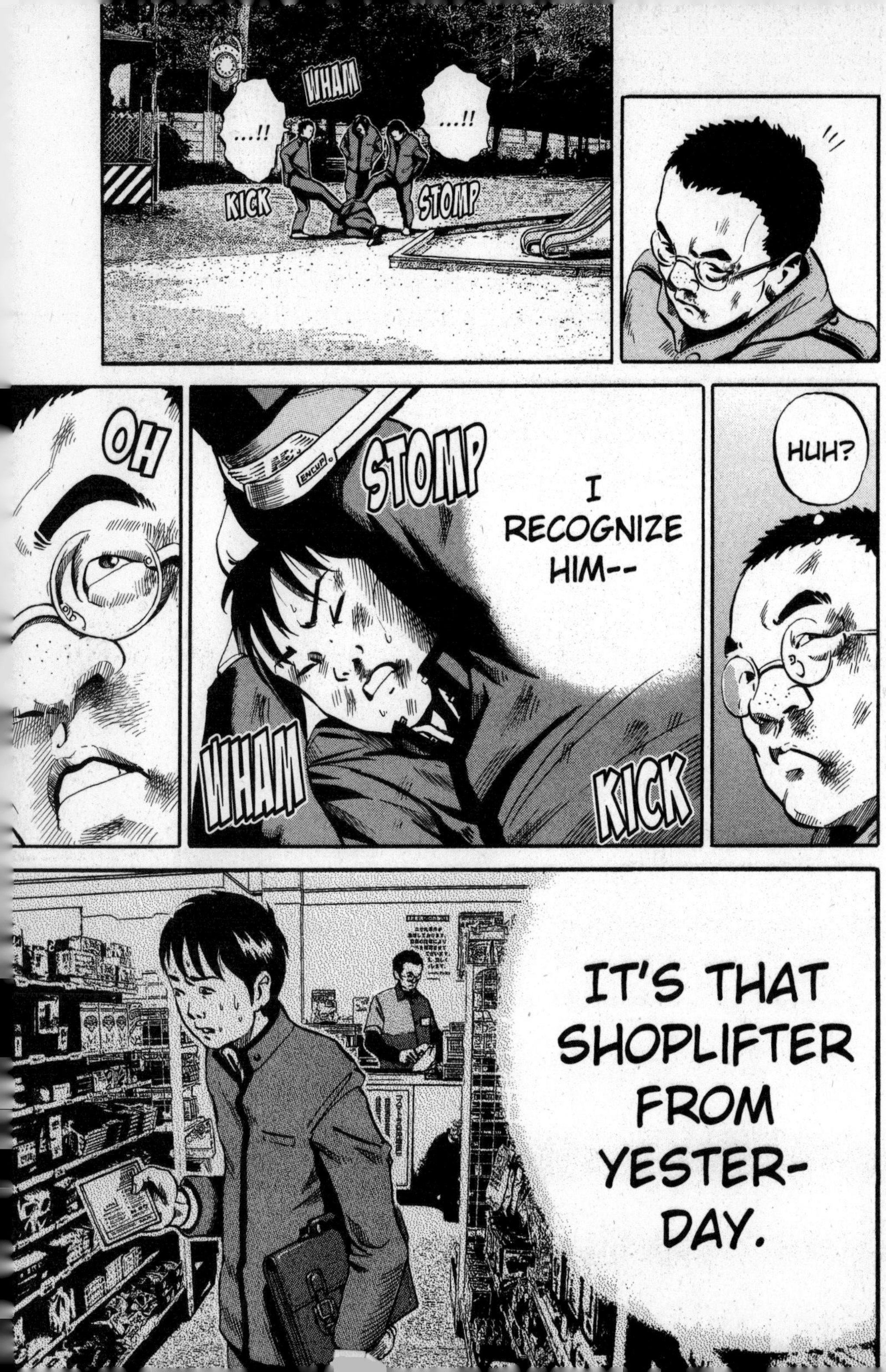
...!!
WHAM
...!!
STOMP
KICK
HUH?
STOMP
I RECOGNIZE HIM--
KICK
WHAM
OH
IT'S THAT SHOPLIFTER FROM YESTER-DAY.

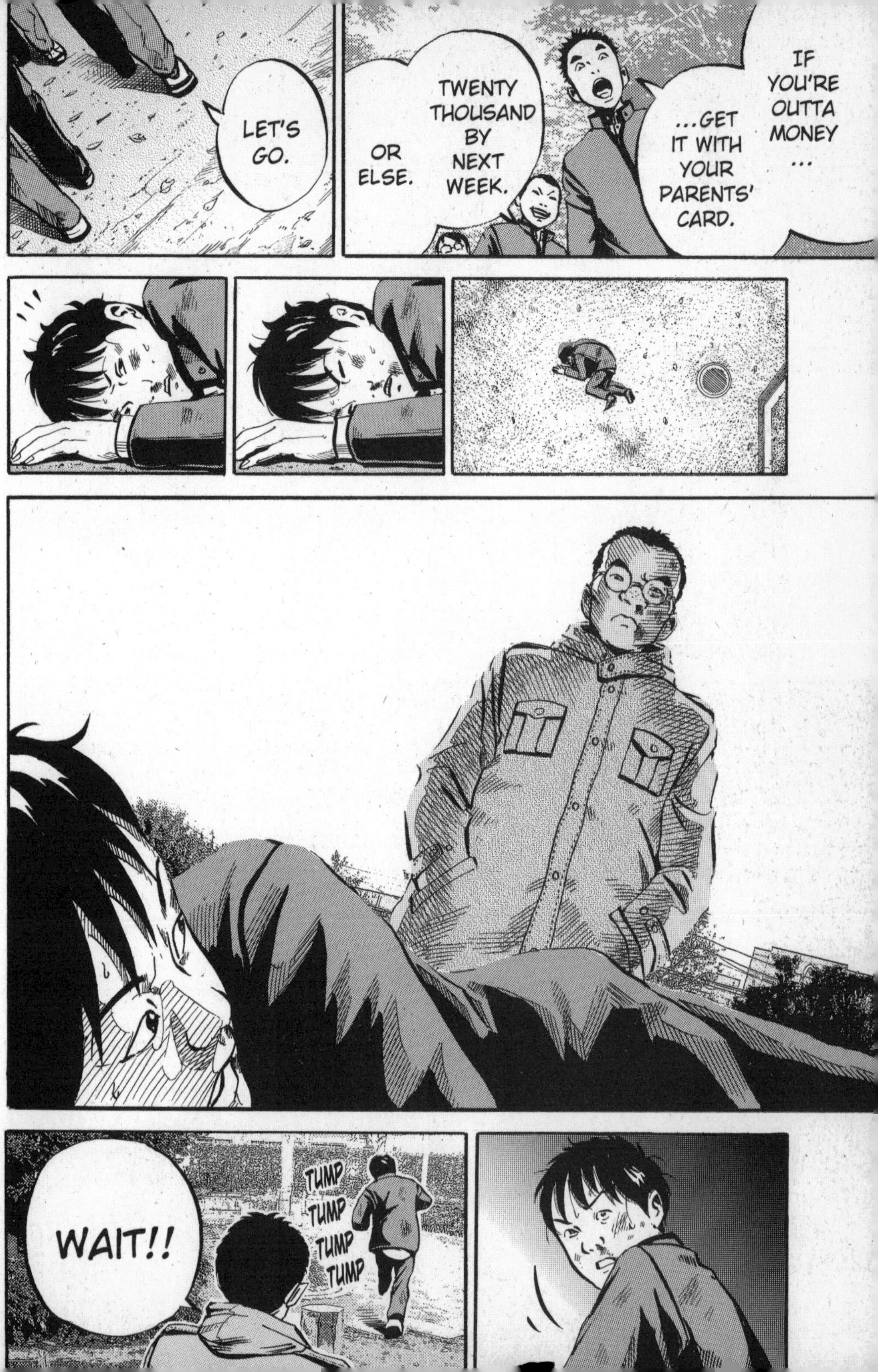
IF YOU'RE OUTTA MONEY ...
...GET IT WITH YOUR PARENTS' CARD.
TWENTY THOUSAND BY NEXT WEEK.
OR ELSE.
LET'S GO.
TUMP TUMP TUMP TUMP
WAIT!!

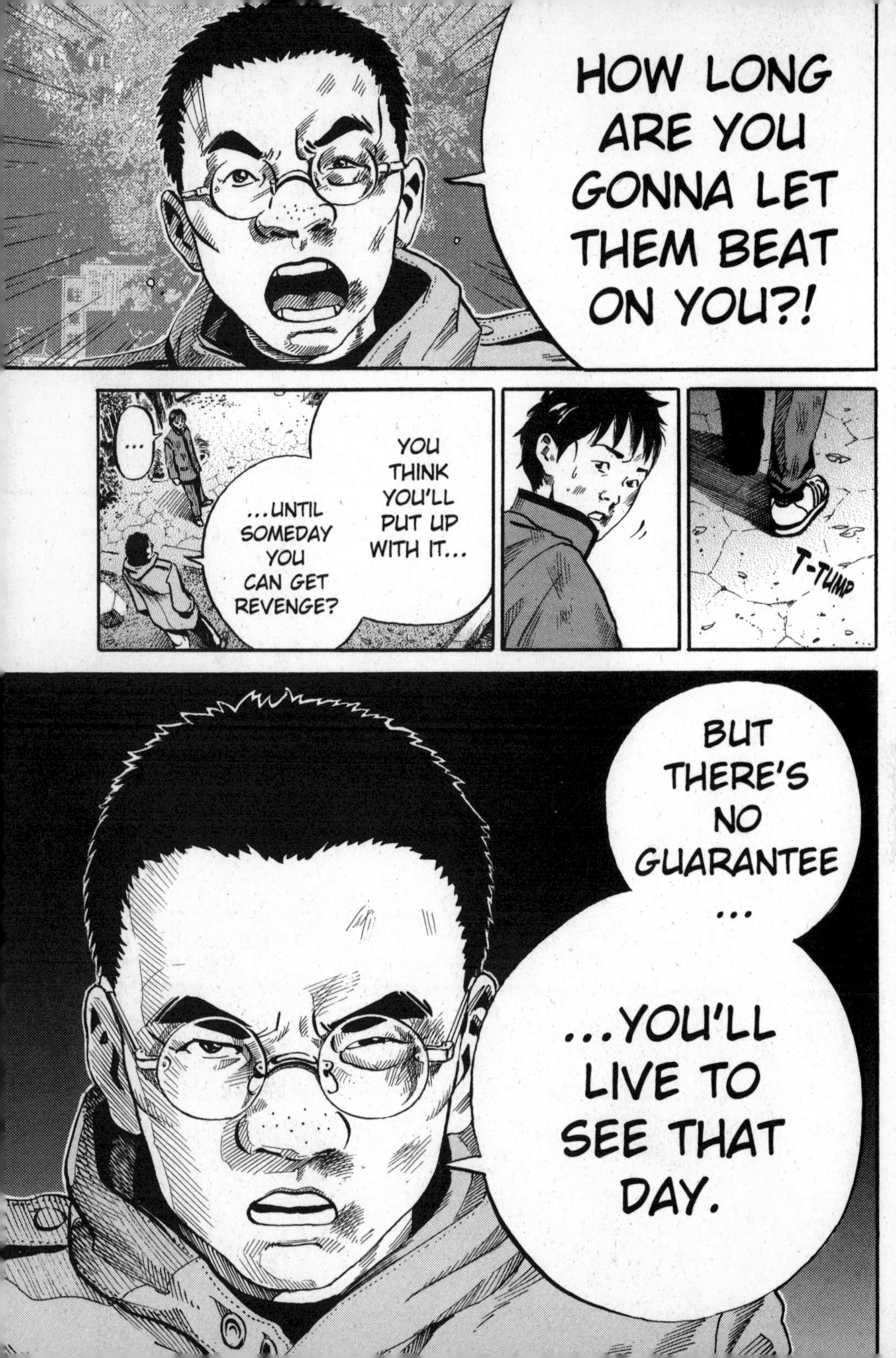
HOW LONG ARE YOU GONNA LET THEM BEAT ON YOU?!
T-TUMP
YOU THINK YOU'LL PUT UP WITH IT...
...UNTIL SOMEDAY YOU CAN GET REVENGE?
...
BUT THERE'S NO GUARANTEE ...
...YOU'LL LIVE TO SEE THAT DAY.

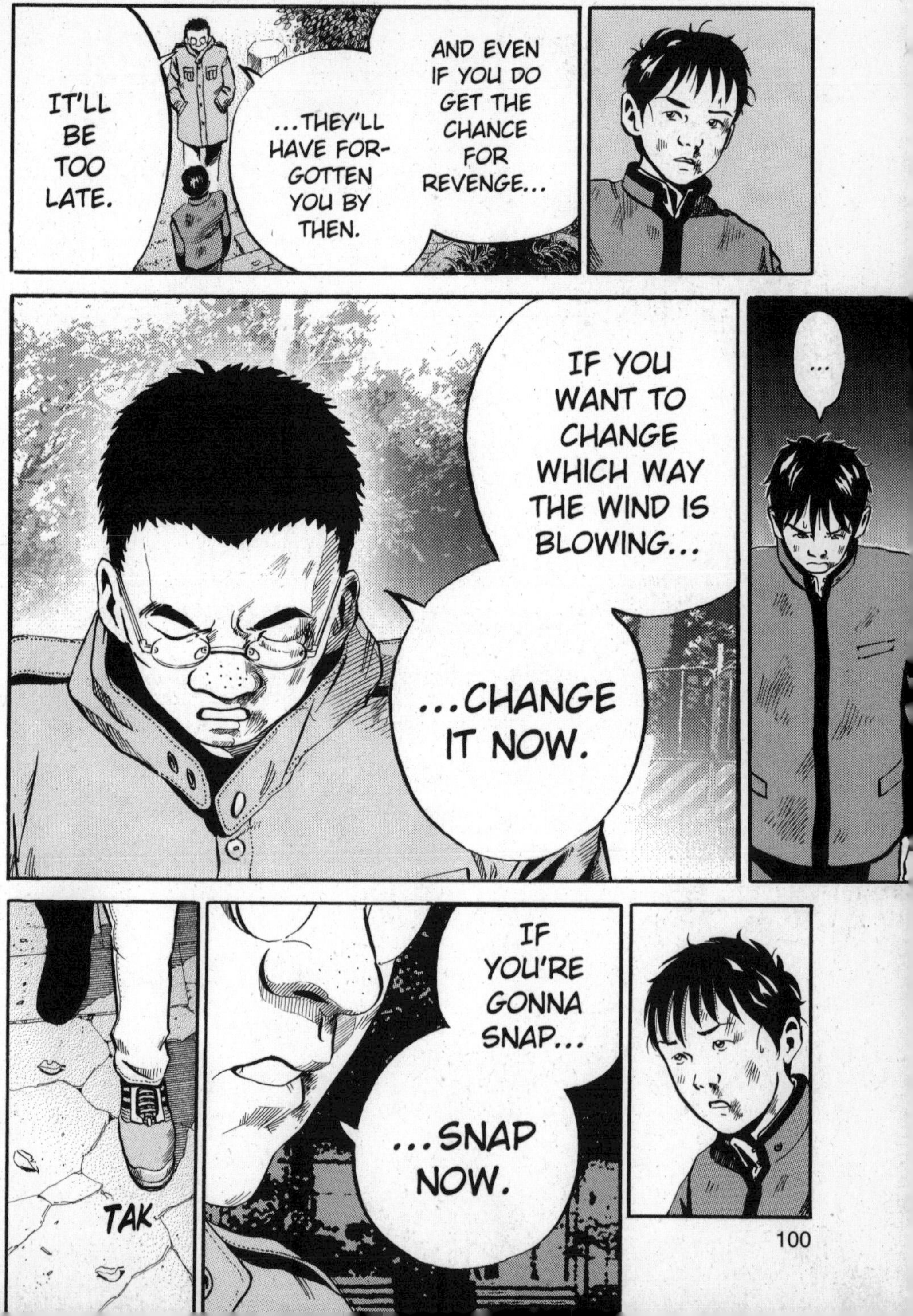
AND EVEN IF YOU DO GET THE CHANCE FOR REVENGE...
...THEY'LL HAVE FOR-GOTTEN YOU BY THEN.
IT'LL BE TOO LATE.
...
IF YOU WANT TO CHANGE WHICH WAY THE WIND IS BLOWING...
...CHANGE IT NOW.
IF YOU'RE GONNA SNAP...
...SNAP NOW.
TAK

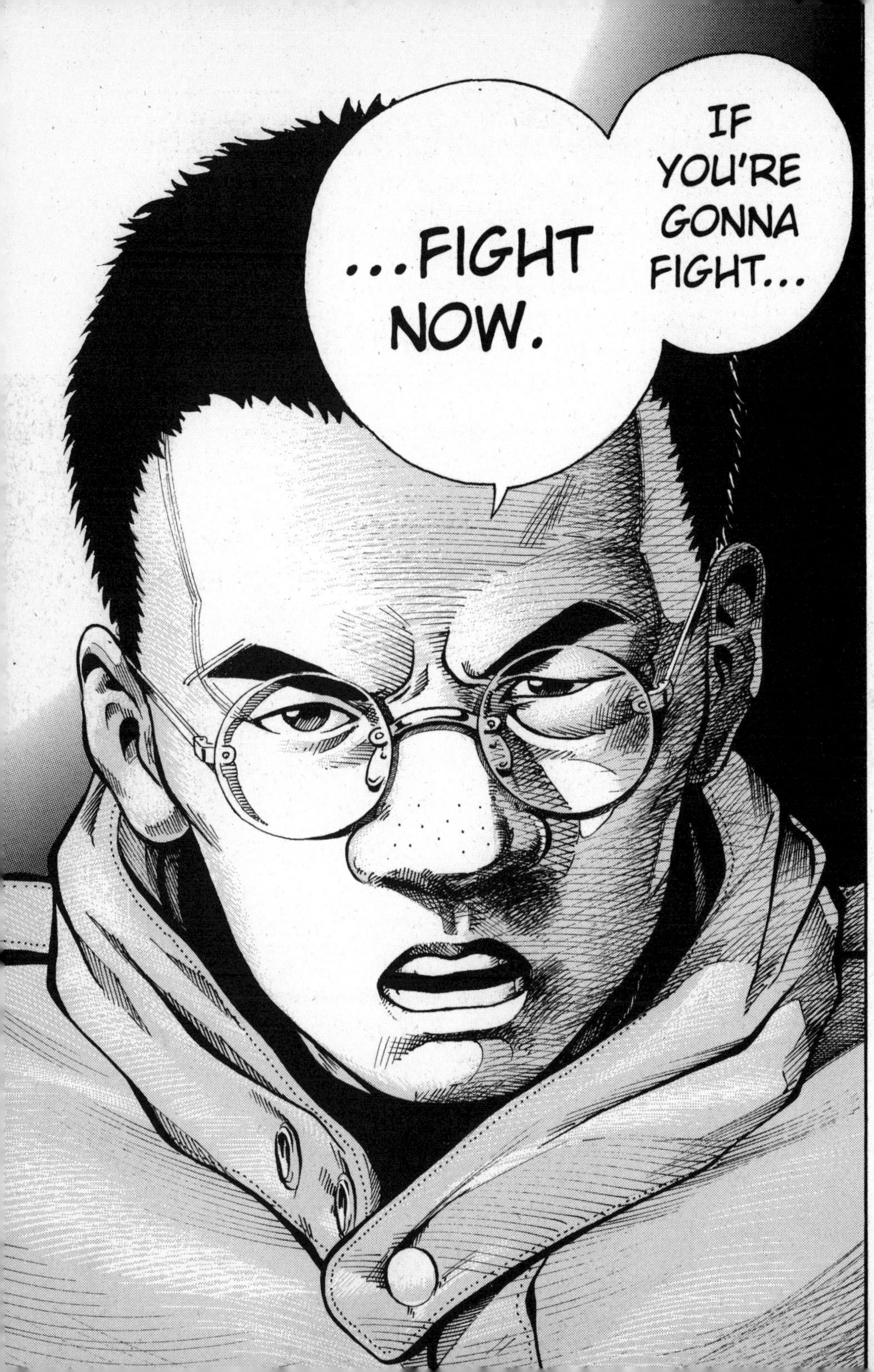
IF YOU'RE GONNA FIGHT...
...FIGHT NOW.

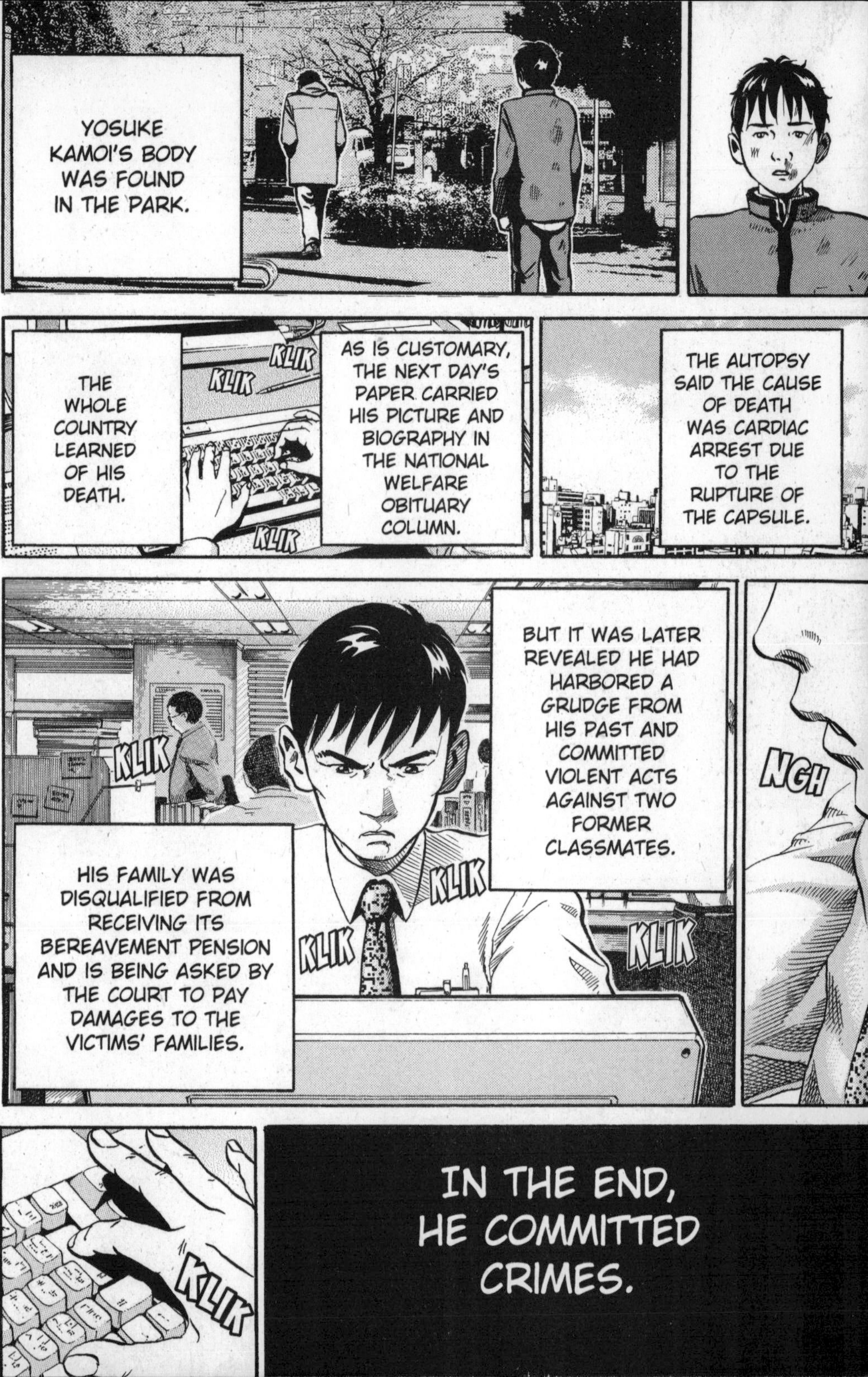
YOSUKE KAMOI'S BODY WAS FOUND IN THE PARK.
THE AUTOPSY SAID THE CAUSE OF DEATH WAS CARDIAC ARREST DUE TO THE RUPTURE OF THE CAPSULE.
KLIK
AS IS CUSTOMARY, THE NEXT DAY'S PAPER CARRIED HIS PICTURE AND BIOGRAPHY IN THE NATIONAL WELFARE OBITUARY COLUMN.
KLIK
THE WHOLE COUNTRY LEARNED OF HIS DEATH.
KLIK
NGH
BUT IT WAS LATER REVEALED HE HAD HARBORED A GRUDGE FROM HIS PAST AND COMMITTED VIOLENT ACTS AGAINST TWO FORMER CLASSMATES.
KLIK
KLIK
KLIK
HIS FAMILY WAS DISQUALIFIED FROM RECEIVING ITS BEREAVEMENT PENSION AND IS BEING ASKED BY THE COURT TO PAY DAMAGES TO THE VICTIMS' FAMILIES.
KLIK
IN THE END, HE COMMITTED CRIMES.
KLIK

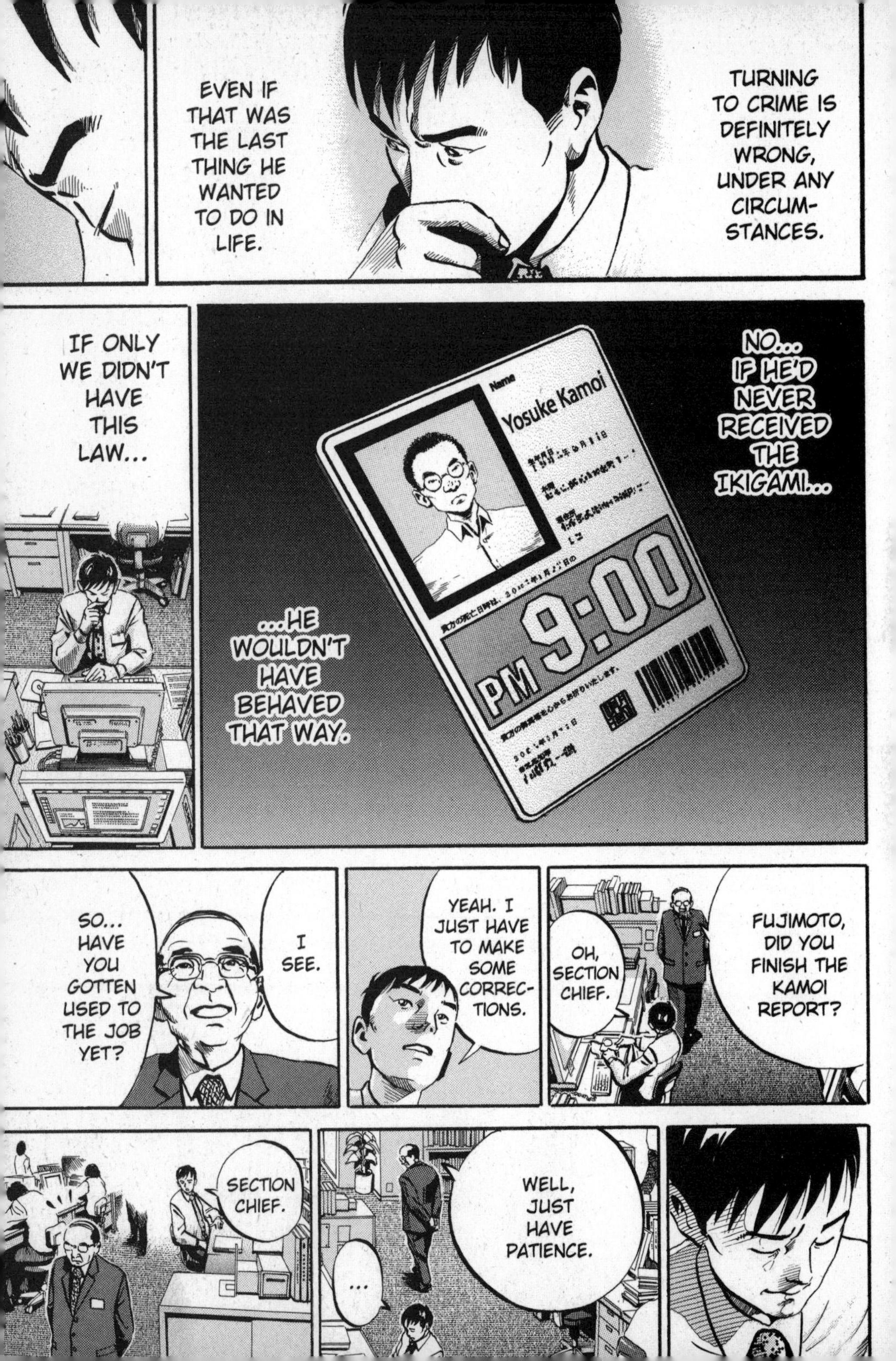
TURNING TO CRIME IS DEFINITELY WRONG, UNDER ANY CIRCUMSTANCES.
EVEN IF THAT WAS THE LAST THING HE WANTED TO DO IN LIFE.
NO... IF HE'D NEVER RECEIVED THE IKIGAMI...
Name
Yosuke Kamoi
PM 9:00
...HE WOULDN'T HAVE BEHAVED THAT WAY.
IF ONLY WE DIDN'T HAVE THIS LAW...
FUJIMOTO, DID YOU FINISH THE KAMOI REPORT?
OH, SECTION CHIEF.
YEAH. I JUST HAVE TO MAKE SOME CORRECTIONS.
I SEE.
SO... HAVE YOU GOTTEN USED TO THE JOB YET?
WELL, JUST HAVE PATIENCE.
...
SECTION CHIEF.

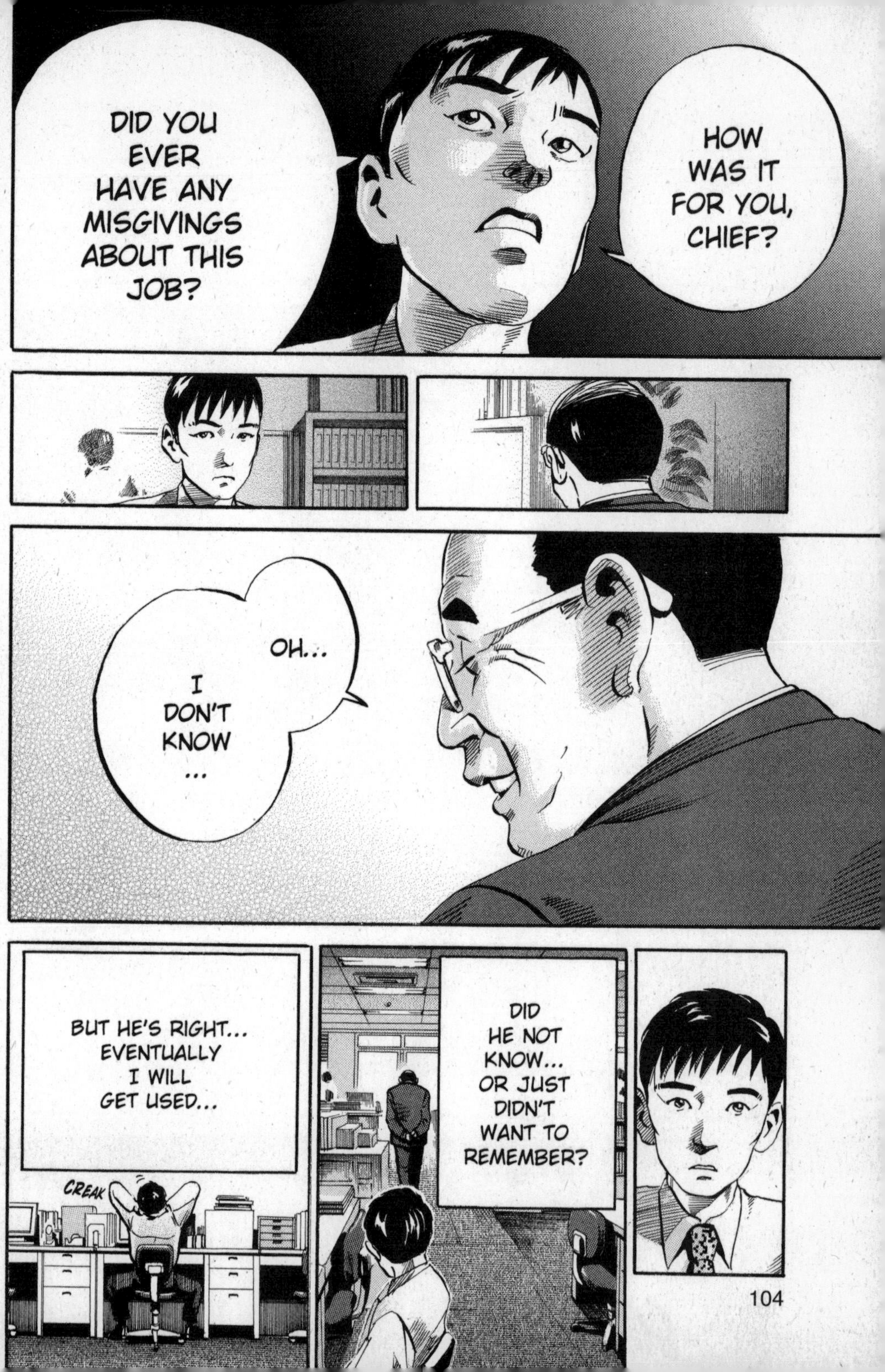
HOW WAS IT FOR YOU, CHIEF?
DID YOU EVER HAVE ANY MISGIVINGS ABOUT THIS JOB?
OH... I DON'T KNOW ...
DID HE NOT KNOW... OR JUST DIDN'T WANT TO REMEMBER?
BUT HE'S RIGHT... EVENTUALLY I WILL GET USED...
CREAK

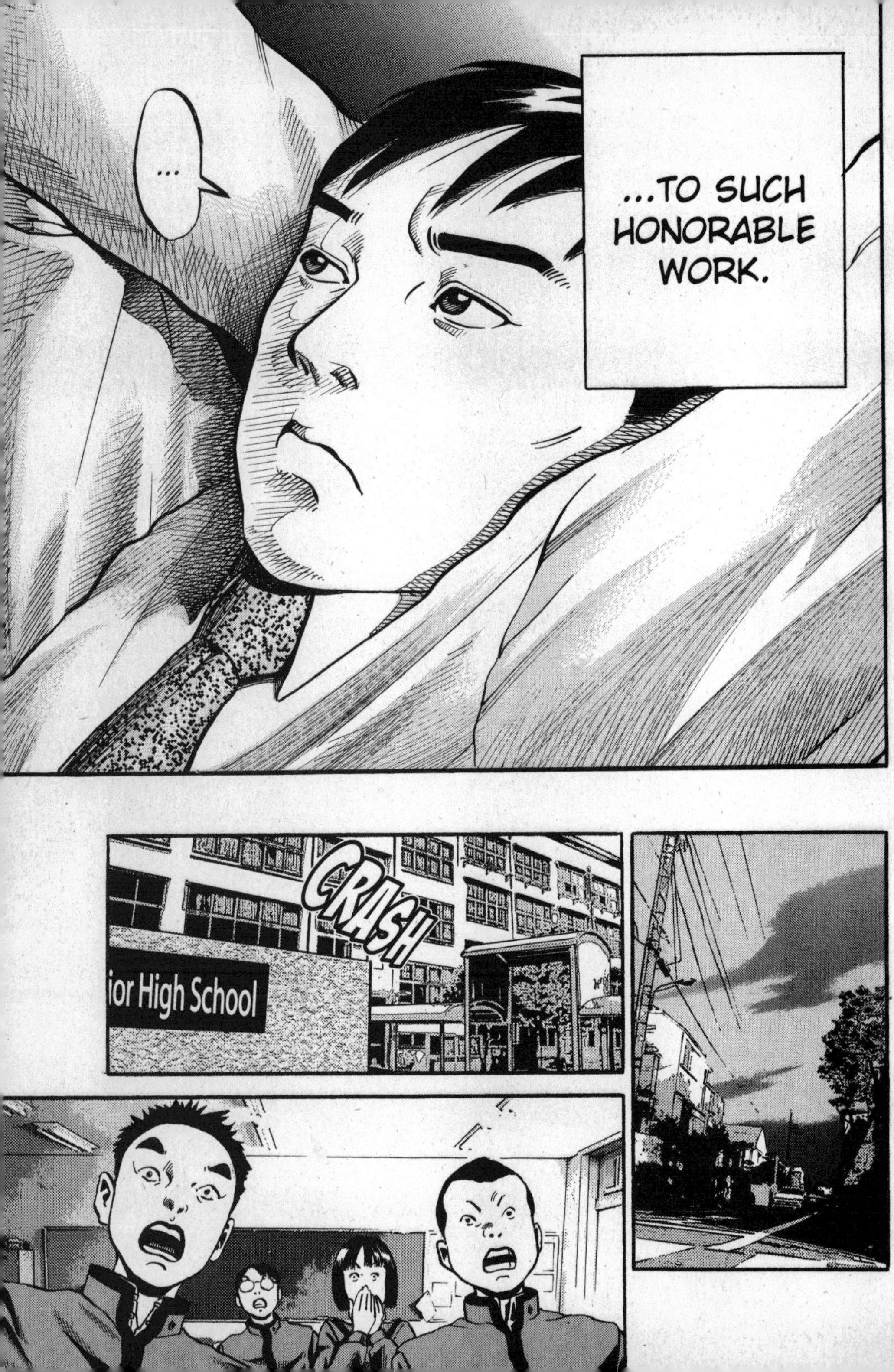
...TO SUCH HONORABLE WORK.
...
CRASH
ior High School

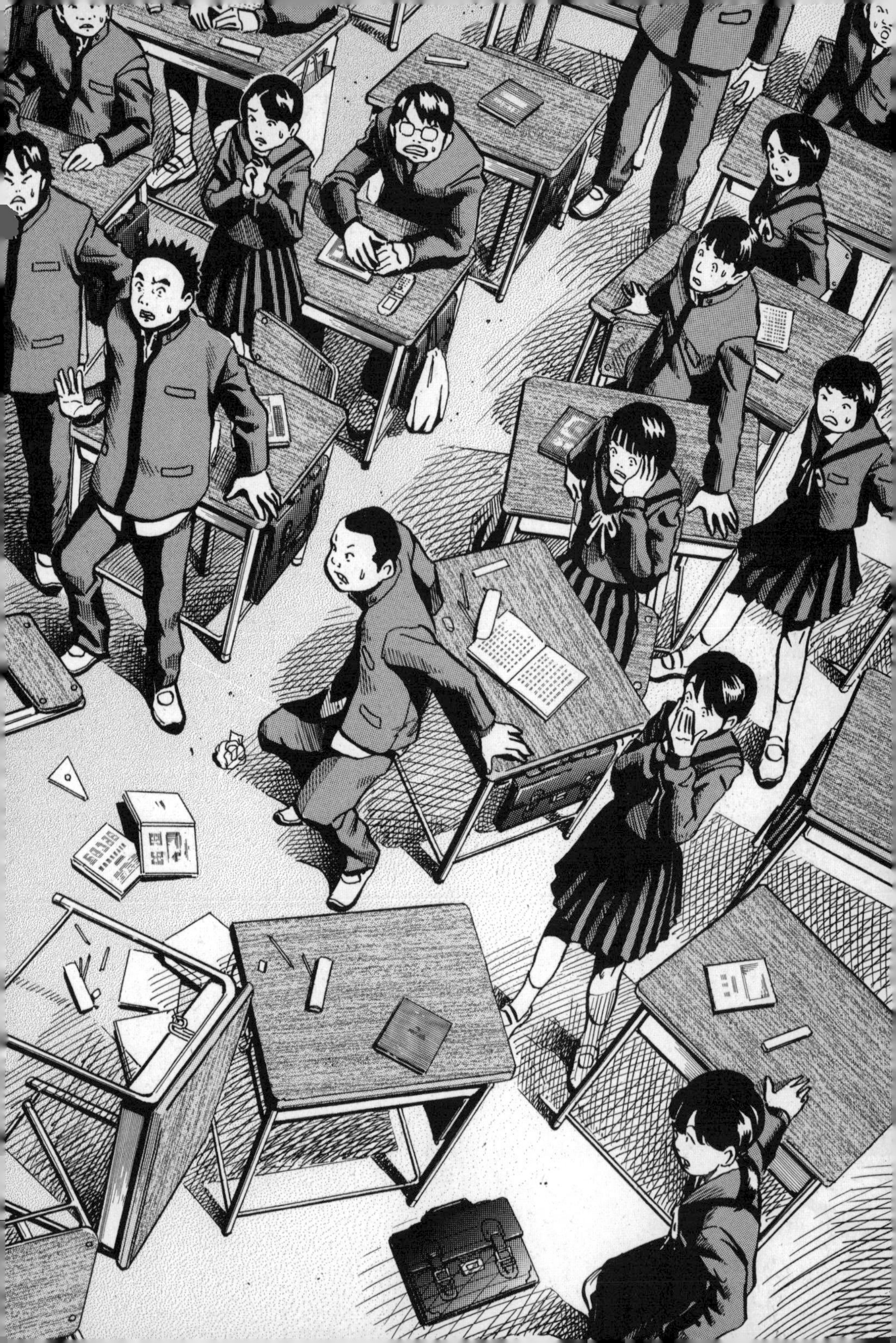

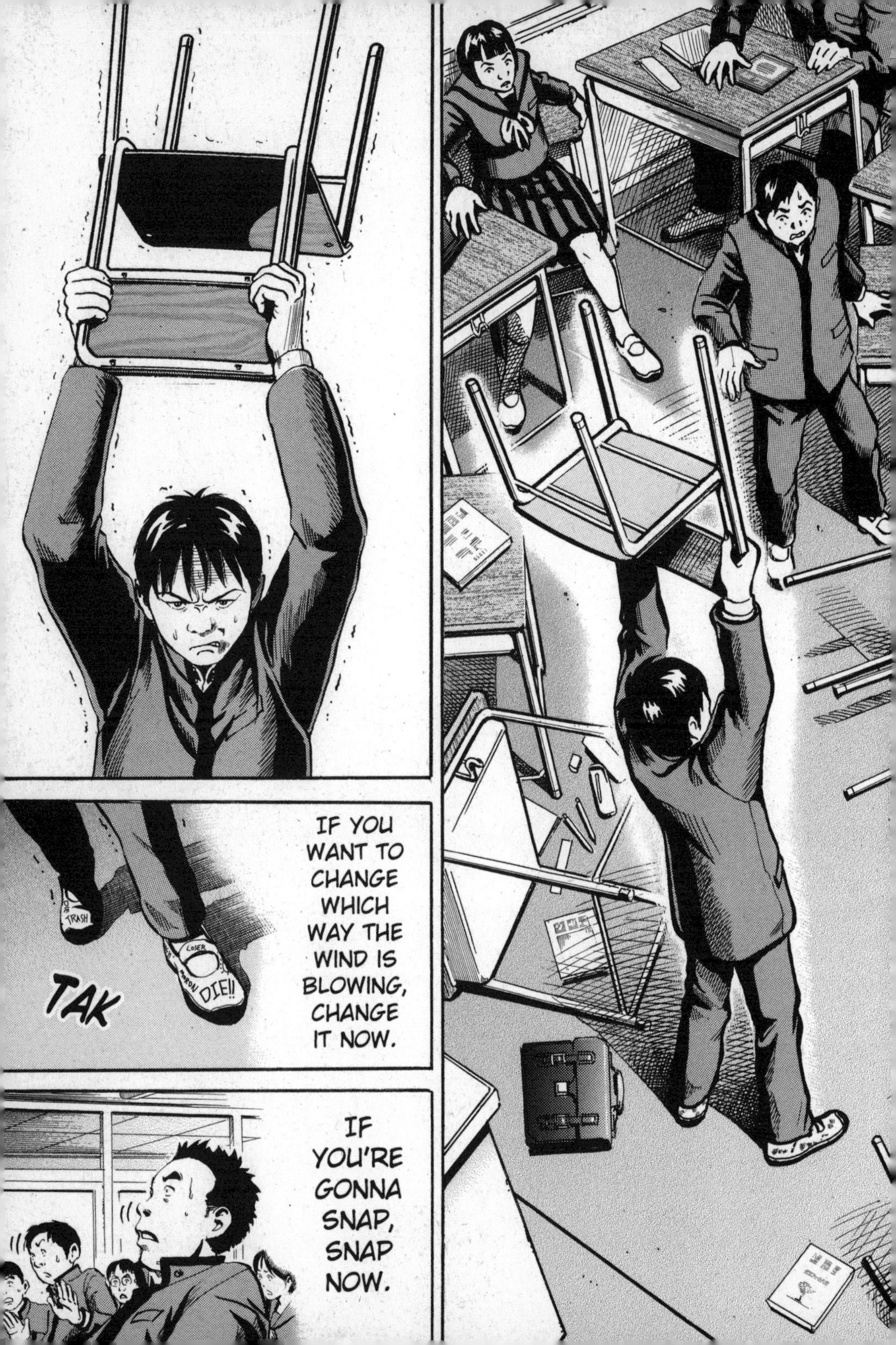
IF YOU WANT TO CHANGE WHICH WAY THE WIND IS BLOWING, CHANGE IT NOW.
LOSER
MORON
DIE!!
TRASH
TAK
IF YOU'RE GONNA SNAP, SNAP NOW.

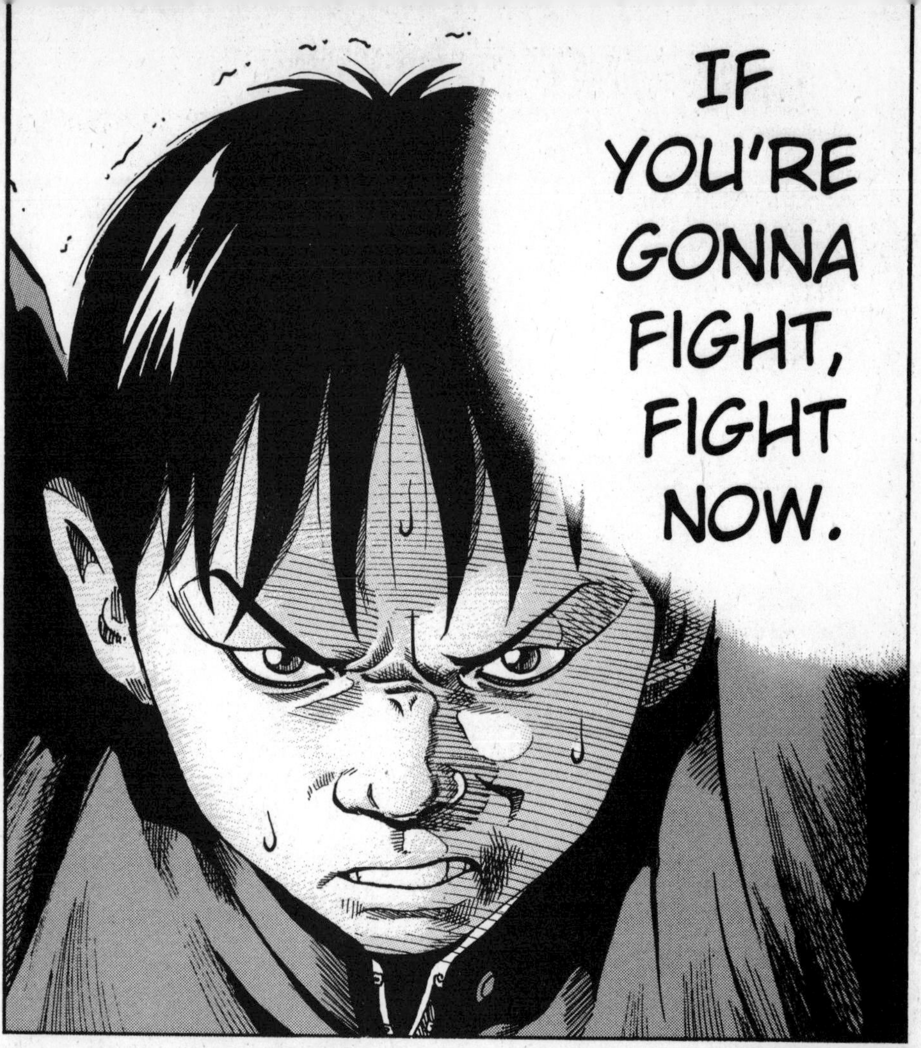
IF YOU'RE GONNA FIGHT, FIGHT NOW.

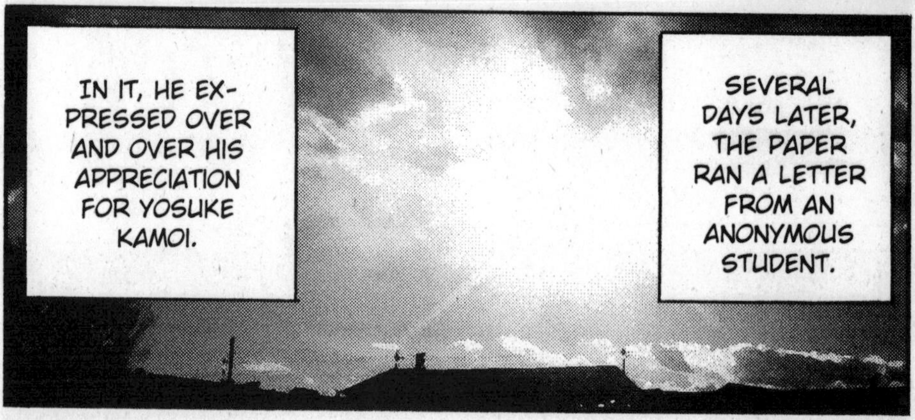
SEVERAL DAYS LATER, THE PAPER RAN A LETTER FROM AN ANONYMOUS STUDENT.
IN IT, HE EX-PRESSED OVER AND OVER HIS APPRECIATION FOR YOSUKE KAMOI.

Episode 2 The Last Song Act1

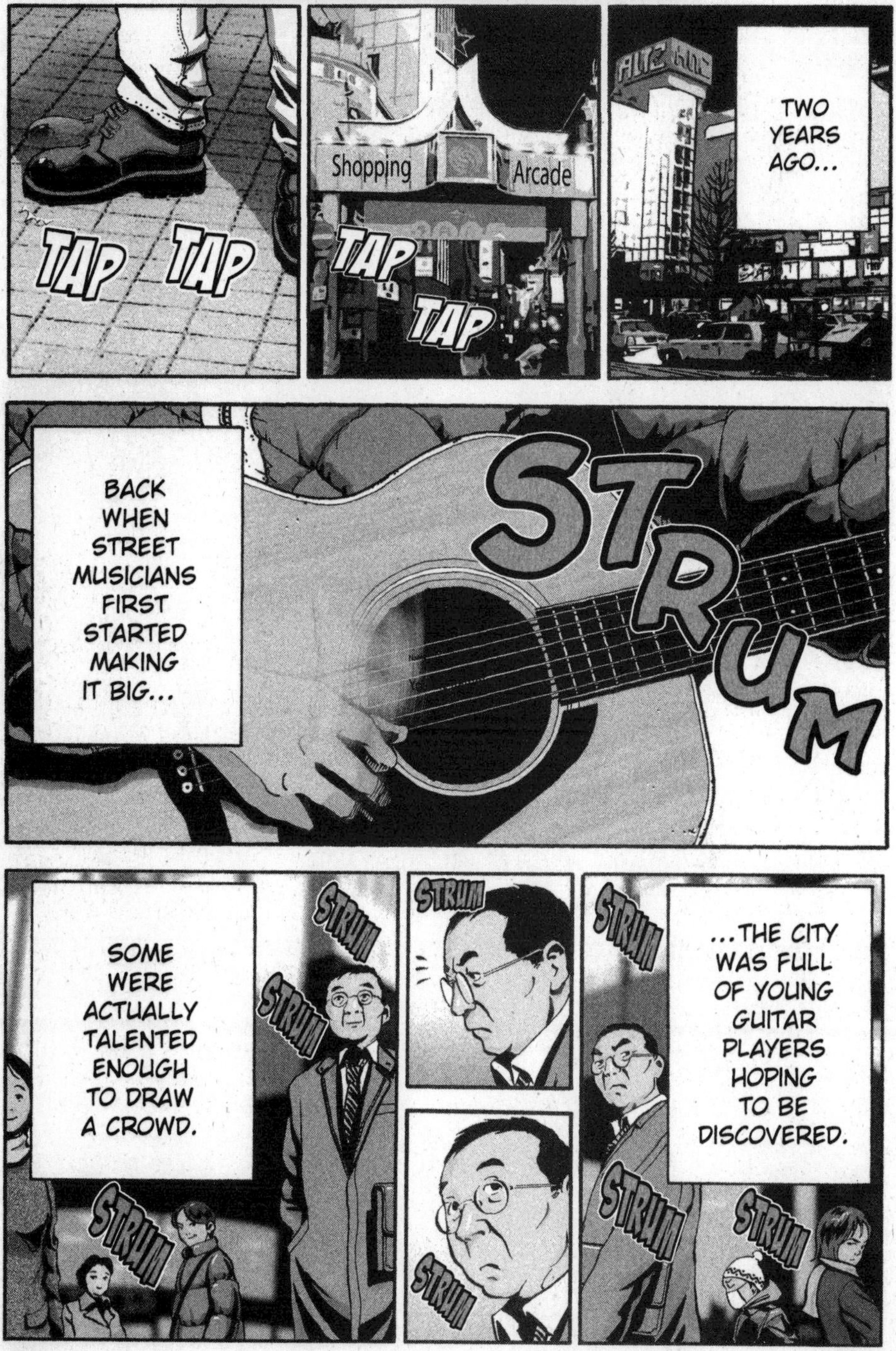

TWO YEARS AGO...
Shopping Arcade
TAP
TAP
TAP TAP
BACK WHEN STREET MUSICIANS FIRST STARTED MAKING IT BIG...
STRUM
...THE CITY WAS FULL OF YOUNG GUITAR PLAYERS HOPING TO BE DISCOVERED.
STRUM
STRUM
STRUM
STRUM
STRUM
STRUM
SOME WERE ACTUALLY TALENTED ENOUGH TO DRAW A CROWD.
STRUM
STRUM

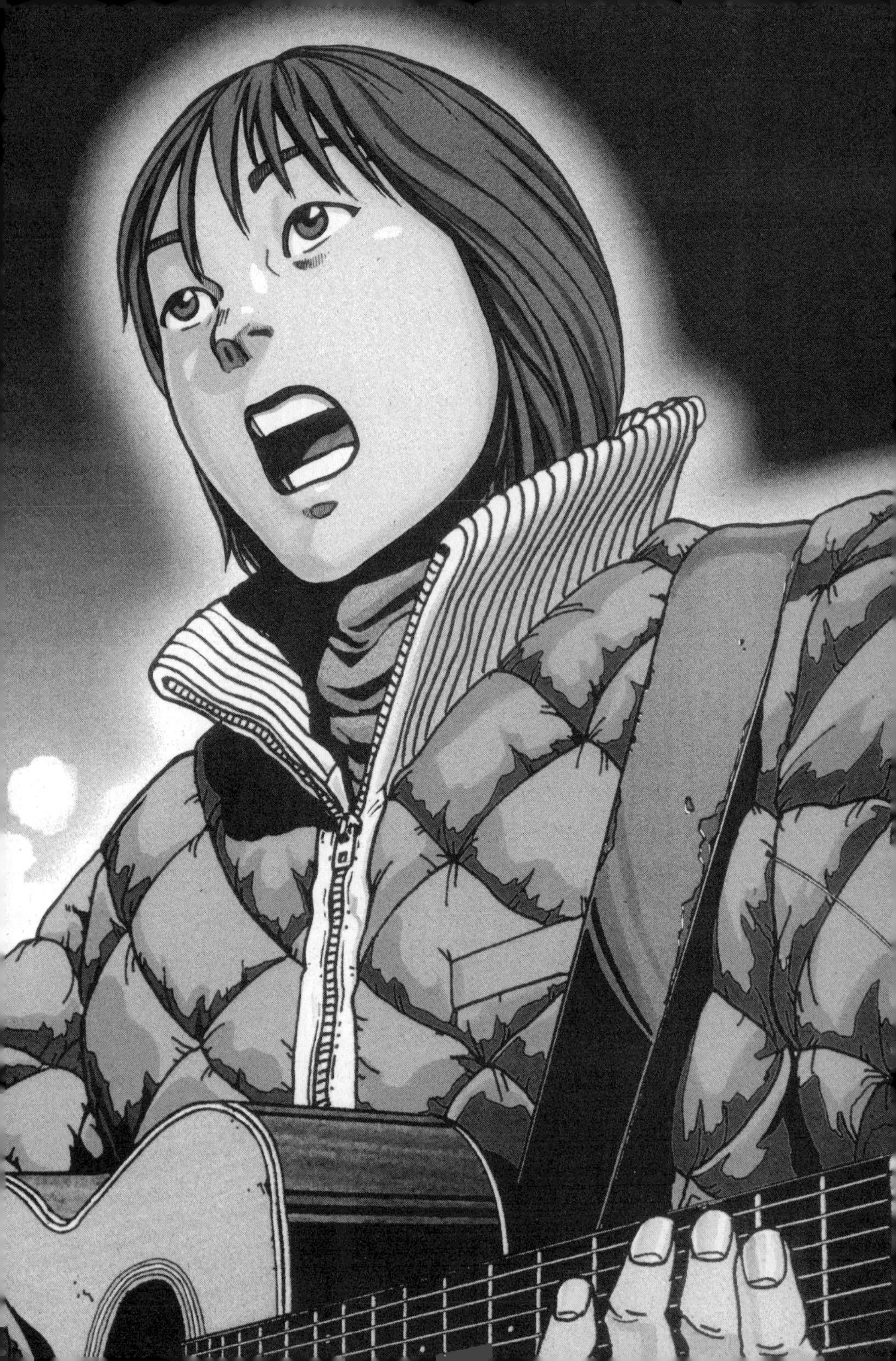

Episode 2 The Last Song Act1

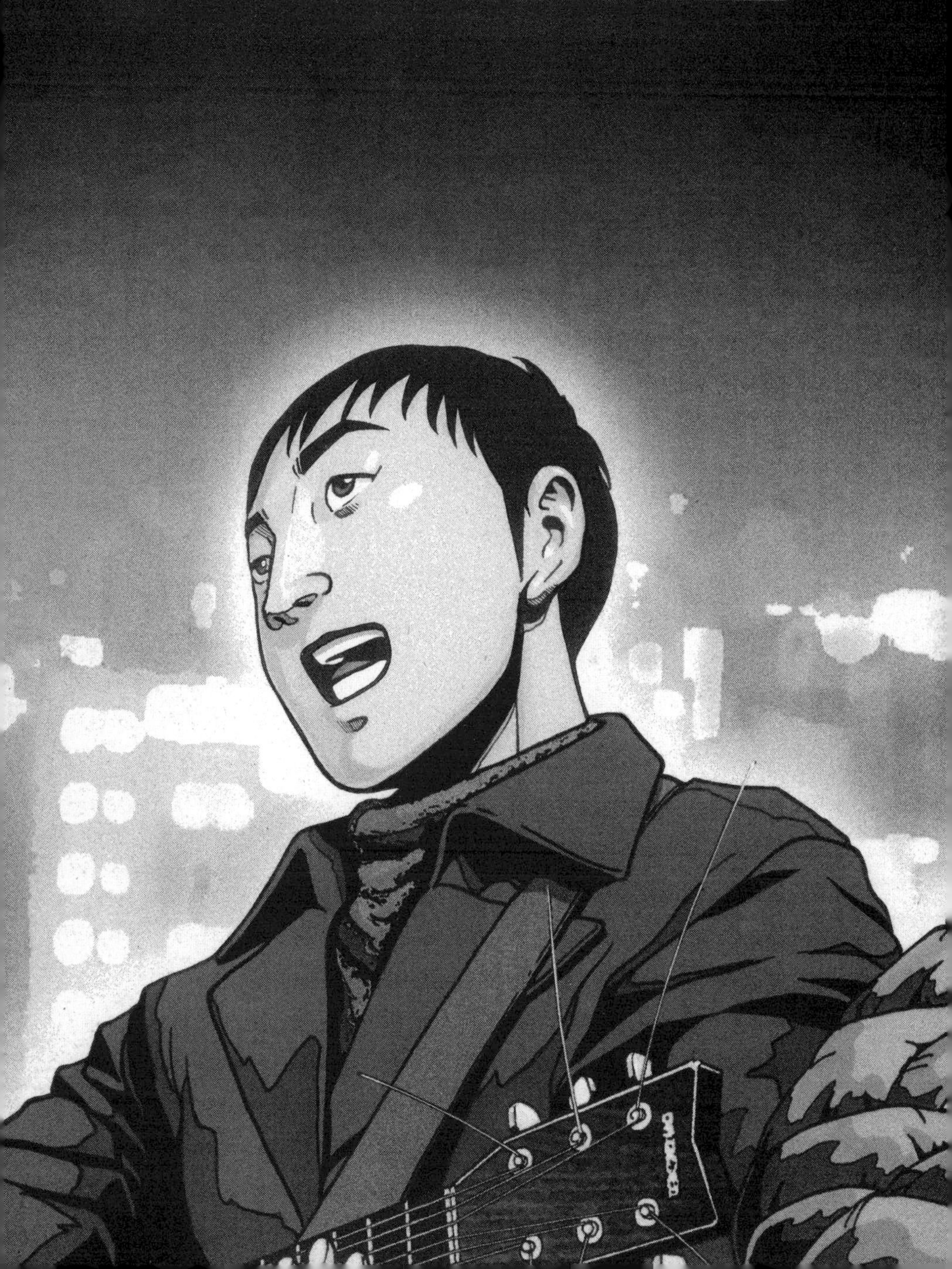

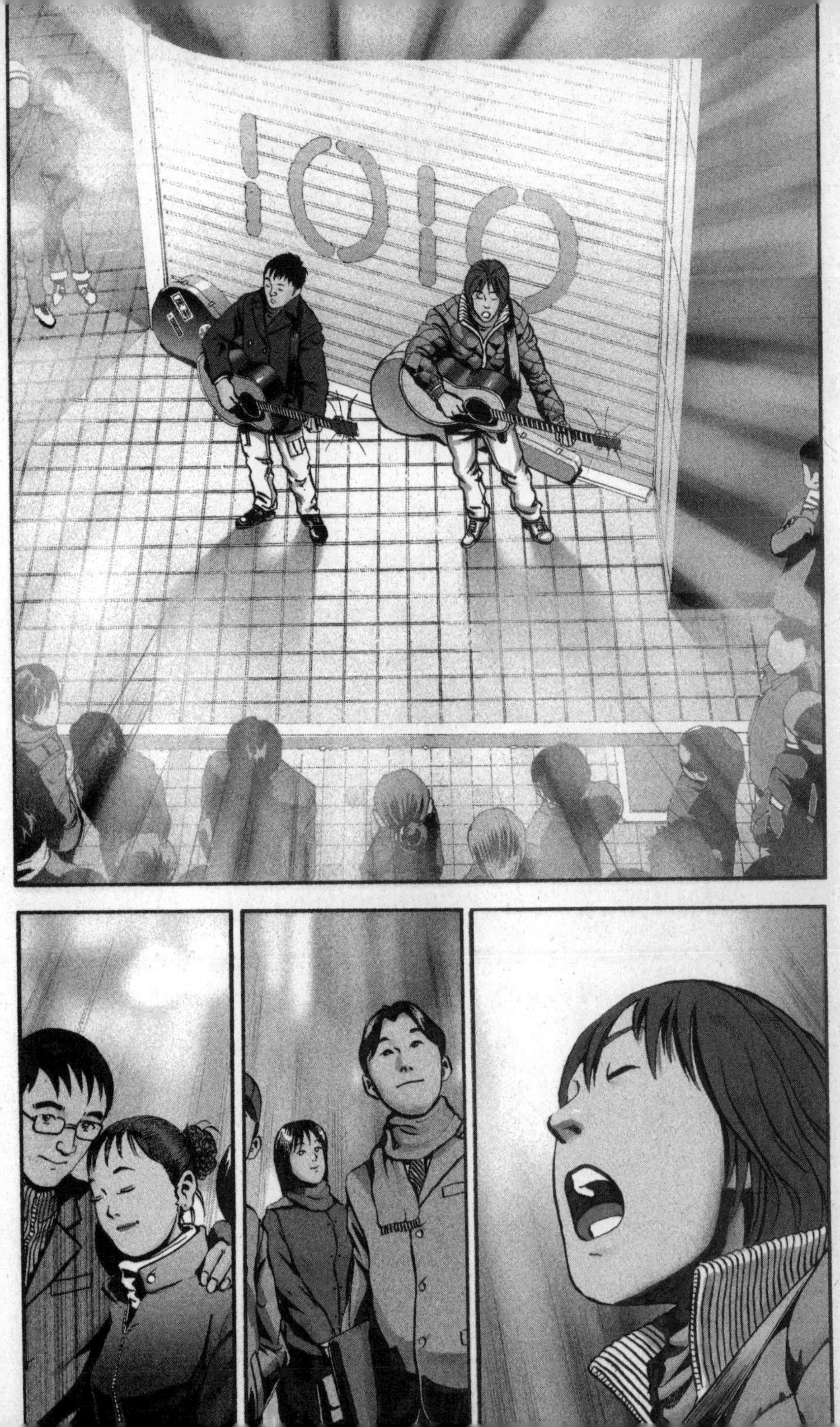

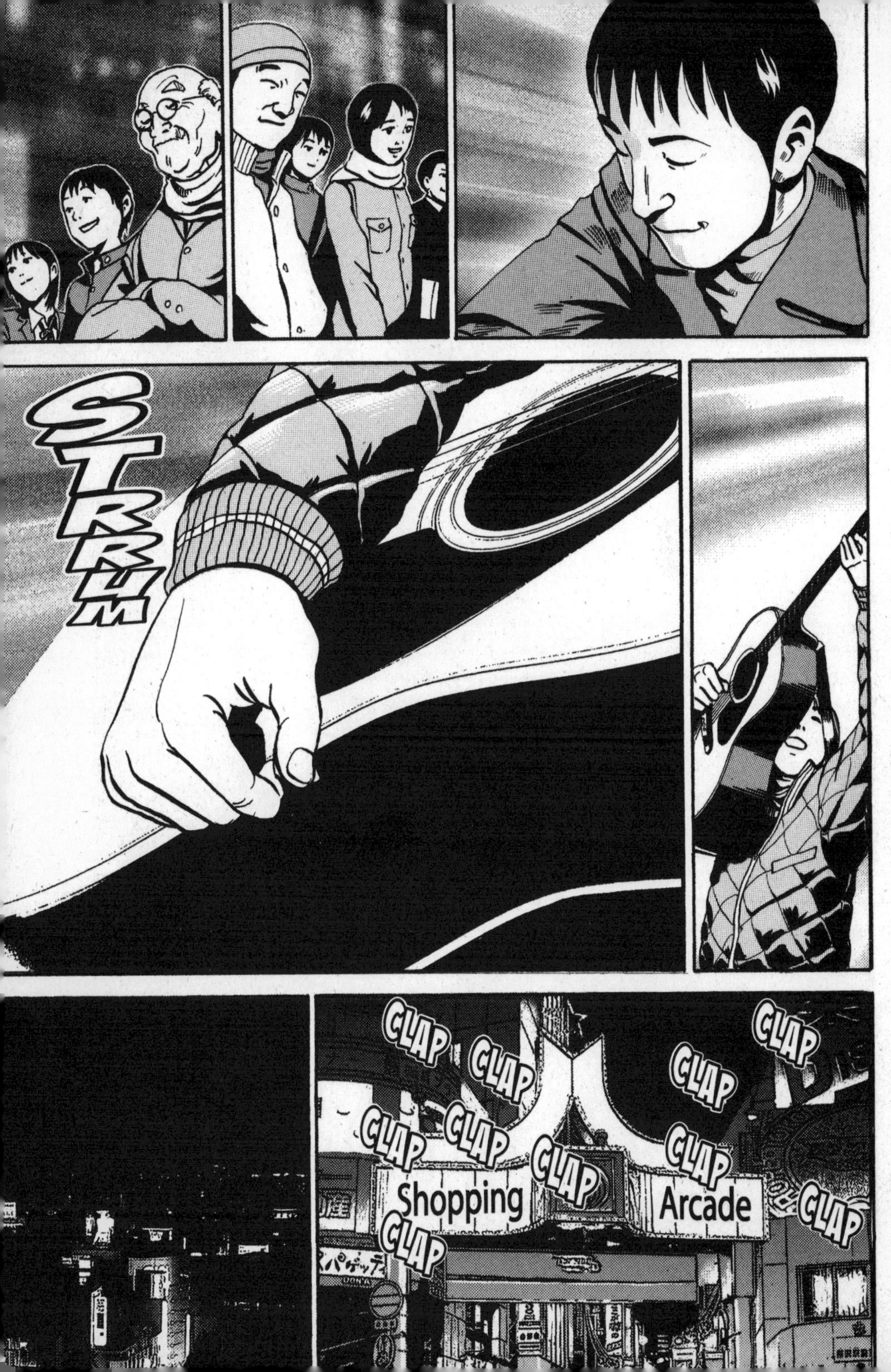
STRUM
CLAP
CLAP
CLAP
CLAP
CLAP
CLAP
CLAP
CLAP
CLAP
Shopping
Arcade

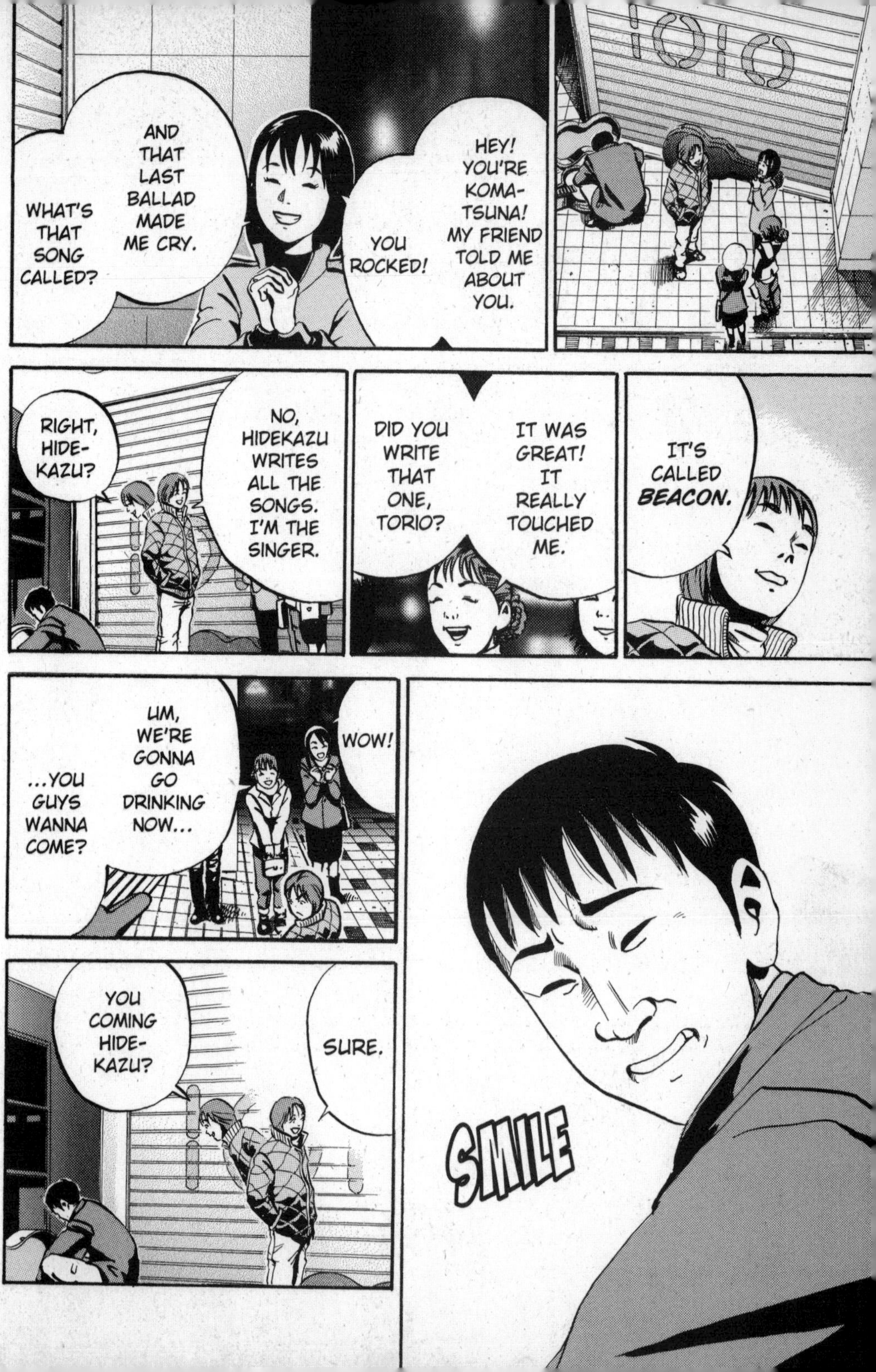
HEY! YOU'RE KOMA-TSUNA! MY FRIEND TOLD ME ABOUT YOU.
YOU ROCKED!
AND THAT LAST BALLAD MADE ME CRY.
WHAT'S THAT SONG CALLED?
IT'S CALLED BEACON.
IT WAS GREAT! IT REALLY TOUCHED ME.
DID YOU WRITE THAT ONE, TORIO?
NO, HIDEKAZU WRITES ALL THE SONGS. I'M THE SINGER.
RIGHT, HIDE-KAZU?
SMILE
WOW!
UM, WE'RE GONNA GO DRINKING NOW...
...YOU GUYS WANNA COME?
SURE.
YOU COMING HIDE-KAZU?

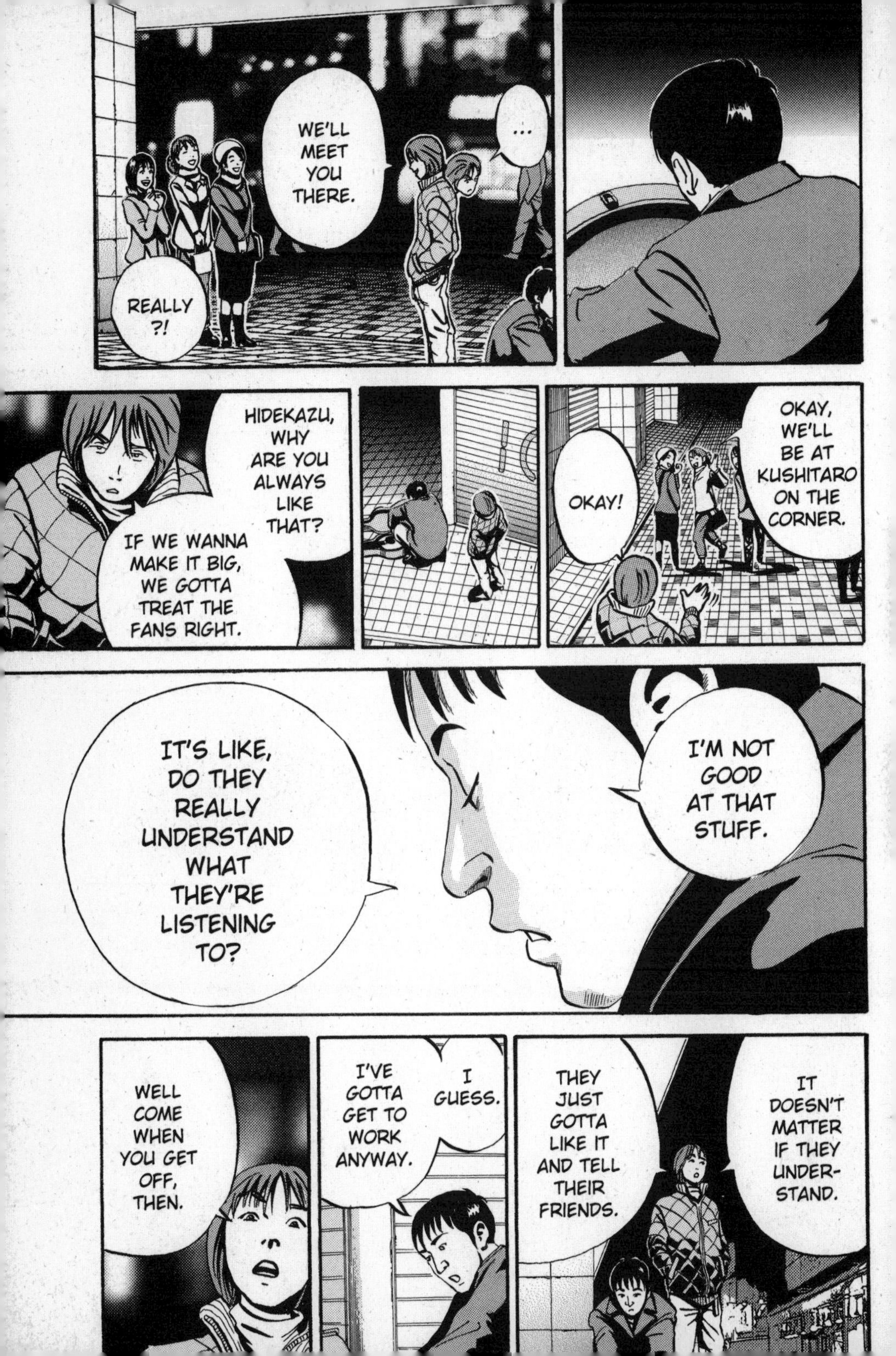
...
WE'LL MEET YOU THERE.
REALLY ?!
OKAY, WE'LL BE AT KUSHITARO ON THE CORNER.
OKAY!
HIDEKAZU, WHY ARE YOU ALWAYS LIKE THAT?
IF WE WANNA MAKE IT BIG, WE GOTTA TREAT THE FANS RIGHT.
I'M NOT GOOD AT THAT STUFF.
IT'S LIKE, DO THEY REALLY UNDERSTAND WHAT THEY'RE LISTENING TO?
IT DOESN'T MATTER IF THEY UNDER-STAND.
THEY JUST GOTTA LIKE IT AND TELL THEIR FRIENDS.
I GUESS.
I'VE GOTTA GET TO WORK ANYWAY.
WELL COME WHEN YOU GET OFF, THEN.

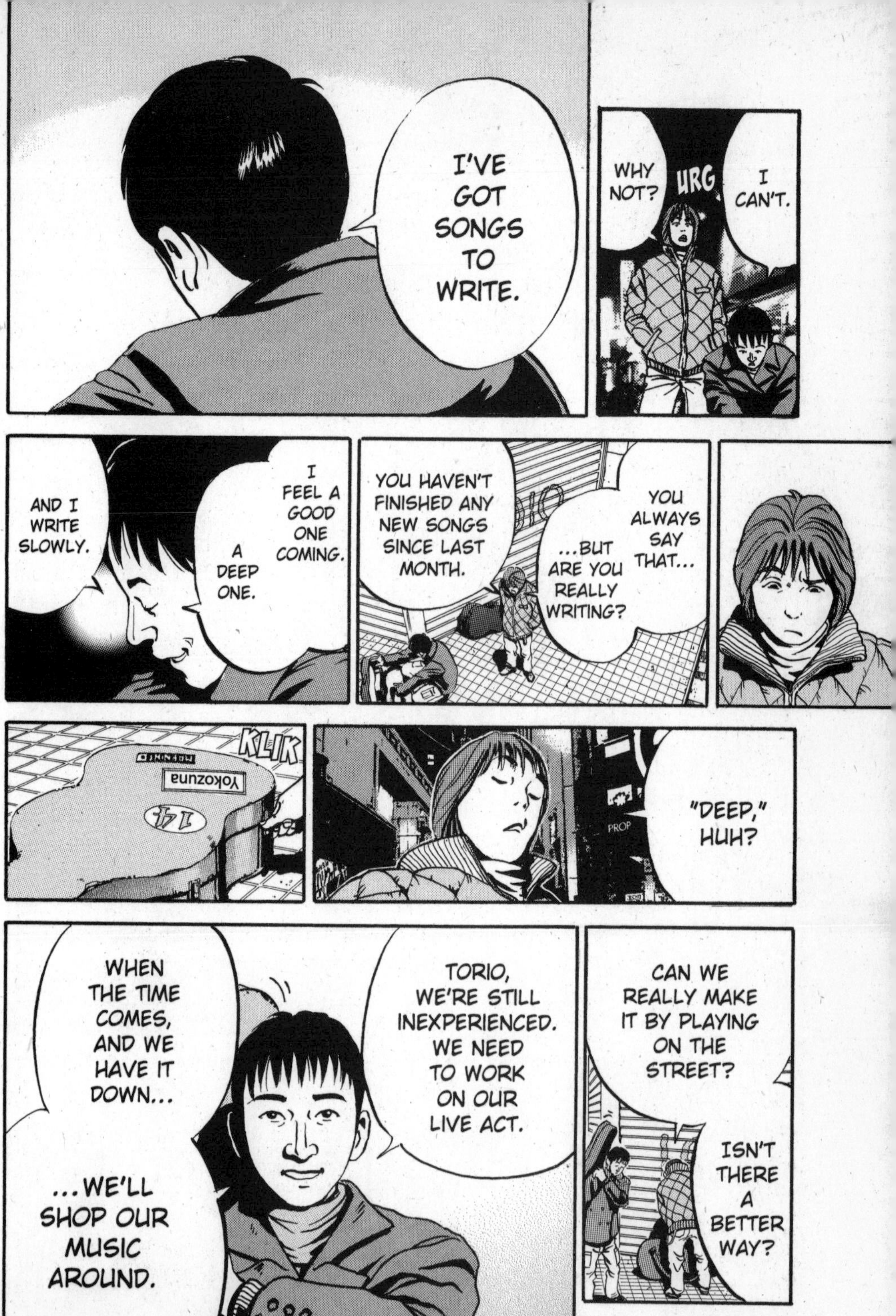
I CAN'T.
URG
WHY NOT?
I'VE GOT SONGS TO WRITE.
YOU ALWAYS SAY THAT...
...BUT ARE YOU REALLY WRITING?
YOU HAVEN'T FINISHED ANY NEW SONGS SINCE LAST MONTH.
I FEEL A GOOD ONE COMING.
A DEEP ONE.
AND I WRITE SLOWLY.
"DEEP," HUH?
PROP
KLIK
Yokozuna
14
CAN WE REALLY MAKE IT BY PLAYING ON THE STREET?
ISN'T THERE A BETTER WAY?
TORIO, WE'RE STILL INEXPERIENCED. WE NEED TO WORK ON OUR LIVE ACT.
WHEN THE TIME COMES, AND WE HAVE IT DOWN...
...WE'LL SHOP OUR MUSIC AROUND.

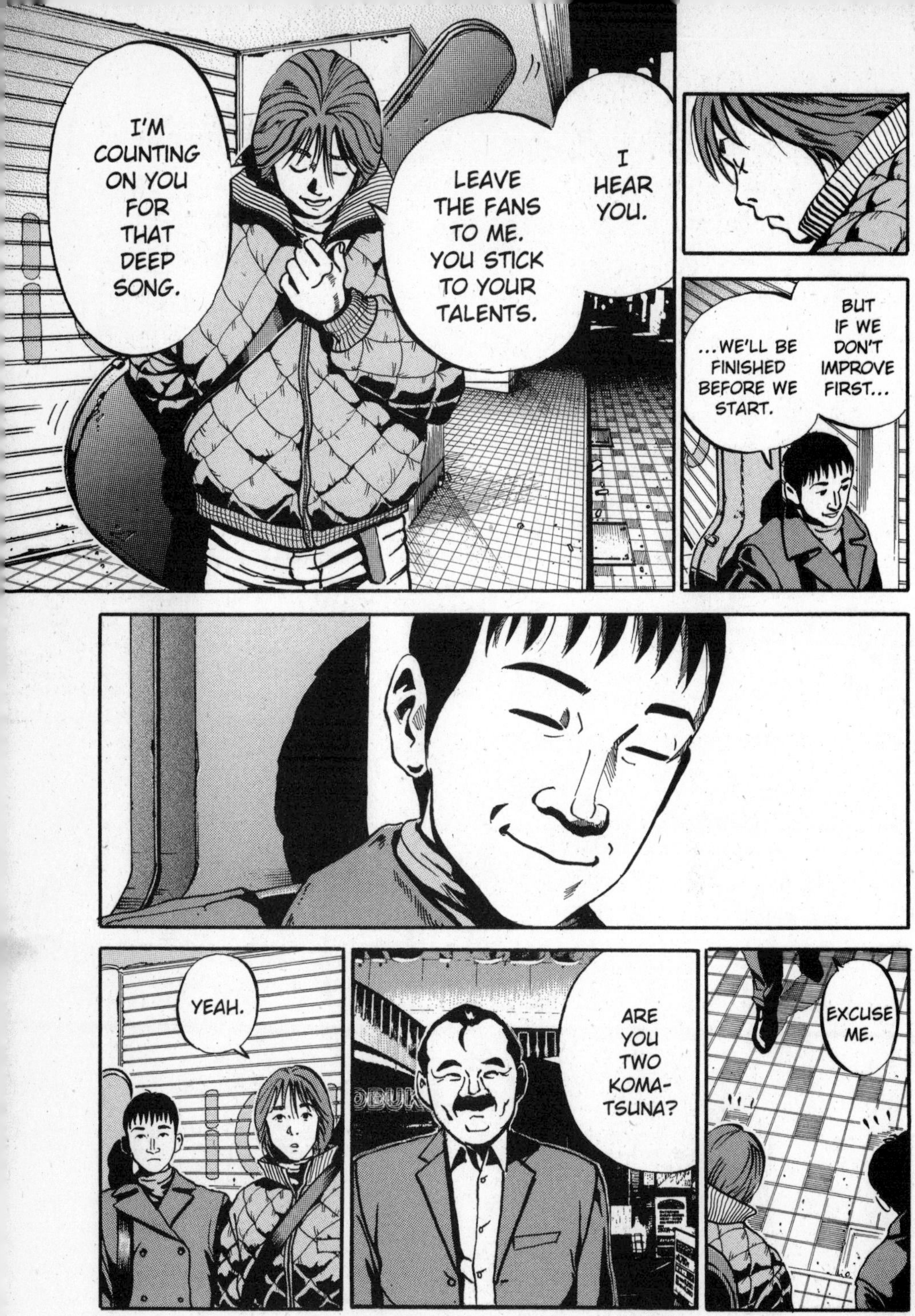
BUT IF WE DON'T IMPROVE FIRST...
...WE'LL BE FINISHED BEFORE WE START.
I HEAR YOU.
LEAVE THE FANS TO ME. YOU STICK TO YOUR TALENTS.
I'M COUNTING ON YOU FOR THAT DEEP SONG.
EXCUSE ME.
ARE YOU TWO KOMA-TSUNA?
YEAH.

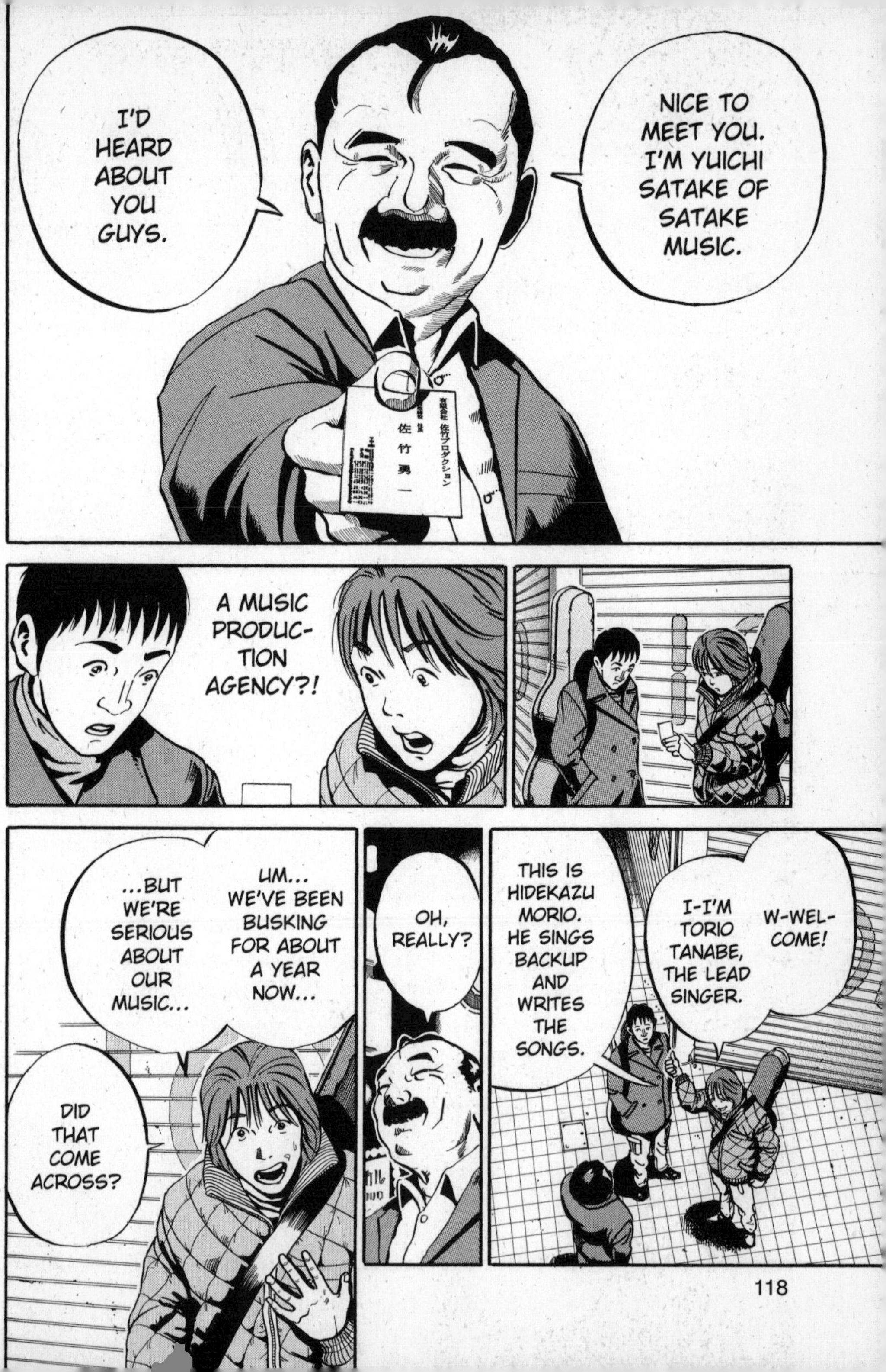
NICE TO MEET YOU. I'M YUICHI SATAKE OF SATAKE MUSIC.
I'D HEARD ABOUT YOU GUYS.
佐竹プロダクション
佐竹 勇一
A MUSIC PRODUCTION AGENCY?!
W-WEL-COME!
I-I'M TORIO TANABE, THE LEAD SINGER.
THIS IS HIDEKAZU MORIO. HE SINGS BACKUP AND WRITES THE SONGS.
OH, REALLY?
UM... WE'VE BEEN BUSKING FOR ABOUT A YEAR NOW...
...BUT WE'RE SERIOUS ABOUT OUR MUSIC...
DID THAT COME ACROSS?

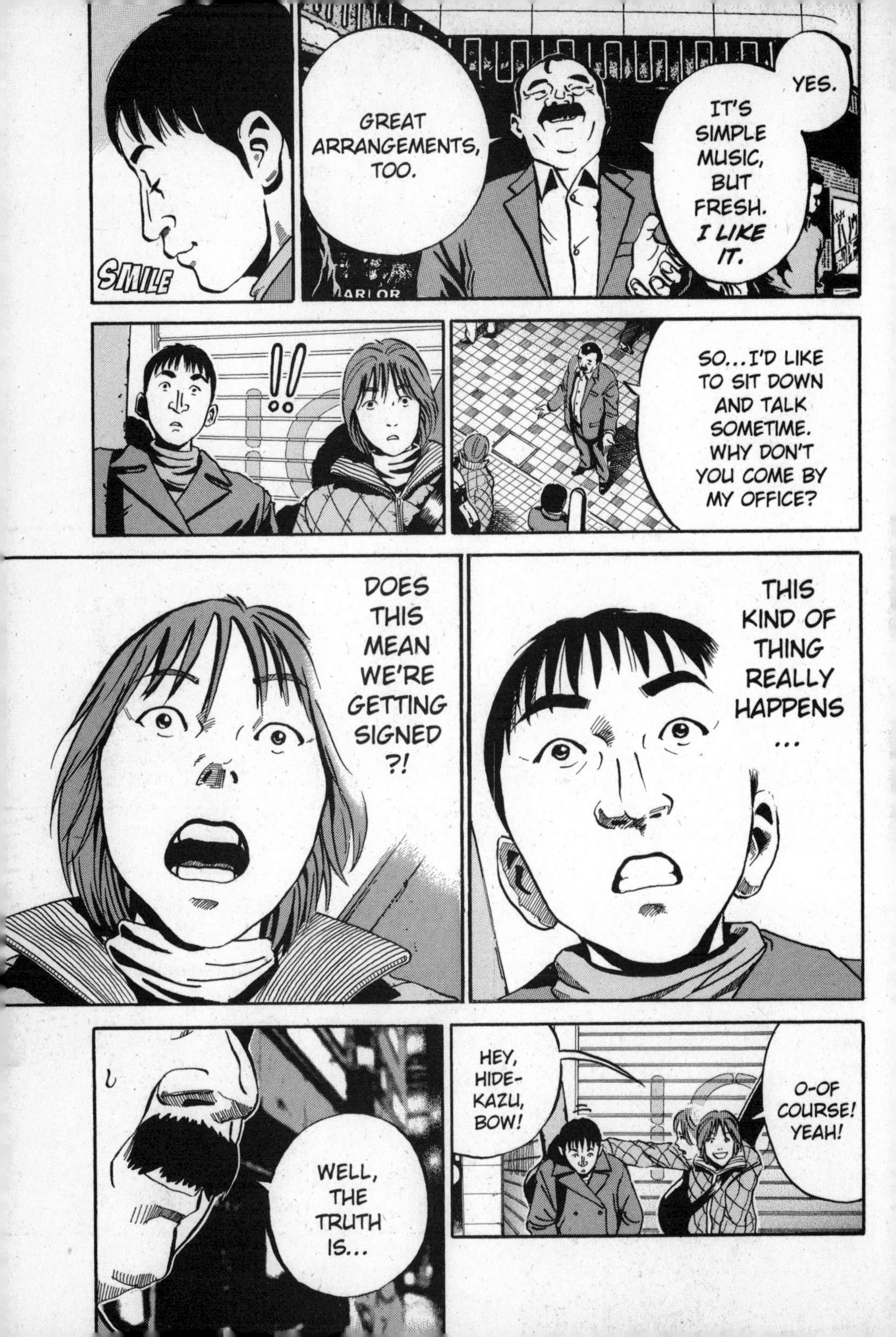
YES.
IT'S SIMPLE MUSIC, BUT FRESH. I LIKE IT.
GREAT ARRANGEMENTS, TOO.
SMILE
SO...I'D LIKE TO SIT DOWN AND TALK SOMETIME. WHY DON'T YOU COME BY MY OFFICE?
!!
THIS KIND OF THING REALLY HAPPENS...
DOES THIS MEAN WE'RE GETTING SIGNED?!
HEY, HIDEKAZU, BOW!
O-OF COURSE! YEAH!
WELL, THE TRUTH IS...

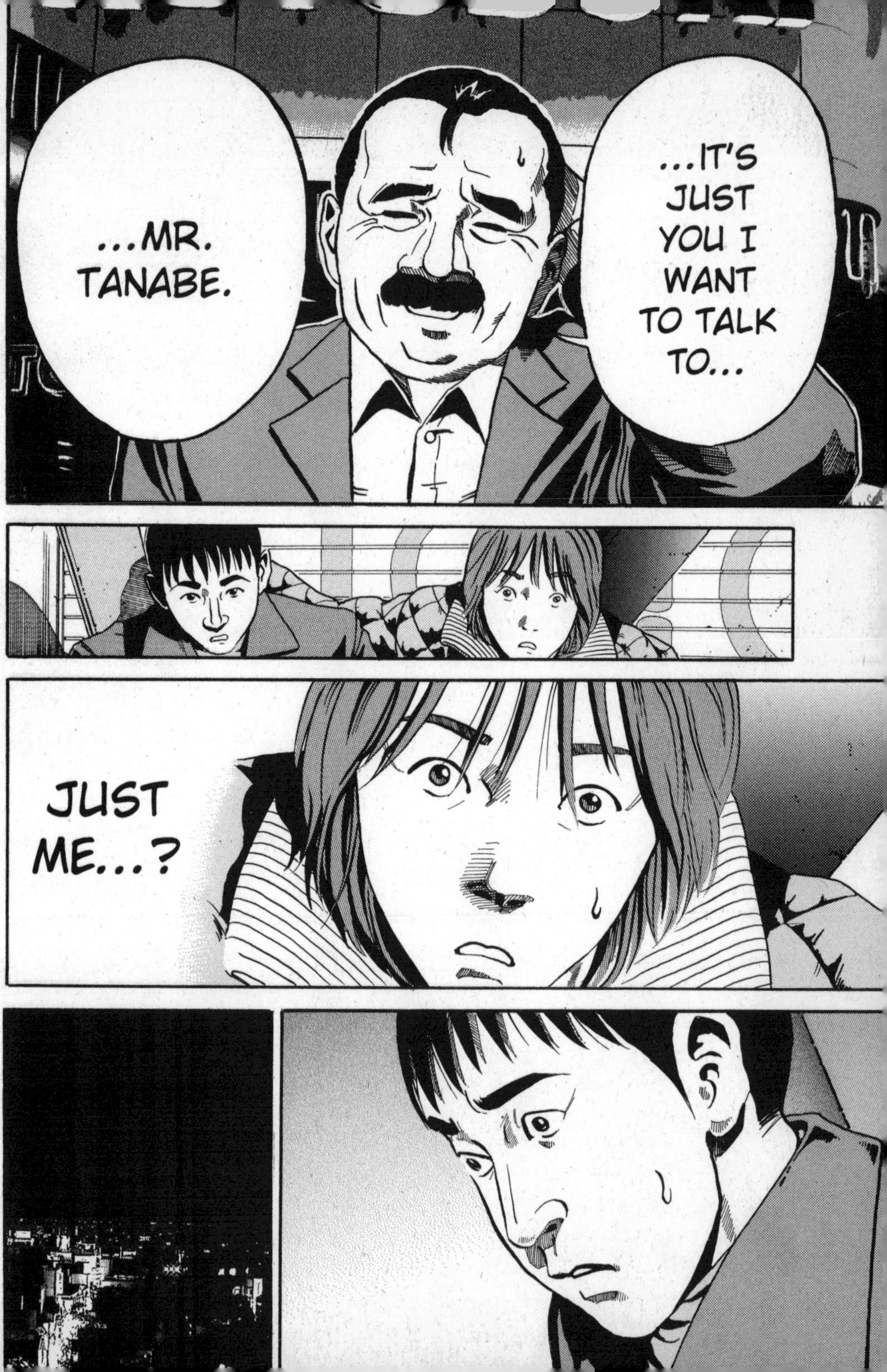
...IT'S JUST YOU I WANT TO TALK TO...
...MR. TANABE.
JUST ME...?

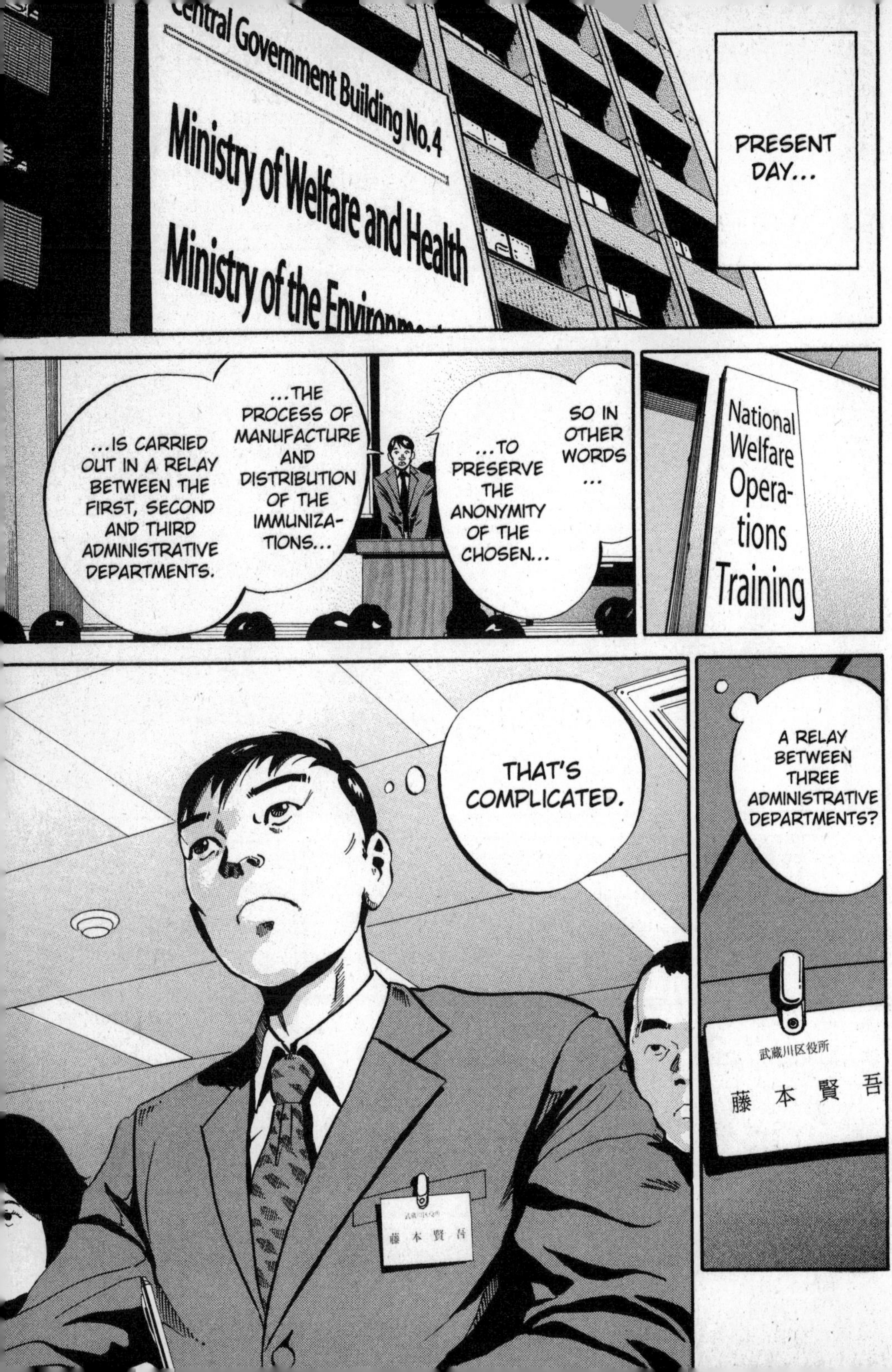
PRESENT DAY...
Central Government Building No.4
Ministry of Welfare and Health
Ministry of the Environm
National Welfare Operations Training
SO IN OTHER WORDS ...
...TO PRESERVE THE ANONYMITY OF THE CHOSEN...
...THE PROCESS OF MANUFACTURE AND DISTRIBUTION OF THE IMMUNIZATIONS...
...IS CARRIED OUT IN A RELAY BETWEEN THE FIRST, SECOND AND THIRD ADMINISTRATIVE DEPARTMENTS.
A RELAY BETWEEN THREE ADMINISTRATIVE DEPARTMENTS?
武蔵川区役所
藤本賢吾
THAT'S COMPLICATED.

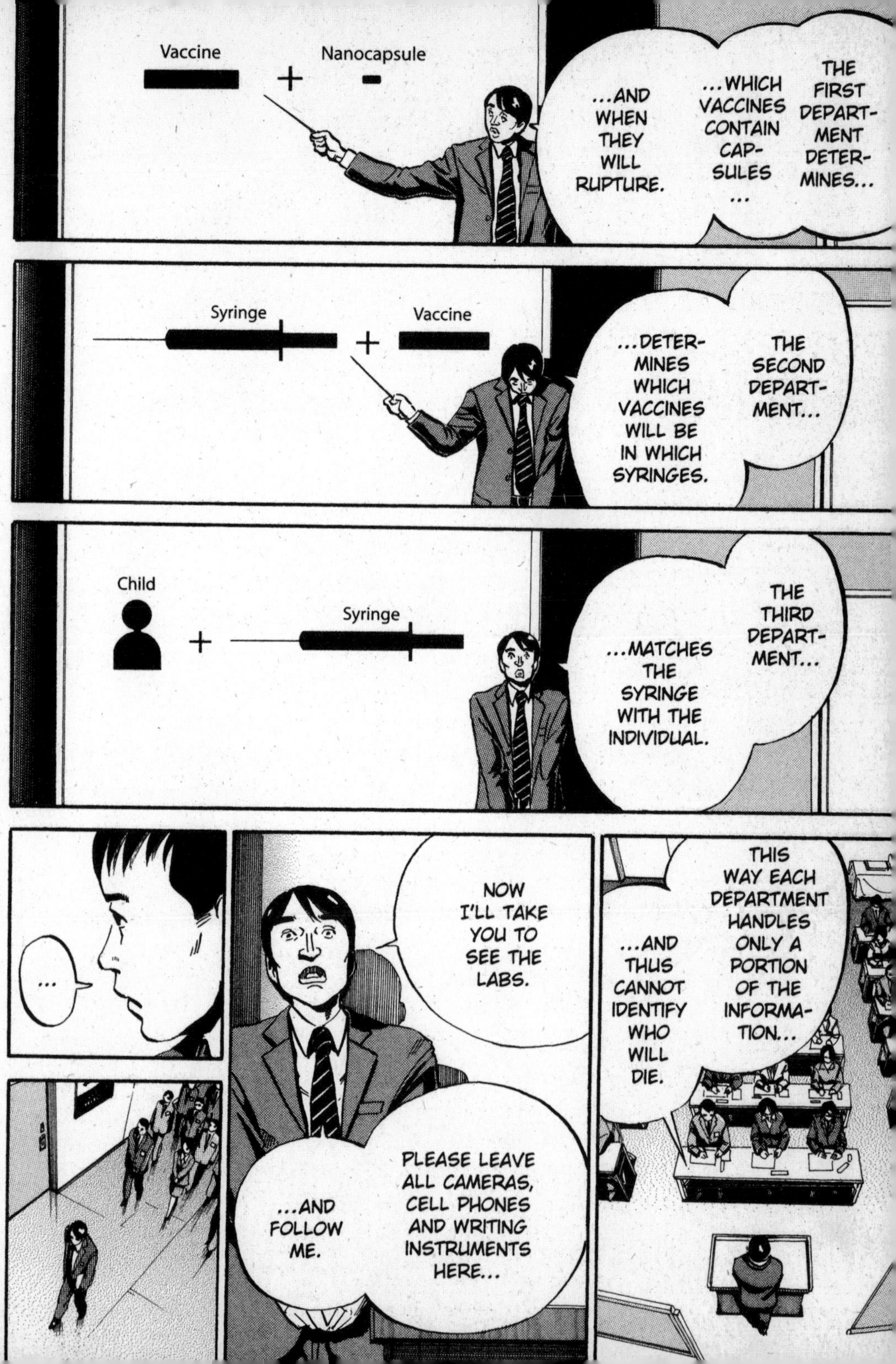
Vaccine
Nanocapsule
THE FIRST DEPARTMENT DETERMINES...
...WHICH VACCINES CONTAIN CAPSULES...
...AND WHEN THEY WILL RUPTURE.
Syringe
Vaccine
THE SECOND DEPARTMENT...
...DETERMINES WHICH VACCINES WILL BE IN WHICH SYRINGES.
Child
Syringe
THE THIRD DEPARTMENT...
...MATCHES THE SYRINGE WITH THE INDIVIDUAL.
THIS WAY EACH DEPARTMENT HANDLES ONLY A PORTION OF THE INFORMATION...
...AND THUS CANNOT IDENTIFY WHO WILL DIE.
NOW I'LL TAKE YOU TO SEE THE LABS.
PLEASE LEAVE ALL CAMERAS, CELL PHONES AND WRITING INSTRUMENTS HERE...
...AND FOLLOW ME.
...

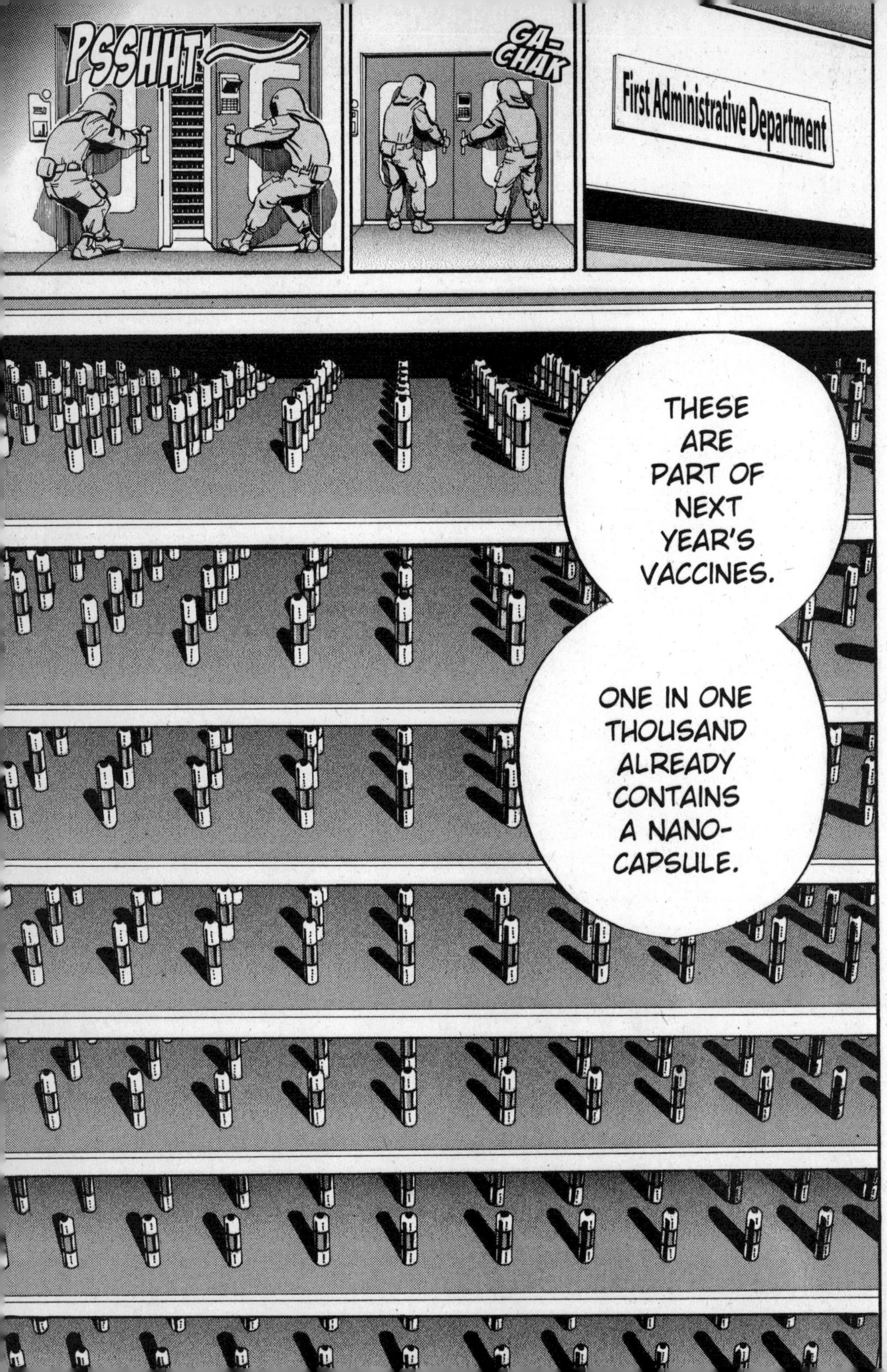
First Administrative Department
GA-CHAK
PSSHHT
THESE ARE PART OF NEXT YEAR'S VACCINES.
ONE IN ONE THOUSAND ALREADY CONTAINS A NANO-CAPSULE.

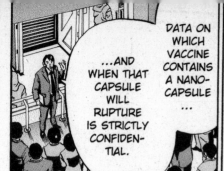

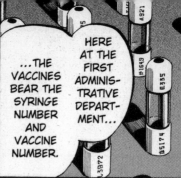

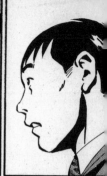

HERE AT THE FIRST ADMINISTRATIVE DEPARTMENT...
...THE VACCINES BEAR THE SYRINGE NUMBER AND VACCINE NUMBER.
DATA ON WHICH VACCINE CONTAINS A NANO-CAPSULE...
...AND WHEN THAT CAPSULE WILL RUPTURE IS STRICTLY CONFIDENTIAL.
MR. FUJIMOTO, PLEASE DON'T TOUCH THE GLASS.
AN ALARM WILL GO OFF.
S-SORRY.
NOBODY KNOWS WHO WILL BE INJECTED WITH A NANO-CAPSULE.
HOW IS THAT INFORMATION KEPT SECRET FOR SO MANY YEARS?
I'VE BEEN AN IKIGAMI MESSENGER FOR HALF A YEAR, BUT I'M ONLY LEARNING ABOUT THE PROCESS NOW.
...

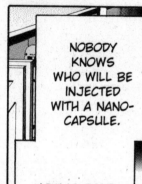

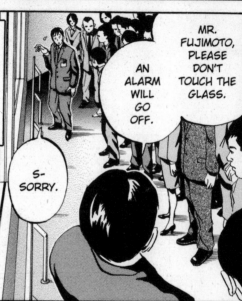

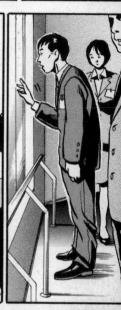

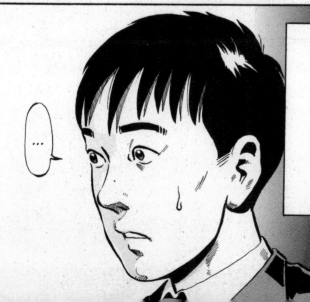

FIVE DAYS BEFORE IMMUNIZATION, THE VACCINES ARE CARRIED FROM THE FIRST ADMINISTRATIVE DEPARTMENT, WHICH YOU JUST SAW...

...AND DELIVERED TO THE SECOND ADMINISTRATIVE DEPARTMENT, WHERE WE ARE GOING NOW.

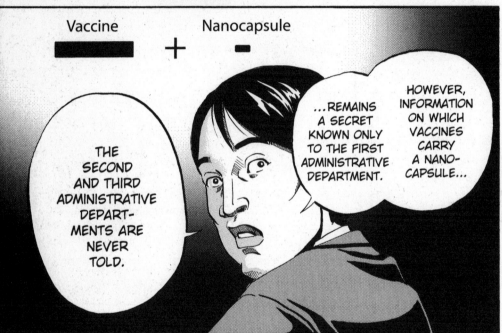

Vaccine   +   Nanocapsule

HOWEVER, INFORMATION ON WHICH VACCINES CARRY A NANO-CAPSULE...

...REMAINS A SECRET KNOWN ONLY TO THE FIRST ADMINISTRATIVE DEPARTMENT.

THE SECOND AND THIRD ADMINISTRATIVE DEPART-MENTS ARE NEVER TOLD.

FROM THIS POINT ON, SOMEONE FROM THE SECOND ADMINISTRATIVE DEPARTMENT WILL GUIDE YOU.

I'M HASEGAWA. PLEASED TO MEET YOU.

Second Administrative Department

THESE ARE THE SYRINGES.

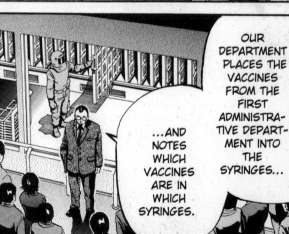

OUR DEPARTMENT PLACES THE VACCINES FROM THE FIRST ADMINISTRATIVE DEPARTMENT INTO THE SYRINGES...

...AND NOTES WHICH VACCINES ARE IN WHICH SYRINGES.

SO THESE SYRINGES DETERMINE WHO WILL LIVE OR DIE...

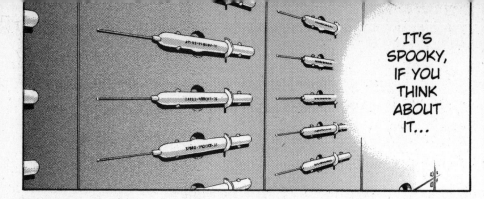

IT'S SPOOKY, IF YOU THINK ABOUT IT...
THEN THE FILLED SYRINGES ARE SENT TO THE THIRD ADMINISTRATIVE DEPARTMENT...
Syringe
Vaccine
...BUT THE SECRET INFORMATION...
...ON WHICH VACCINES HAVE BEEN PLACED IN WHICH SYRINGES...
...IS NEVER CONVEYED TO THE FIRST OR THIRD ADMINISTRATIVE DEPARTMENTS.
Third Administrative Department
FROM THIS POINT ON, ISOMURA OF THE THIRD ADMINISTRATIVE DEPARTMENT WILL GUIDE YOU.
PLEASED TO MEET YOU.

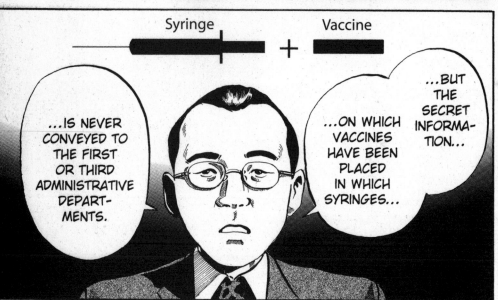

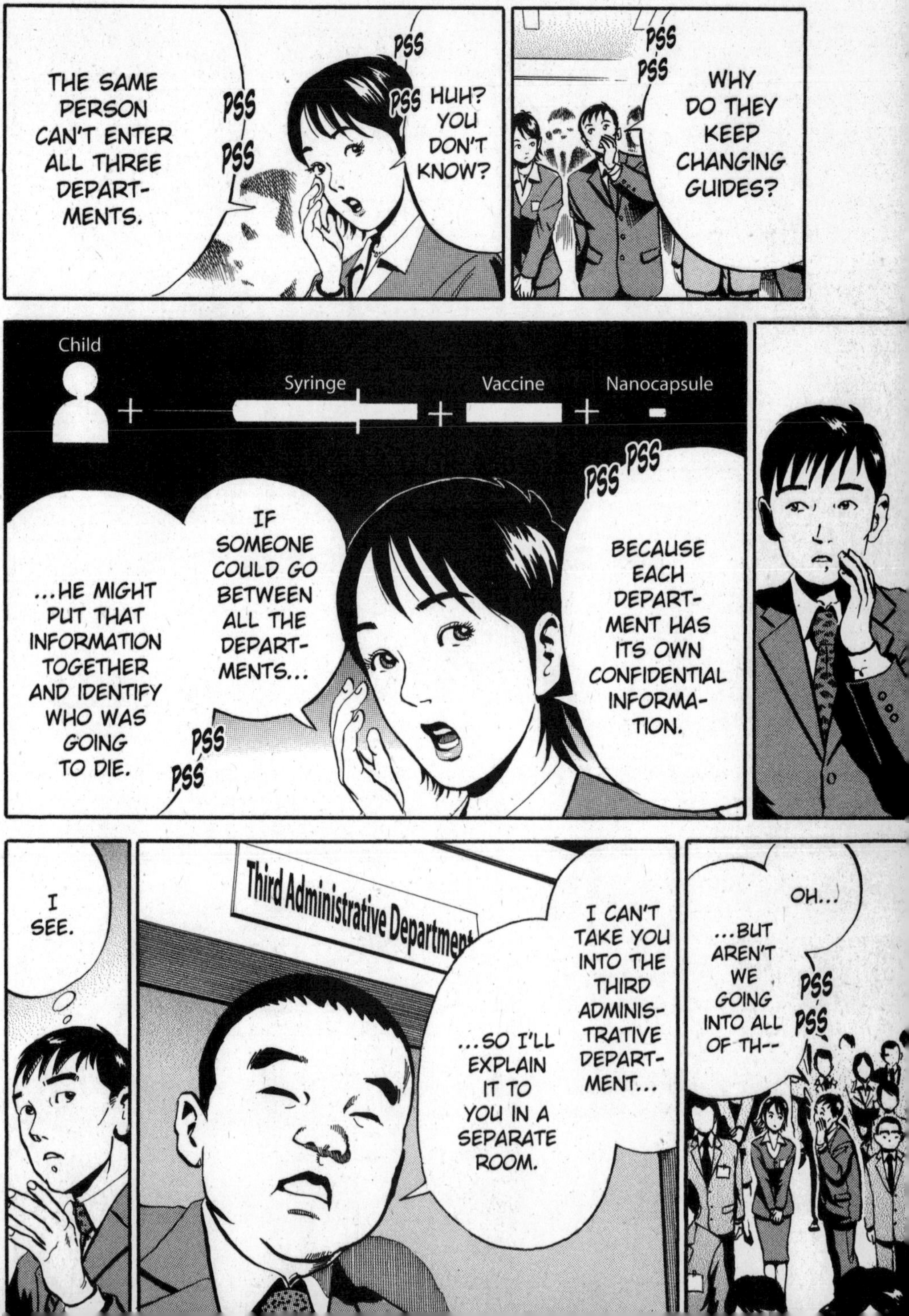
PSS PSS
WHY DO THEY KEEP CHANGING GUIDES?
PSS PSS
HUH? YOU DON'T KNOW?
THE SAME PERSON CAN'T ENTER ALL THREE DEPART-MENTS.
PSS PSS
Child
Syringe
Vaccine
Nanocapsule
PSS PSS
BECAUSE EACH DEPART-MENT HAS ITS OWN CONFIDENTIAL INFORMA-TION.
IF SOMEONE COULD GO BETWEEN ALL THE DEPART-MENTS...
...HE MIGHT PUT THAT INFORMATION TOGETHER AND IDENTIFY WHO WAS GOING TO DIE.
PSS PSS
OH...
...BUT AREN'T WE GOING INTO ALL OF TH--
PSS PSS
Third Administrative Department
I CAN'T TAKE YOU INTO THE THIRD ADMINIS-TRATIVE DEPART-MENT...
...SO I'LL EXPLAIN IT TO YOU IN A SEPARATE ROOM.
I SEE.

IN THIS DEPARTMENT, WE DETERMINE WHO IS INJECTED WITH THE SYRINGES FROM THE SECOND ADMINISTRATIVE DEPARTMENT...
...AND WE ISSUE THE IKIGAMI.
ISSUE THE IKIGAMI ?!
FIRST, WE SEND THE SYRINGES TO ELEMENTARY SCHOOLS ACROSS THE NATION.
AT THE TIME OF IMMUNIZATION, WE RECORD WHICH SYRINGES WERE USED ON WHICH STUDENTS.
Tadokoro, Susumu
Tanaka, Yuko
NOT KNOWING, OF COURSE, WHICH SYRINGES HOLD NANO-CAPSULES.
AND THE OTHER DEPARTMENTS DON'T KNOW OUR SECRET-- WHICH SYRINGE WAS INJECTED INTO WHICH STUDENT.
THROUGH THIS PROCESS, THE IMMUNIZATION ENDS WITHOUT ANYONE KNOWING WHO WAS INJECTED WITH A CAPSULE.

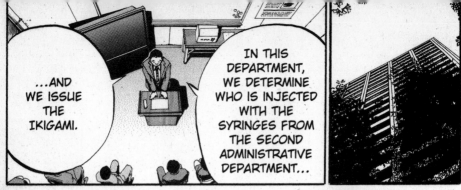

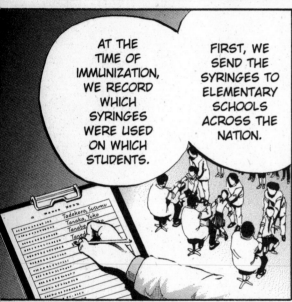

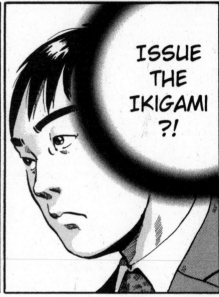

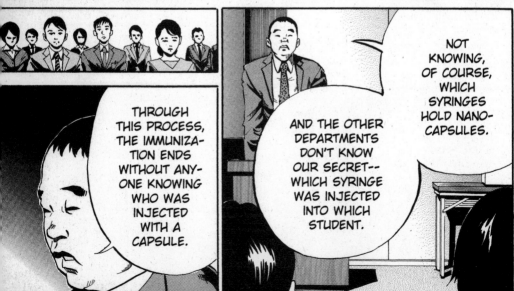

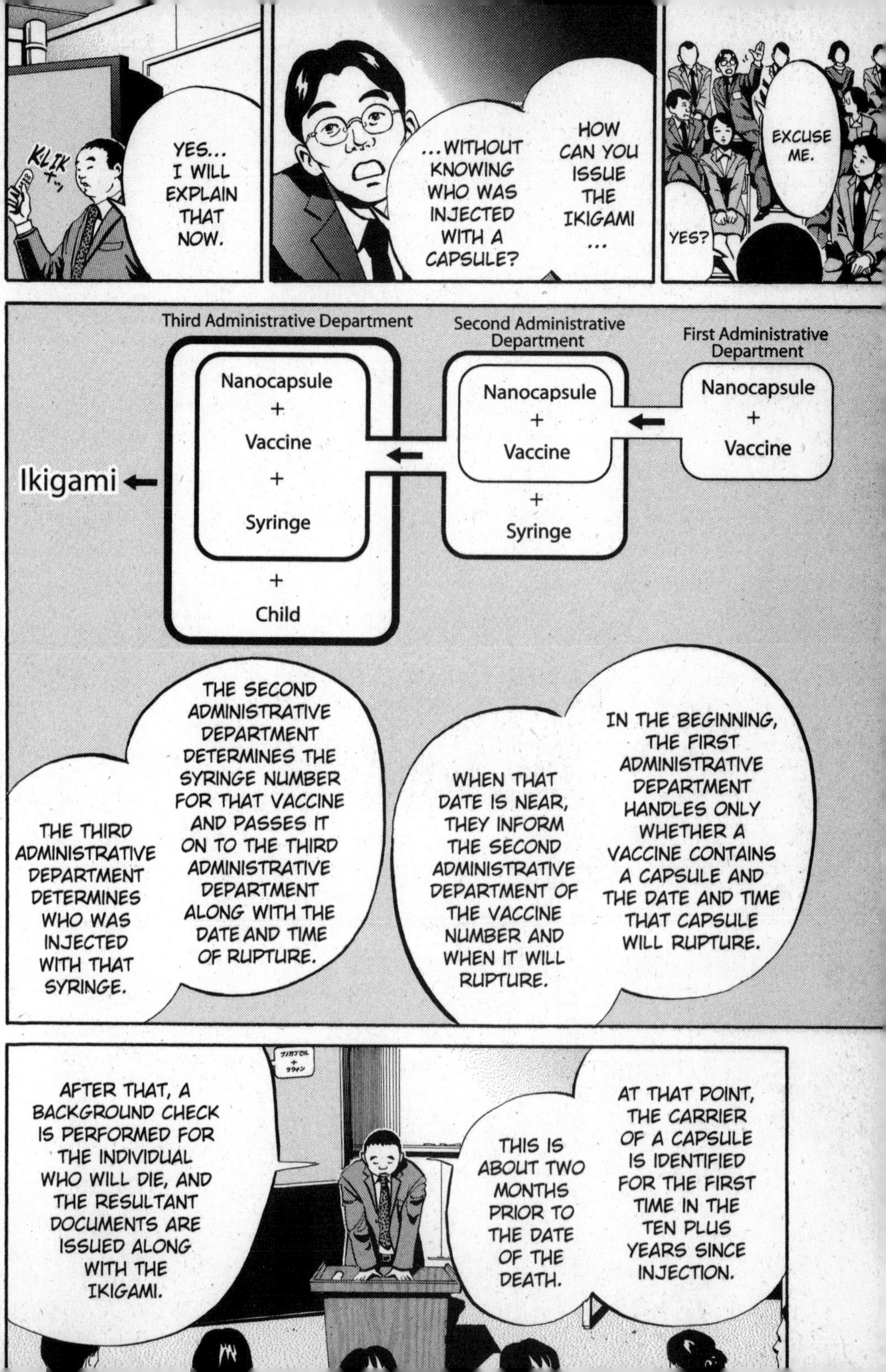
EXCUSE ME.
YES?
HOW CAN YOU ISSUE THE IKIGAMI...
...WITHOUT KNOWING WHO WAS INJECTED WITH A CAPSULE?
KLIK
YES... I WILL EXPLAIN THAT NOW.
First Administrative Department
Nanocapsule + Vaccine
Second Administrative Department
Nanocapsule + Vaccine + Syringe
Third Administrative Department
Nanocapsule + Vaccine + Syringe + Child
Ikigami
IN THE BEGINNING, THE FIRST ADMINISTRATIVE DEPARTMENT HANDLES ONLY WHETHER A VACCINE CONTAINS A CAPSULE AND THE DATE AND TIME THAT CAPSULE WILL RUPTURE.
WHEN THAT DATE IS NEAR, THEY INFORM THE SECOND ADMINISTRATIVE DEPARTMENT OF THE VACCINE NUMBER AND WHEN IT WILL RUPTURE.
THE SECOND ADMINISTRATIVE DEPARTMENT DETERMINES THE SYRINGE NUMBER FOR THAT VACCINE AND PASSES IT ON TO THE THIRD ADMINISTRATIVE DEPARTMENT ALONG WITH THE DATE AND TIME OF RUPTURE.
THE THIRD ADMINISTRATIVE DEPARTMENT DETERMINES WHO WAS INJECTED WITH THAT SYRINGE.
AT THAT POINT, THE CARRIER OF A CAPSULE IS IDENTIFIED FOR THE FIRST TIME IN THE TEN PLUS YEARS SINCE INJECTION.
THIS IS ABOUT TWO MONTHS PRIOR TO THE DATE OF THE DEATH.
AFTER THAT, A BACKGROUND CHECK IS PERFORMED FOR THE INDIVIDUAL WHO WILL DIE, AND THE RESULTANT DOCUMENTS ARE ISSUED ALONG WITH THE IKIGAMI.

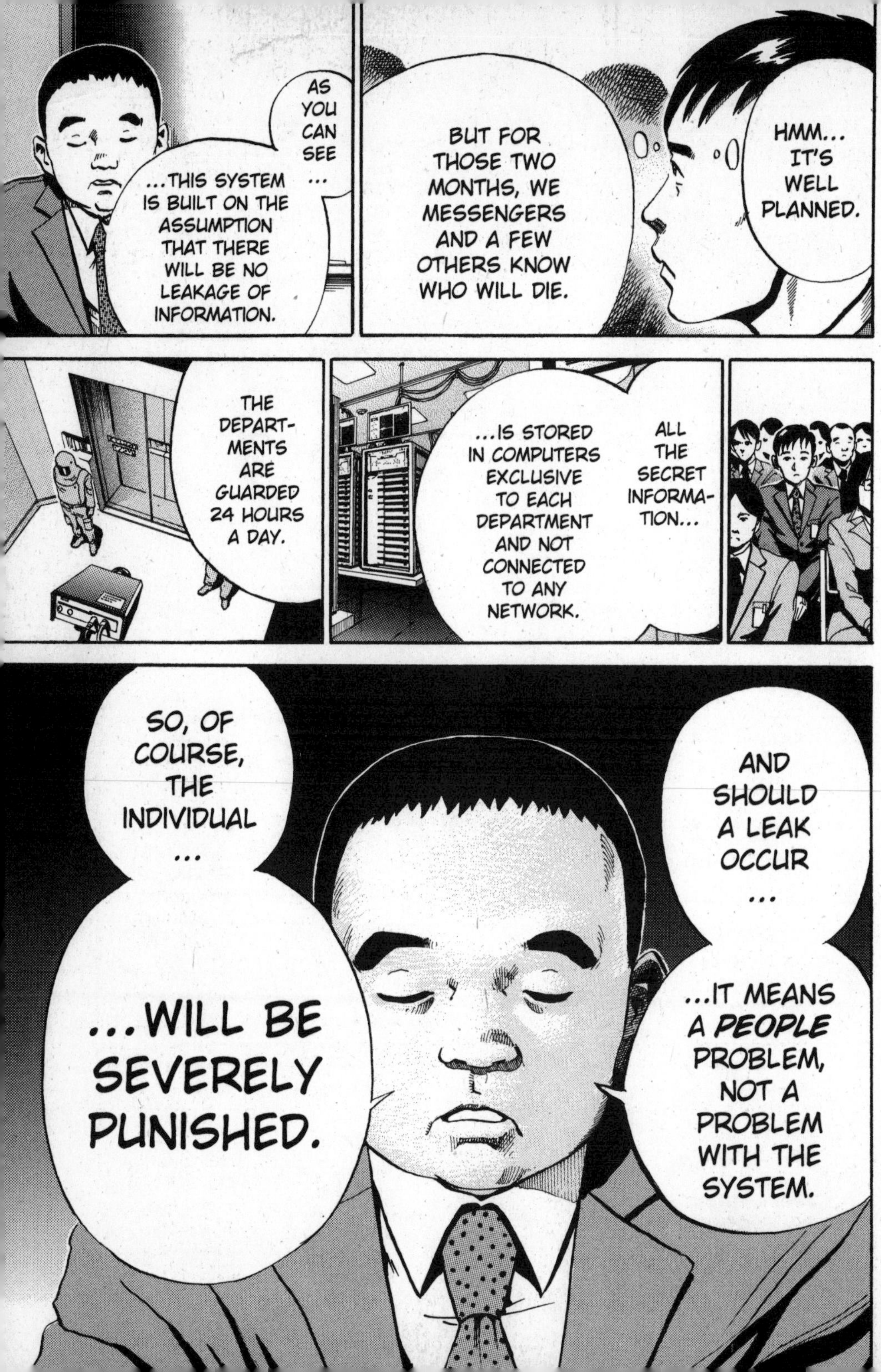
HMM... IT'S WELL PLANNED.
BUT FOR THOSE TWO MONTHS, WE MESSENGERS AND A FEW OTHERS KNOW WHO WILL DIE.
AS YOU CAN SEE ...
...THIS SYSTEM IS BUILT ON THE ASSUMPTION THAT THERE WILL BE NO LEAKAGE OF INFORMATION.
ALL THE SECRET INFORMATION...
...IS STORED IN COMPUTERS EXCLUSIVE TO EACH DEPARTMENT AND NOT CONNECTED TO ANY NETWORK.
THE DEPARTMENTS ARE GUARDED 24 HOURS A DAY.
AND SHOULD A LEAK OCCUR ...
...IT MEANS A *PEOPLE* PROBLEM, NOT A PROBLEM WITH THE SYSTEM.
SO, OF COURSE, THE INDIVIDUAL ...
...WILL BE SEVERELY PUNISHED.

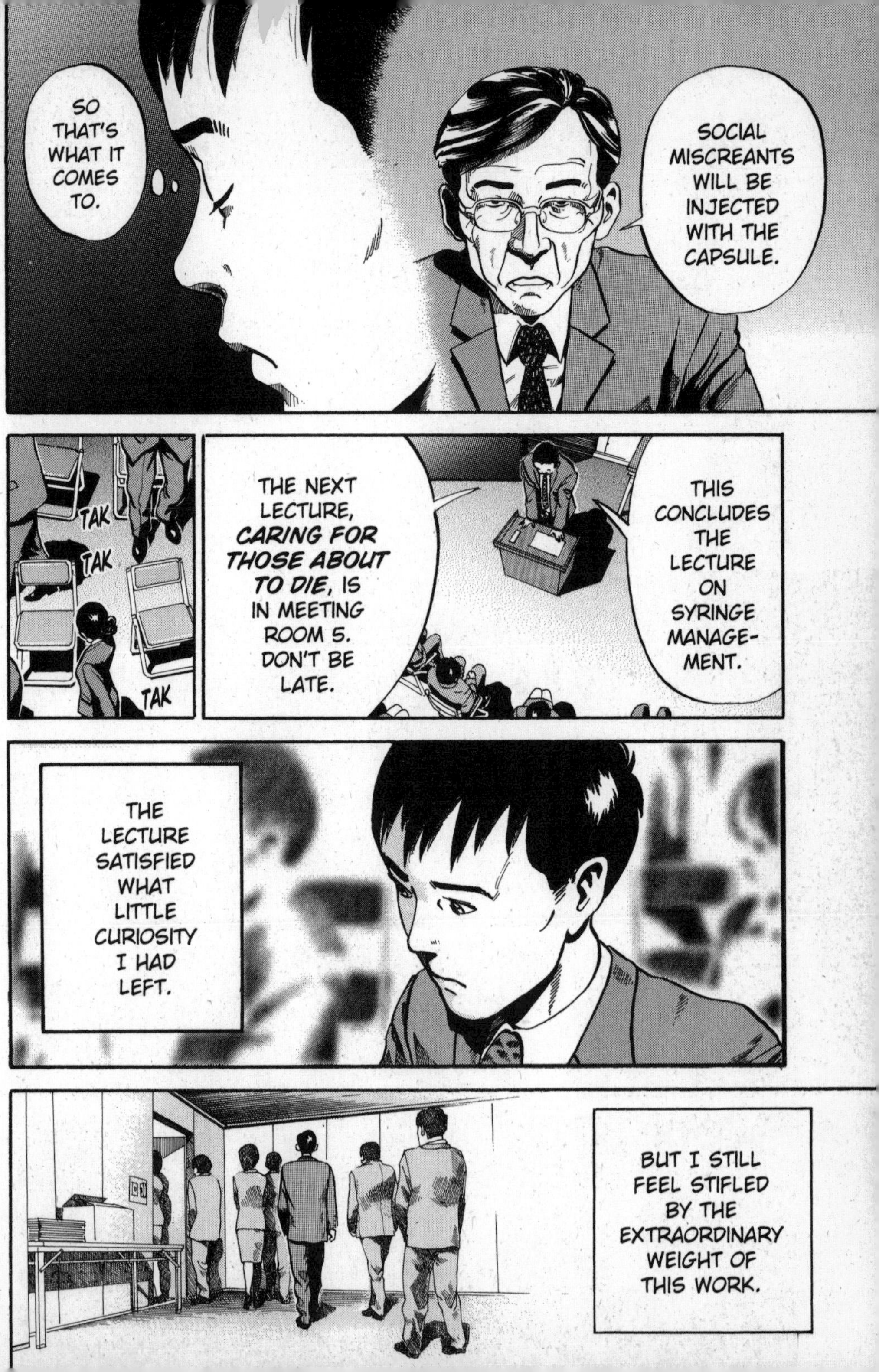
SOCIAL MISCREANTS WILL BE INJECTED WITH THE CAPSULE.
SO THAT'S WHAT IT COMES TO.
THIS CONCLUDES THE LECTURE ON SYRINGE MANAGE-MENT.
THE NEXT LECTURE, *CARING FOR THOSE ABOUT TO DIE*, IS IN MEETING ROOM 5. DON'T BE LATE.
TAK
TAK
TAK
THE LECTURE SATISFIED WHAT LITTLE CURIOSITY I HAD LEFT.
BUT I STILL FEEL STIFLED BY THE EXTRAORDINARY WEIGHT OF THIS WORK.

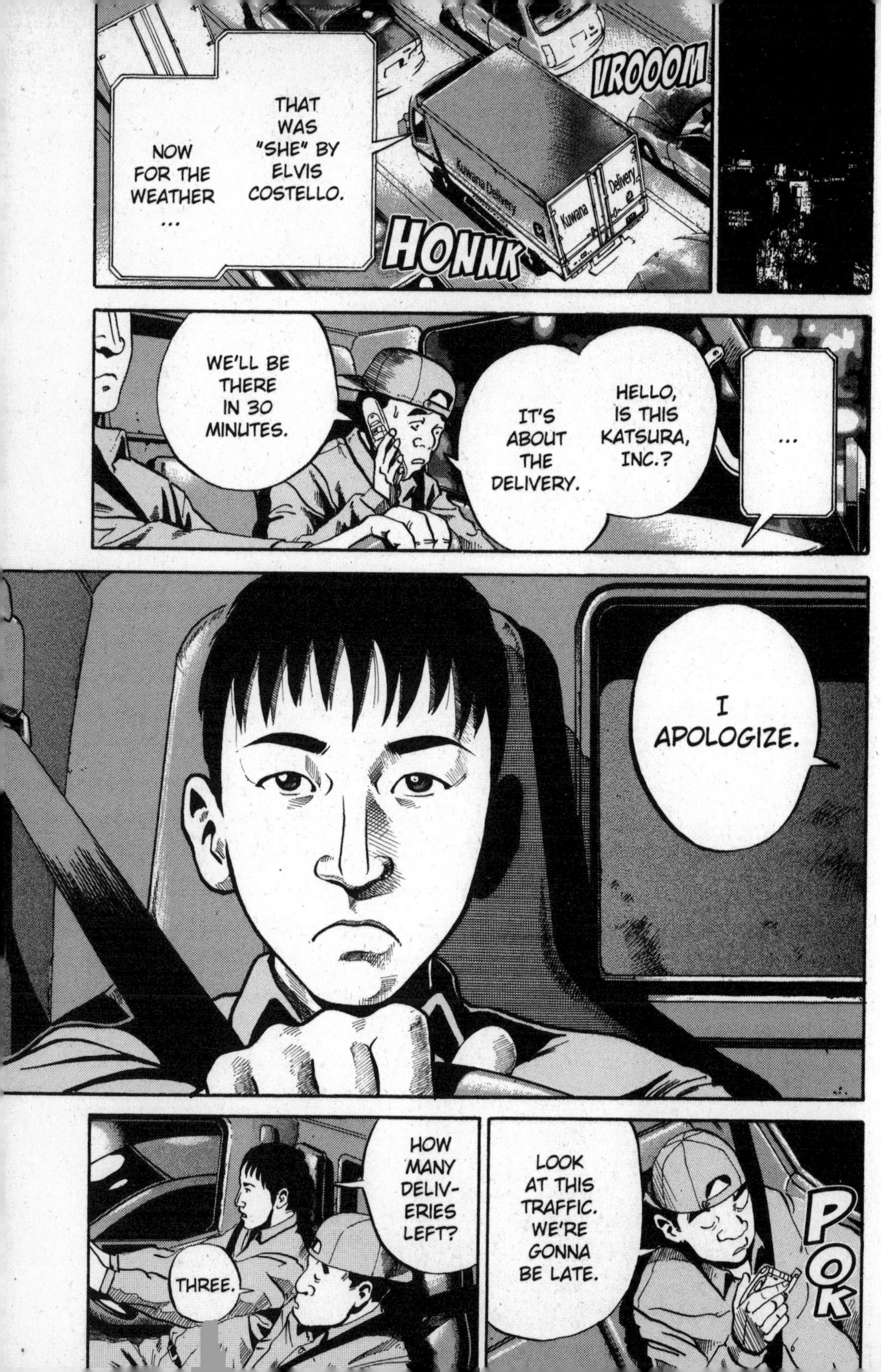
VROOOM
THAT WAS "SHE" BY ELVIS COSTELLO.
NOW FOR THE WEATHER ...
HONNK
...
HELLO, IS THIS KATSURA, INC.?
IT'S ABOUT THE DELIVERY.
WE'LL BE THERE IN 30 MINUTES.
I APOLOGIZE.
POK
LOOK AT THIS TRAFFIC. WE'RE GONNA BE LATE.
HOW MANY DELIV-ERIES LEFT?
THREE.

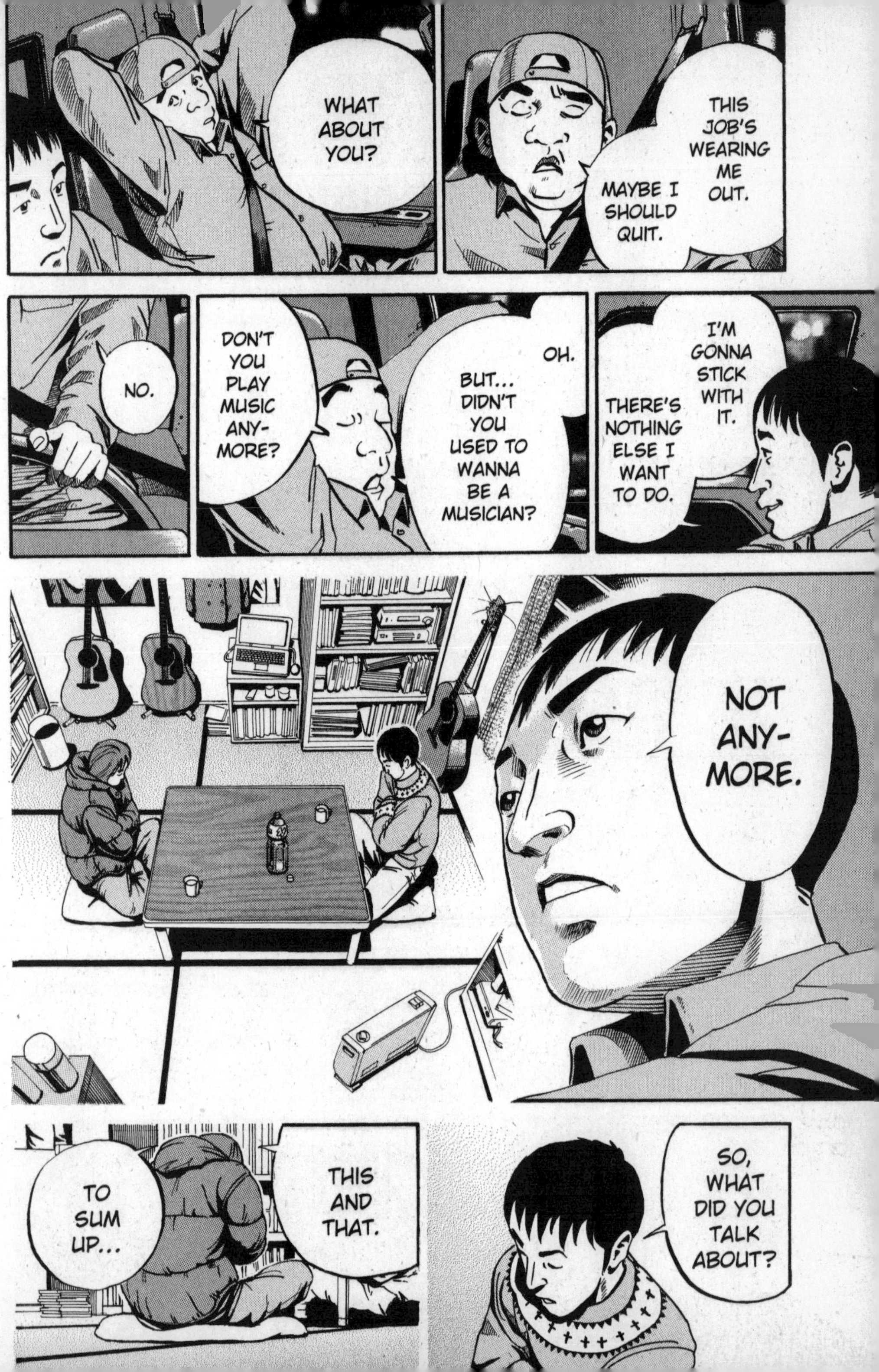
THIS JOB'S WEARING ME OUT.
MAYBE I SHOULD QUIT.
WHAT ABOUT YOU?
I'M GONNA STICK WITH IT.
THERE'S NOTHING ELSE I WANT TO DO.
OH.
BUT... DIDN'T YOU USED TO WANNA BE A MUSICIAN?
DON'T YOU PLAY MUSIC ANY-MORE?
NO.
NOT ANY-MORE.
SO, WHAT DID YOU TALK ABOUT?
THIS AND THAT.
TO SUM UP...

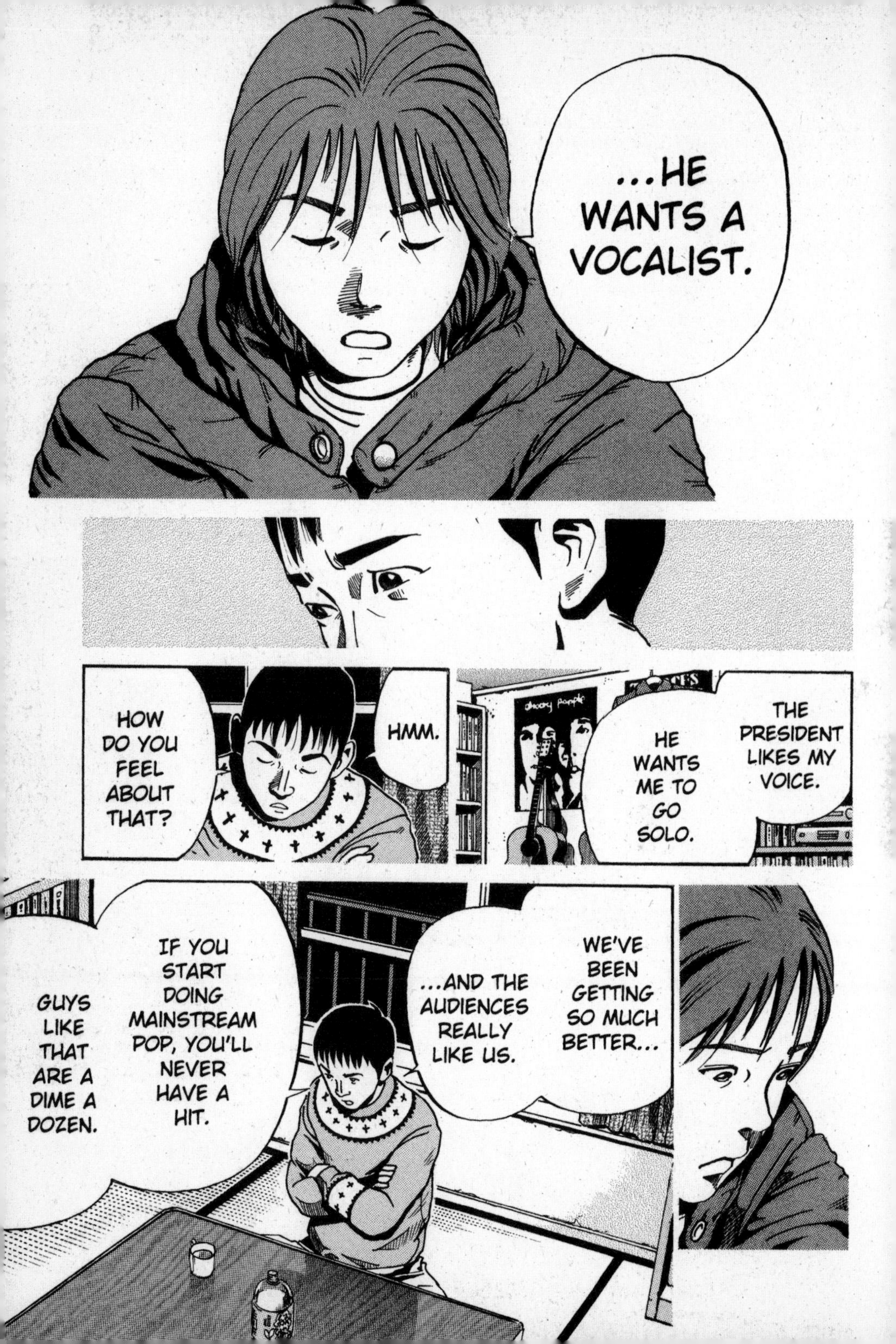
...HE WANTS A VOCALIST.
THE PRESIDENT LIKES MY VOICE.
HE WANTS ME TO GO SOLO.
HMM.
HOW DO YOU FEEL ABOUT THAT?
WE'VE BEEN GETTING SO MUCH BETTER...
...AND THE AUDIENCES REALLY LIKE US.
IF YOU START DOING MAINSTREAM POP, YOU'LL NEVER HAVE A HIT.
GUYS LIKE THAT ARE A DIME A DOZEN.

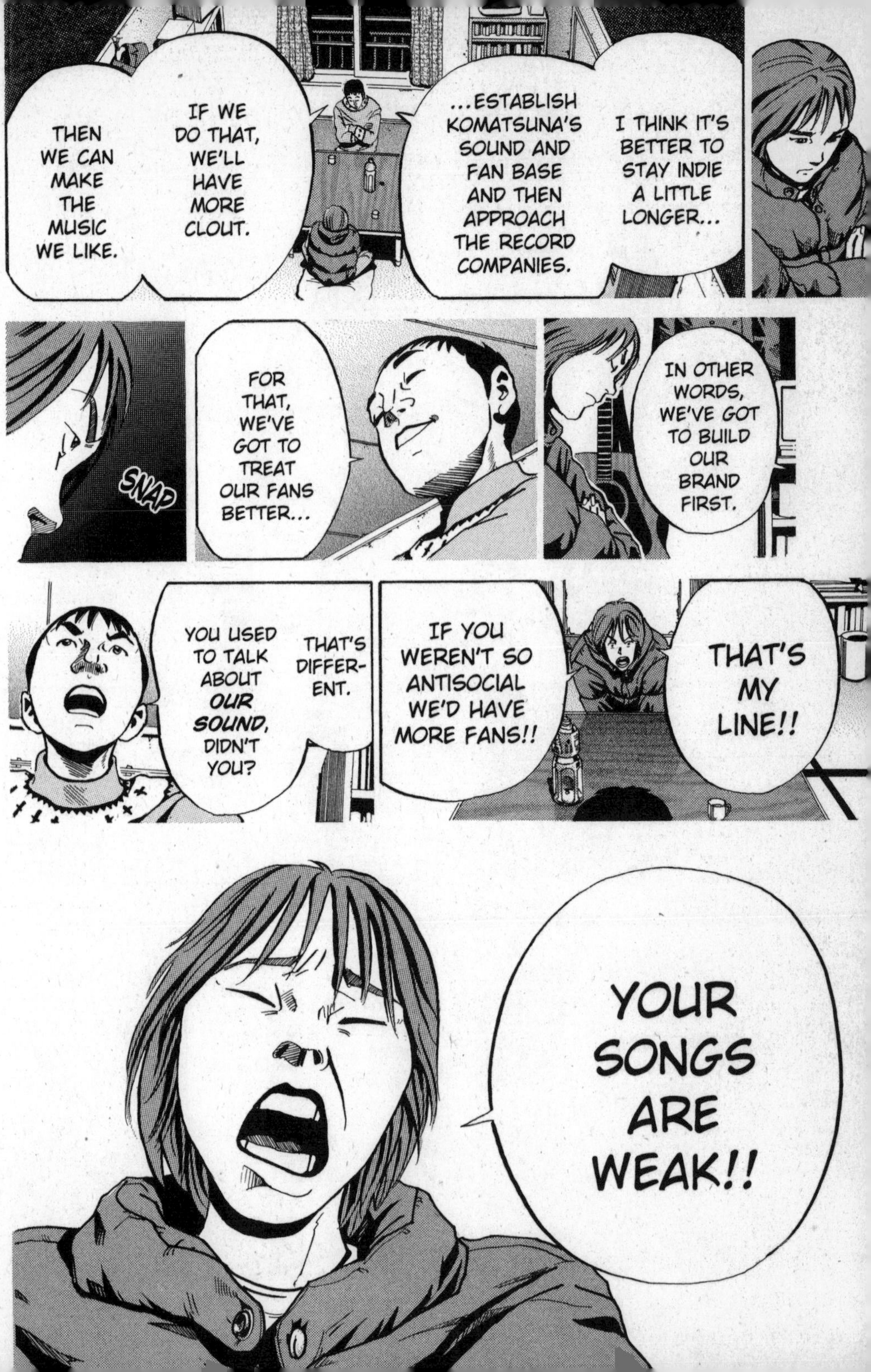
I THINK IT'S BETTER TO STAY INDIE A LITTLE LONGER...
...ESTABLISH KOMATSUNA'S SOUND AND FAN BASE AND THEN APPROACH THE RECORD COMPANIES.
IF WE DO THAT, WE'LL HAVE MORE CLOUT.
THEN WE CAN MAKE THE MUSIC WE LIKE.
IN OTHER WORDS, WE'VE GOT TO BUILD OUR BRAND FIRST.
FOR THAT, WE'VE GOT TO TREAT OUR FANS BETTER...
SNAP
THAT'S MY LINE!!
IF YOU WEREN'T SO ANTISOCIAL WE'D HAVE MORE FANS!!
THAT'S DIFFERENT.
YOU USED TO TALK ABOUT *OUR SOUND*, DIDN'T YOU?
YOUR SONGS ARE WEAK!!

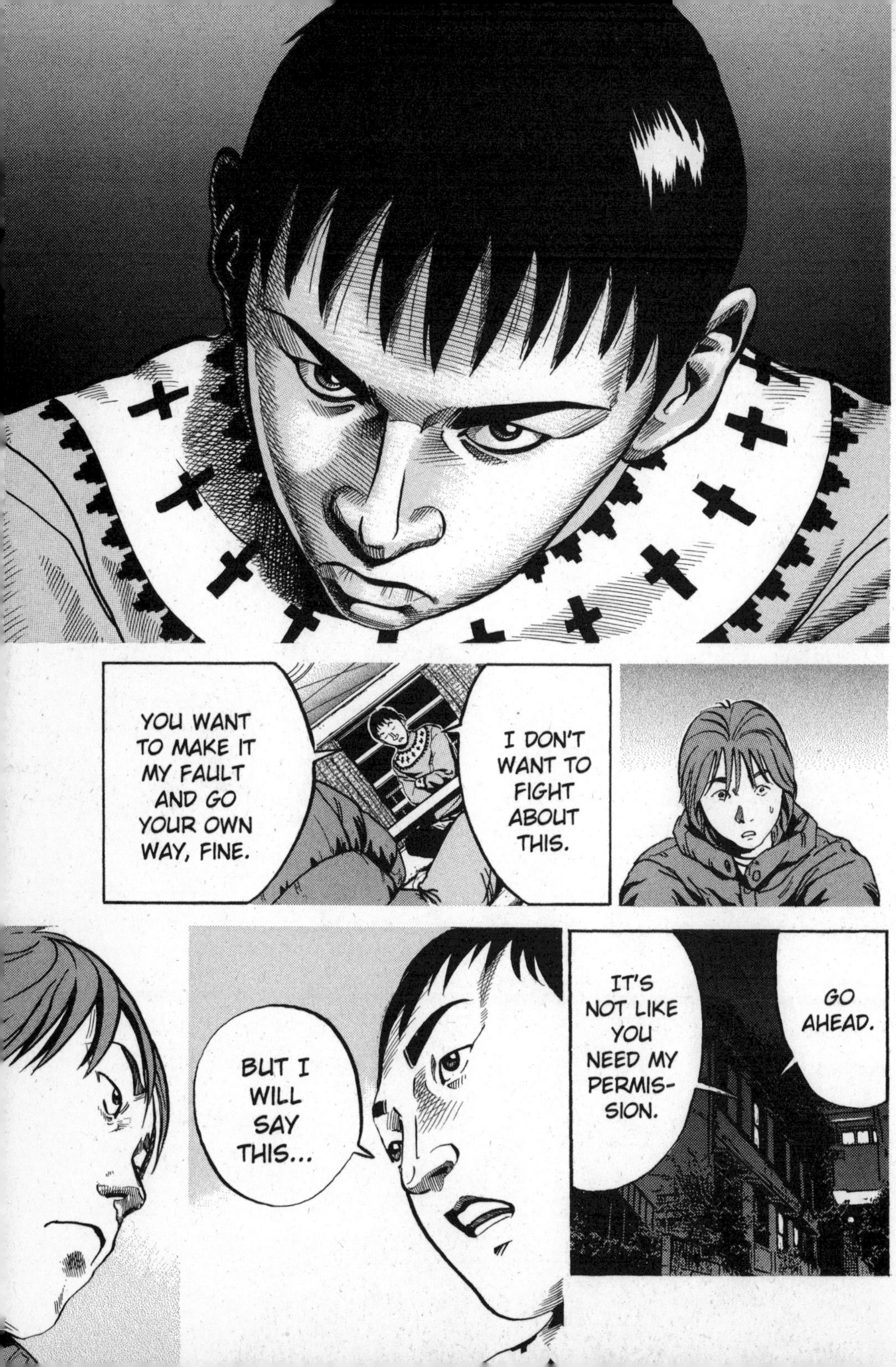
I DON'T WANT TO FIGHT ABOUT THIS.
YOU WANT TO MAKE IT MY FAULT AND GO YOUR OWN WAY, FINE.
GO AHEAD.
IT'S NOT LIKE YOU NEED MY PERMISSION.
BUT I WILL SAY THIS...

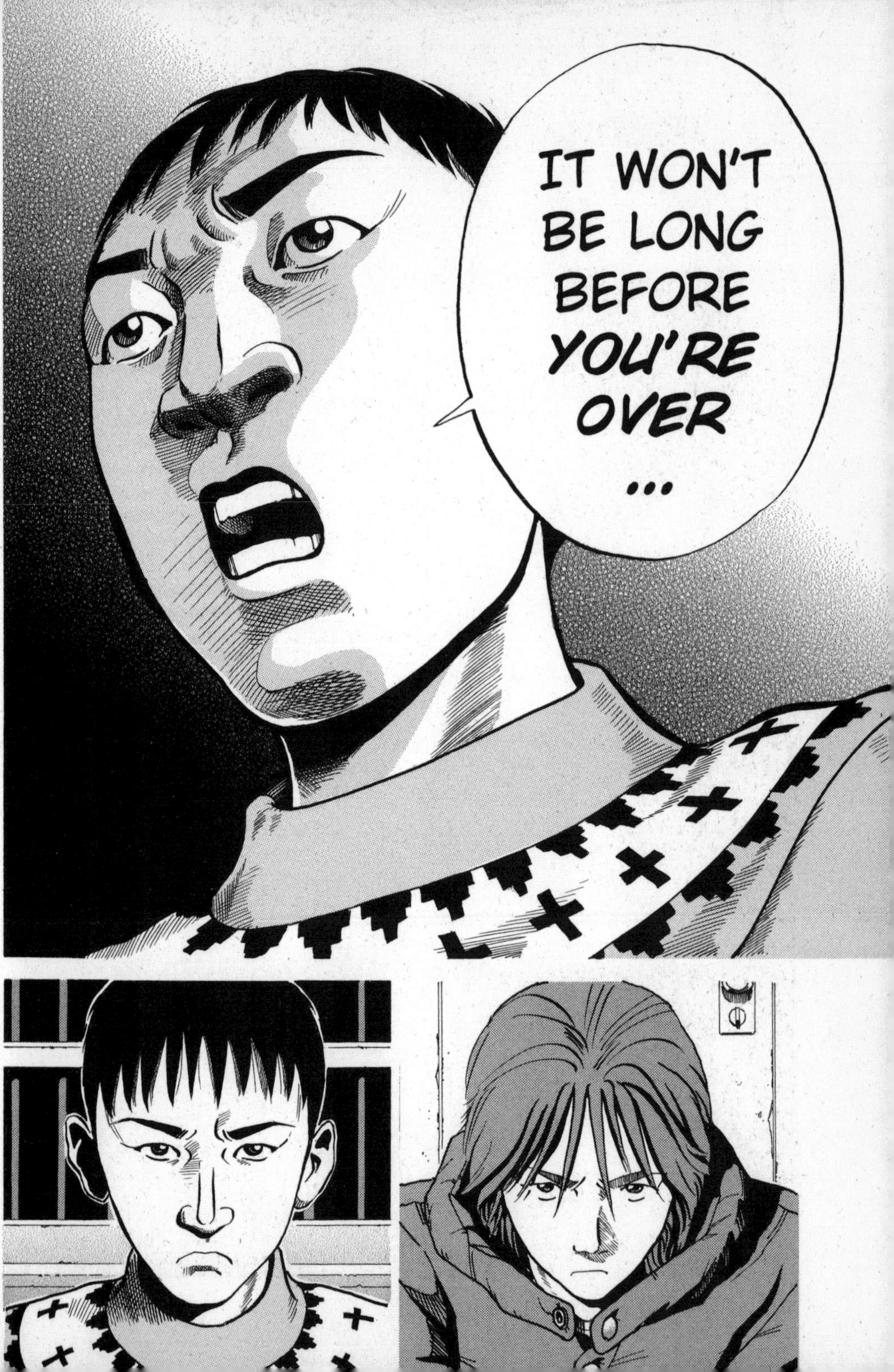
IT WON'T BE LONG BEFORE YOU'RE OVER ...

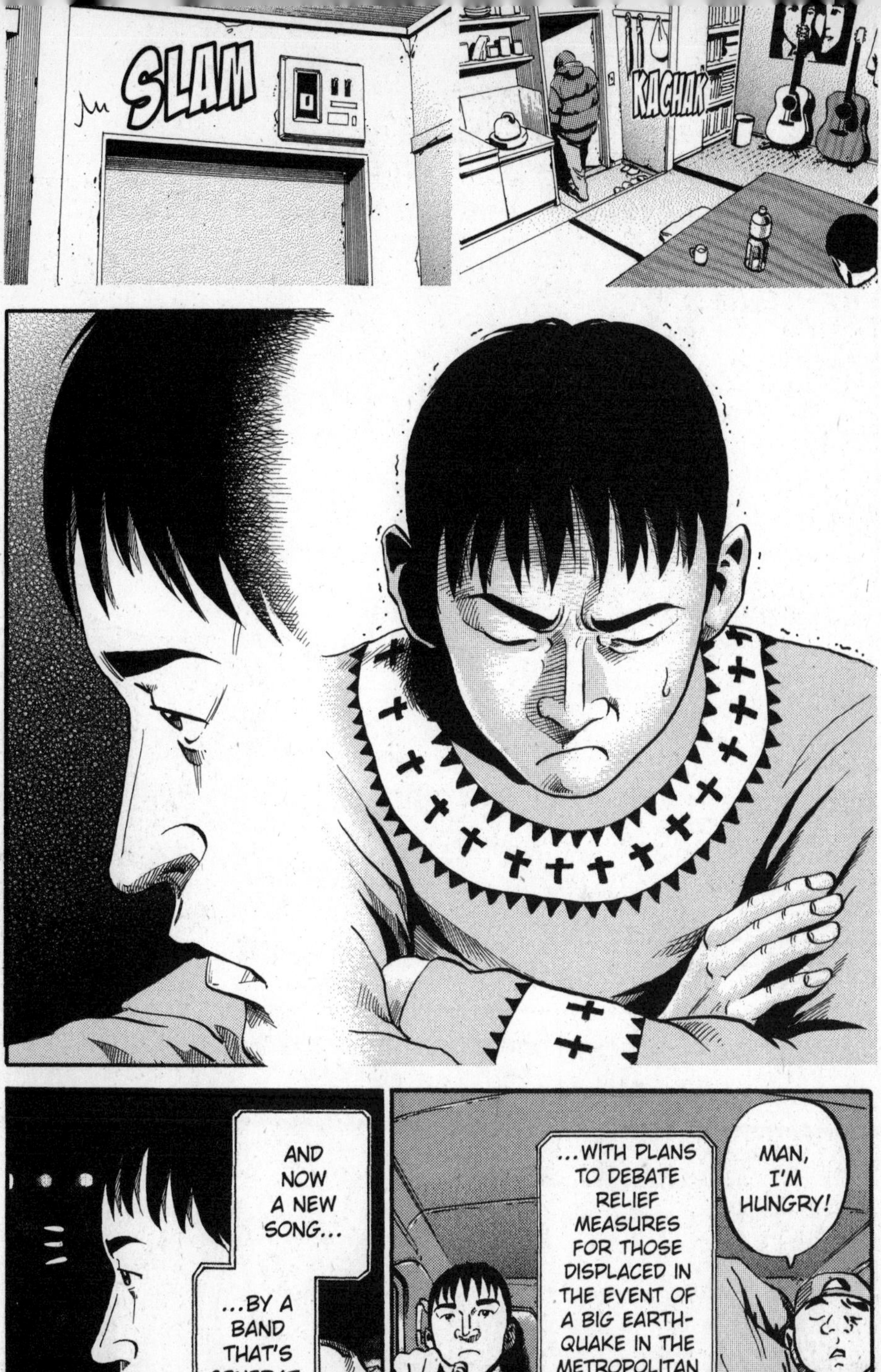
KACHAK
SLAM
MAN, I'M HUNGRY!
...WITH PLANS TO DEBATE RELIEF MEASURES FOR THOSE DISPLACED IN THE EVENT OF A BIG EARTH-QUAKE IN THE METROPOLITAN REGION.
AND NOW A NEW SONG...
...BY A BAND THAT'S GENERAT-ING A BUZZ.

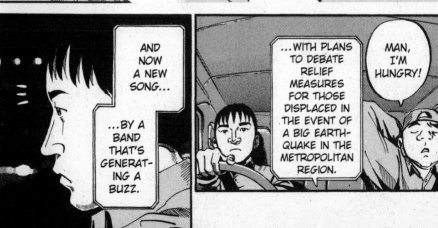

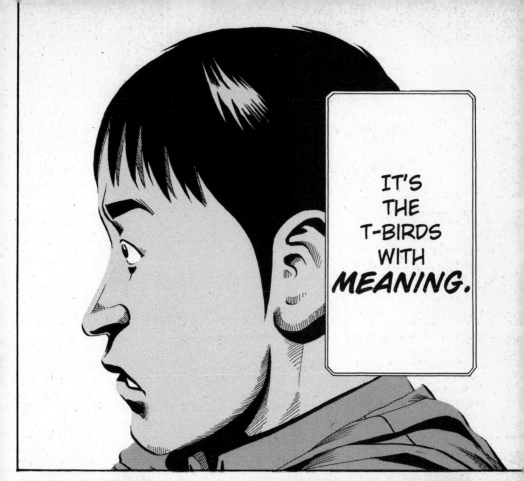

IT'S
THE
T-BIRDS
WITH
MEANING.

HEY,
WHY'D YA
SHUT IT
OFF?

KLIK

HONNK

VROOM

...

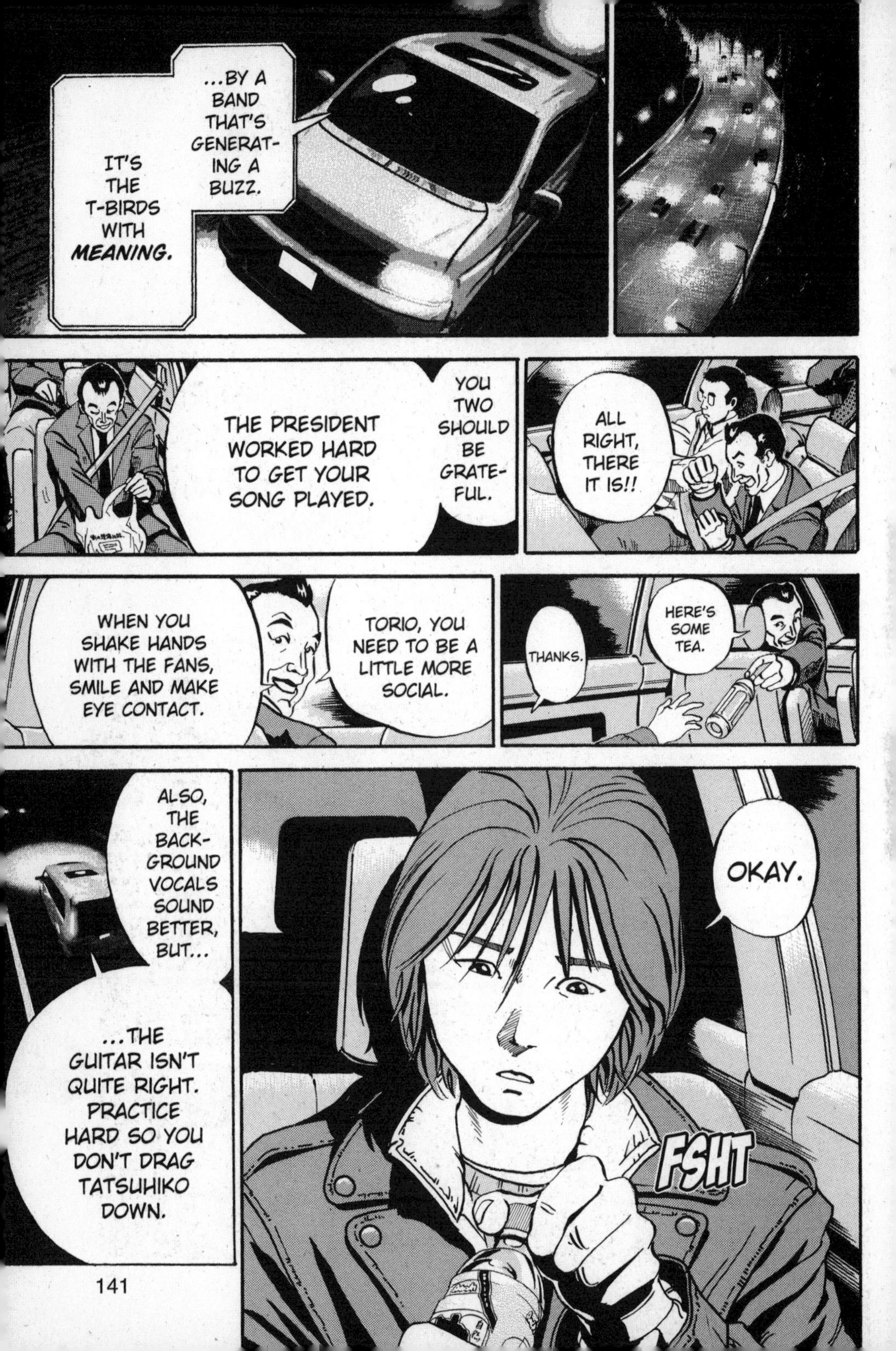
...BY A BAND THAT'S GENERAT-ING A BUZZ.
IT'S THE T-BIRDS WITH ***MEANING.***
ALL RIGHT, THERE IT IS!!
YOU TWO SHOULD BE GRATE-FUL.
THE PRESIDENT WORKED HARD TO GET YOUR SONG PLAYED.
HERE'S SOME TEA.
THANKS.
TORIO, YOU NEED TO BE A LITTLE MORE SOCIAL.
WHEN YOU SHAKE HANDS WITH THE FANS, SMILE AND MAKE EYE CONTACT.
OKAY.
FSHT
ALSO, THE BACK-GROUND VOCALS SOUND BETTER, BUT...
...THE GUITAR ISN'T QUITE RIGHT. PRACTICE HARD SO YOU DON'T DRAG TATSUHIKO DOWN.

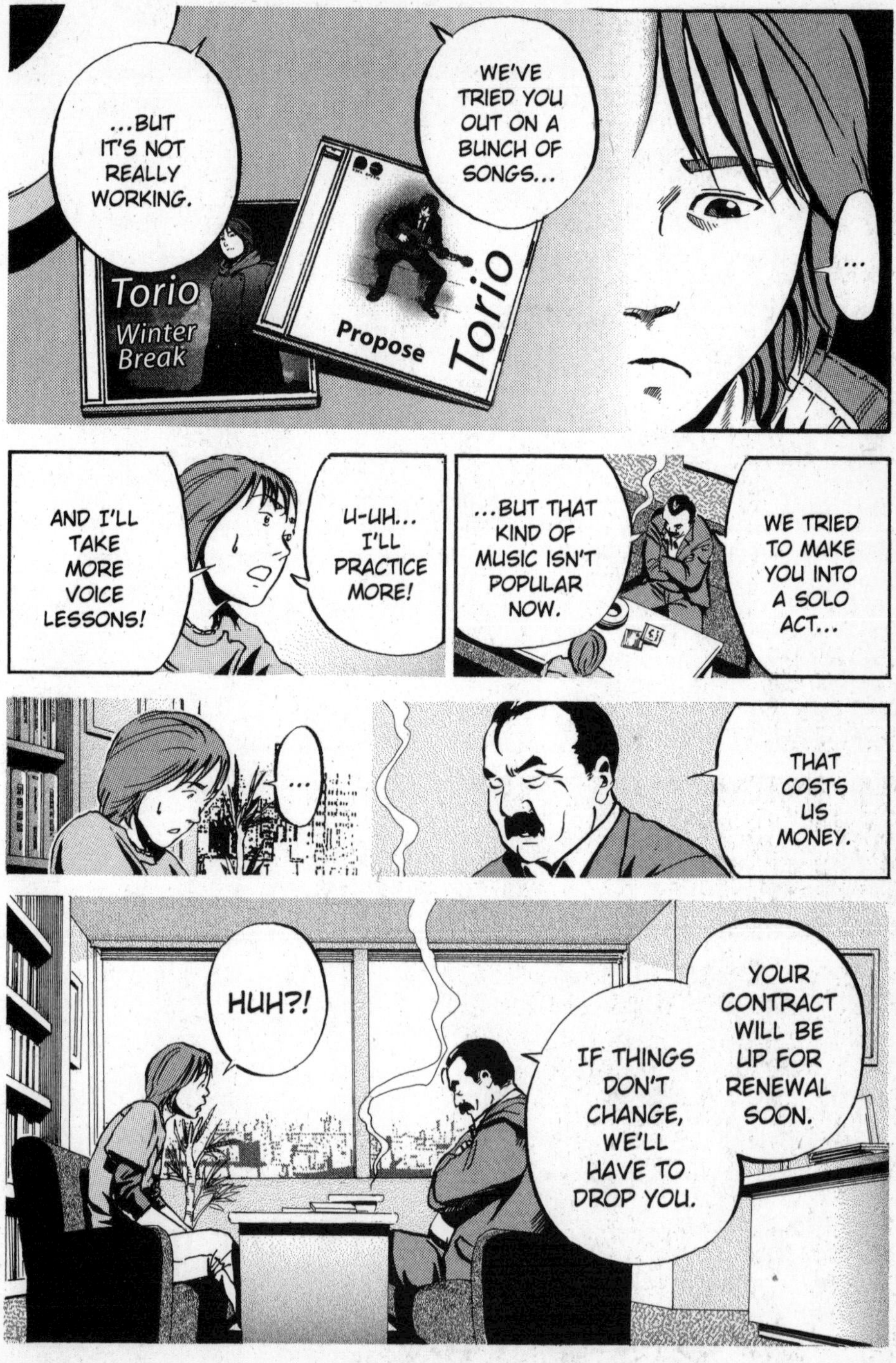
WE'VE TRIED YOU OUT ON A BUNCH OF SONGS...
...BUT IT'S NOT REALLY WORKING.
Torio Winter Break
Propose Torio
...
WE TRIED TO MAKE YOU INTO A SOLO ACT...
...BUT THAT KIND OF MUSIC ISN'T POPULAR NOW.
U-UH... I'LL PRACTICE MORE!
AND I'LL TAKE MORE VOICE LESSONS!
THAT COSTS US MONEY.
...
YOUR CONTRACT WILL BE UP FOR RENEWAL SOON.
IF THINGS DON'T CHANGE, WE'LL HAVE TO DROP YOU.
HUH?!

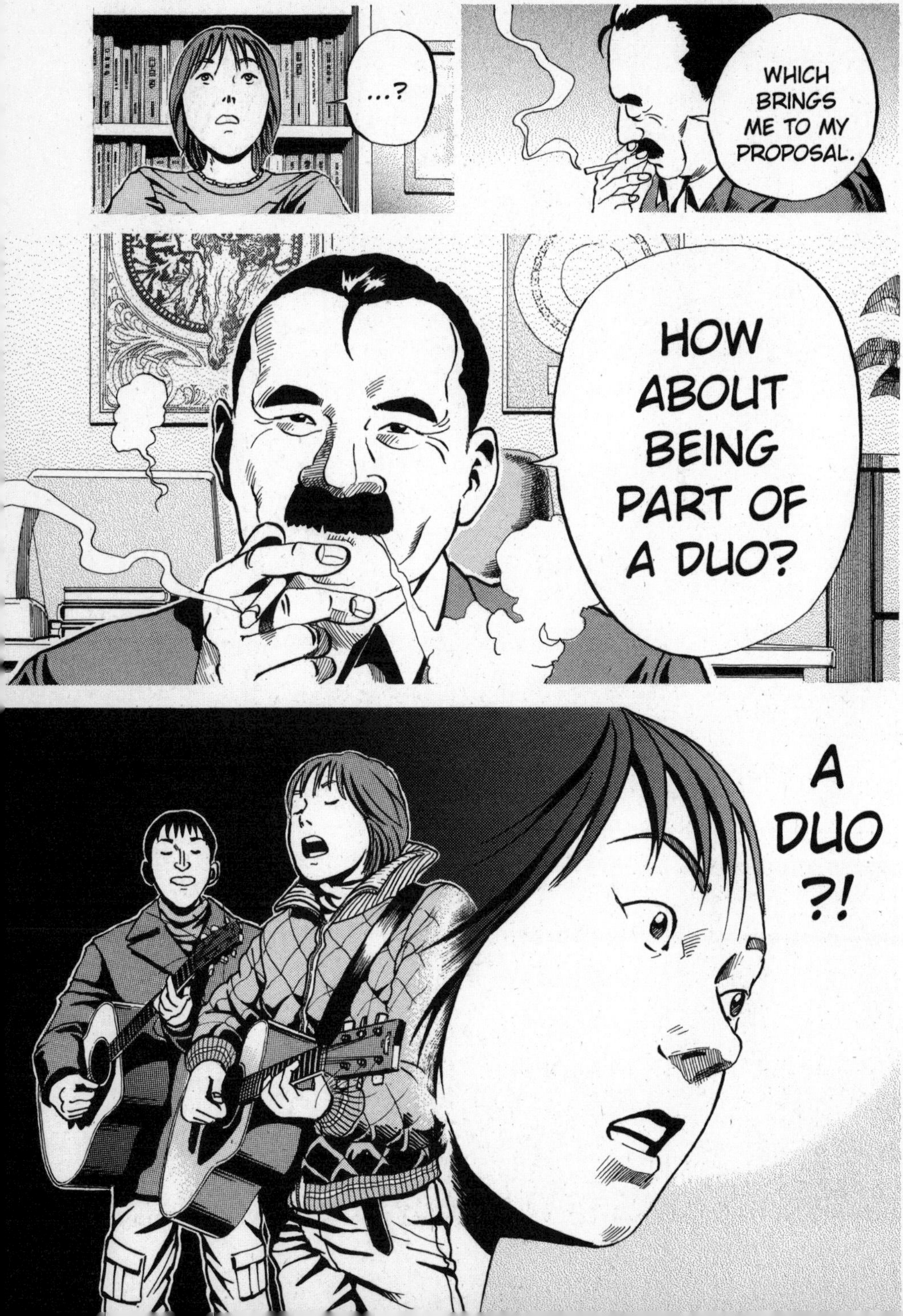
WHICH BRINGS ME TO MY PROPOSAL.
...?
HOW ABOUT BEING PART OF A DUO?
A DUO ?!

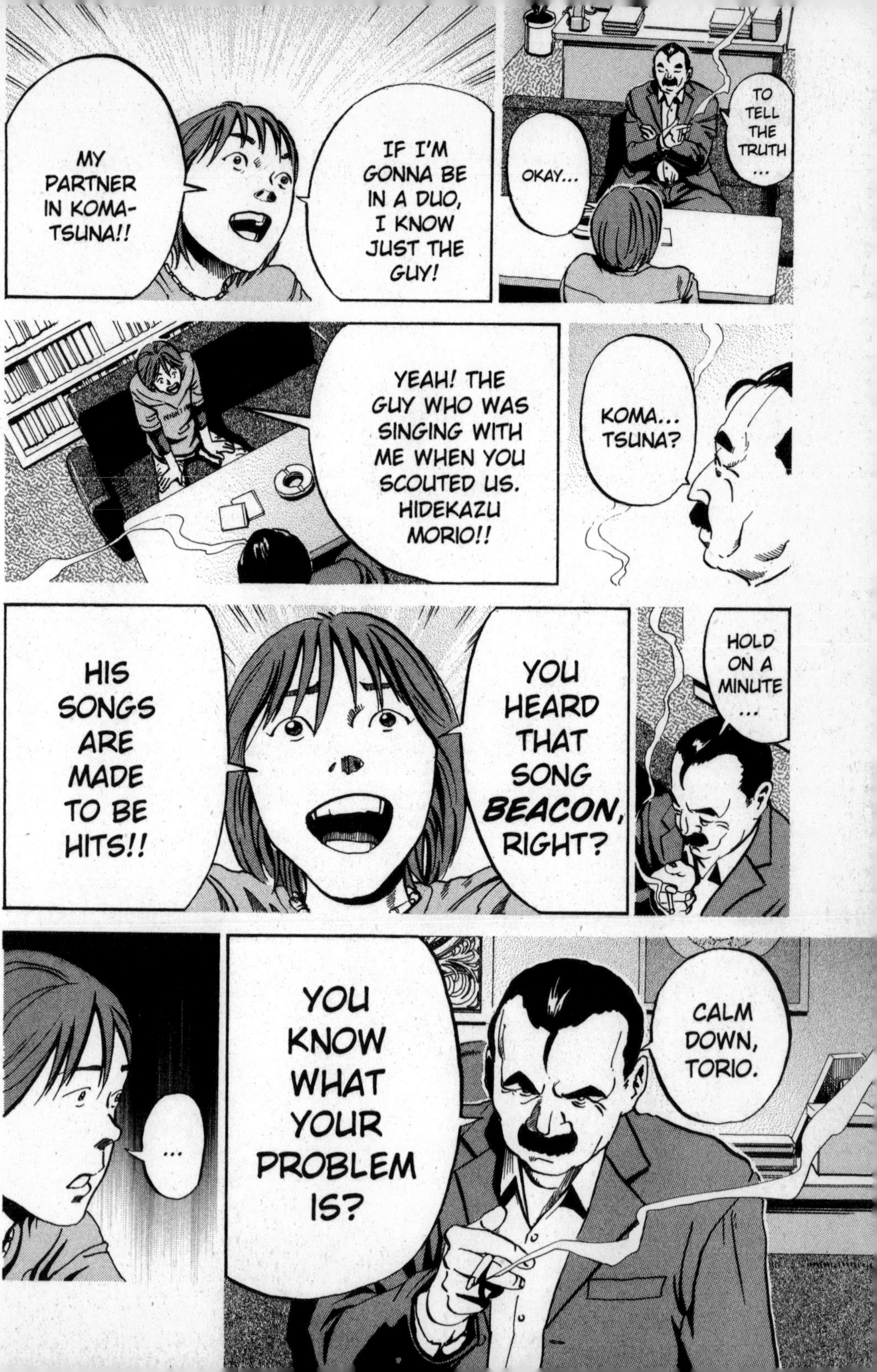
TO TELL THE TRUTH...
OKAY...
IF I'M GONNA BE IN A DUO, I KNOW JUST THE GUY!
MY PARTNER IN KOMATSUNA!!
KOMA... TSUNA?
YEAH! THE GUY WHO WAS SINGING WITH ME WHEN YOU SCOUTED US. HIDEKAZU MORIO!!
HOLD ON A MINUTE...
YOU HEARD THAT SONG *BEACON*, RIGHT?
HIS SONGS ARE MADE TO BE HITS!!
CALM DOWN, TORIO.
YOU KNOW WHAT YOUR PROBLEM IS?
...

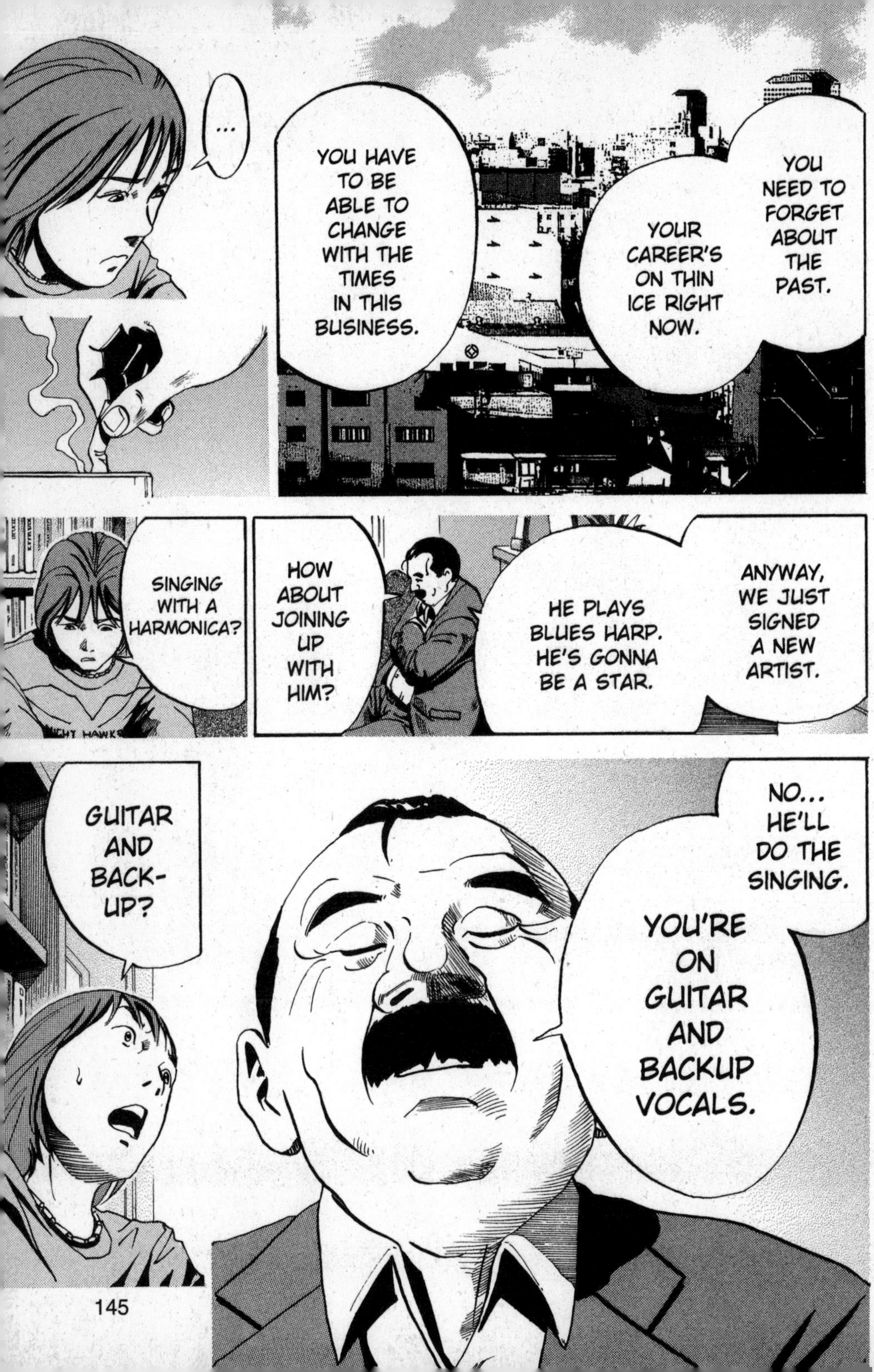
YOU NEED TO FORGET ABOUT THE PAST.
YOUR CAREER'S ON THIN ICE RIGHT NOW.
YOU HAVE TO BE ABLE TO CHANGE WITH THE TIMES IN THIS BUSINESS.
...
ANYWAY, WE JUST SIGNED A NEW ARTIST.
HE PLAYS BLUES HARP. HE'S GONNA BE A STAR.
HOW ABOUT JOINING UP WITH HIM?
SINGING WITH A HARMONICA?
NO... HE'LL DO THE SINGING.
YOU'RE ON GUITAR AND BACKUP VOCALS.
GUITAR AND BACK-UP?

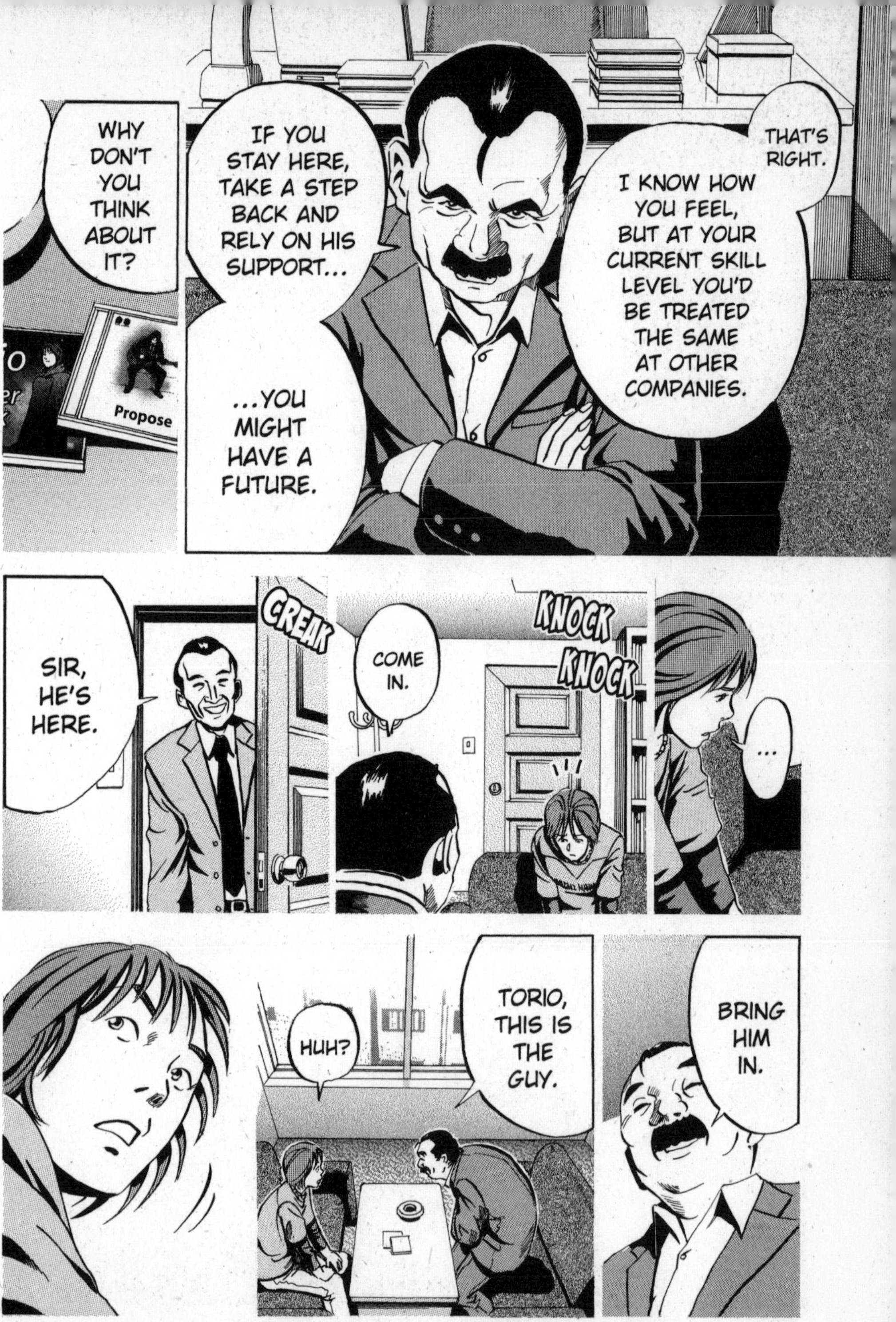
THAT'S RIGHT.
I KNOW HOW YOU FEEL, BUT AT YOUR CURRENT SKILL LEVEL YOU'D BE TREATED THE SAME AT OTHER COMPANIES.
IF YOU STAY HERE, TAKE A STEP BACK AND RELY ON HIS SUPPORT...
...YOU MIGHT HAVE A FUTURE.
WHY DON'T YOU THINK ABOUT IT?
Propose
...
KNOCK KNOCK
COME IN.
CREAK
SIR, HE'S HERE.
BRING HIM IN.
TORIO, THIS IS THE GUY.
HUH?

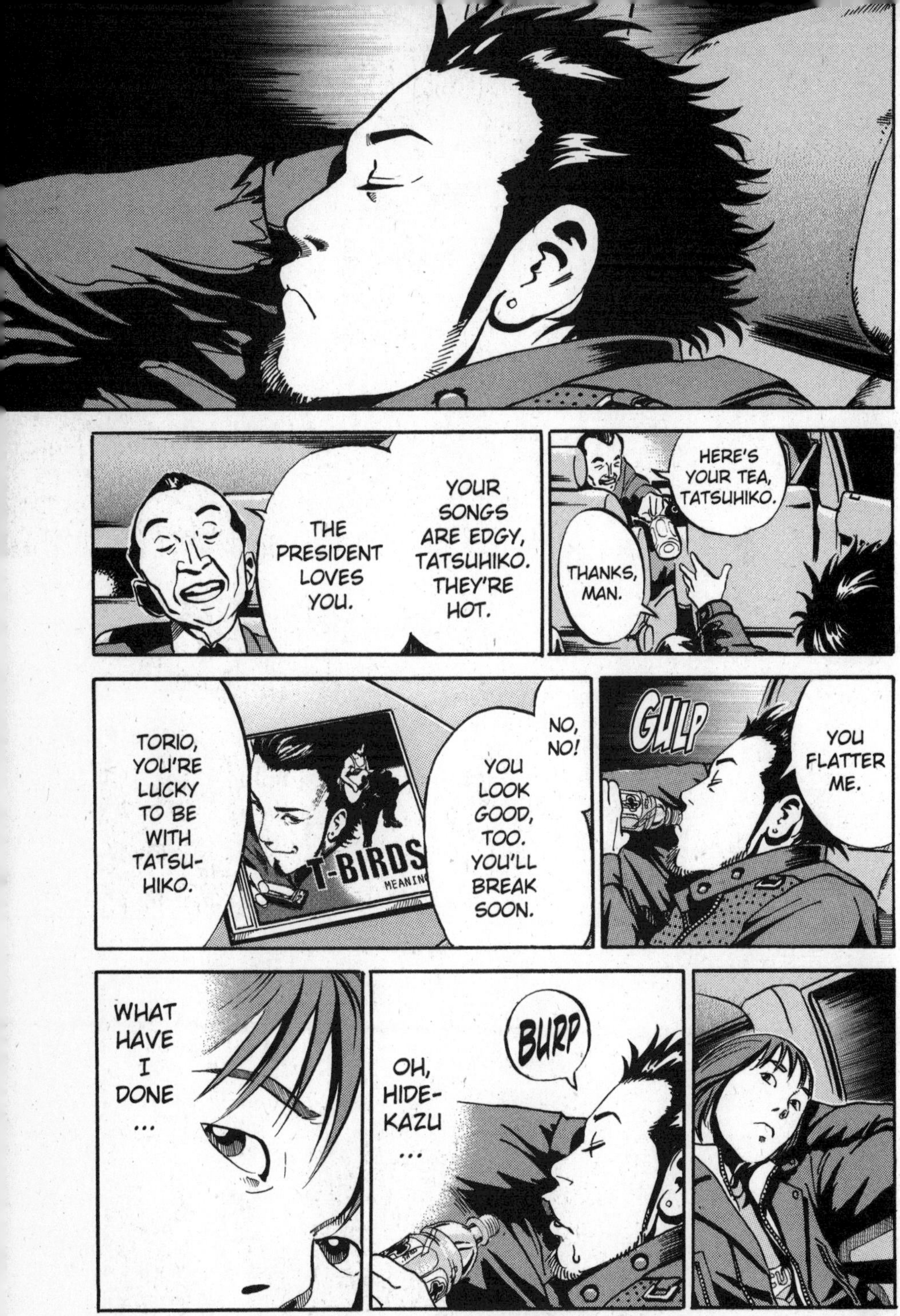
HERE'S YOUR TEA, TATSUHIKO.
THANKS, MAN.
YOUR SONGS ARE EDGY, TATSUHIKO. THEY'RE HOT.
THE PRESIDENT LOVES YOU.
GULP
YOU FLATTER ME.
NO, NO!
YOU LOOK GOOD, TOO. YOU'LL BREAK SOON.
T-BIRDS
TORIO, YOU'RE LUCKY TO BE WITH TATSUHIKO.
BURP
OH, HIDEKAZU ...
WHAT HAVE I DONE ...

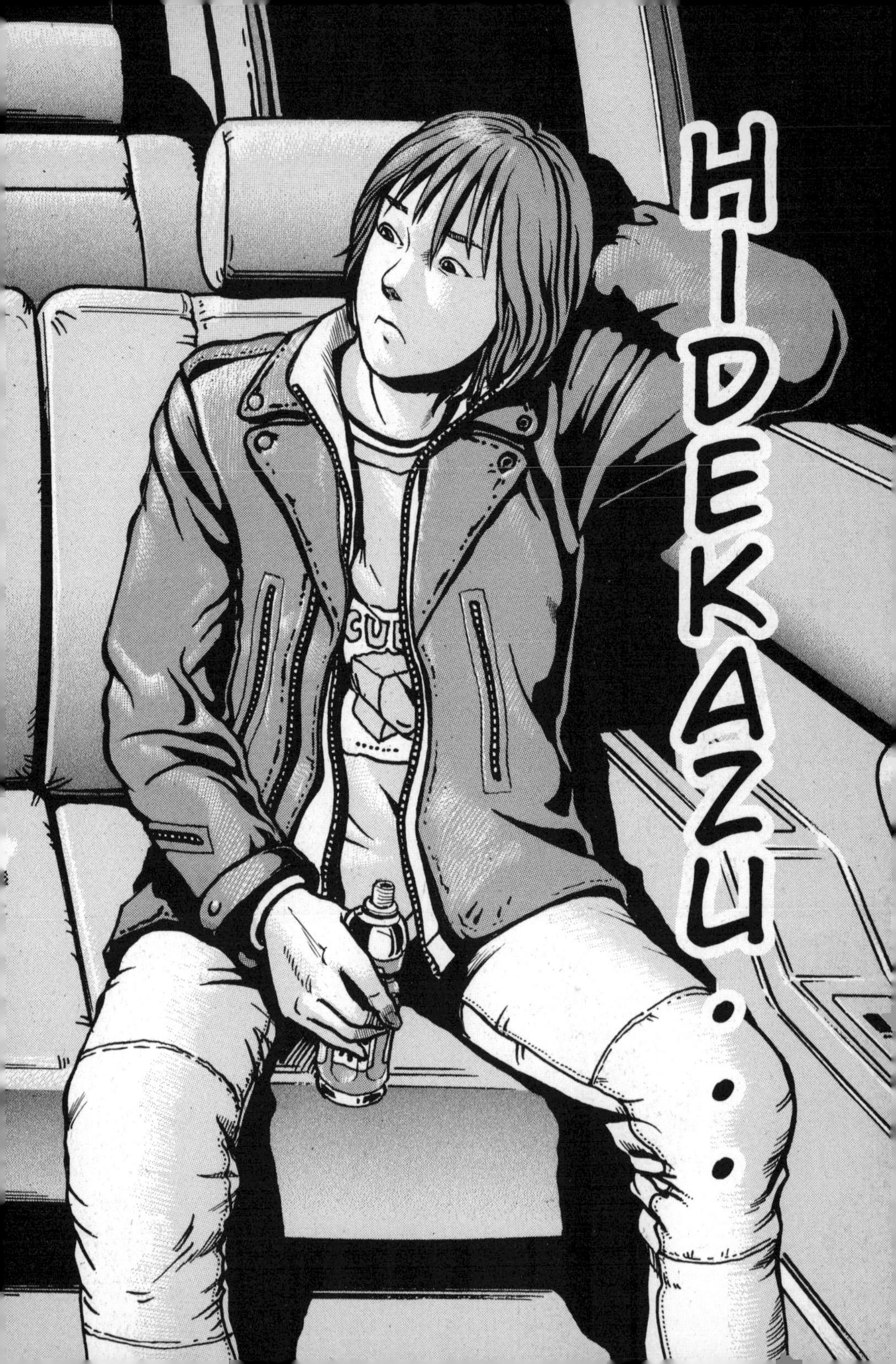
HIDEKAZU...

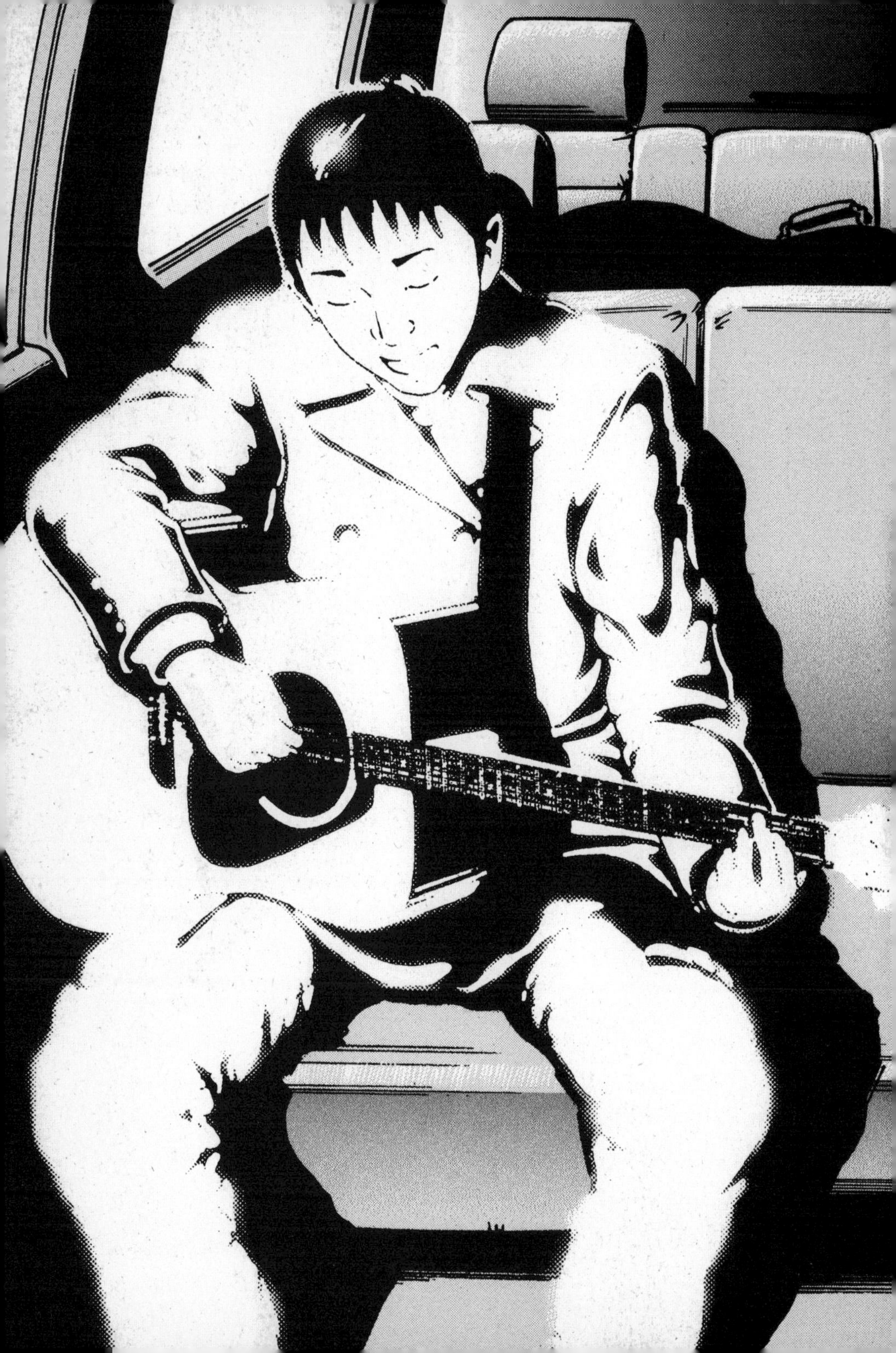

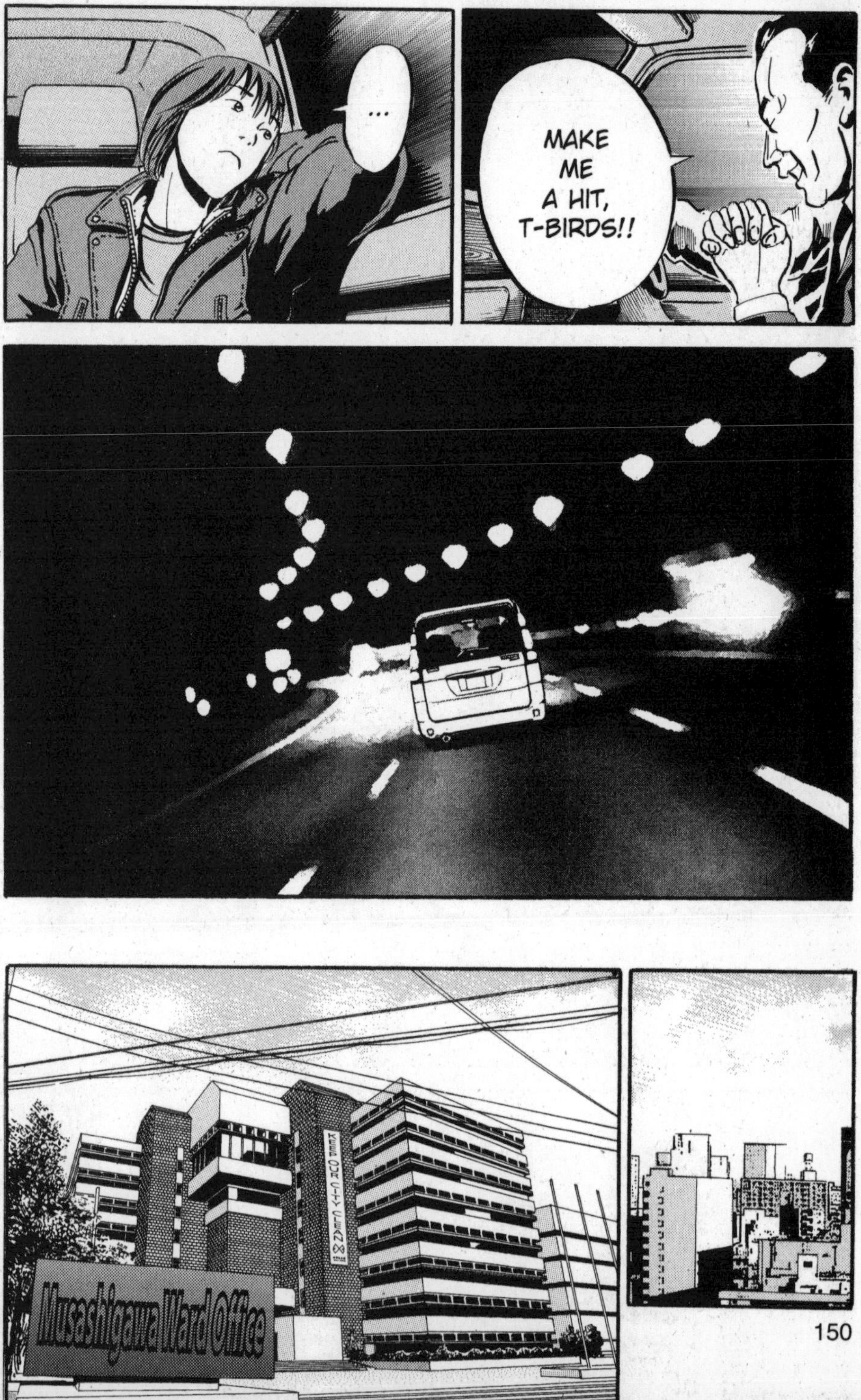
MAKE ME A HIT, T-BIRDS!!
...
KEEP OUR CITY CLEAN
Musashigawa Ward Office

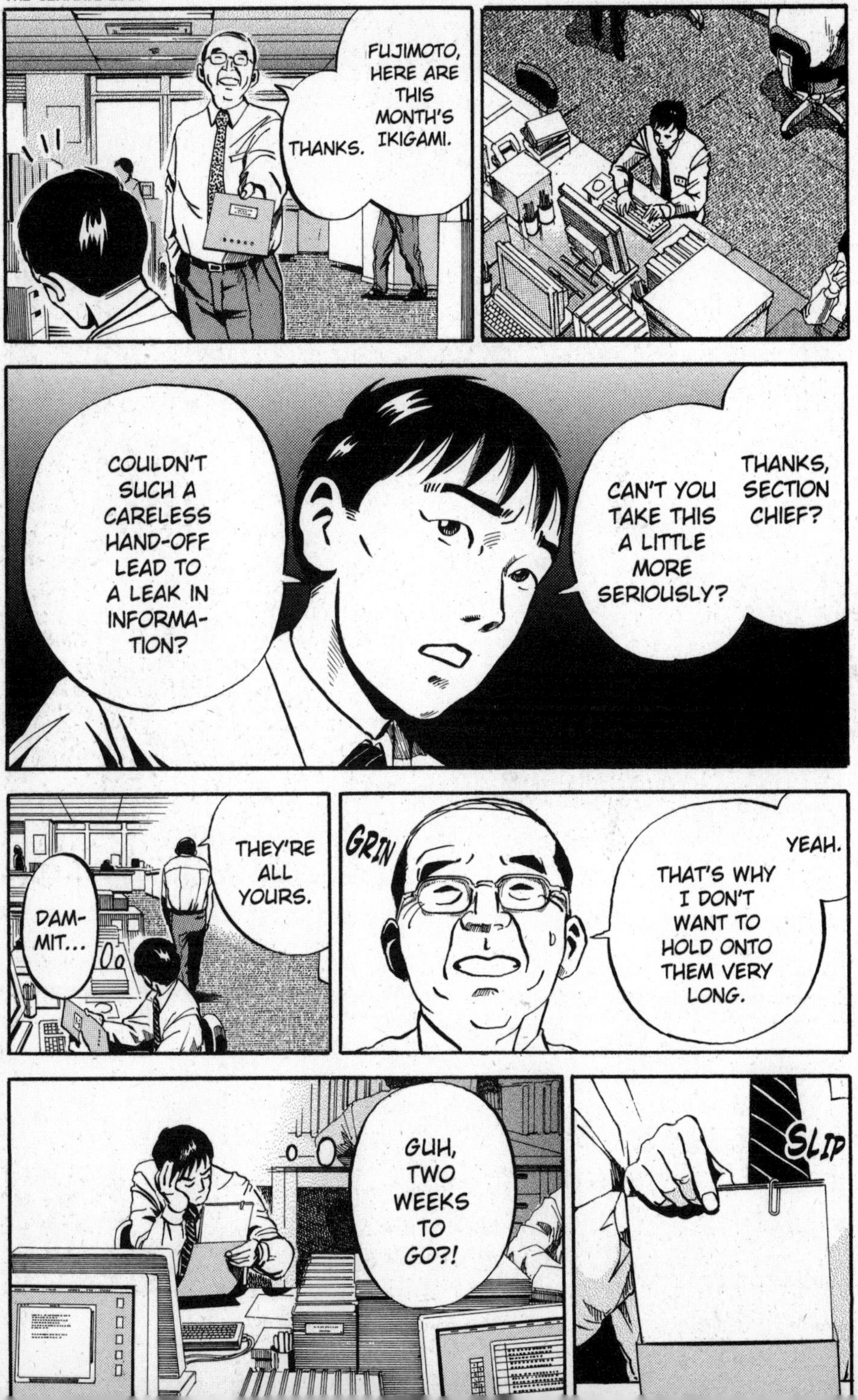
FUJIMOTO, HERE ARE THIS MONTH'S IKIGAMI.
THANKS.
THANKS, SECTION CHIEF?
CAN'T YOU TAKE THIS A LITTLE MORE SERIOUSLY?
COULDN'T SUCH A CARELESS HAND-OFF LEAD TO A LEAK IN INFORMATION?
GRIN
YEAH.
THAT'S WHY I DON'T WANT TO HOLD ONTO THEM VERY LONG.
THEY'RE ALL YOURS.
DAM-MIT...
SLIP
GUH, TWO WEEKS TO GO?!

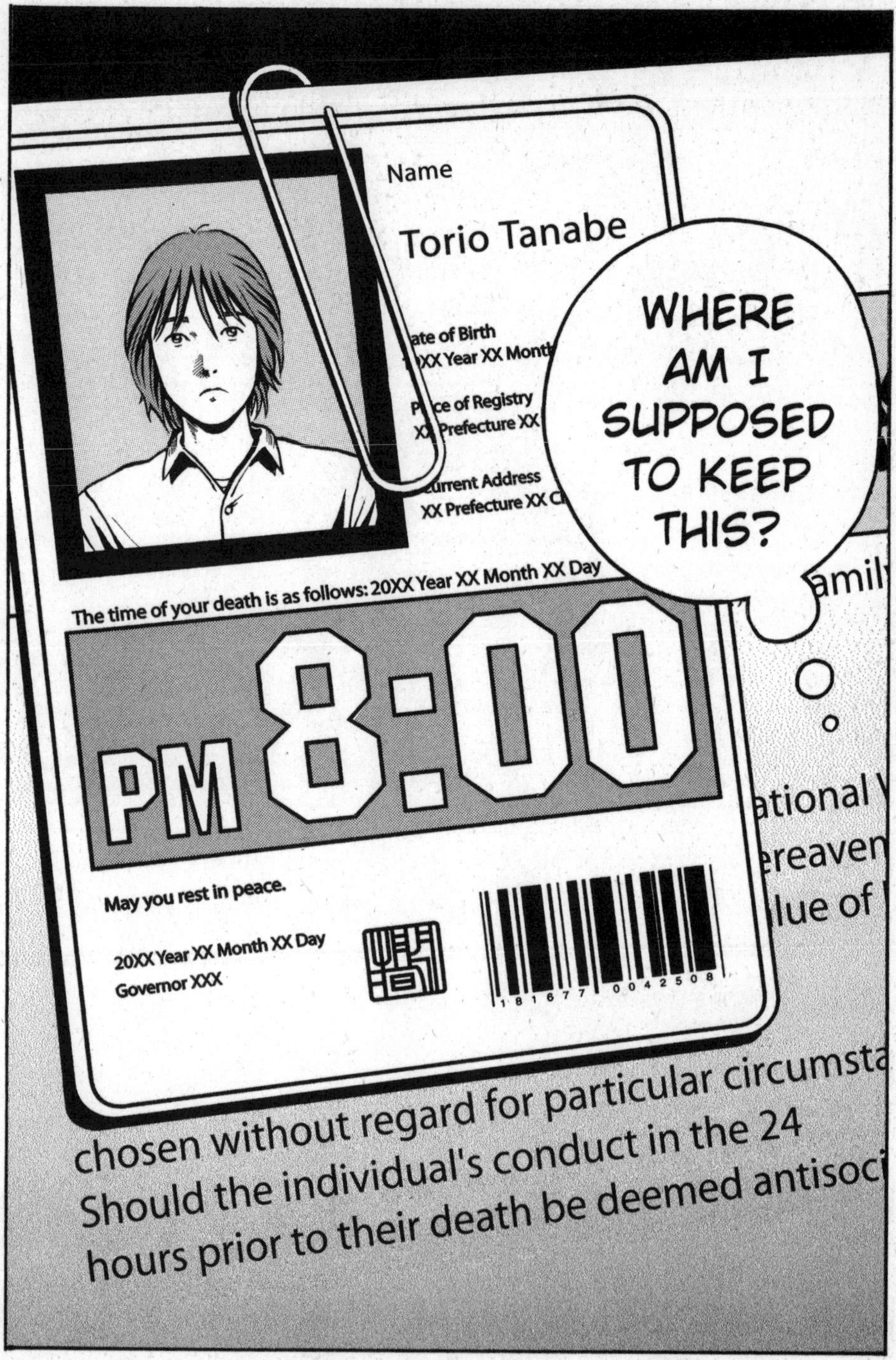

Name
Torio Tanabe
WHERE AM I SUPPOSED TO KEEP THIS?
The time of your death is as follows: 20XX Year XX Month XX Day
PM 8:00
May you rest in peace.
20XX Year XX Month XX Day
Governor XXX
chosen without regard for particular circumsta
Should the individual's conduct in the 24
hours prior to their death be deemed antisoci

Episode 2 The Last Song Act2

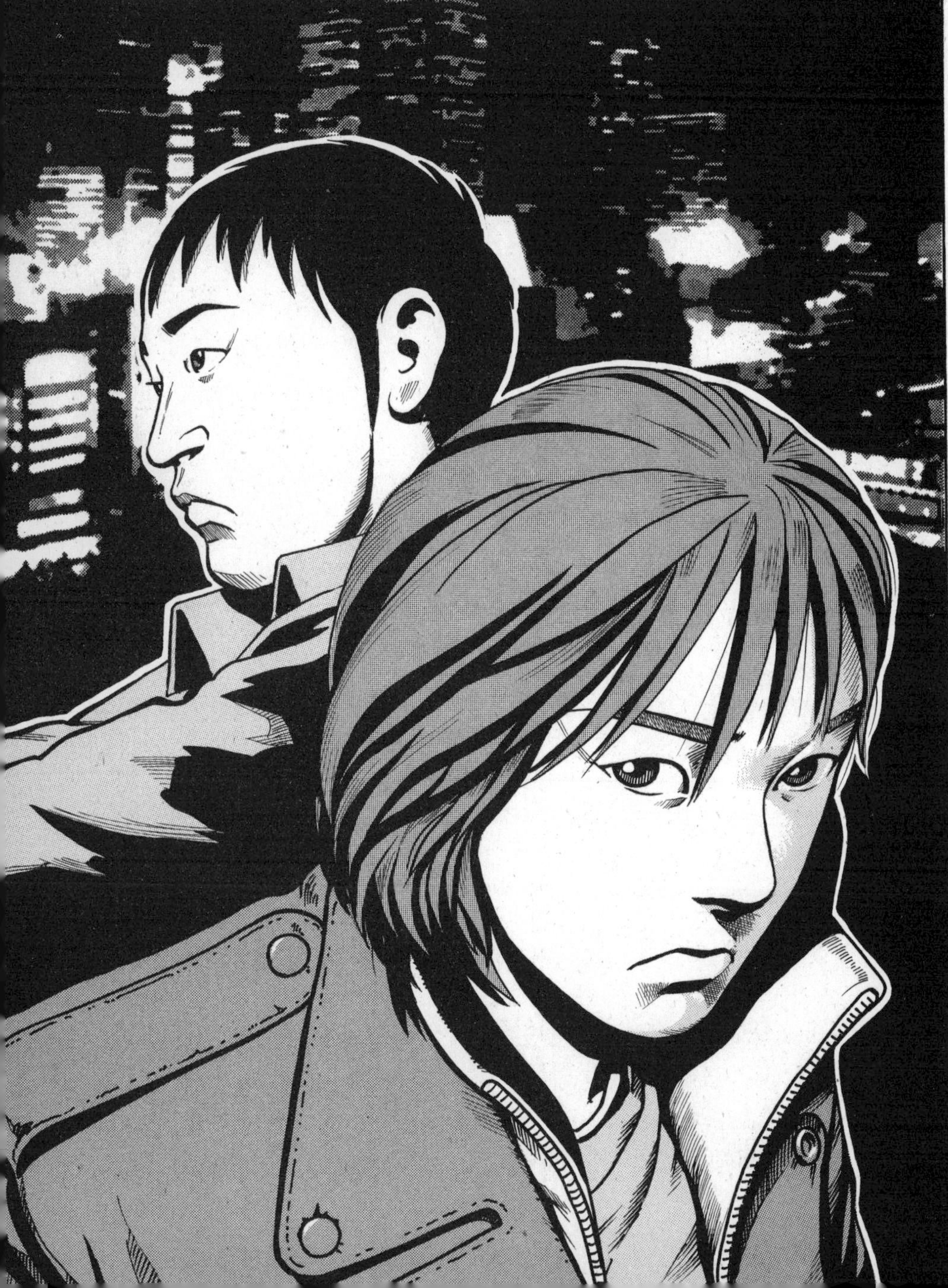

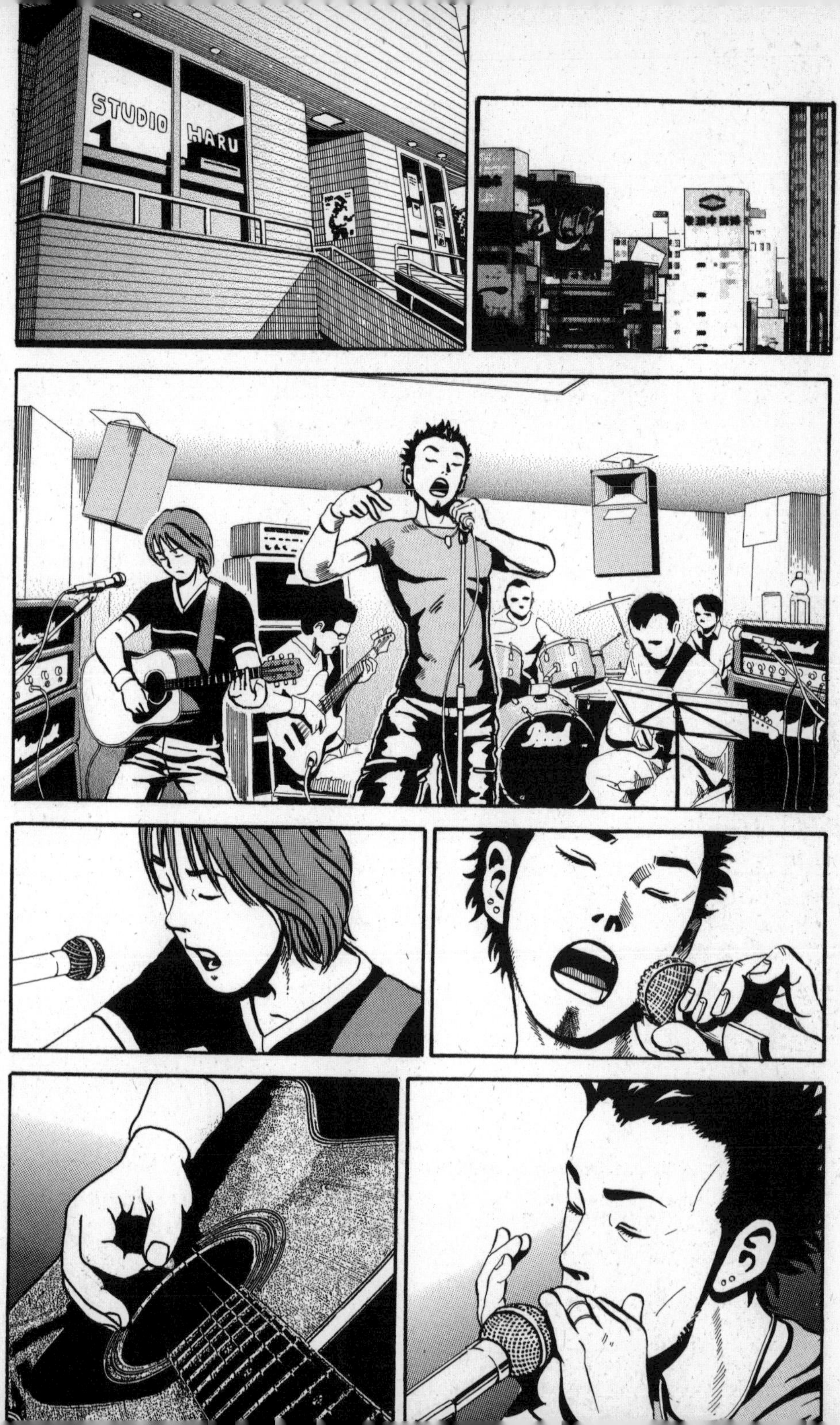
STUDIO HARU

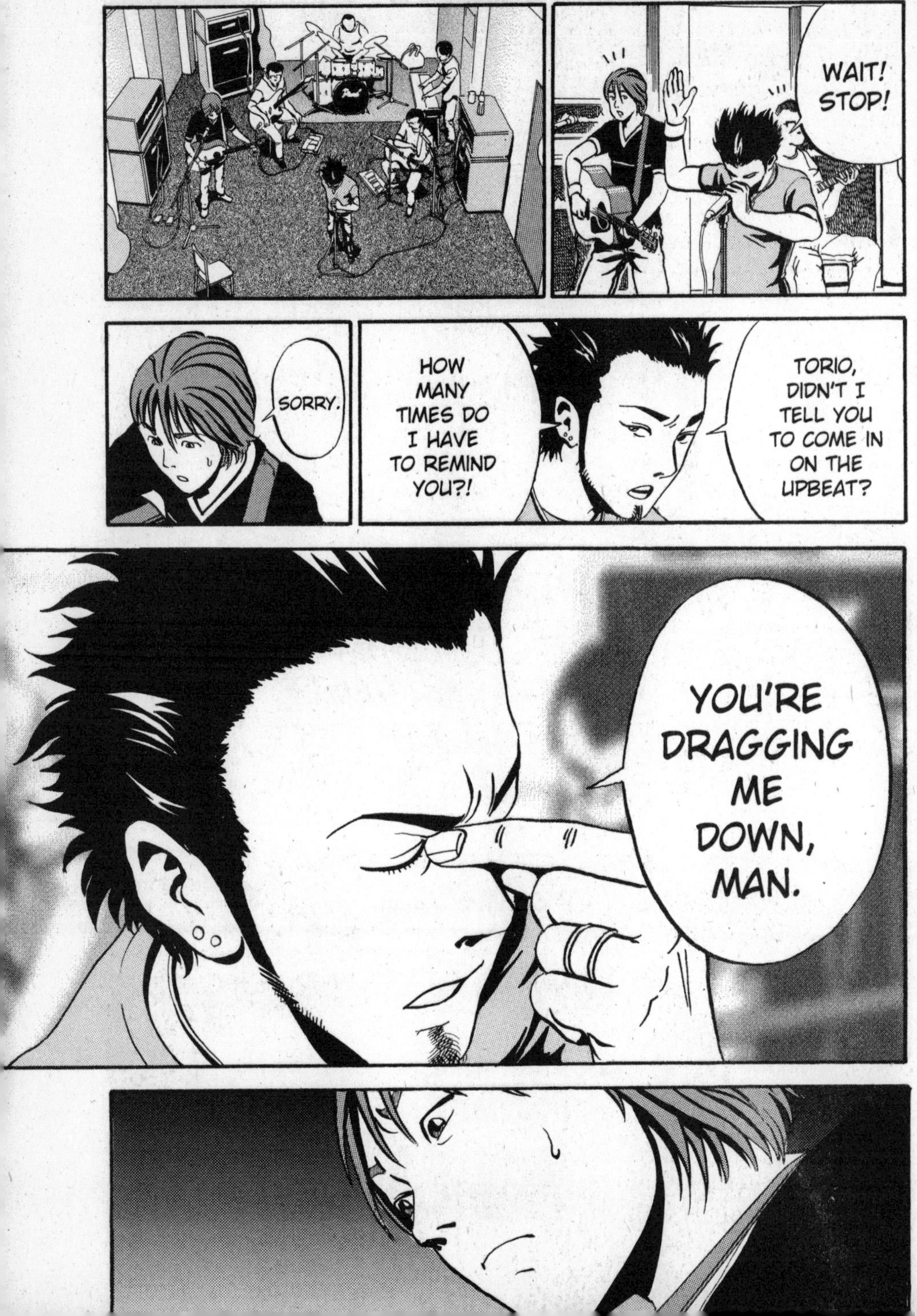
WAIT! STOP!
TORIO, DIDN'T I TELL YOU TO COME IN ON THE UPBEAT?
HOW MANY TIMES DO I HAVE TO REMIND YOU?!
SORRY.
YOU'RE DRAGGING ME DOWN, MAN.

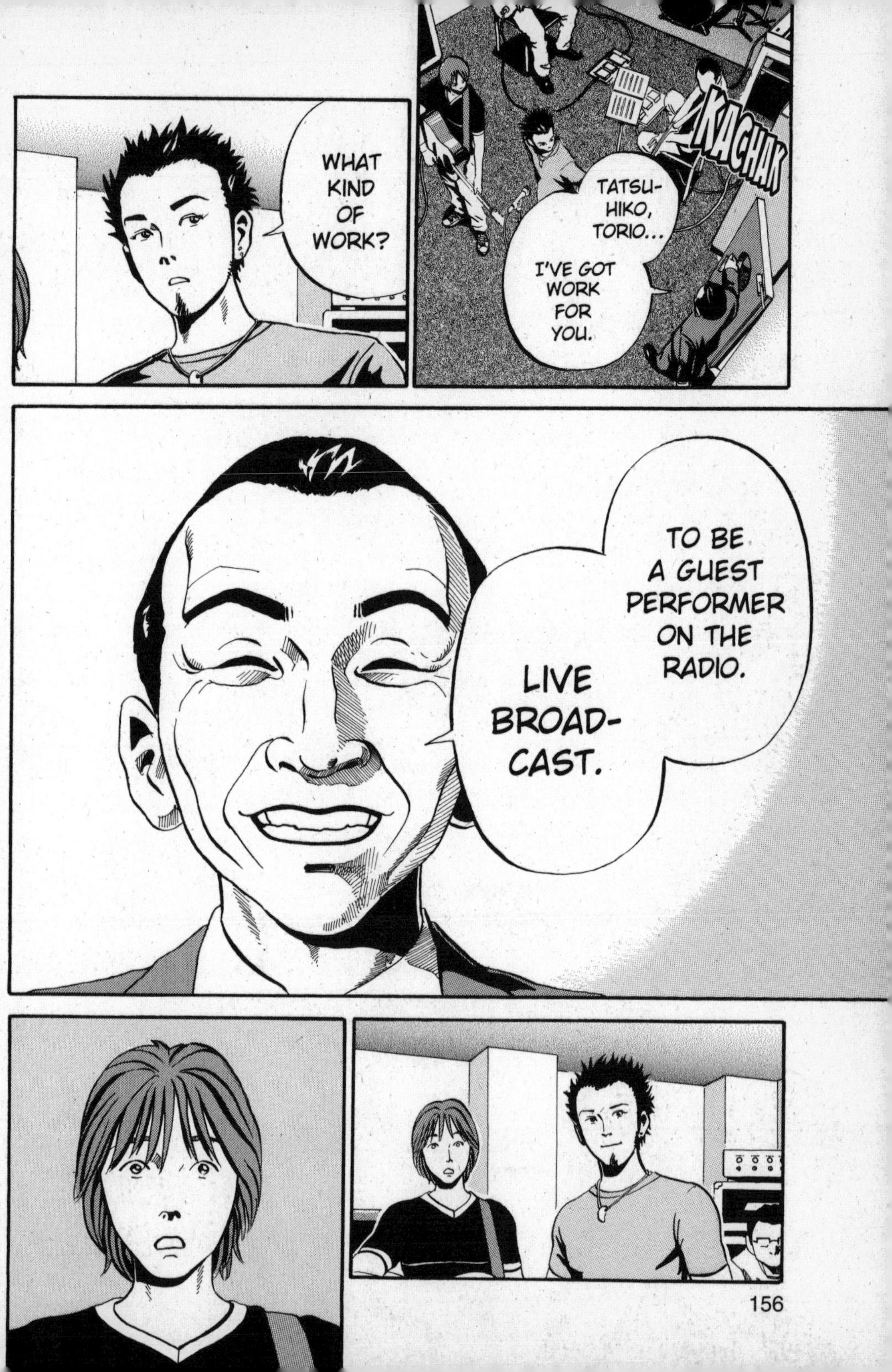
KACHAK
TATSU-HIKO, TORIO...
I'VE GOT WORK FOR YOU.
WHAT KIND OF WORK?
TO BE A GUEST PERFORMER ON THE RADIO.
LIVE BROADCAST.

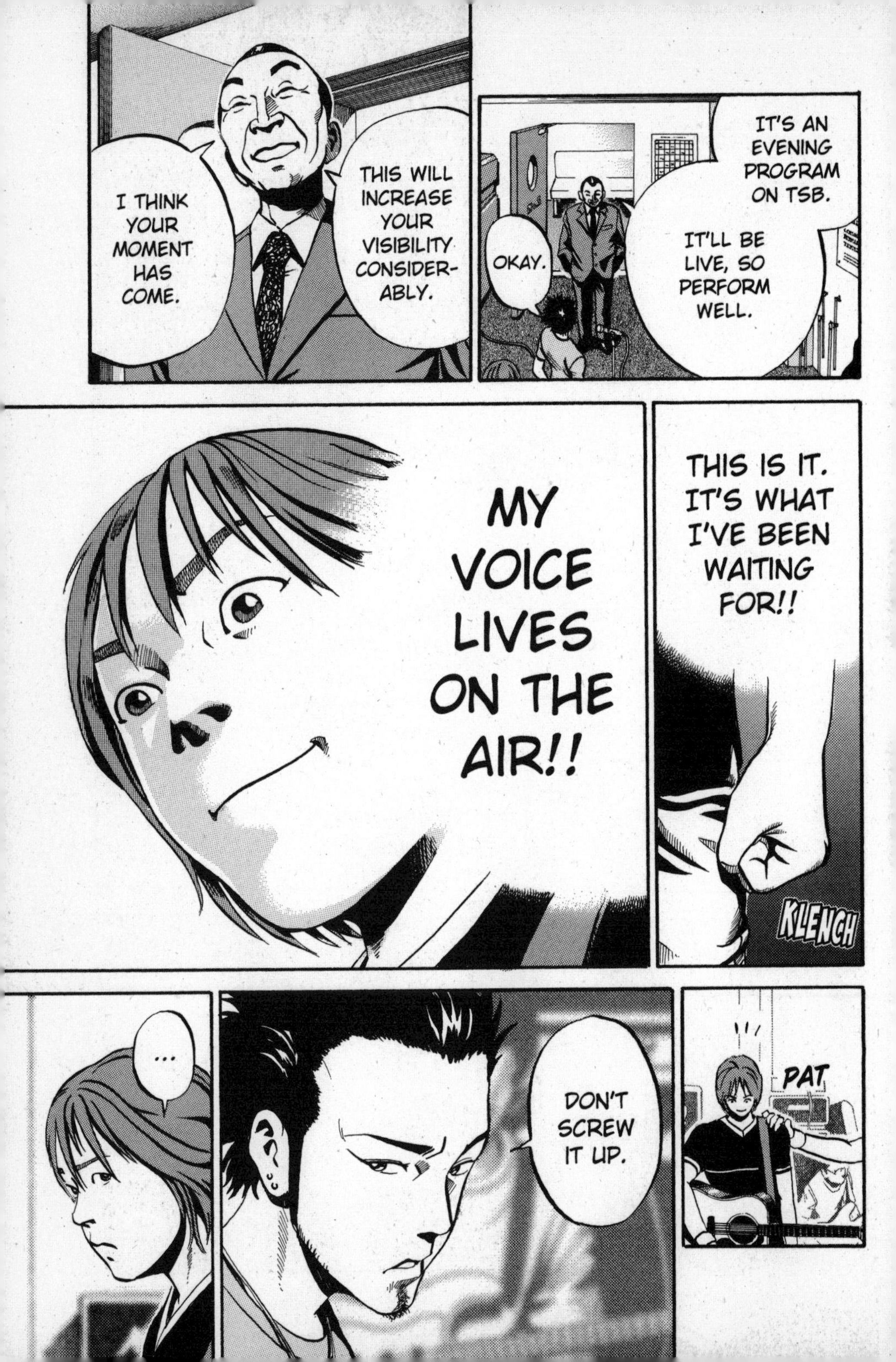
IT'S AN EVENING PROGRAM ON TSB.
IT'LL BE LIVE, SO PERFORM WELL.
OKAY.
THIS WILL INCREASE YOUR VISIBILITY CONSIDERABLY.
I THINK YOUR MOMENT HAS COME.
THIS IS IT. IT'S WHAT I'VE BEEN WAITING FOR!!
KLENCH
MY VOICE LIVES ON THE AIR!!
PAT
DON'T SCREW IT UP.
...

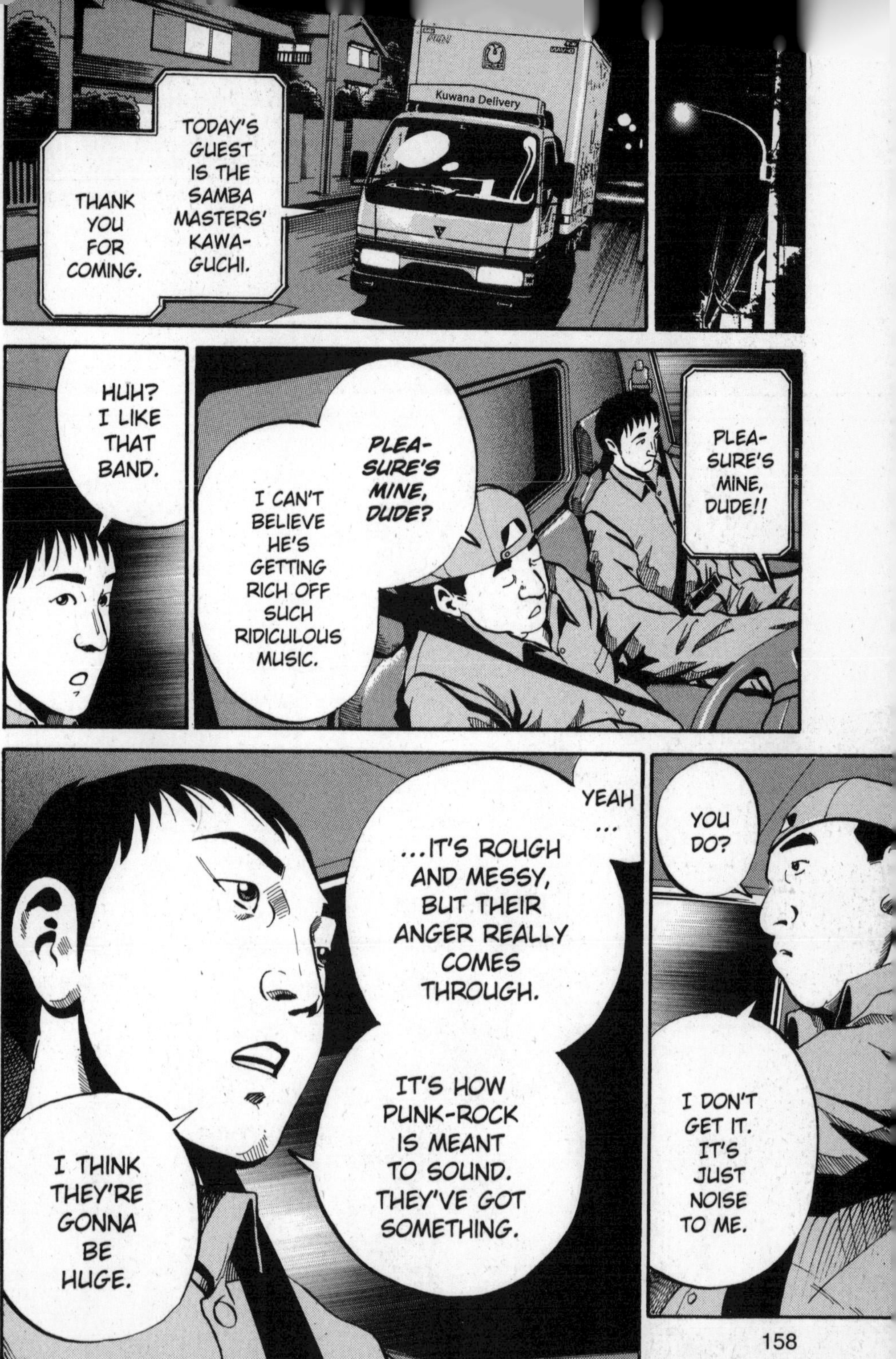
Kuwana Delivery
TODAY'S GUEST IS THE SAMBA MASTERS' KAWA-GUCHI.
THANK YOU FOR COMING.
PLEA-SURE'S MINE, DUDE!!
PLEA-SURE'S MINE, DUDE?
I CAN'T BELIEVE HE'S GETTING RICH OFF SUCH RIDICULOUS MUSIC.
HUH? I LIKE THAT BAND.
YOU DO?
I DON'T GET IT. IT'S JUST NOISE TO ME.
YEAH ...
...IT'S ROUGH AND MESSY, BUT THEIR ANGER REALLY COMES THROUGH.
IT'S HOW PUNK-ROCK IS MEANT TO SOUND. THEY'VE GOT SOMETHING.
I THINK THEY'RE GONNA BE HUGE.

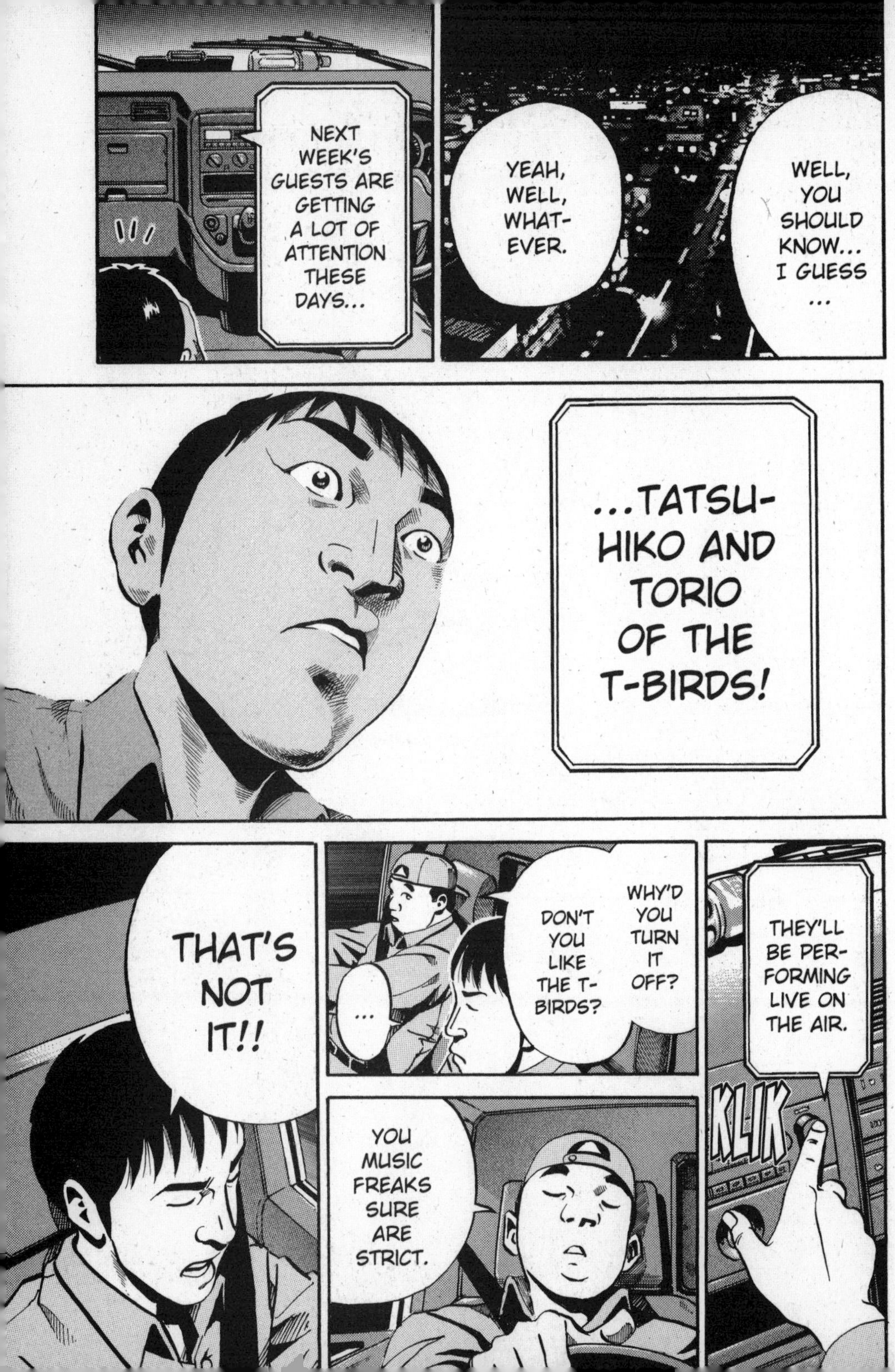
WELL, YOU SHOULD KNOW... I GUESS...
YEAH, WELL, WHATEVER.
NEXT WEEK'S GUESTS ARE GETTING A LOT OF ATTENTION THESE DAYS...
...TATSUHIKO AND TORIO OF THE T-BIRDS!
THEY'LL BE PERFORMING LIVE ON THE AIR.
KLIK
WHY'D YOU TURN IT OFF?
DON'T YOU LIKE THE T-BIRDS?
...
YOU MUSIC FREAKS SURE ARE STRICT.
THAT'S NOT IT!!

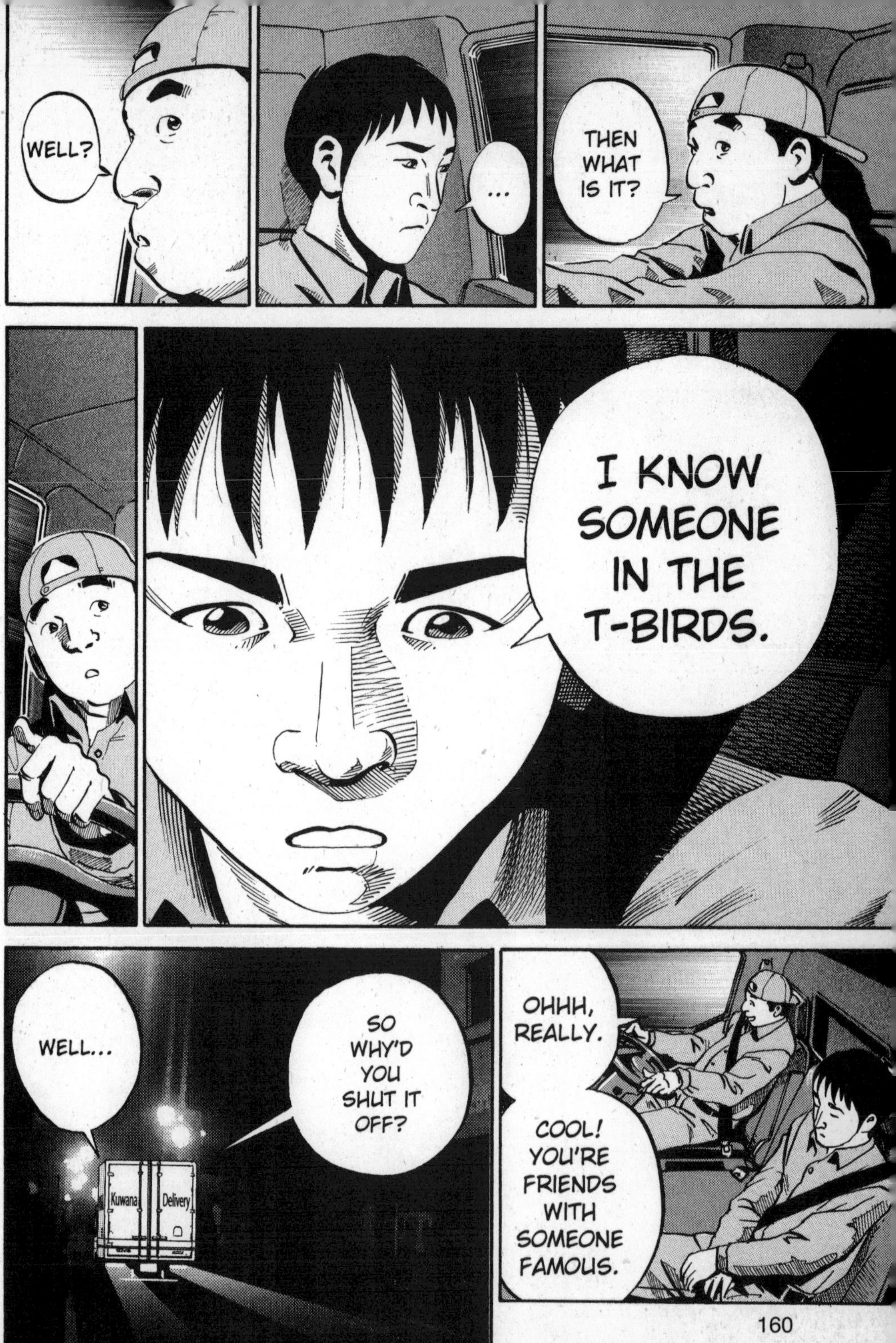
THEN WHAT IS IT?
...
WELL?
I KNOW SOMEONE IN THE T-BIRDS.
OHHH, REALLY.
COOL! YOU'RE FRIENDS WITH SOMEONE FAMOUS.
SO WHY'D YOU SHUT IT OFF?
WELL...
Kuwana Delivery

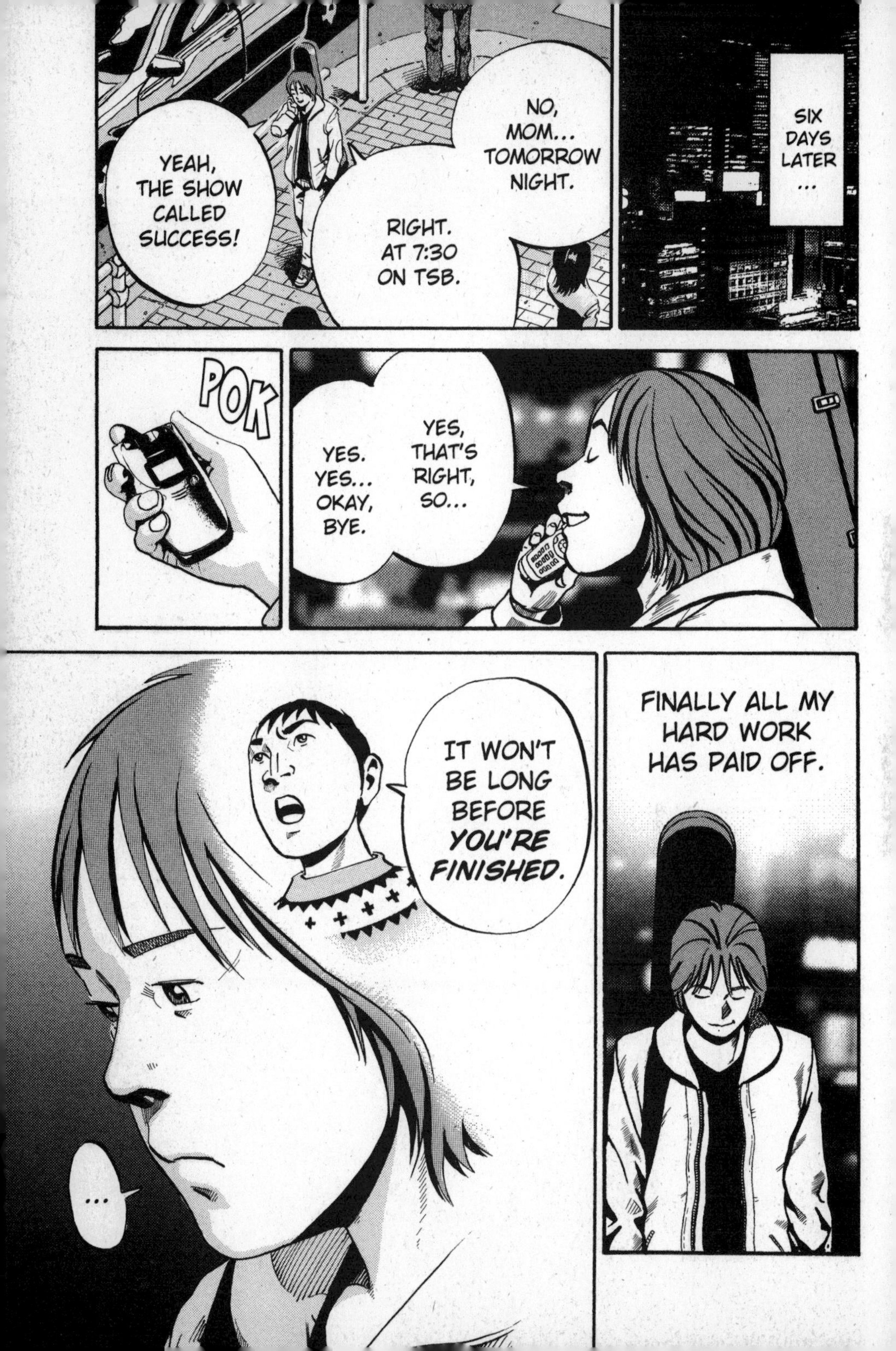
SIX DAYS LATER ...
NO, MOM... TOMORROW NIGHT.
RIGHT. AT 7:30 ON TSB.
YEAH, THE SHOW CALLED SUCCESS!
YES, THAT'S RIGHT, SO...
YES. YES... OKAY, BYE.
POK
FINALLY ALL MY HARD WORK HAS PAID OFF.
IT WON'T BE LONG BEFORE *YOU'RE FINISHED*.
...

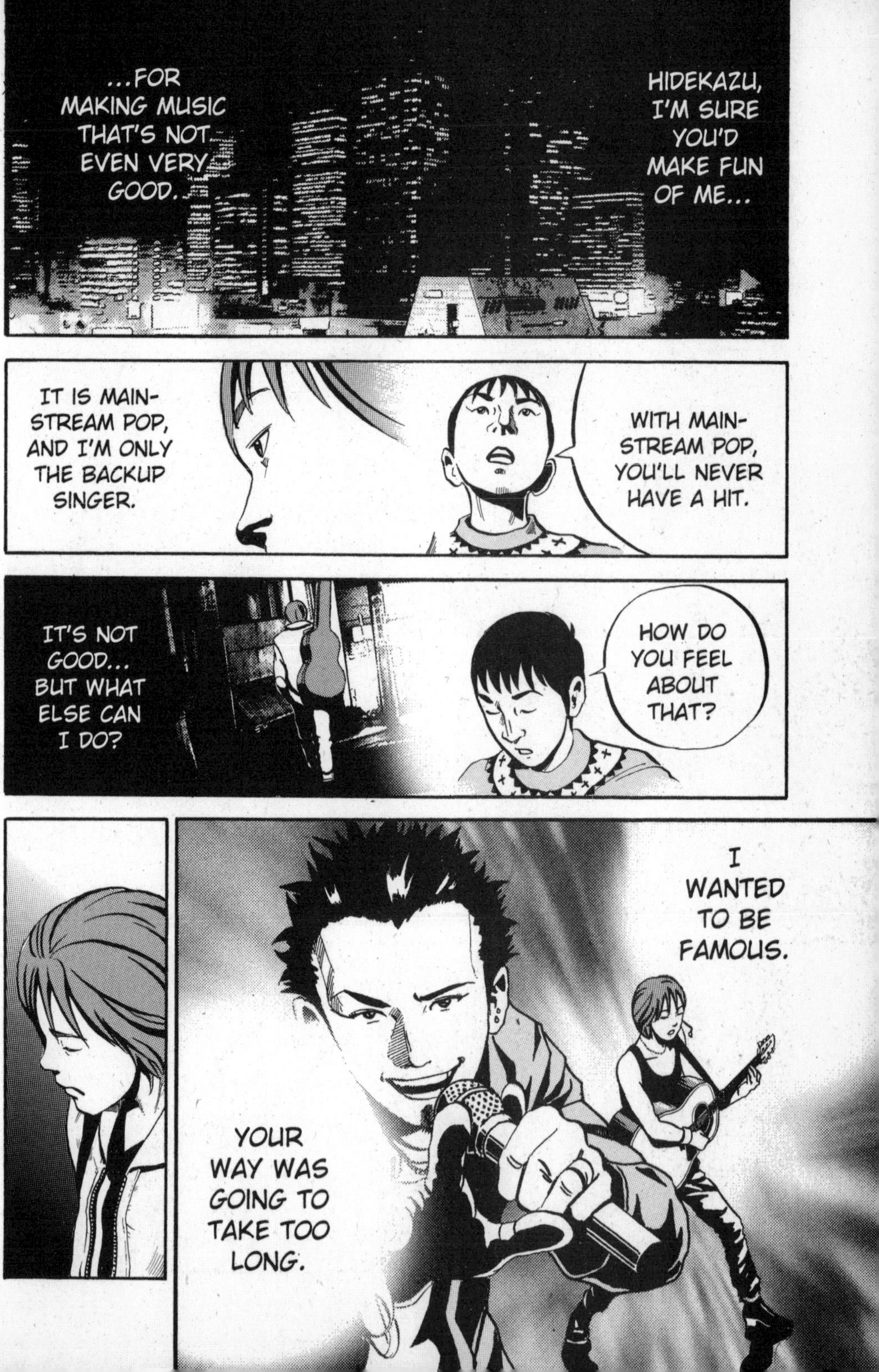
HIDEKAZU, I'M SURE YOU'D MAKE FUN OF ME...
...FOR MAKING MUSIC THAT'S NOT EVEN VERY GOOD.
WITH MAIN-STREAM POP, YOU'LL NEVER HAVE A HIT.
IT IS MAIN-STREAM POP, AND I'M ONLY THE BACKUP SINGER.
HOW DO YOU FEEL ABOUT THAT?
IT'S NOT GOOD... BUT WHAT ELSE CAN I DO?
I WANTED TO BE FAMOUS.
YOUR WAY WAS GOING TO TAKE TOO LONG.

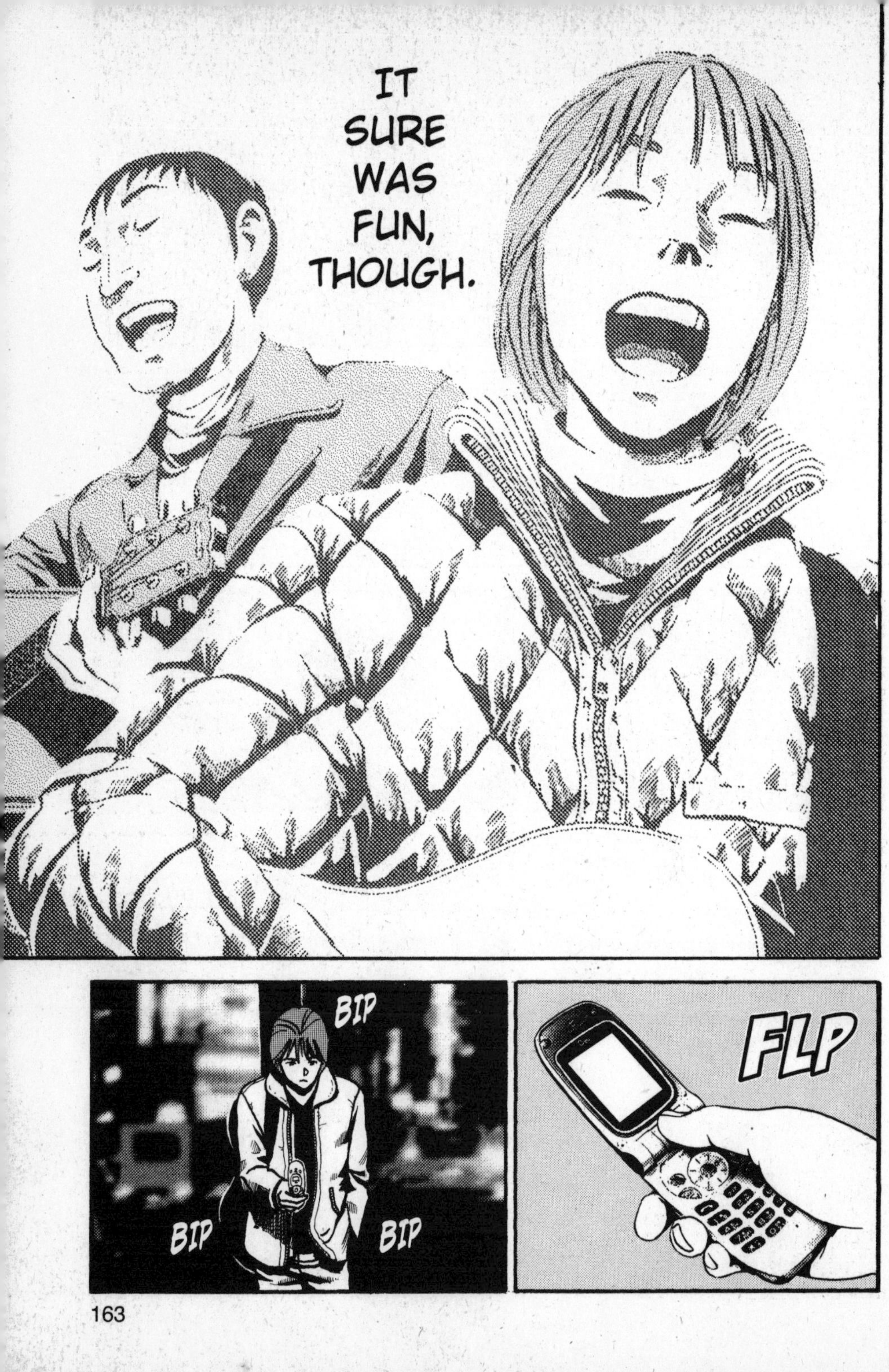
IT SURE WAS FUN, THOUGH.
FLP
BIP
BIP
BIP

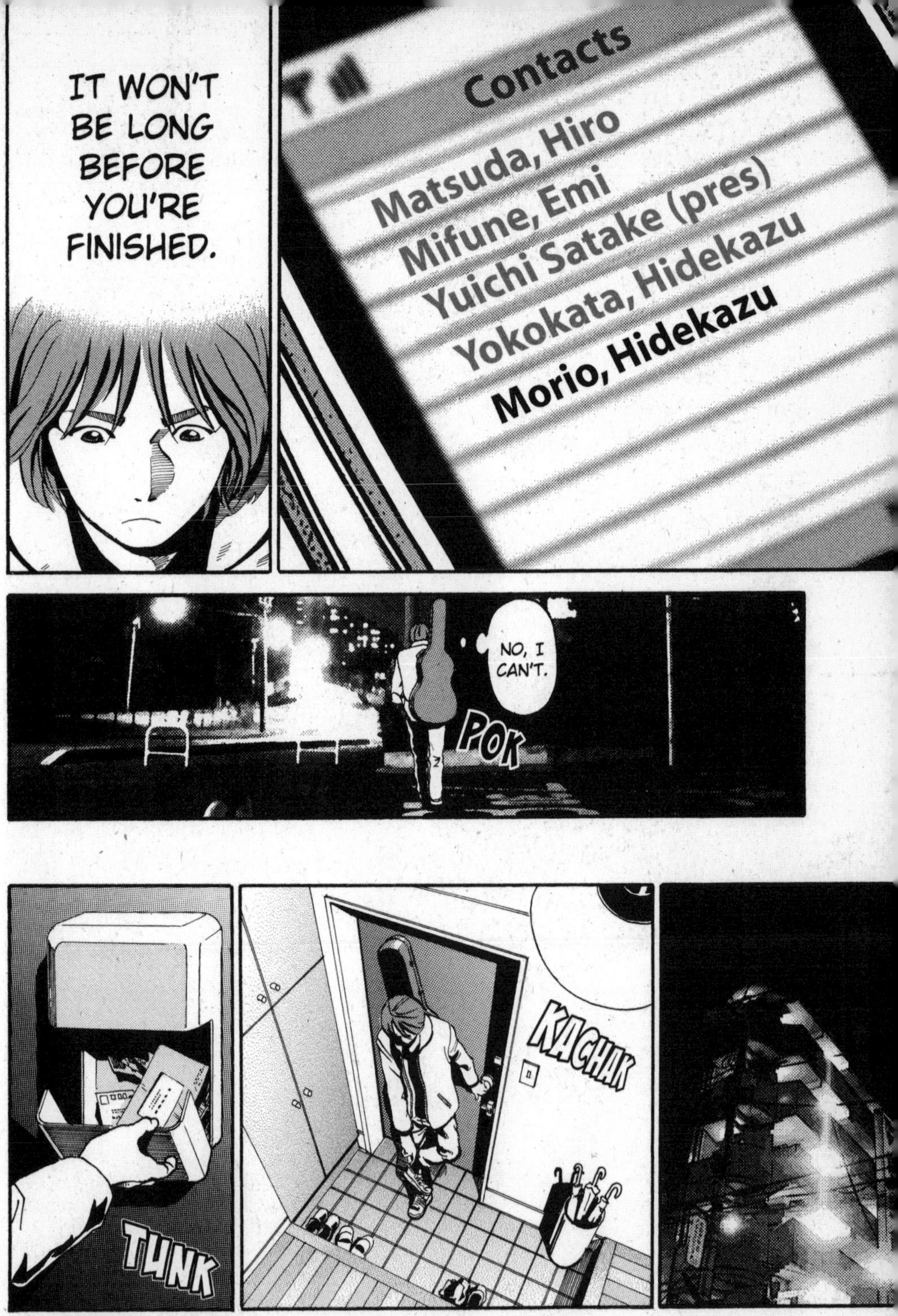
Contacts
Matsuda, Hiro
Mifune, Emi
Yuichi Satake (pres)
Yokokata, Hidekazu
Morio, Hidekazu
IT WON'T BE LONG BEFORE YOU'RE FINISHED.
NO, I CAN'T.
POK
KACHAK
TUNK

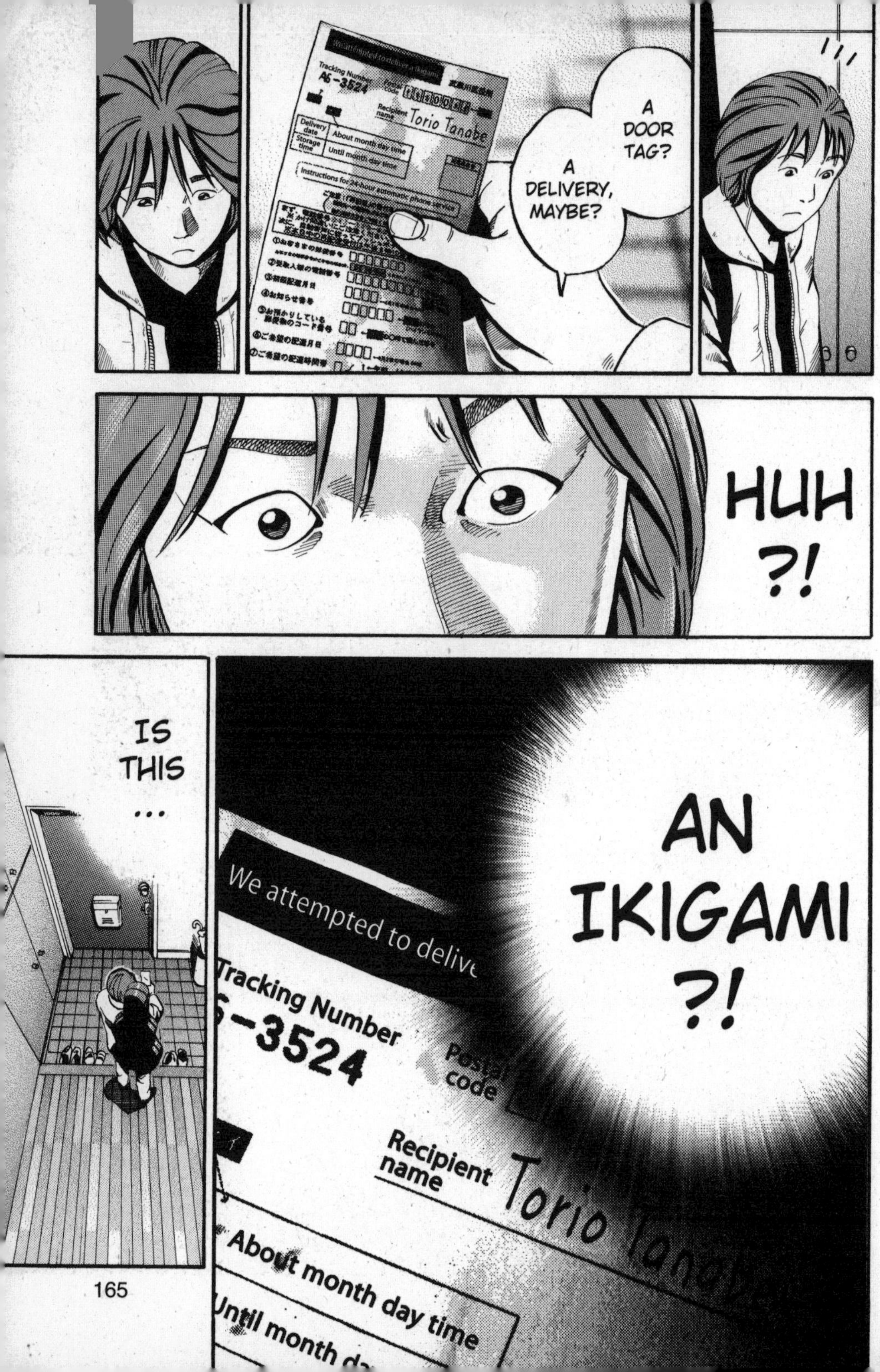

A DOOR TAG?
A DELIVERY, MAYBE?
Tracking Number
A6-3524
Postal code
Recipient name
Torio Tanabe
Delivery date
About month day time
Storage time
Until month day time
HUH?!
AN IKIGAMI?!
We attempted to delive
Tracking Number
6-3524
Postal code
Recipient name
Torio Tanab
About month day time
Until month da
IS THIS...

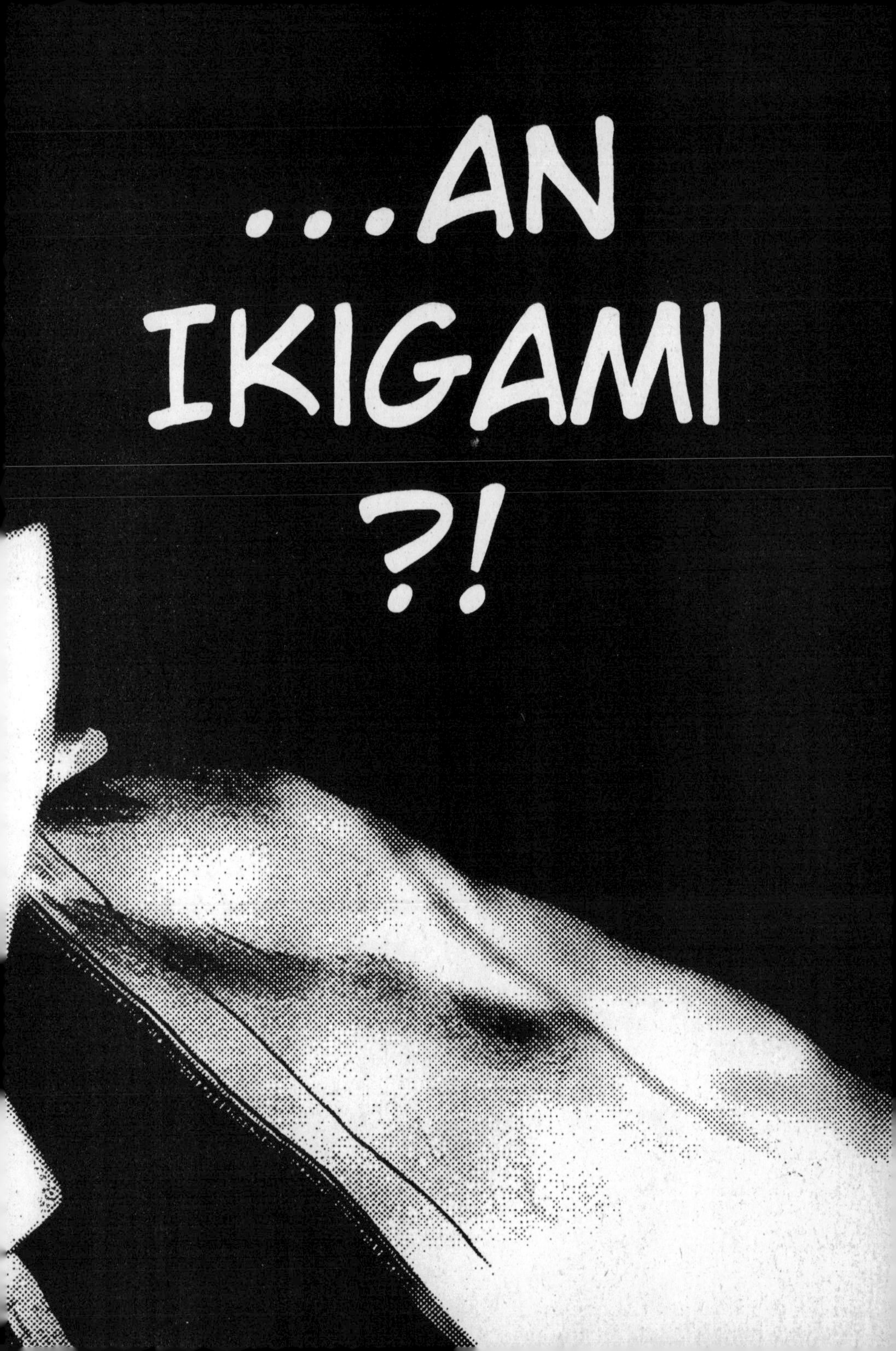
...AN IKIGAMI ?!

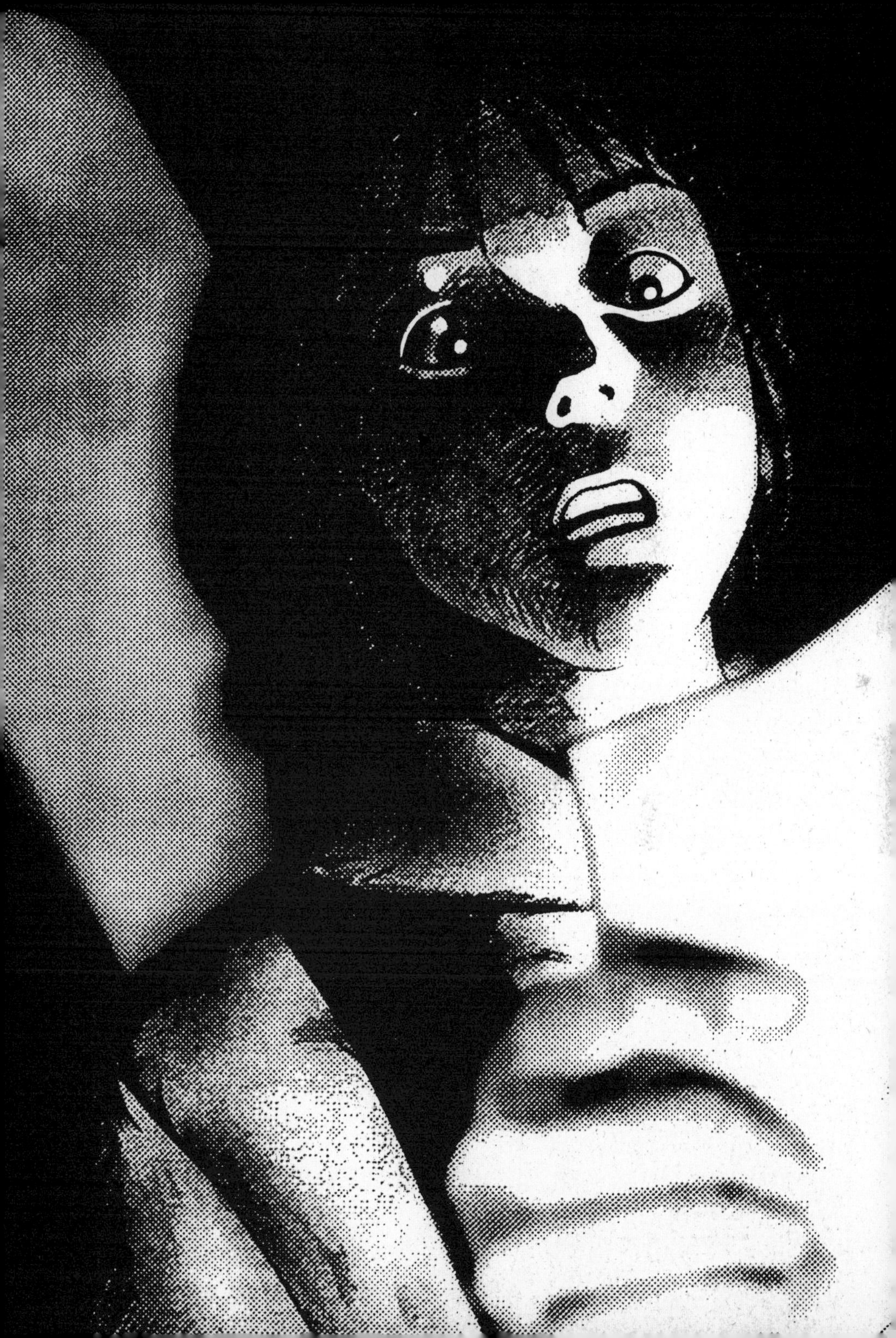

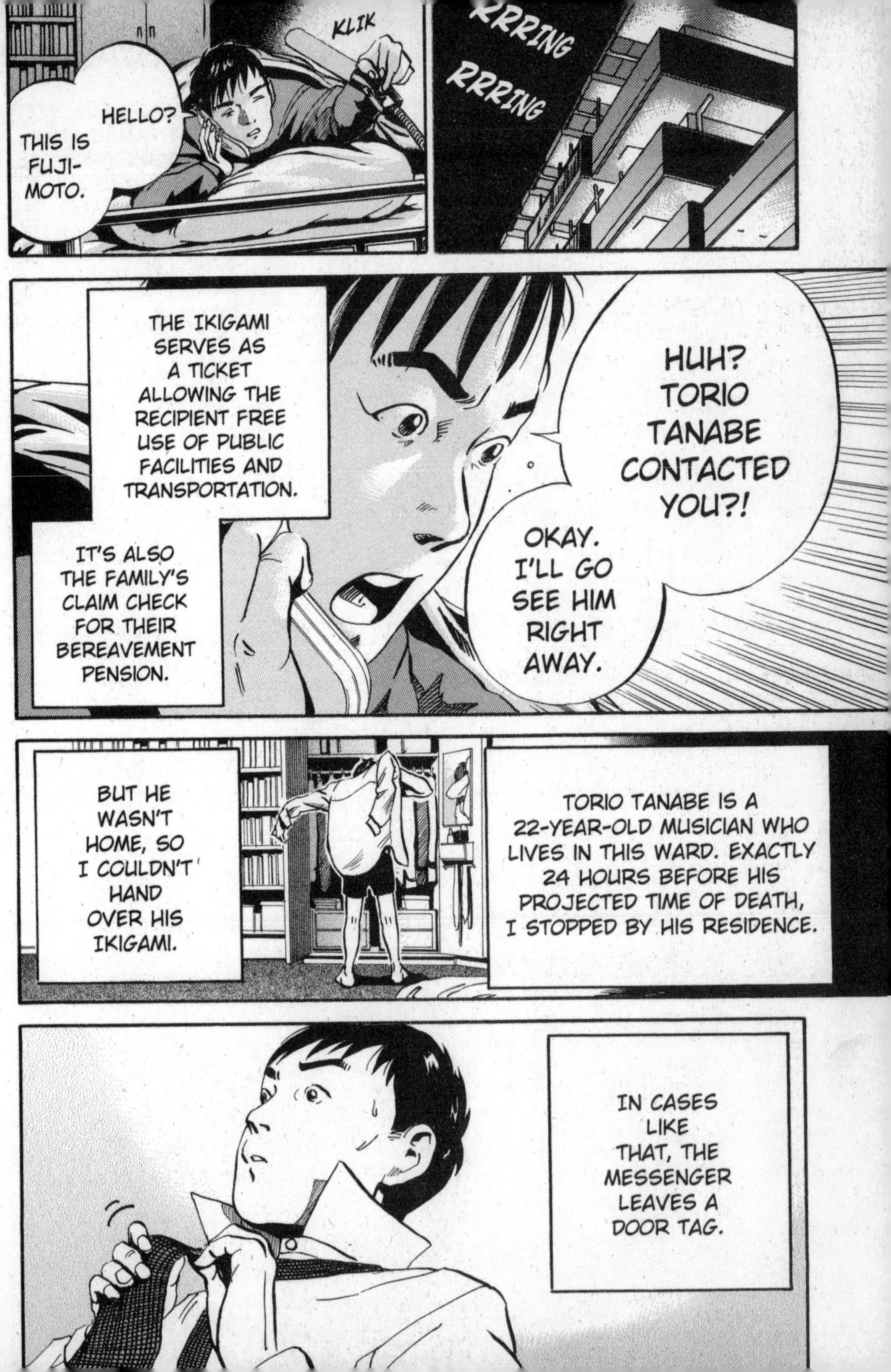
RRRING
RRRING
KLIK
HELLO? THIS IS FUJI-MOTO.
HUH? TORIO TANABE CONTACTED YOU?!
OKAY. I'LL GO SEE HIM RIGHT AWAY.
THE IKIGAMI SERVES AS A TICKET ALLOWING THE RECIPIENT FREE USE OF PUBLIC FACILITIES AND TRANSPORTATION.
IT'S ALSO THE FAMILY'S CLAIM CHECK FOR THEIR BEREAVEMENT PENSION.
TORIO TANABE IS A 22-YEAR-OLD MUSICIAN WHO LIVES IN THIS WARD. EXACTLY 24 HOURS BEFORE HIS PROJECTED TIME OF DEATH, I STOPPED BY HIS RESIDENCE.
BUT HE WASN'T HOME, SO I COULDN'T HAND OVER HIS IKIGAMI.
IN CASES LIKE THAT, THE MESSENGER LEAVES A DOOR TAG.

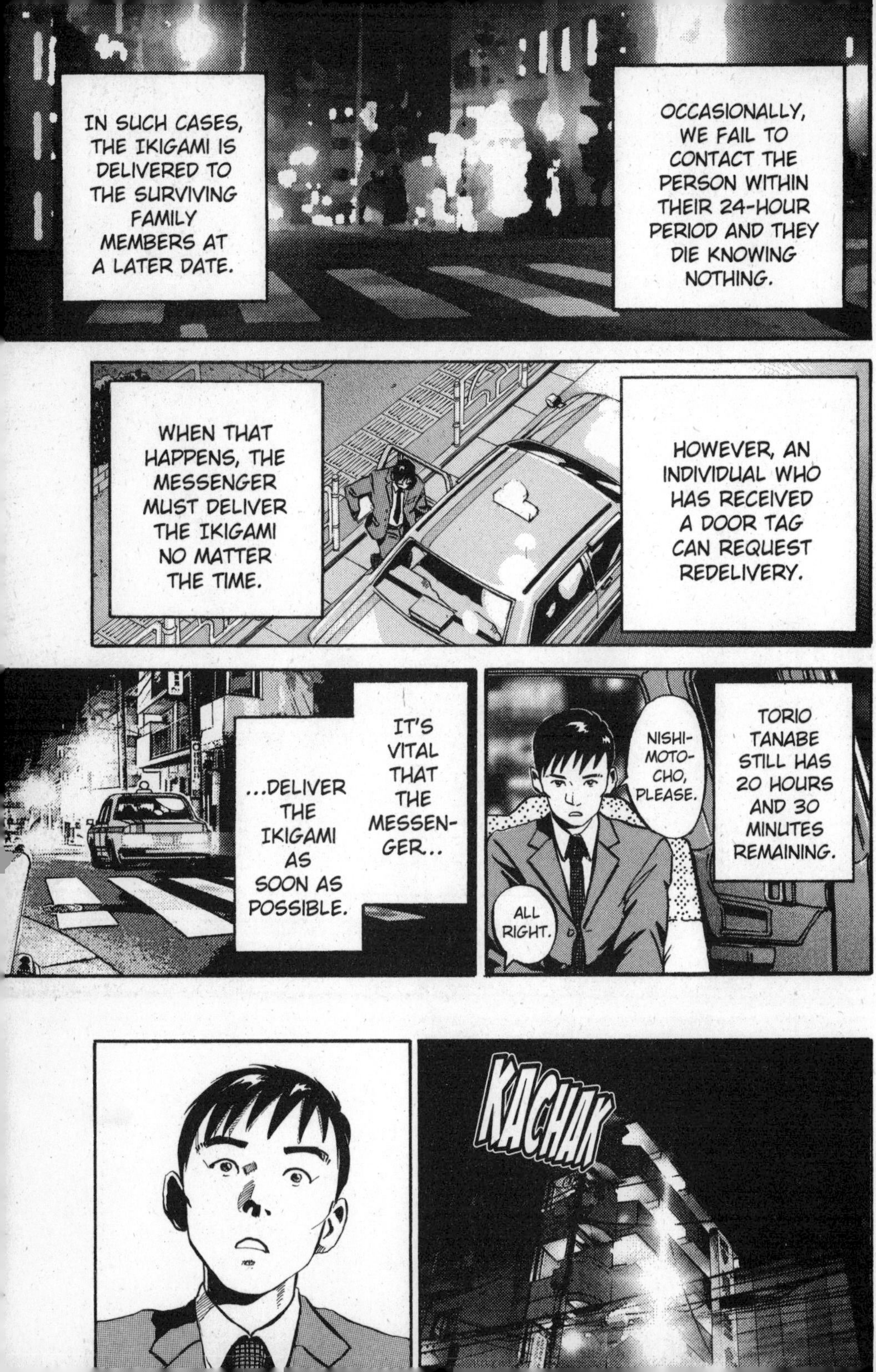
OCCASIONALLY, WE FAIL TO CONTACT THE PERSON WITHIN THEIR 24-HOUR PERIOD AND THEY DIE KNOWING NOTHING.
IN SUCH CASES, THE IKIGAMI IS DELIVERED TO THE SURVIVING FAMILY MEMBERS AT A LATER DATE.
HOWEVER, AN INDIVIDUAL WHO HAS RECEIVED A DOOR TAG CAN REQUEST REDELIVERY.
WHEN THAT HAPPENS, THE MESSENGER MUST DELIVER THE IKIGAMI NO MATTER THE TIME.
TORIO TANABE STILL HAS 20 HOURS AND 30 MINUTES REMAINING.
NISHI-MOTO-CHO, PLEASE.
ALL RIGHT.
IT'S VITAL THAT THE MESSEN-GER...
...DELIVER THE IKIGAMI AS SOON AS POSSIBLE.
KACHAK

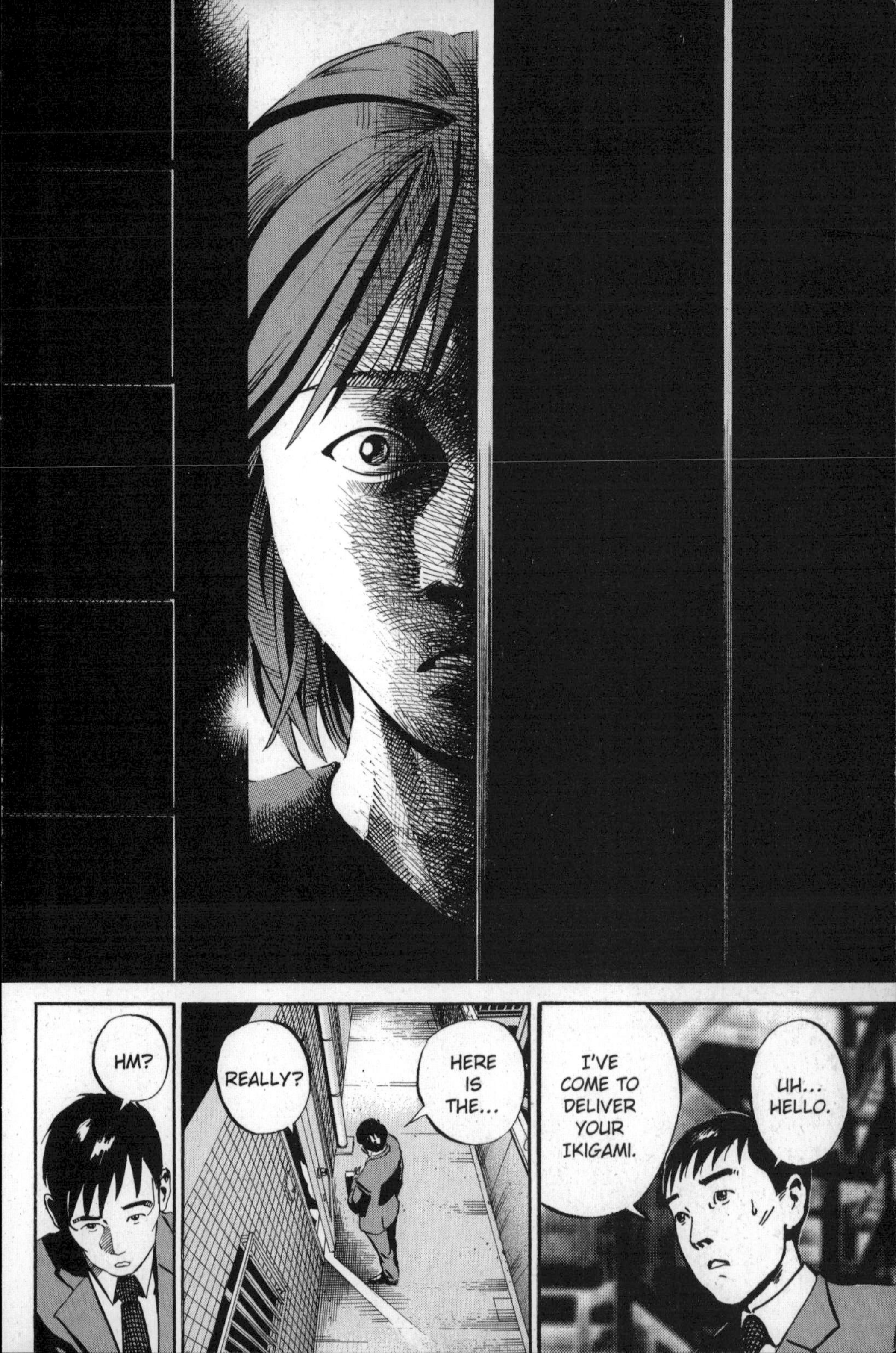
UH... HELLO.
I'VE COME TO DELIVER YOUR IKIGAMI.
HERE IS THE...
REALLY?
HM?

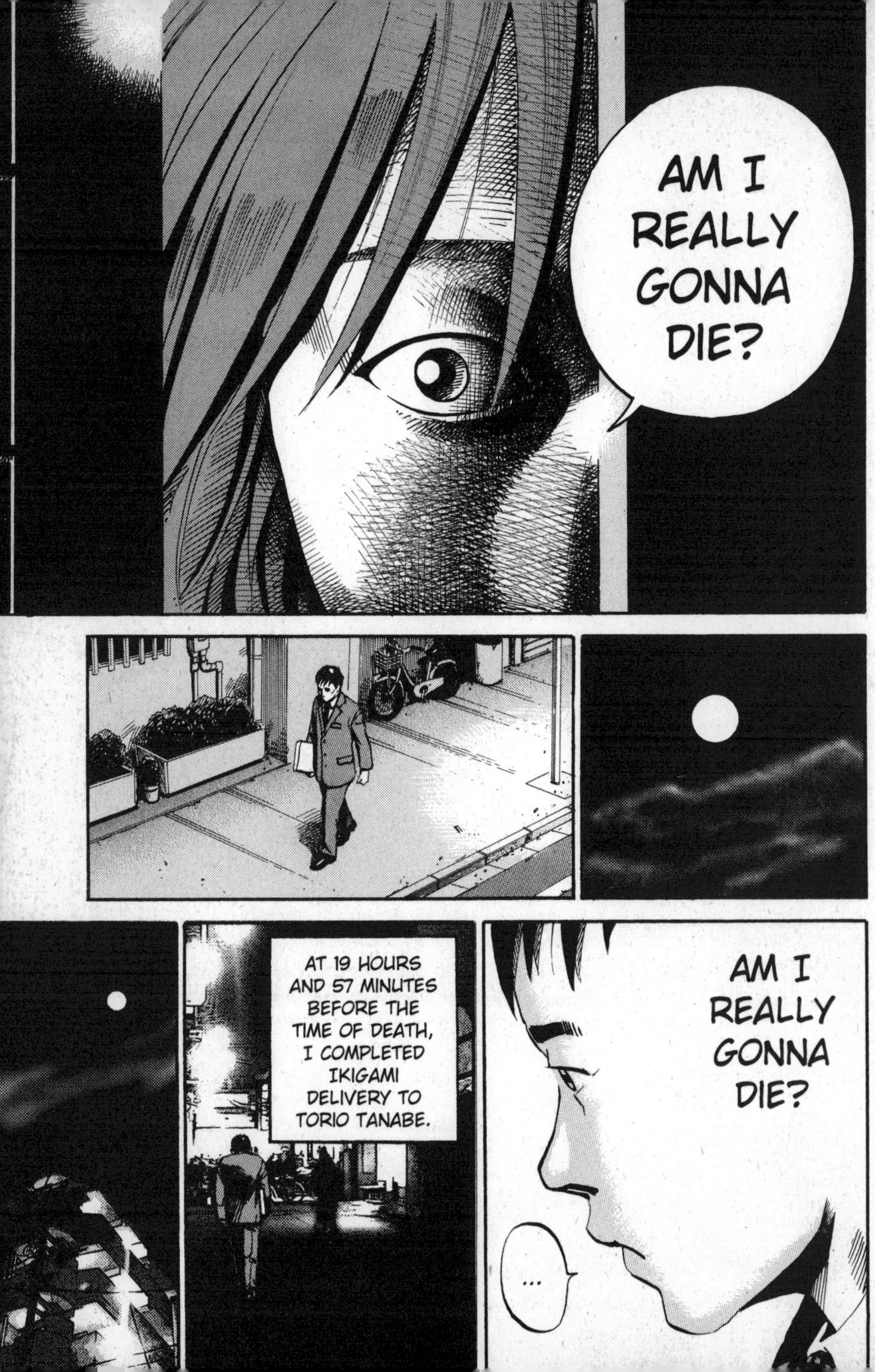
AM I REALLY GONNA DIE?
AM I REALLY GONNA DIE?
...
AT 19 HOURS AND 57 MINUTES BEFORE THE TIME OF DEATH, I COMPLETED IKIGAMI DELIVERY TO TORIO TANABE.

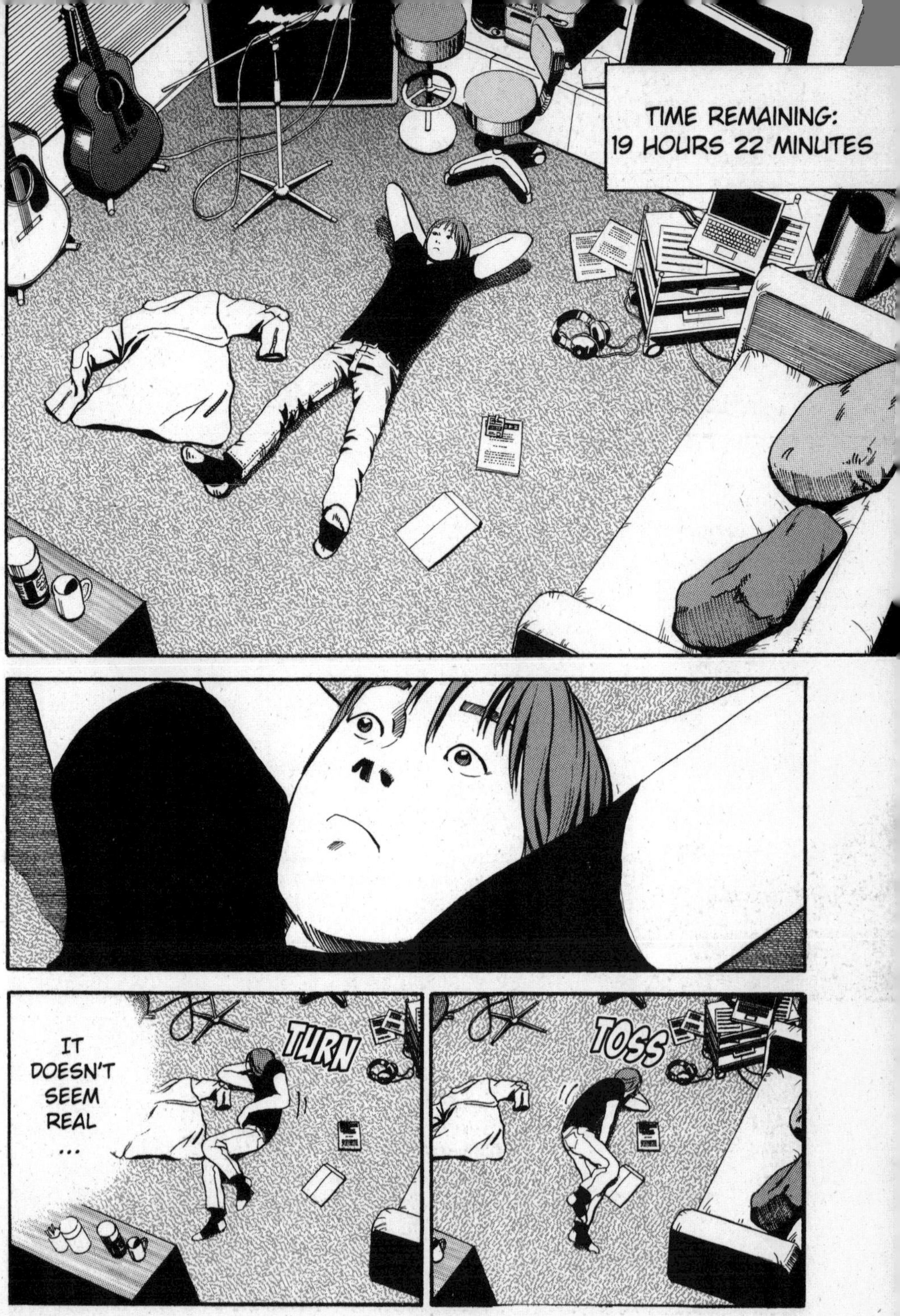
TIME REMAINING:
19 HOURS 22 MINUTES
TOSS
TURN
IT DOESN'T SEEM REAL ...

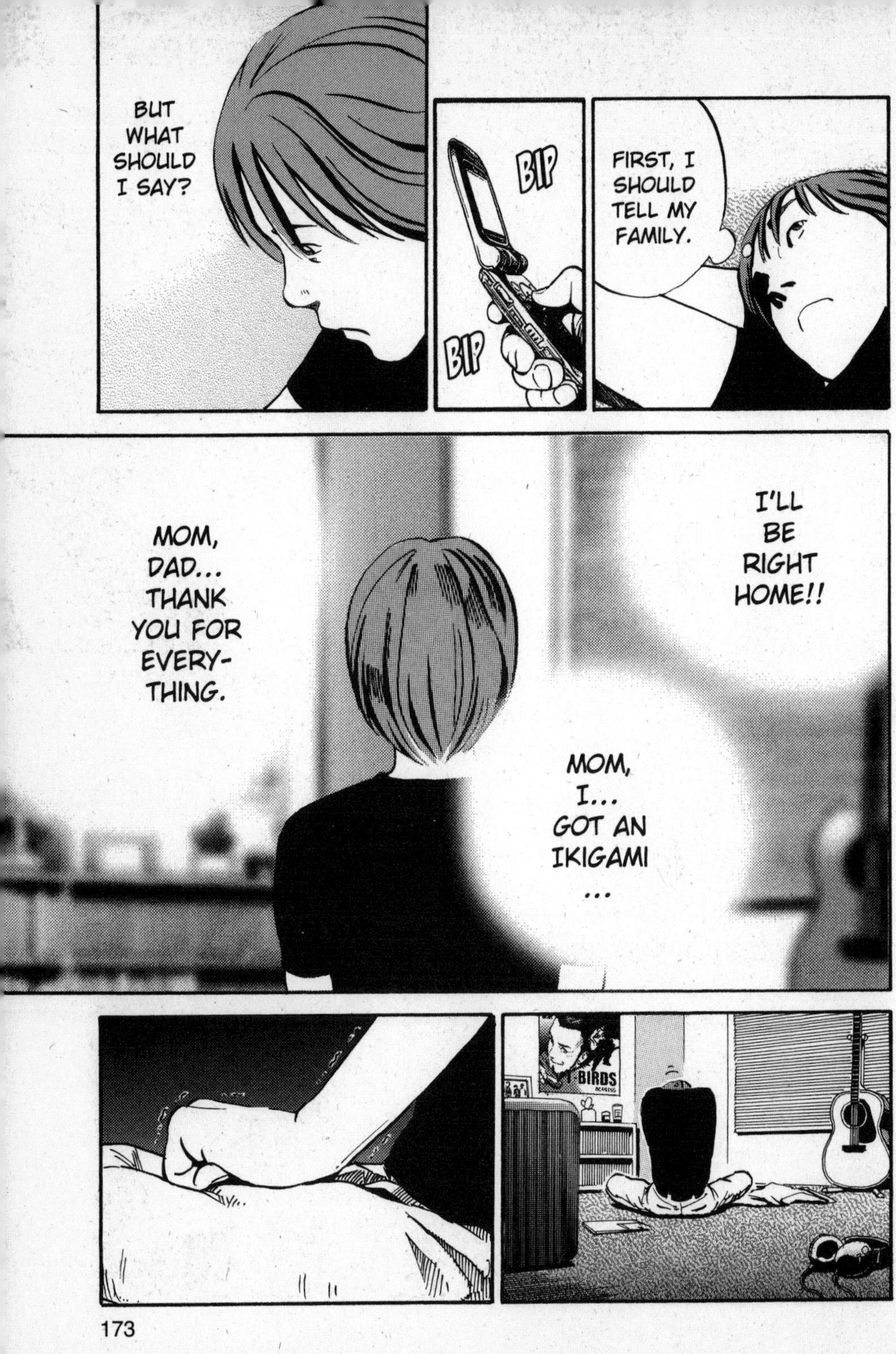
FIRST, I SHOULD TELL MY FAMILY.
BIP
BIP
BUT WHAT SHOULD I SAY?
I'LL BE RIGHT HOME!!
MOM, DAD... THANK YOU FOR EVERY-THING.
MOM, I... GOT AN IKIGAMI ...
T-BIRDS

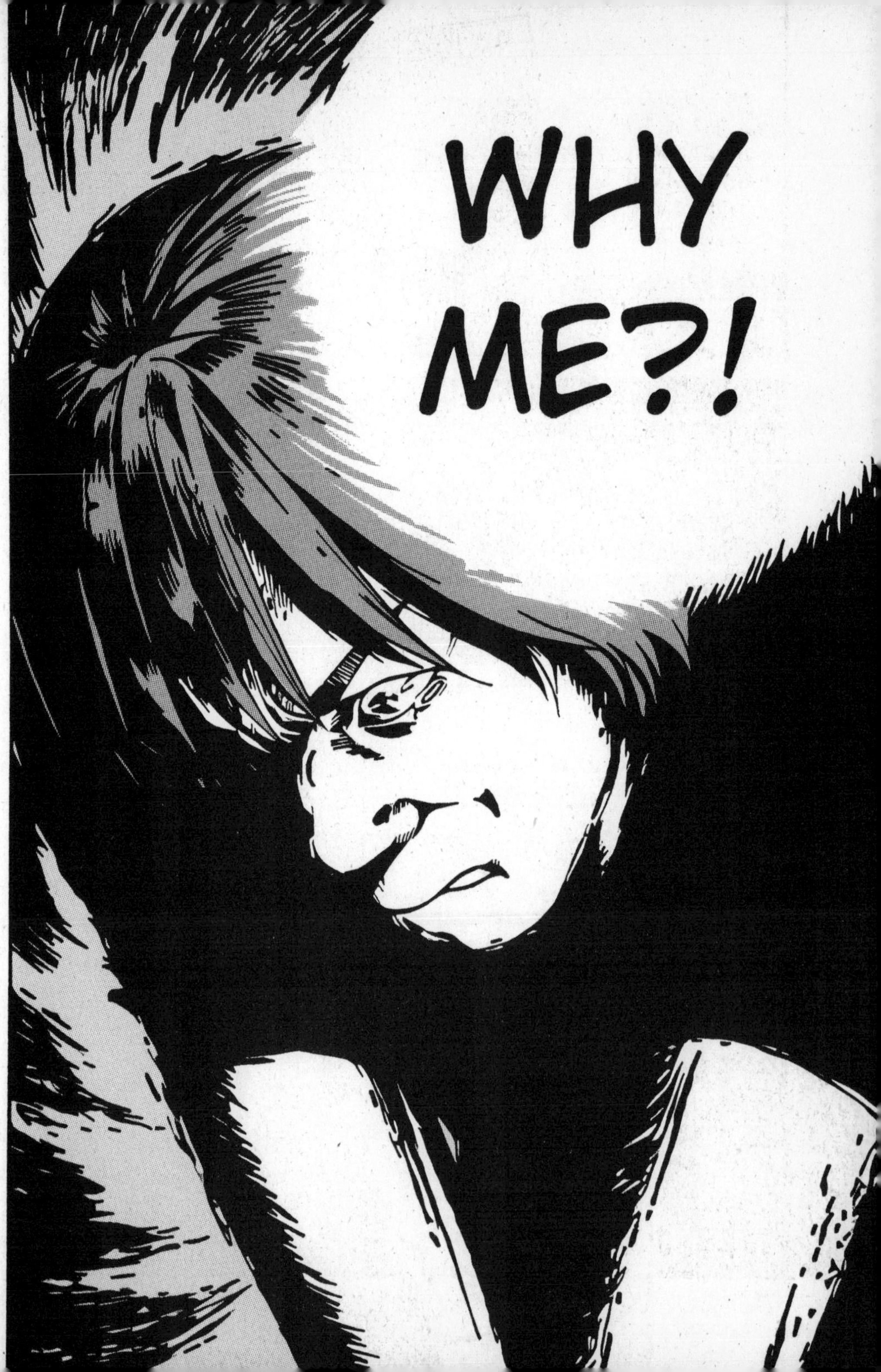
WHY ME?!

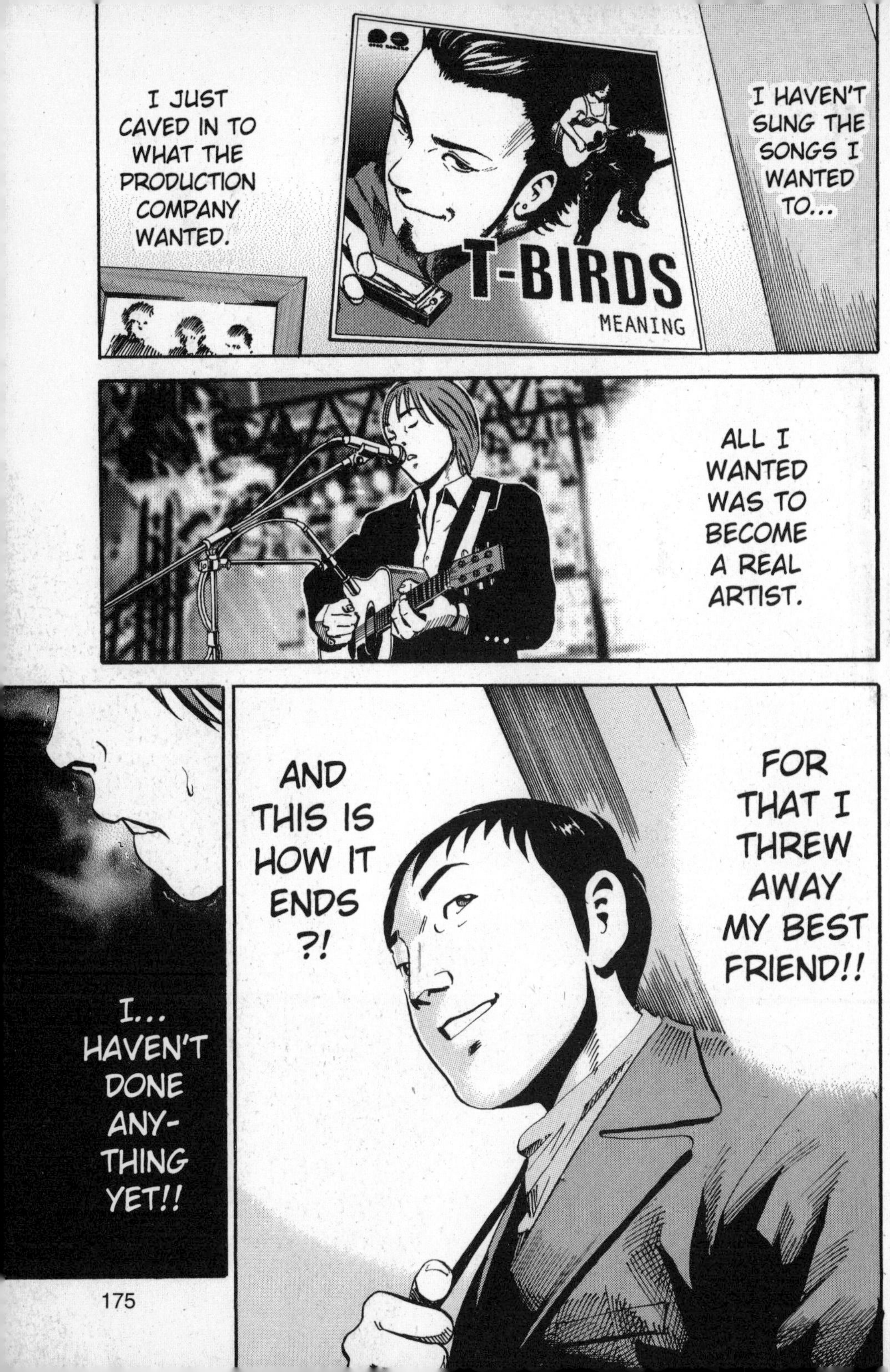
I HAVEN'T SUNG THE SONGS I WANTED TO...
T-BIRDS
MEANING
I JUST CAVED IN TO WHAT THE PRODUCTION COMPANY WANTED.
ALL I WANTED WAS TO BECOME A REAL ARTIST.
FOR THAT I THREW AWAY MY BEST FRIEND!!
AND THIS IS HOW IT ENDS?!
I... HAVEN'T DONE ANYTHING YET!!

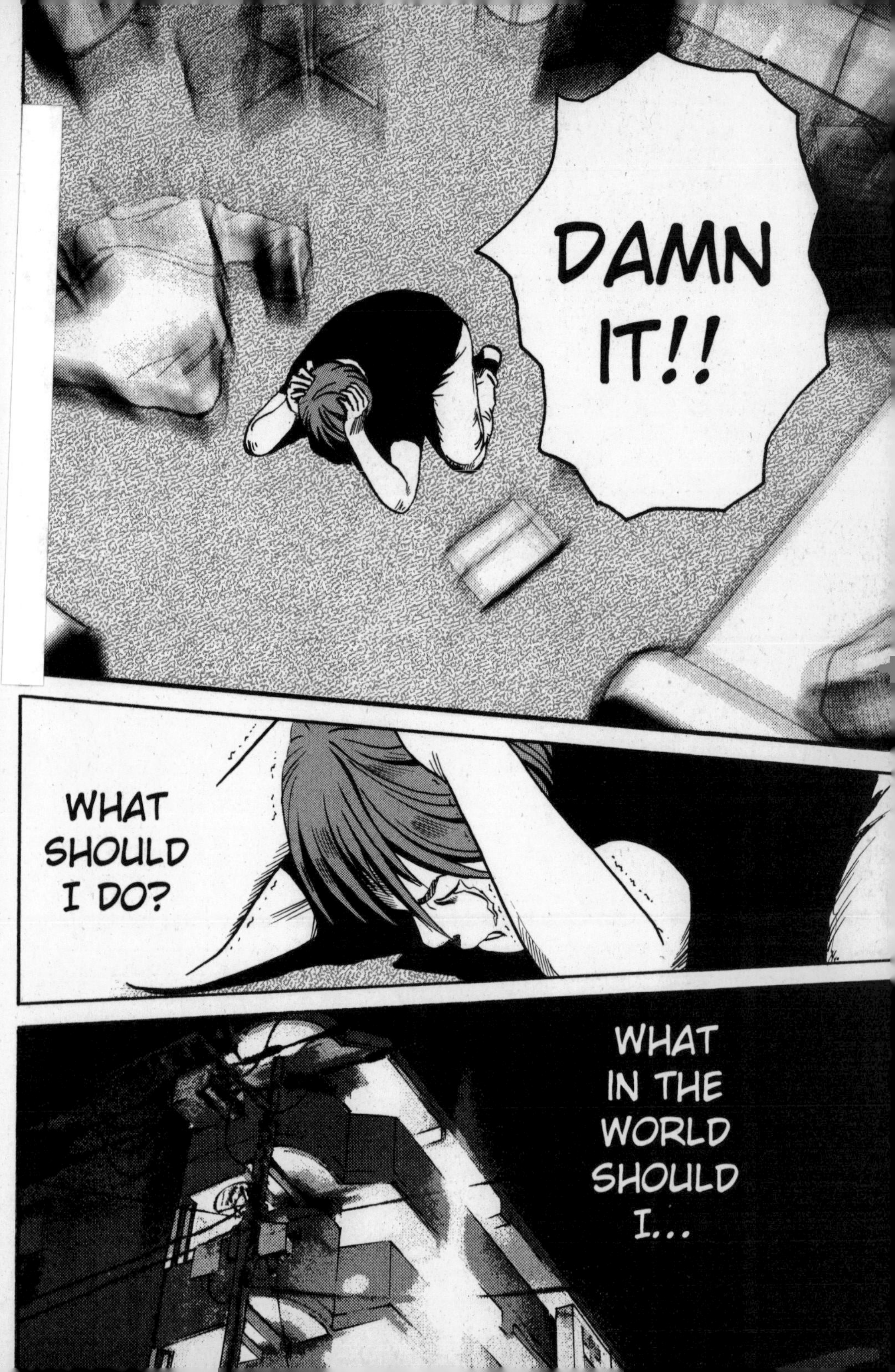
DAMN IT!!
WHAT SHOULD I DO?
WHAT IN THE WORLD SHOULD I...

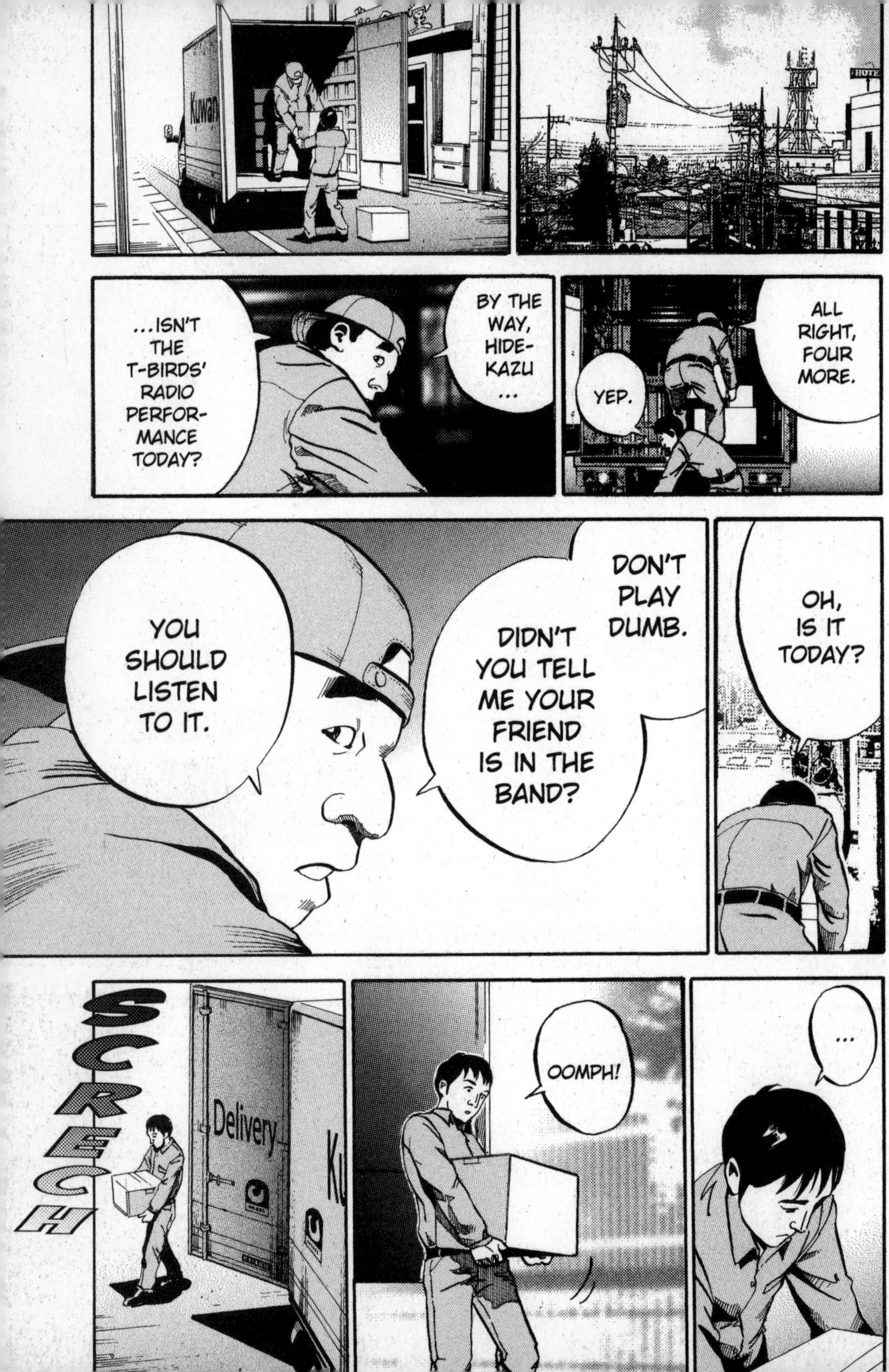
ALL RIGHT, FOUR MORE.
YEP.
BY THE WAY, HIDE-KAZU ...
...ISN'T THE T-BIRDS' RADIO PERFORMANCE TODAY?
OH, IS IT TODAY?
DON'T PLAY DUMB.
DIDN'T YOU TELL ME YOUR FRIEND IS IN THE BAND?
YOU SHOULD LISTEN TO IT.
...
OOMPH!
SCRECH
Delivery

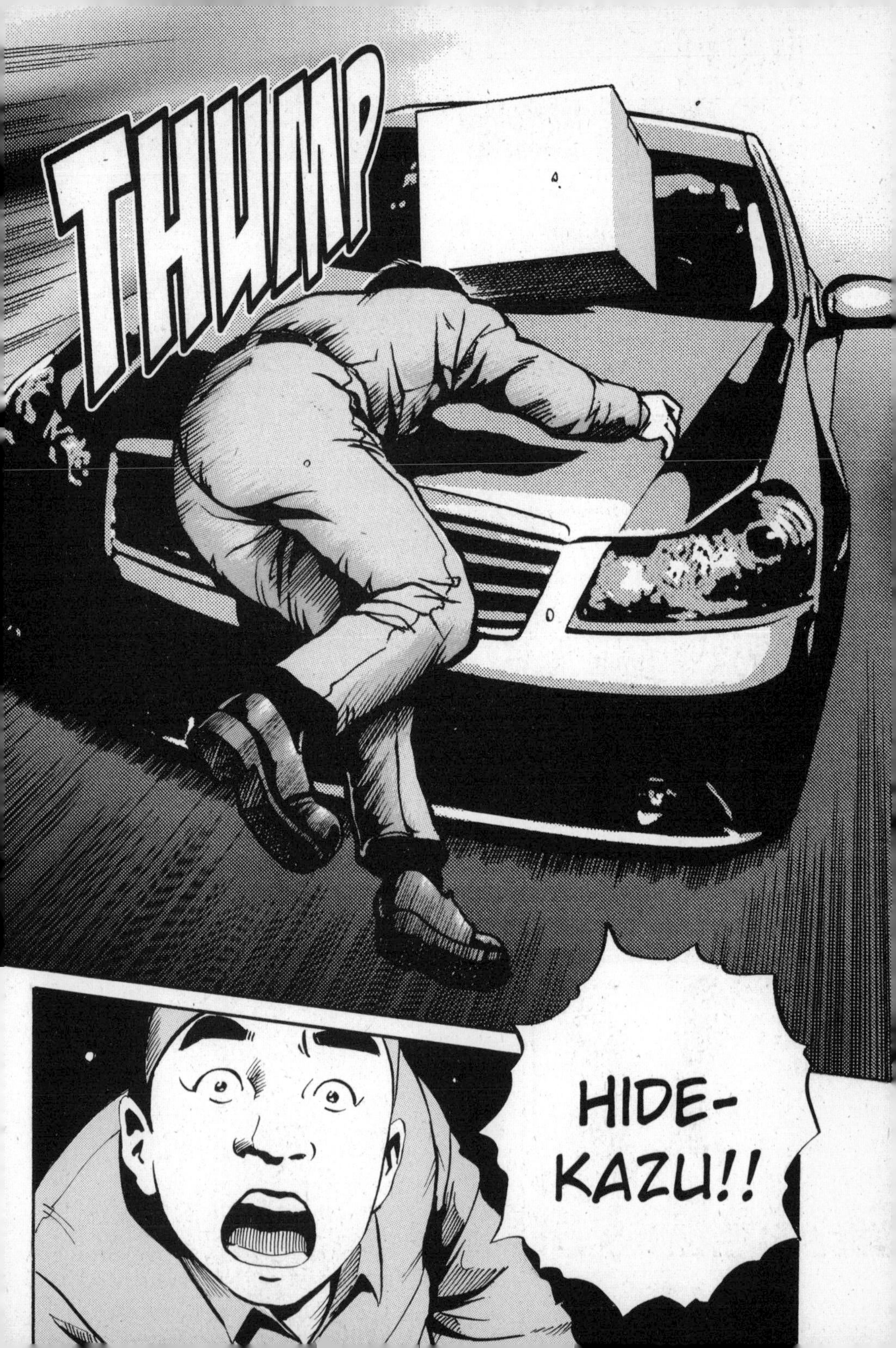
THUMP
HIDE-
KAZU!!

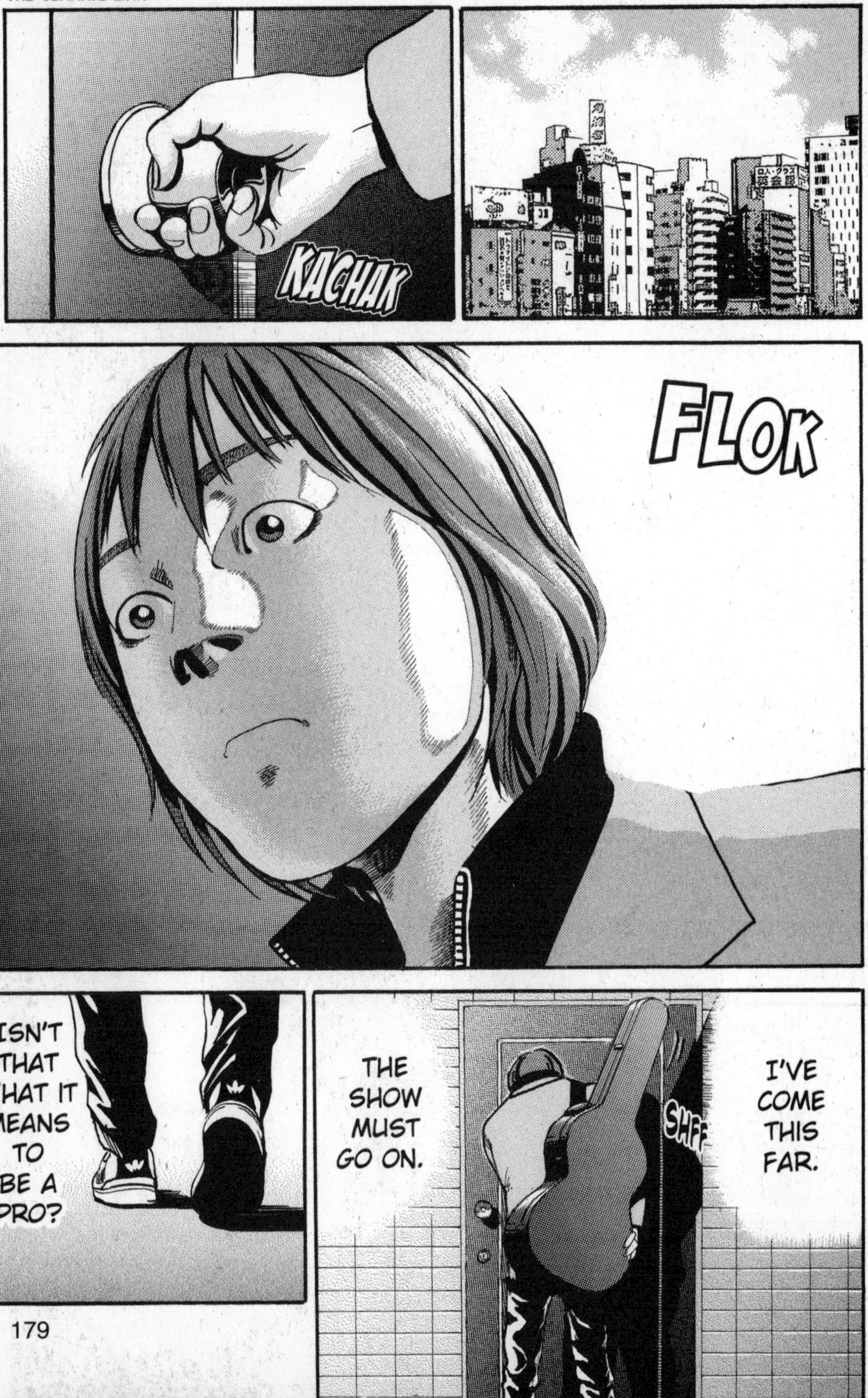
KACHAK
FLOK
I'VE COME THIS FAR.
SHFF
THE SHOW MUST GO ON.
ISN'T THAT WHAT IT MEANS TO BE A PRO?

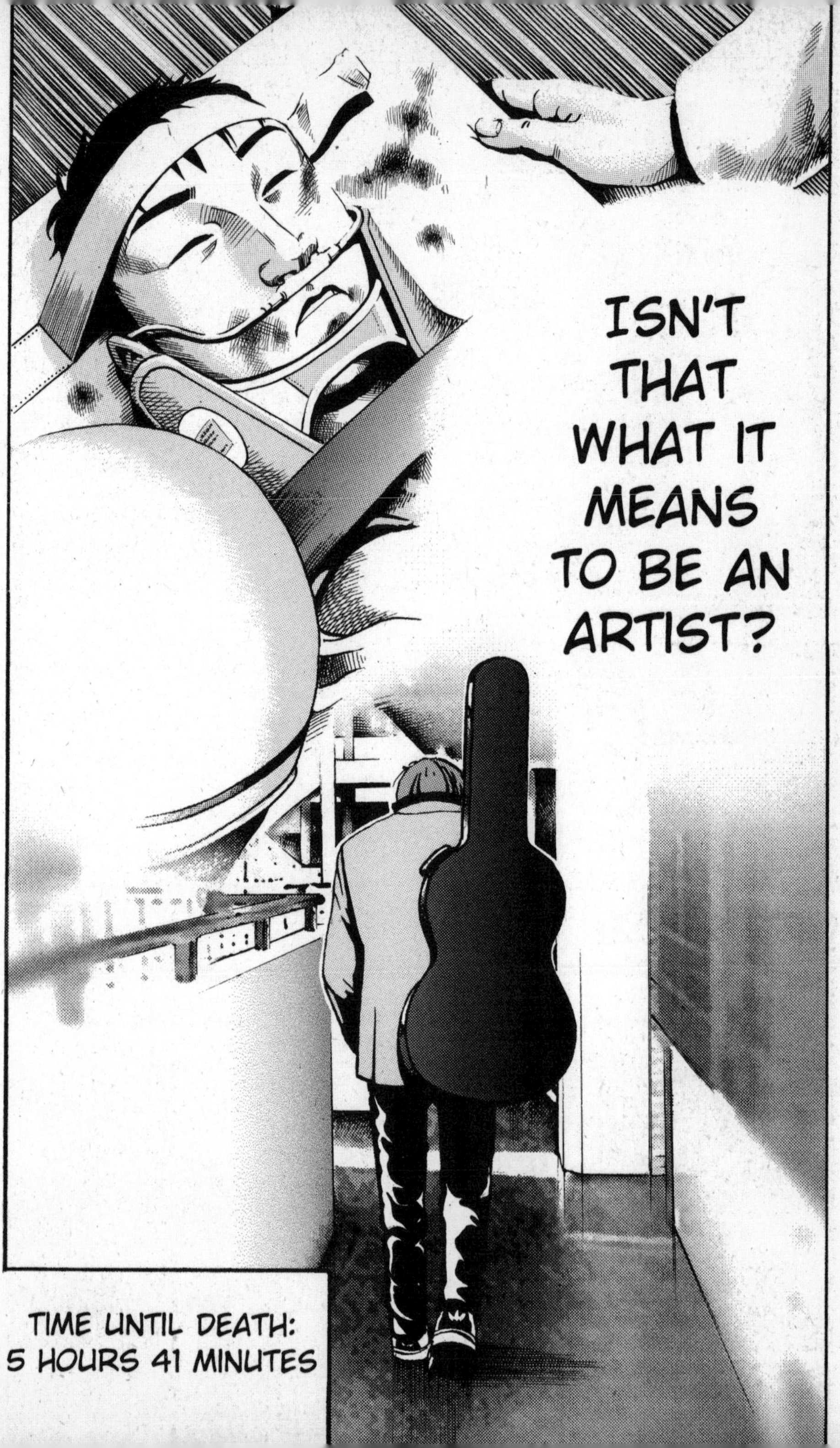
ISN'T THAT WHAT IT MEANS TO BE AN ARTIST?
TIME UNTIL DEATH: 5 HOURS 41 MINUTES

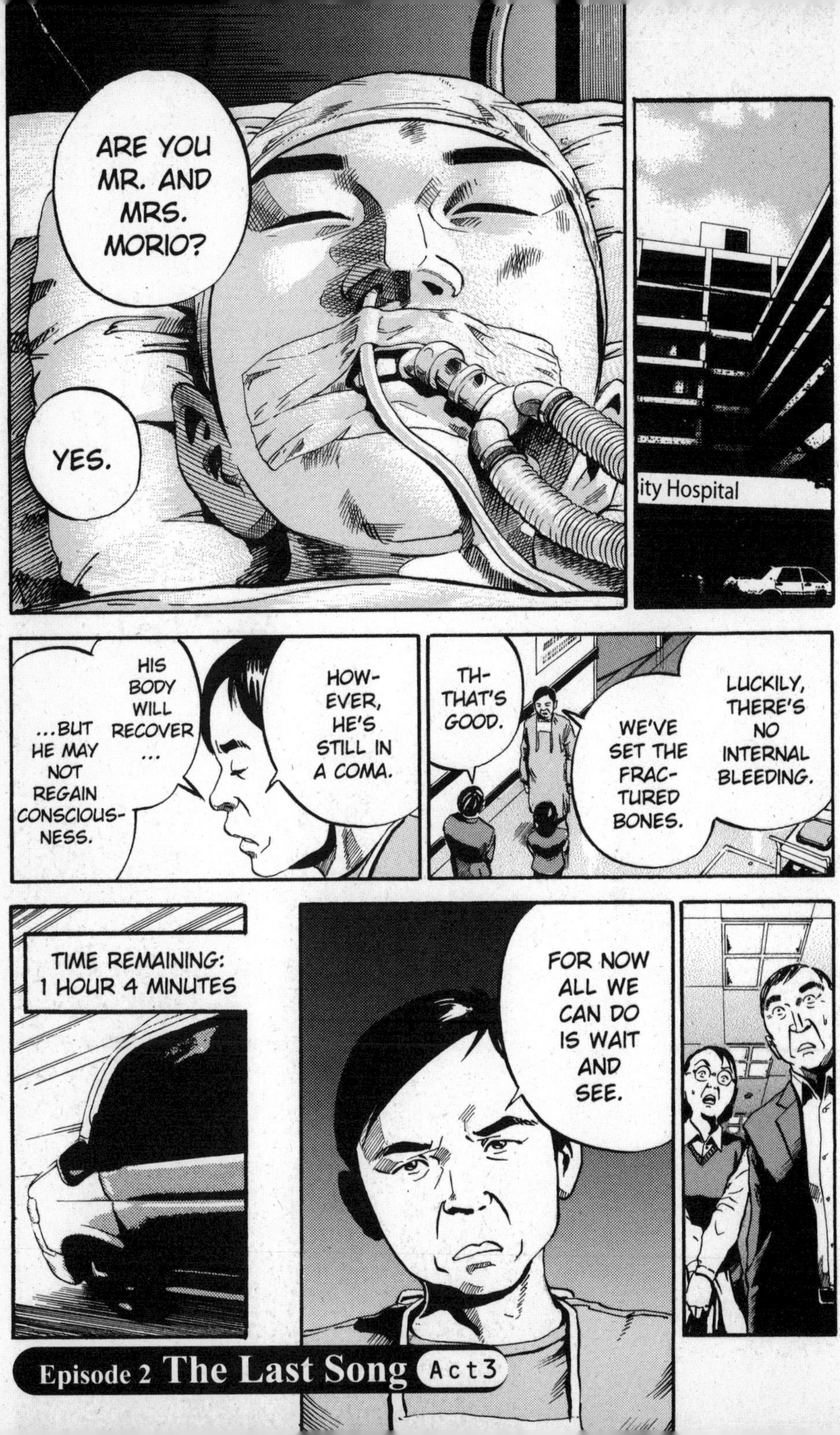
ity Hospital
ARE YOU MR. AND MRS. MORIO?
YES.
LUCKILY, THERE'S NO INTERNAL BLEEDING.
WE'VE SET THE FRACTURED BONES.
TH- THAT'S GOOD.
HOWEVER, HE'S STILL IN A COMA.
HIS BODY WILL RECOVER...
...BUT HE MAY NOT REGAIN CONSCIOUSNESS.
FOR NOW ALL WE CAN DO IS WAIT AND SEE.
TIME REMAINING: 1 HOUR 4 MINUTES

Episode 2 The Last Song Act3

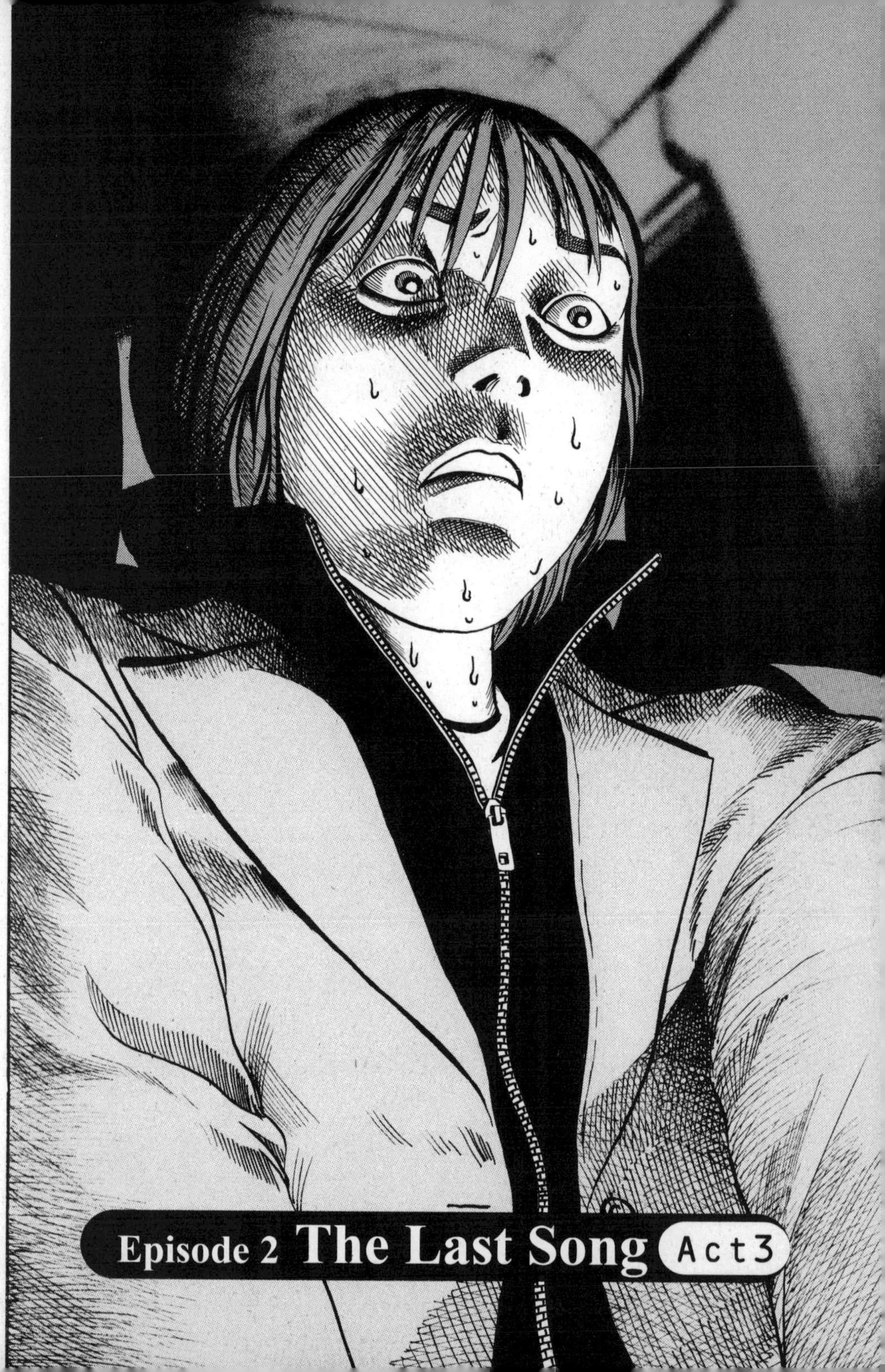

Episode 2 The Last Song Act3

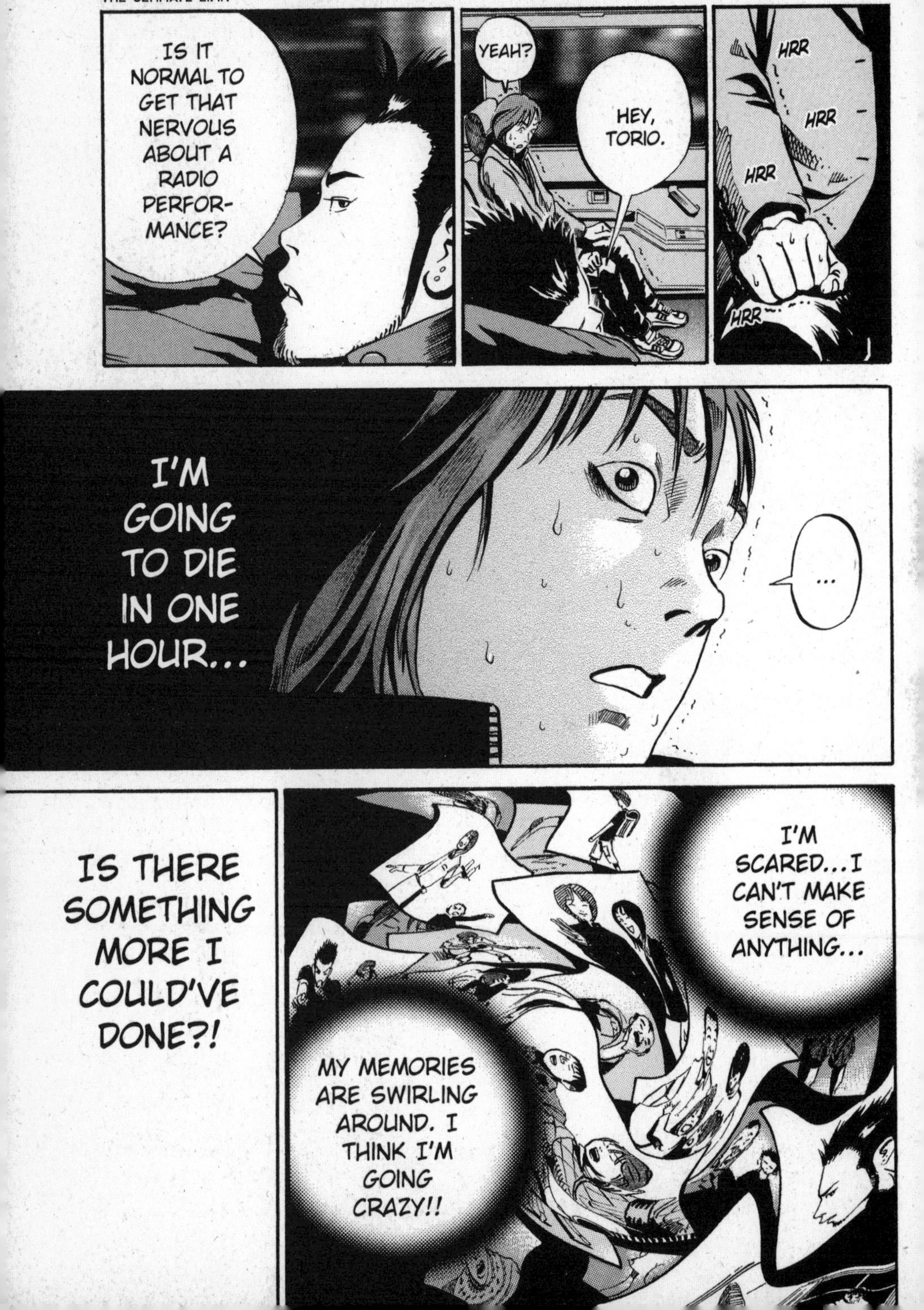
HRR
HRR
HRR
HRR
HEY, TORIO.
YEAH?
IS IT NORMAL TO GET THAT NERVOUS ABOUT A RADIO PERFORMANCE?
...
I'M GOING TO DIE IN ONE HOUR...
I'M SCARED...I CAN'T MAKE SENSE OF ANYTHING...
MY MEMORIES ARE SWIRLING AROUND. I THINK I'M GOING CRAZY!!
IS THERE SOMETHING MORE I COULD'VE DONE?!

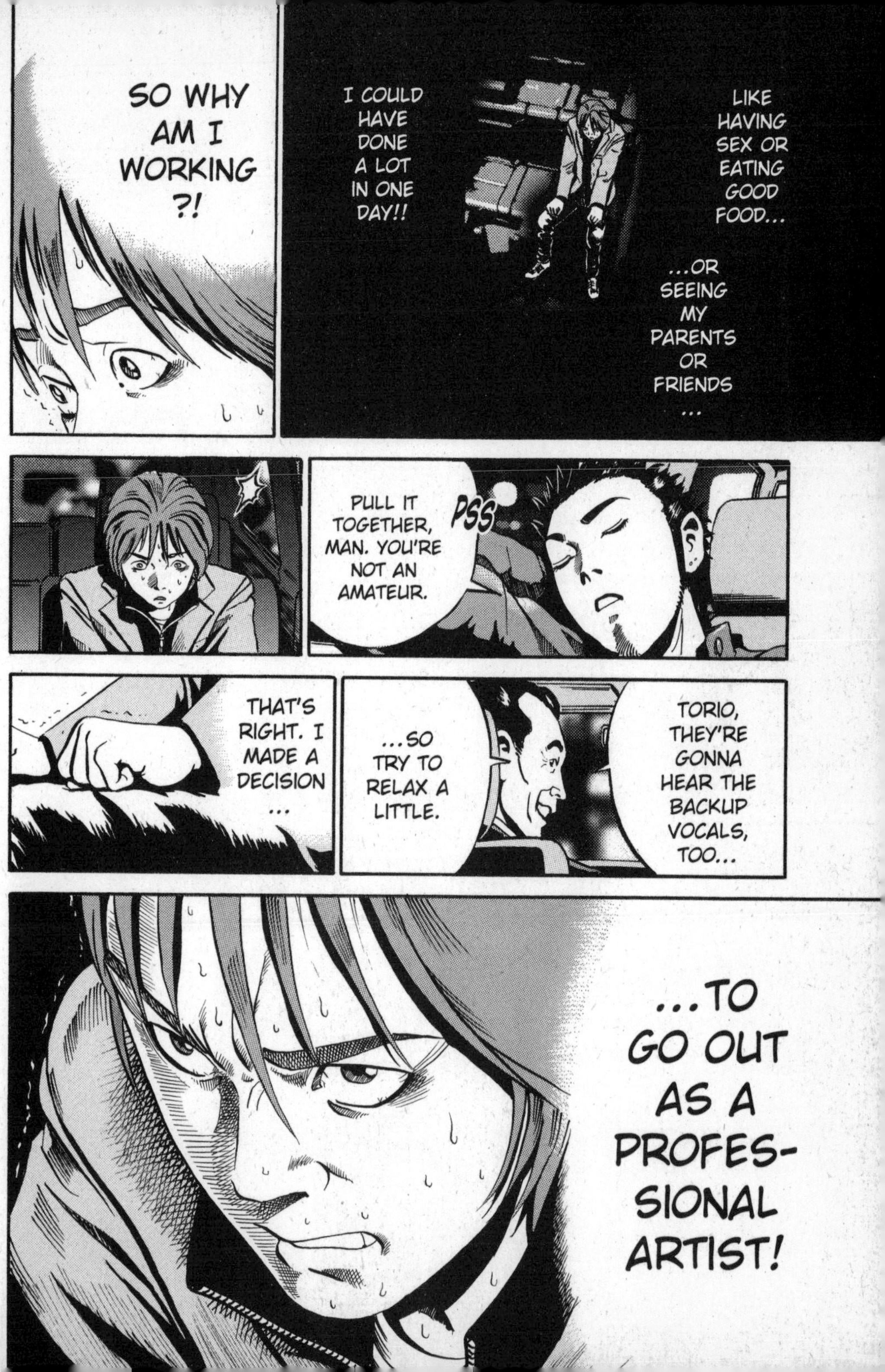
LIKE HAVING SEX OR EATING GOOD FOOD...
...OR SEEING MY PARENTS OR FRIENDS...
I COULD HAVE DONE A LOT IN ONE DAY!!
SO WHY AM I WORKING ?!
PSS
PULL IT TOGETHER, MAN. YOU'RE NOT AN AMATEUR.
TORIO, THEY'RE GONNA HEAR THE BACKUP VOCALS, TOO...
...SO TRY TO RELAX A LITTLE.
THAT'S RIGHT. I MADE A DECISION...
...TO GO OUT AS A PROFES-SIONAL ARTIST!

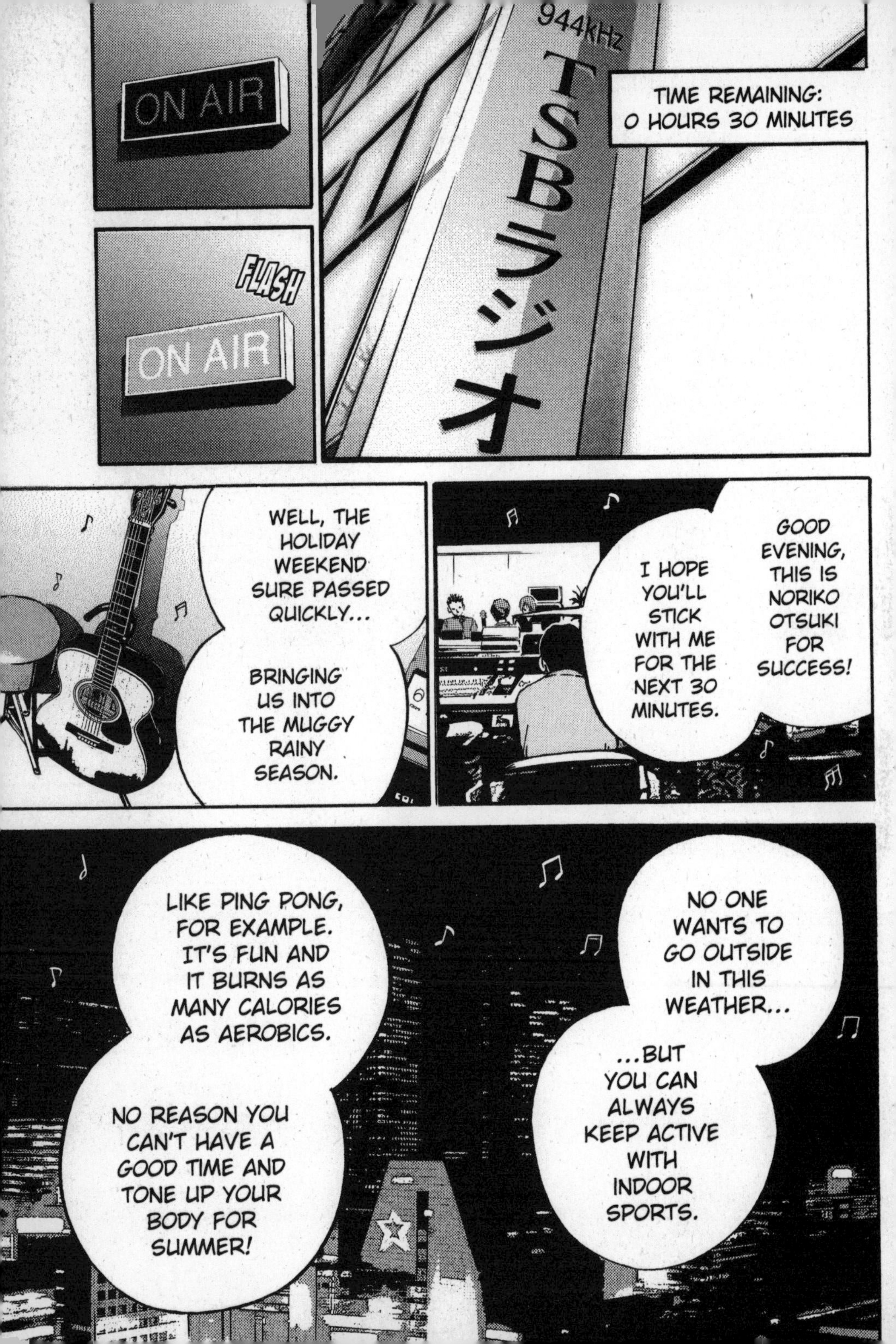
944kHz
TSBラジオ
TIME REMAINING: 0 HOURS 30 MINUTES
ON AIR
FLASH
ON AIR
GOOD EVENING, THIS IS NORIKO OTSUKI FOR SUCCESS!
I HOPE YOU'LL STICK WITH ME FOR THE NEXT 30 MINUTES.
WELL, THE HOLIDAY WEEKEND SURE PASSED QUICKLY...
BRINGING US INTO THE MUGGY RAINY SEASON.
NO ONE WANTS TO GO OUTSIDE IN THIS WEATHER...
...BUT YOU CAN ALWAYS KEEP ACTIVE WITH INDOOR SPORTS.
LIKE PING PONG, FOR EXAMPLE. IT'S FUN AND IT BURNS AS MANY CALORIES AS AEROBICS.
NO REASON YOU CAN'T HAVE A GOOD TIME AND TONE UP YOUR BODY FOR SUMMER!

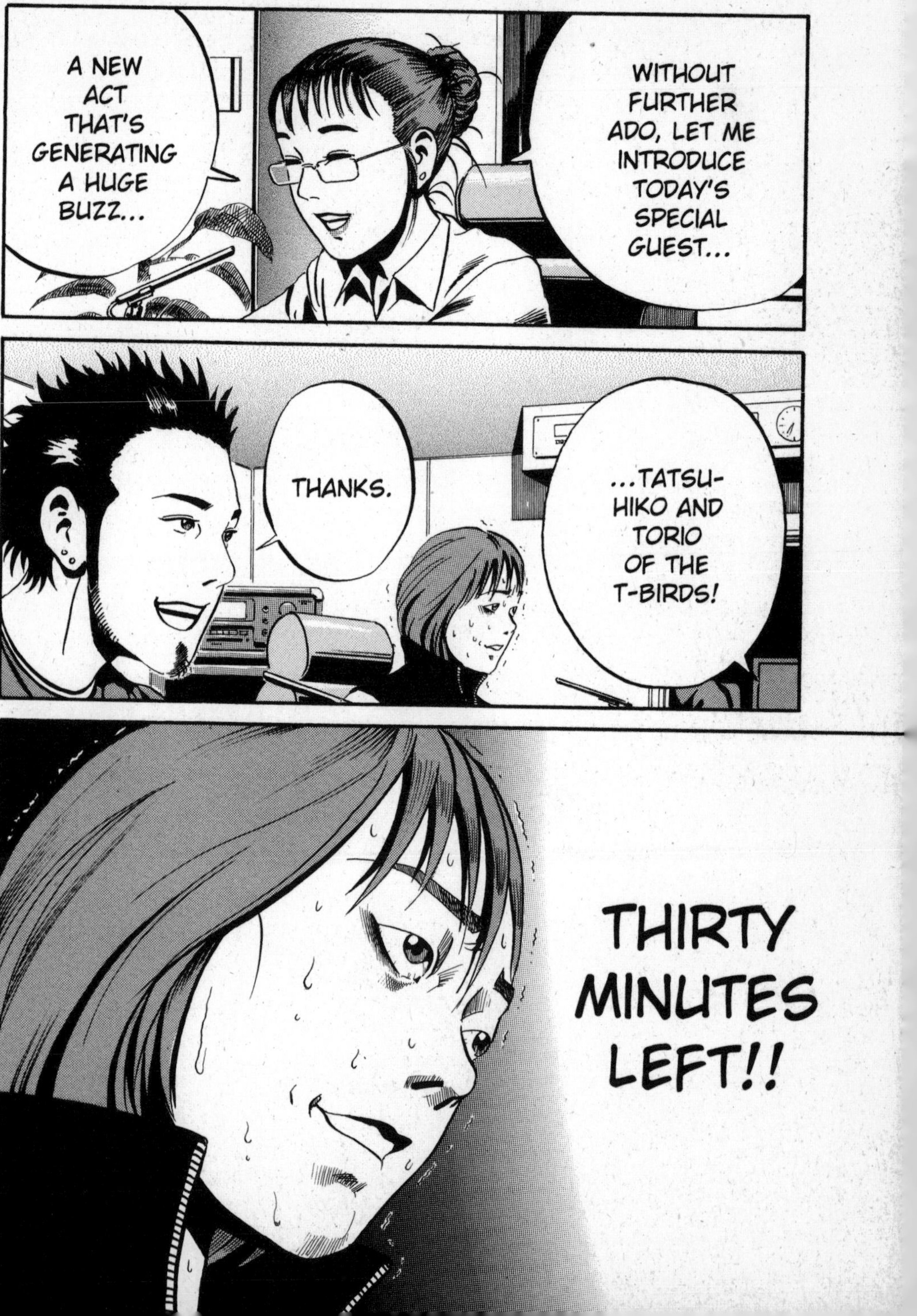
WITHOUT FURTHER ADO, LET ME INTRODUCE TODAY'S SPECIAL GUEST...
A NEW ACT THAT'S GENERATING A HUGE BUZZ...
...TATSU-HIKO AND TORIO OF THE T-BIRDS!
THANKS.
THIRTY MINUTES LEFT!!

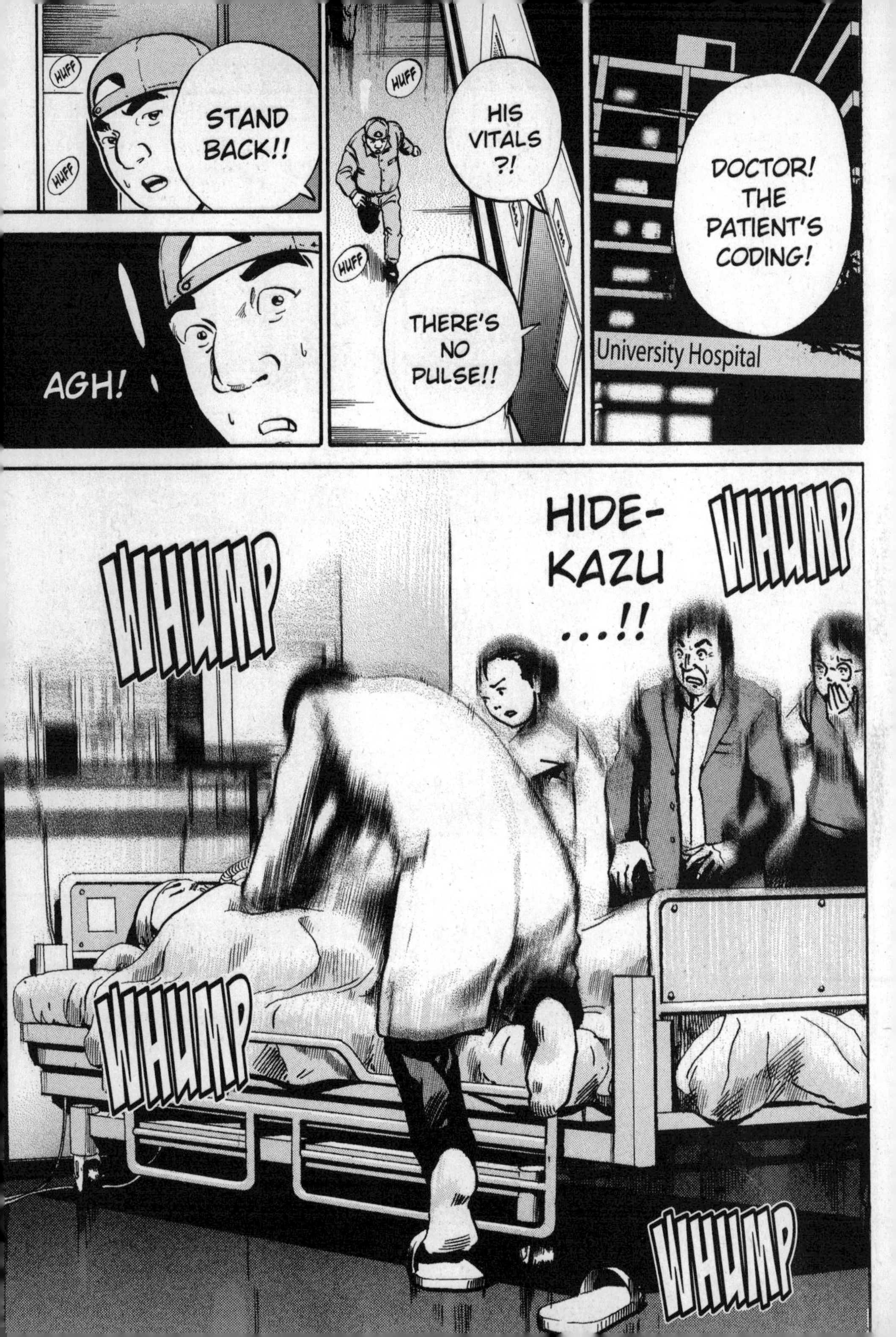
DOCTOR! THE PATIENT'S CODING!
University Hospital
HUFF
HIS VITALS ?!
HUFF
THERE'S NO PULSE!!
HUFF
HUFF
STAND BACK!!
AGH!
WHUMP
HIDE-KAZU ...!!
WHUMP
WHUMP
WHUMP

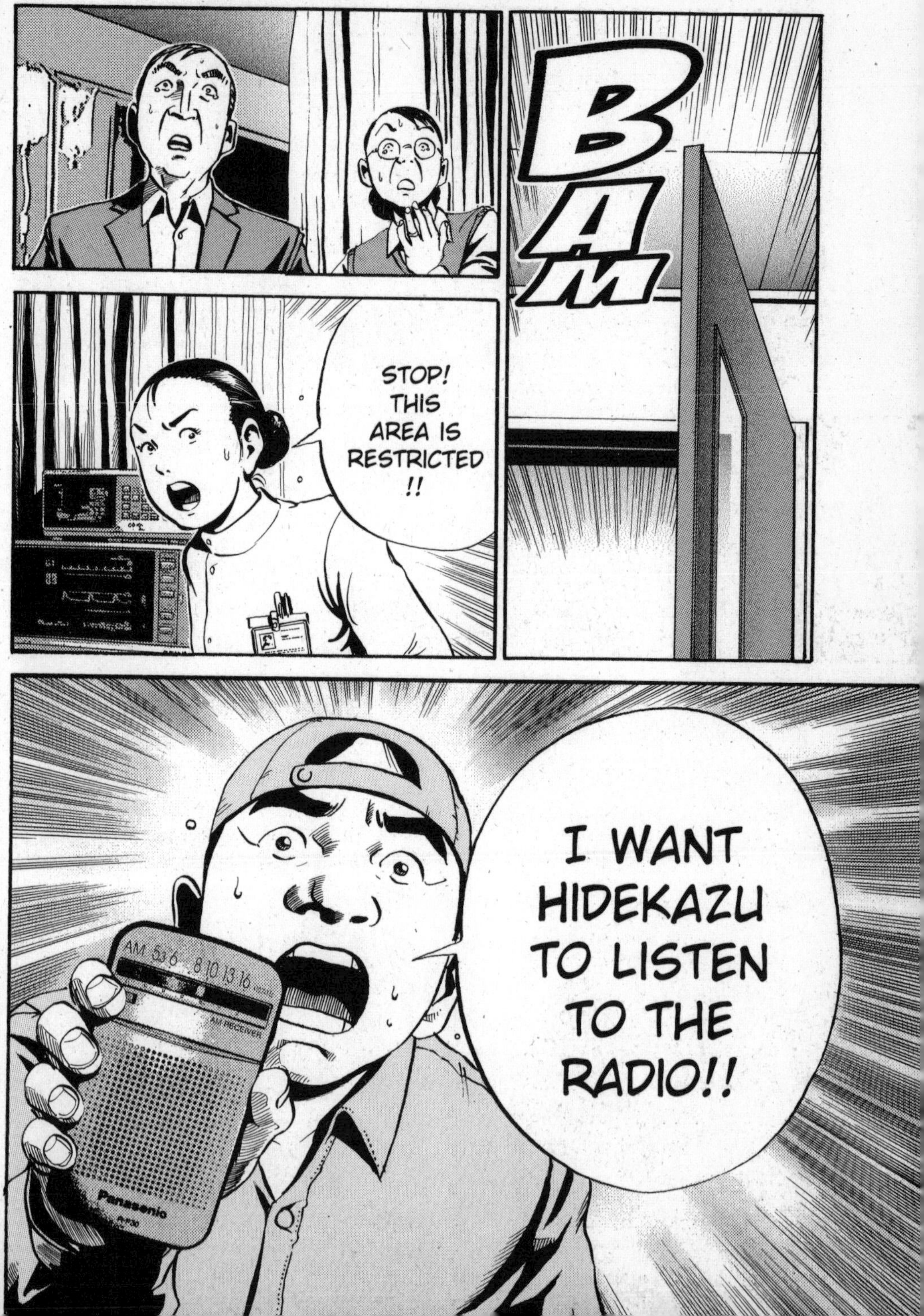
BAM
STOP! THIS AREA IS RESTRICTED!!
I WANT HIDEKAZU TO LISTEN TO THE RADIO!!
AM RECEIVER
Panasonic

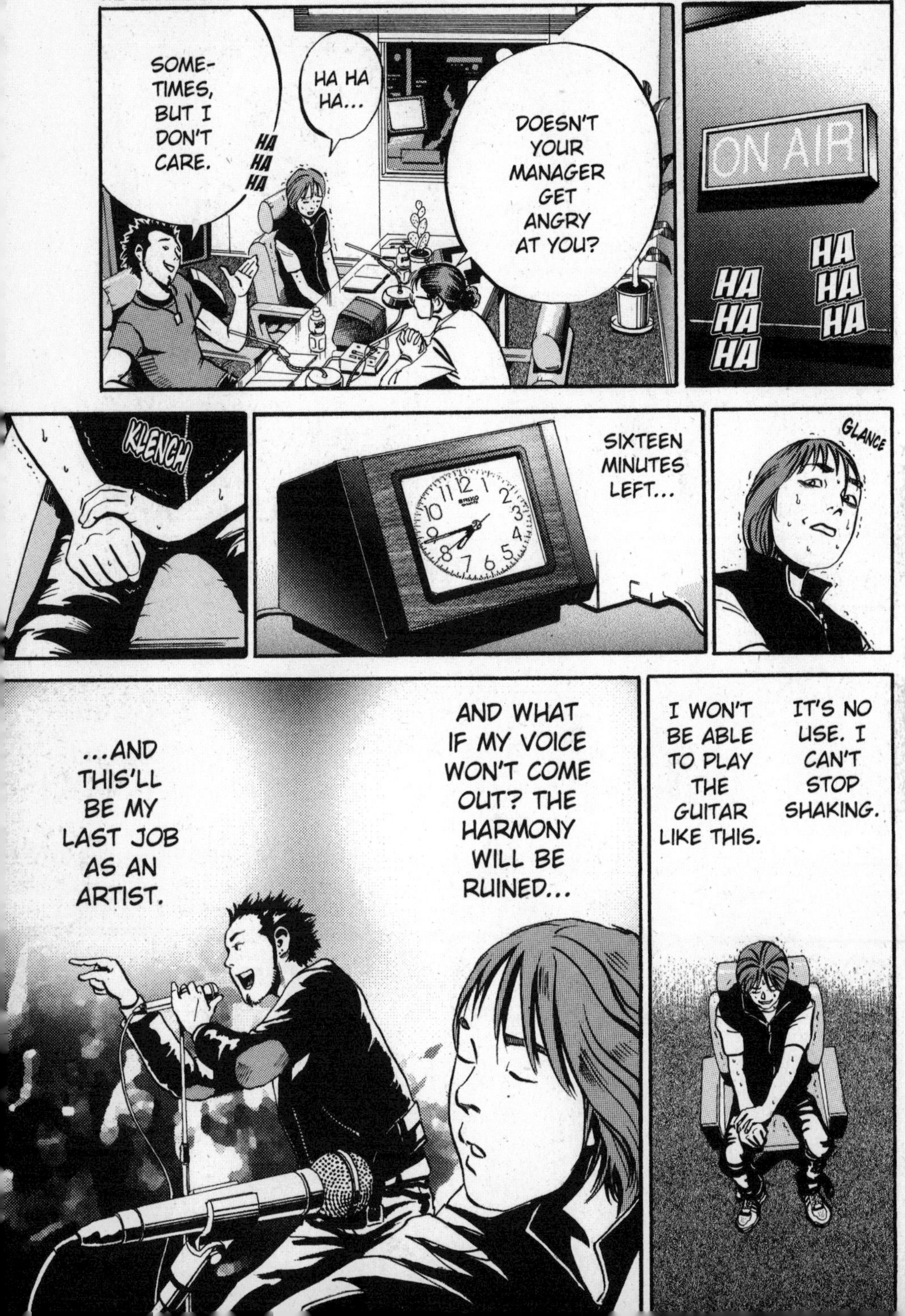
ON AIR
HA HA HA
HA HA HA
DOESN'T YOUR MANAGER GET ANGRY AT YOU?
HA HA HA...
SOME-TIMES, BUT I DON'T CARE.
HA HA HA
GLANCE
SIXTEEN MINUTES LEFT...
KLENCH
IT'S NO USE. I CAN'T STOP SHAKING.
I WON'T BE ABLE TO PLAY THE GUITAR LIKE THIS.
AND WHAT IF MY VOICE WON'T COME OUT? THE HARMONY WILL BE RUINED...
...AND THIS'LL BE MY LAST JOB AS AN ARTIST.

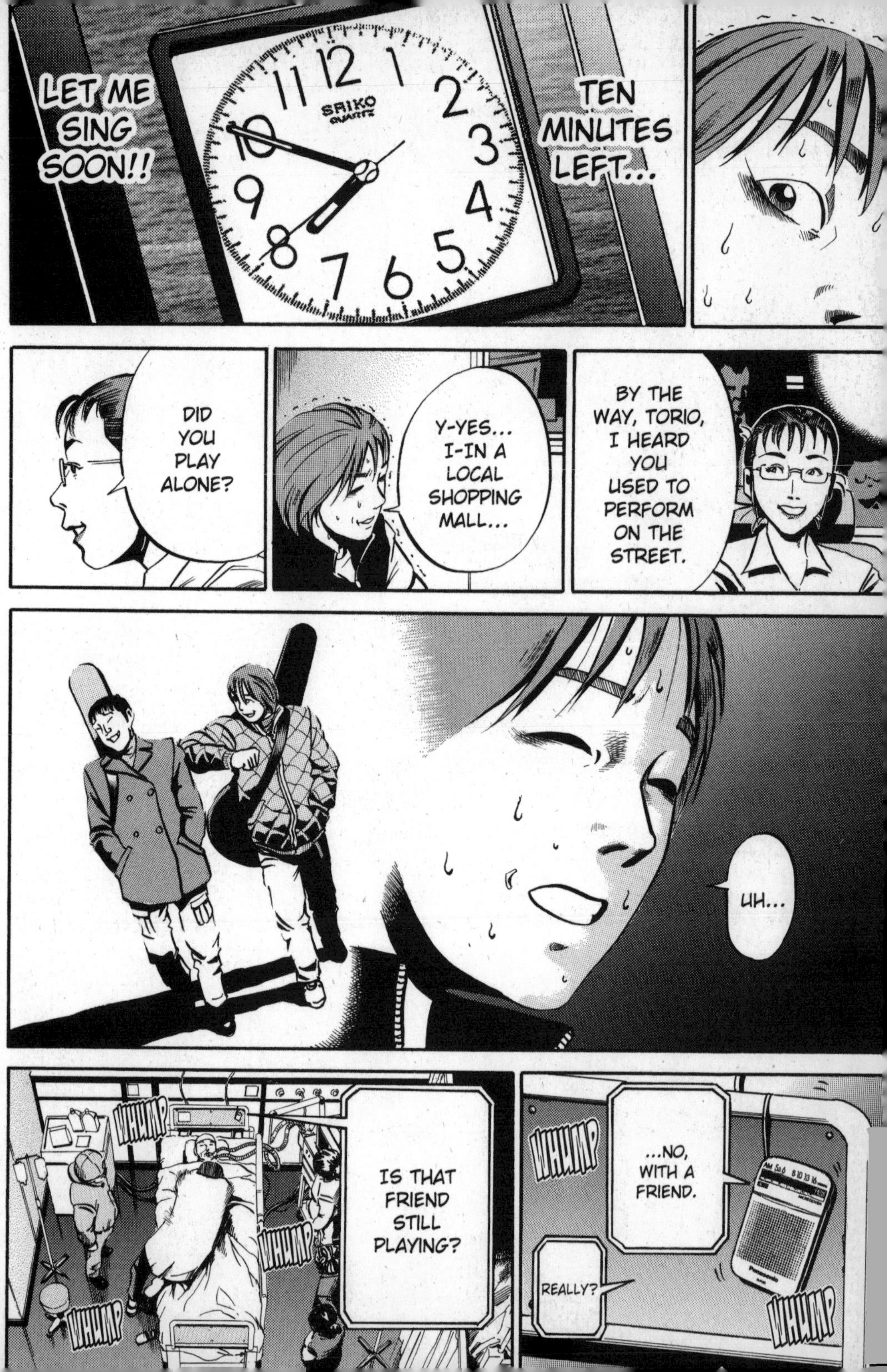
TEN MINUTES LEFT...
LET ME SING SOON!!
BY THE WAY, TORIO, I HEARD YOU USED TO PERFORM ON THE STREET.
Y-YES... I-IN A LOCAL SHOPPING MALL...
DID YOU PLAY ALONE?
UH...
WHUMP
...NO, WITH A FRIEND.
REALLY?
WHUMP
WHUMP
IS THAT FRIEND STILL PLAYING?
WHUMP
WHUMP

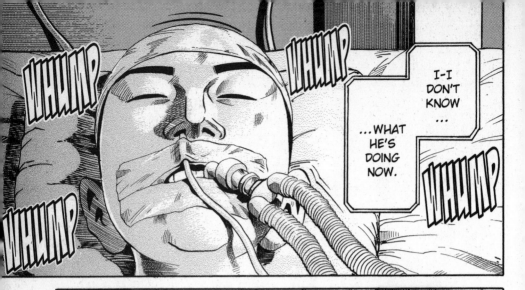

WHUMP WHUMP WHUMP WHUMP

I-I DON'T KNOW...

...WHAT HE'S DOING NOW.

WELL, LOTS OF PEOPLE PLAY ON THE STREET...

...BUT IF YOU DON'T HAVE A GOOD SOUND, IT'S HARD TO MAKE A LIVING.

BUT TORIO'S DIFFERENT.

WHEN IT COMES TO SOUND, THIS GUY'S GOT IT.

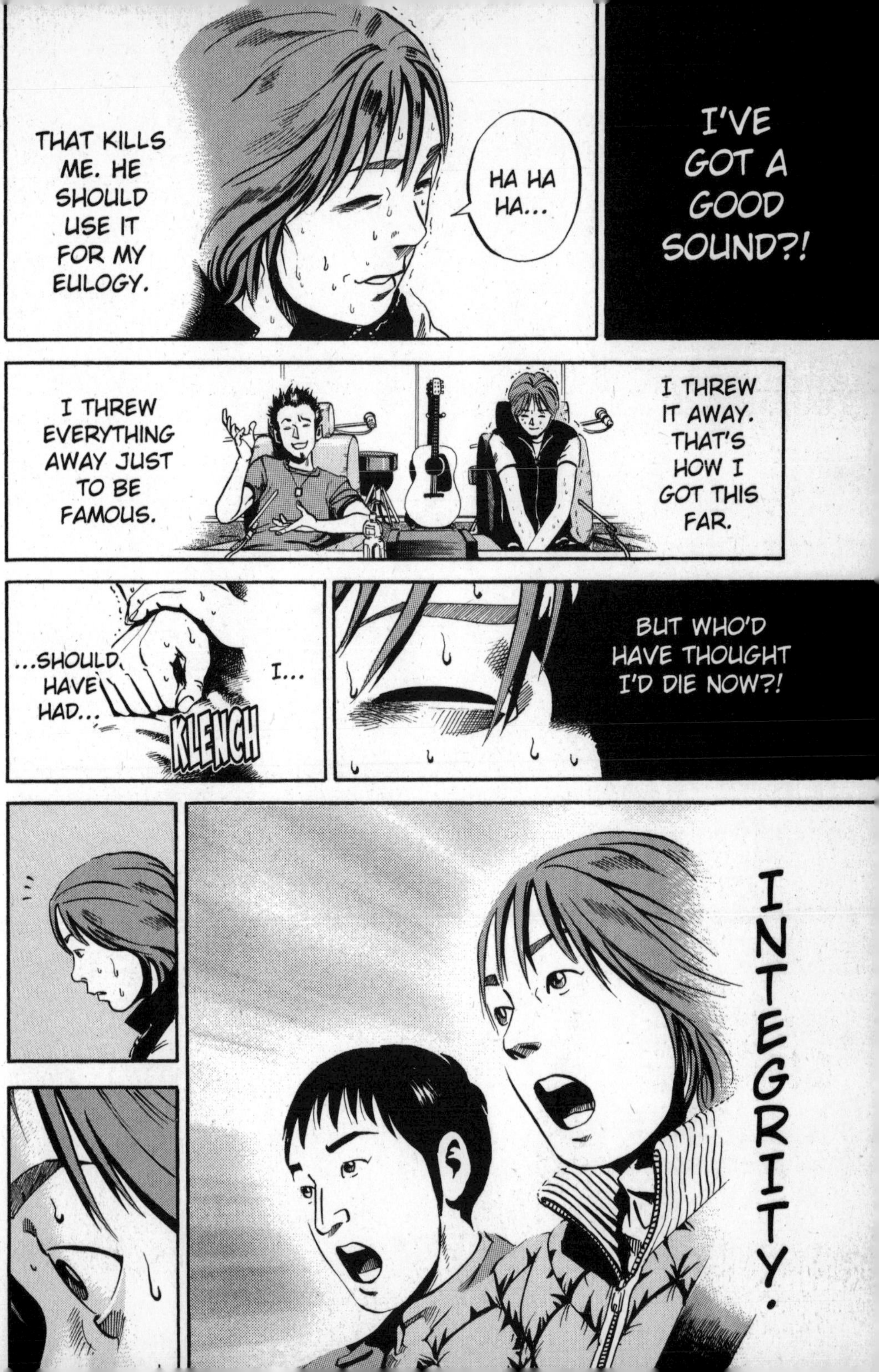
I'VE GOT A GOOD SOUND?!
HA HA HA...
THAT KILLS ME. HE SHOULD USE IT FOR MY EULOGY.
I THREW IT AWAY. THAT'S HOW I GOT THIS FAR.
I THREW EVERYTHING AWAY JUST TO BE FAMOUS.
BUT WHO'D HAVE THOUGHT I'D DIE NOW?!
I...
...SHOULD HAVE HAD...
KLENCH
INTEGRITY.

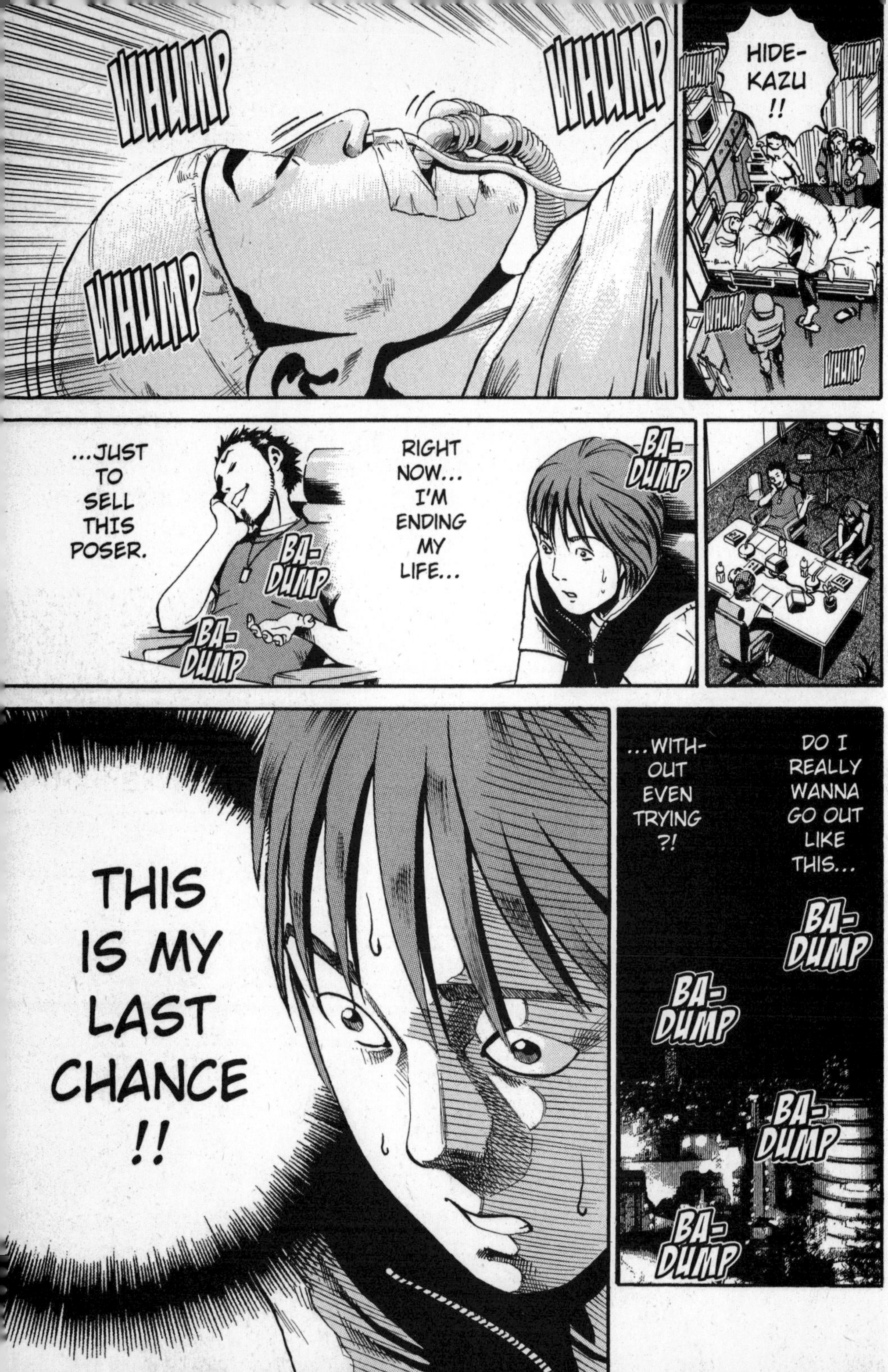
WHUMP
HIDE-KAZU!!
WHUMP
WHUMP
WHUMP
WHUMP
WHUMP
WHUMP
BA-DUMP
RIGHT NOW... I'M ENDING MY LIFE...
...JUST TO SELL THIS POSER.
BA-DUMP
BA-DUMP
DO I REALLY WANNA GO OUT LIKE THIS...
...WITH-OUT EVEN TRYING?!
BA-DUMP
BA-DUMP
BA-DUMP
BA-DUMP
THIS IS MY LAST CHANCE!!

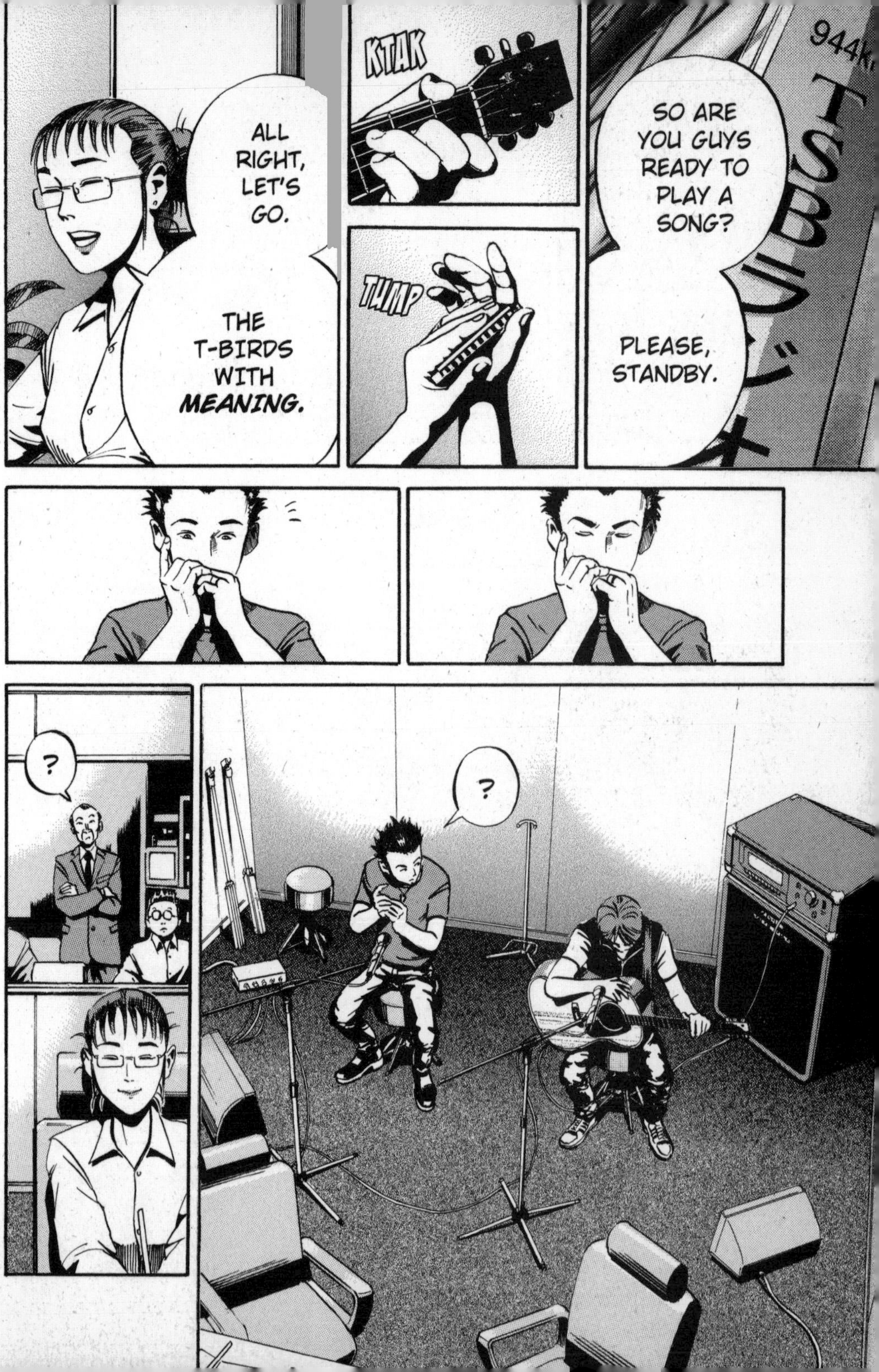
SO ARE YOU GUYS READY TO PLAY A SONG?
PLEASE, STANDBY.
KTAK
THMP
ALL RIGHT, LET'S GO.
THE T-BIRDS WITH *MEANING.*
?
?

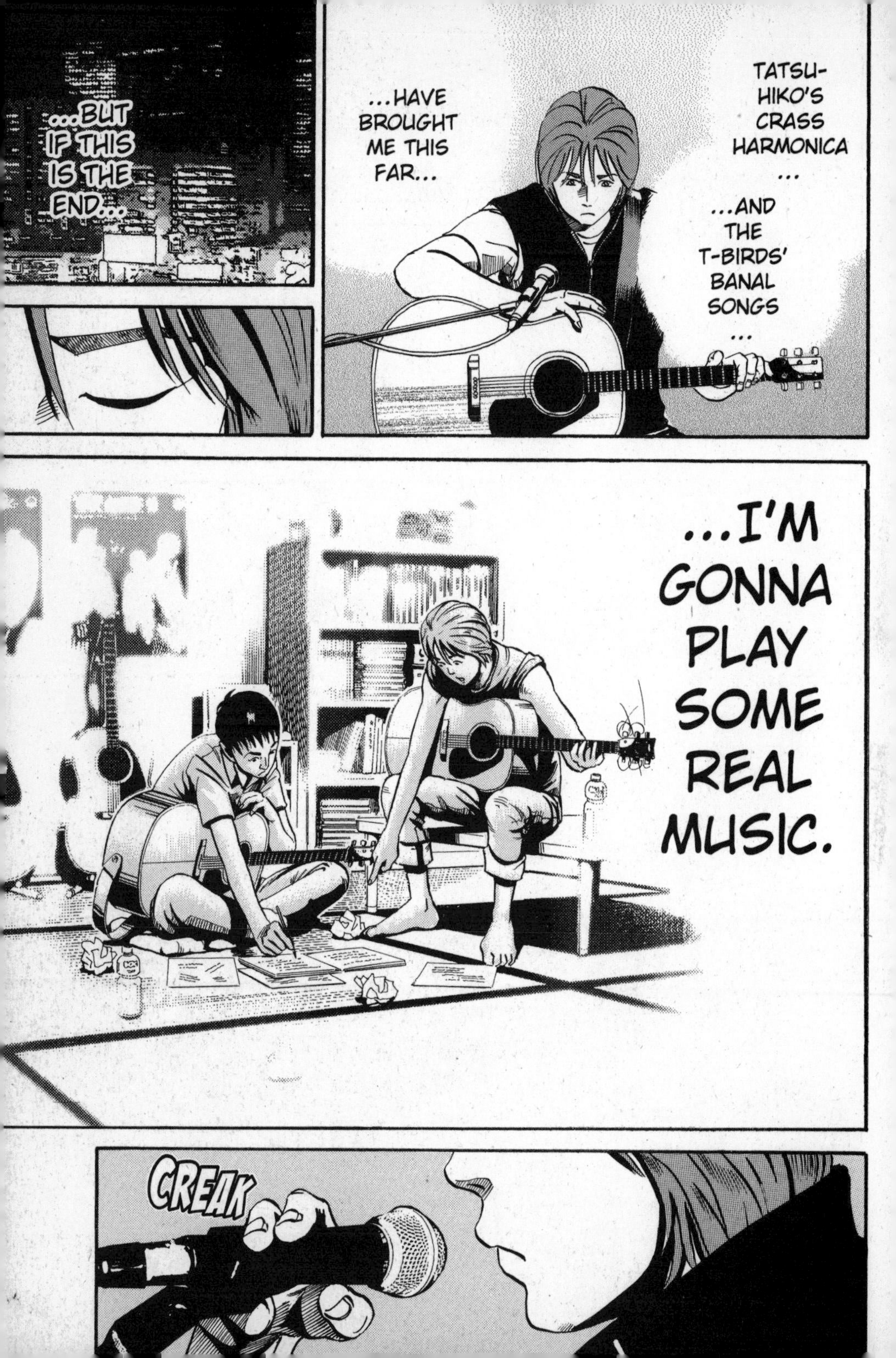
TATSU-HIKO'S CRASS HARMONICA ...
...AND THE T-BIRDS' BANAL SONGS ...
...HAVE BROUGHT ME THIS FAR...
...BUT IF THIS IS THE END...
...I'M GONNA PLAY SOME REAL MUSIC.
CREAK

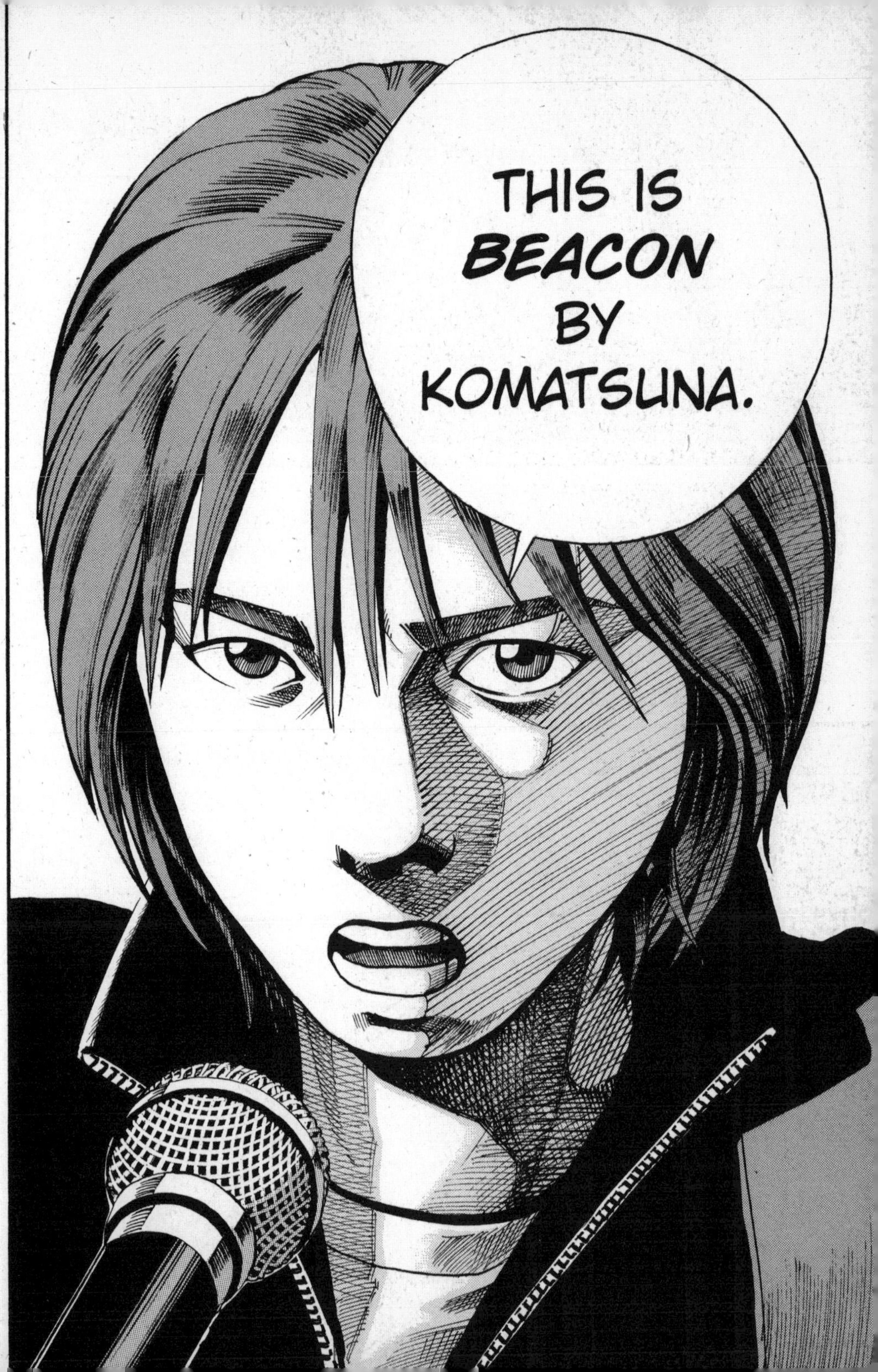
THIS IS BEACON BY KOMATSUNA.

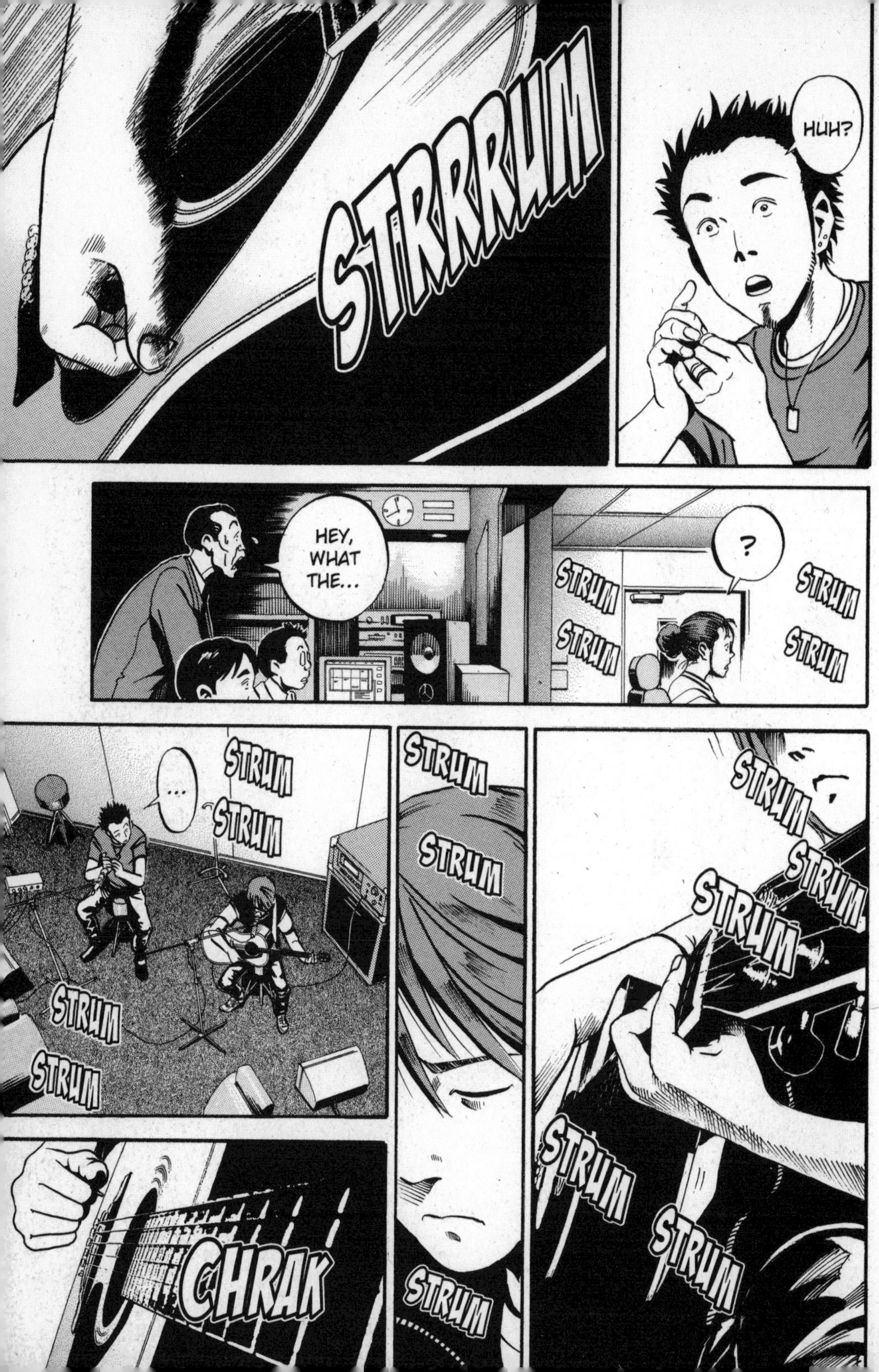
HUH?
STRRRUM
STRUM
STRUM
?
STRUM
STRUM
HEY, WHAT THE...
STRUM
STRUM
STRUM
STRUM
STRUM
STRUM
STRUM
STRUM
...
STRUM
STRUM
STRUM
STRUM
CHRAK

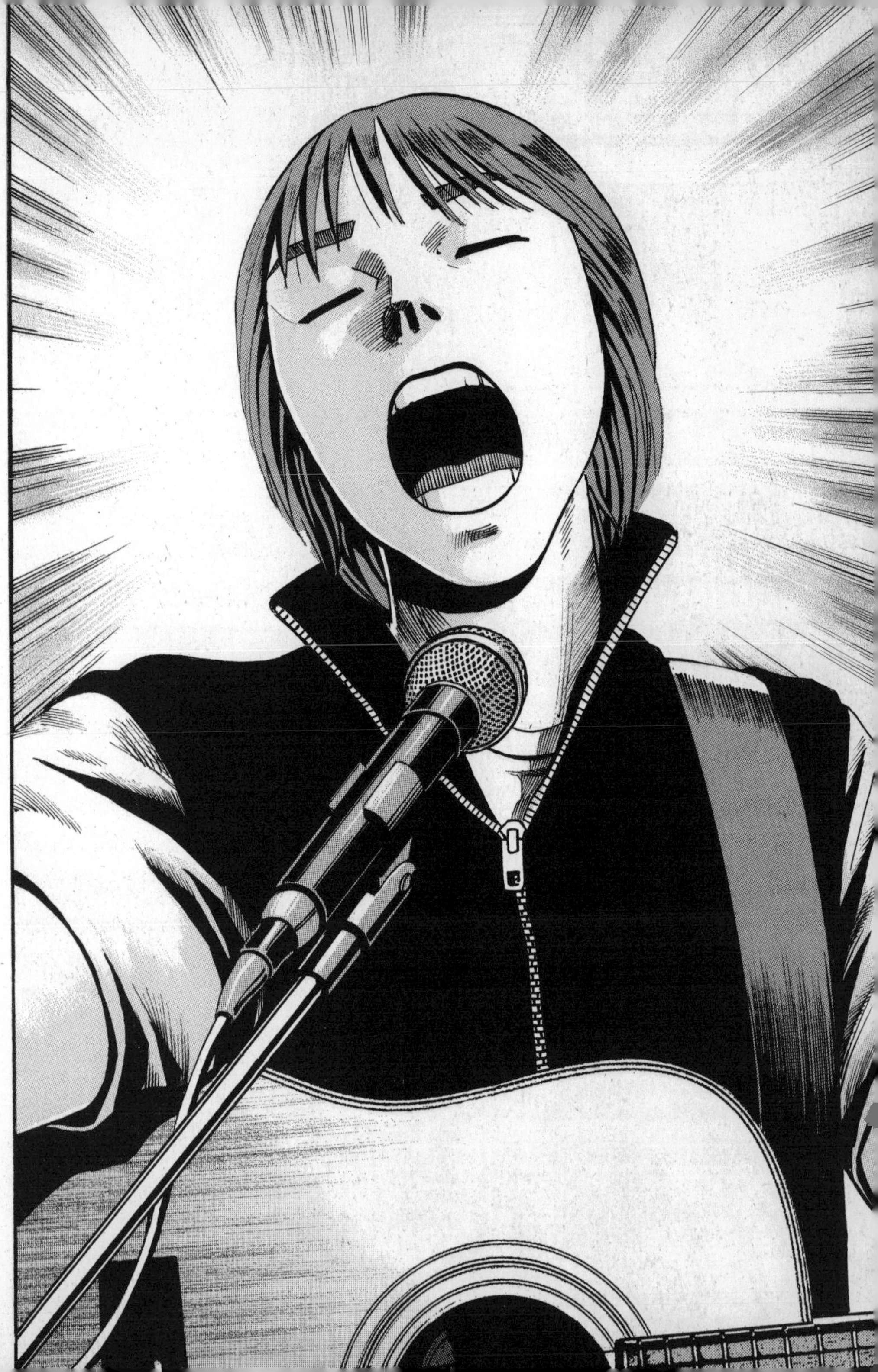

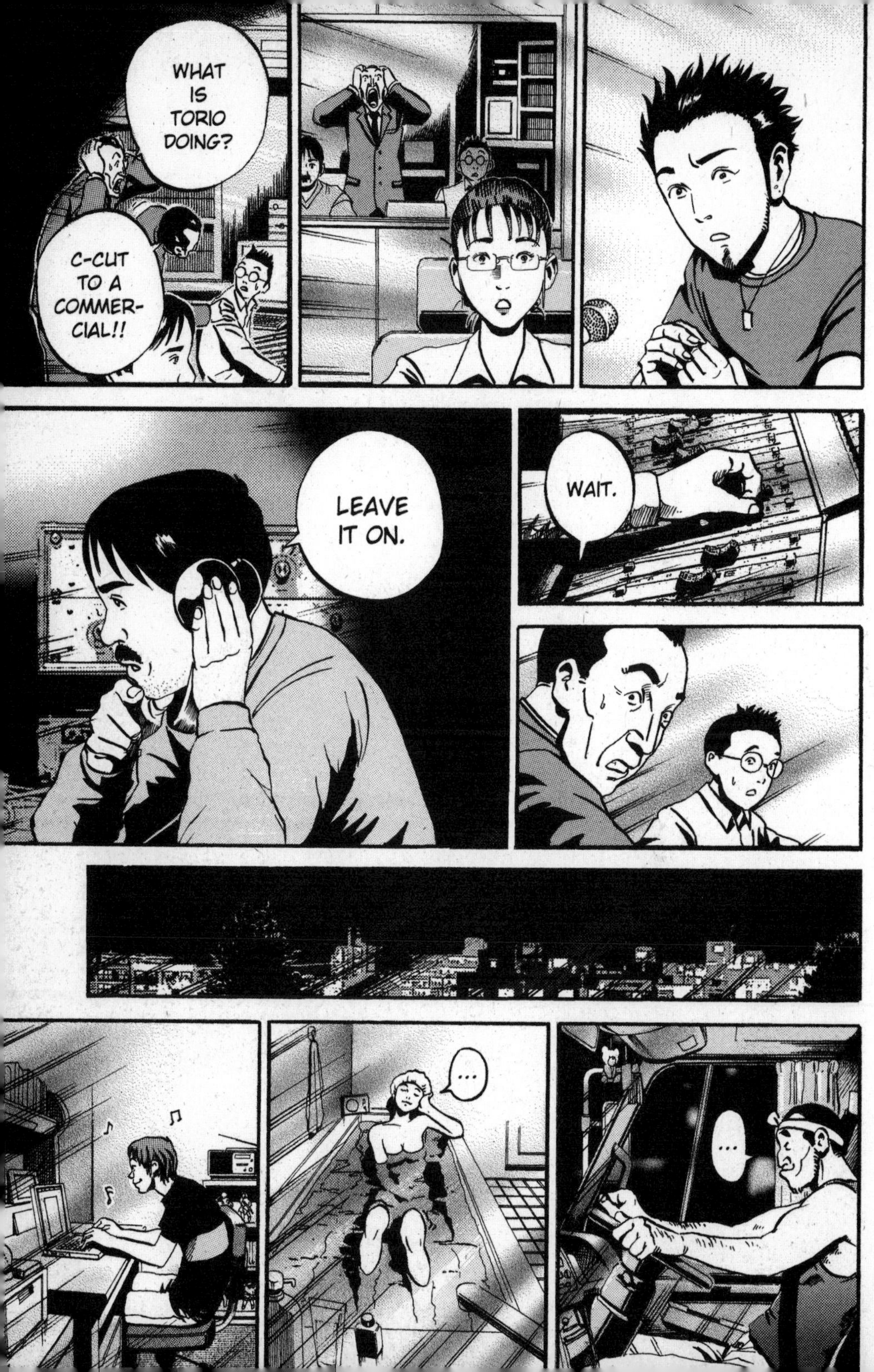
WHAT IS TORIO DOING?
C-CUT TO A COMMERCIAL!!
WAIT.
LEAVE IT ON.
...
...

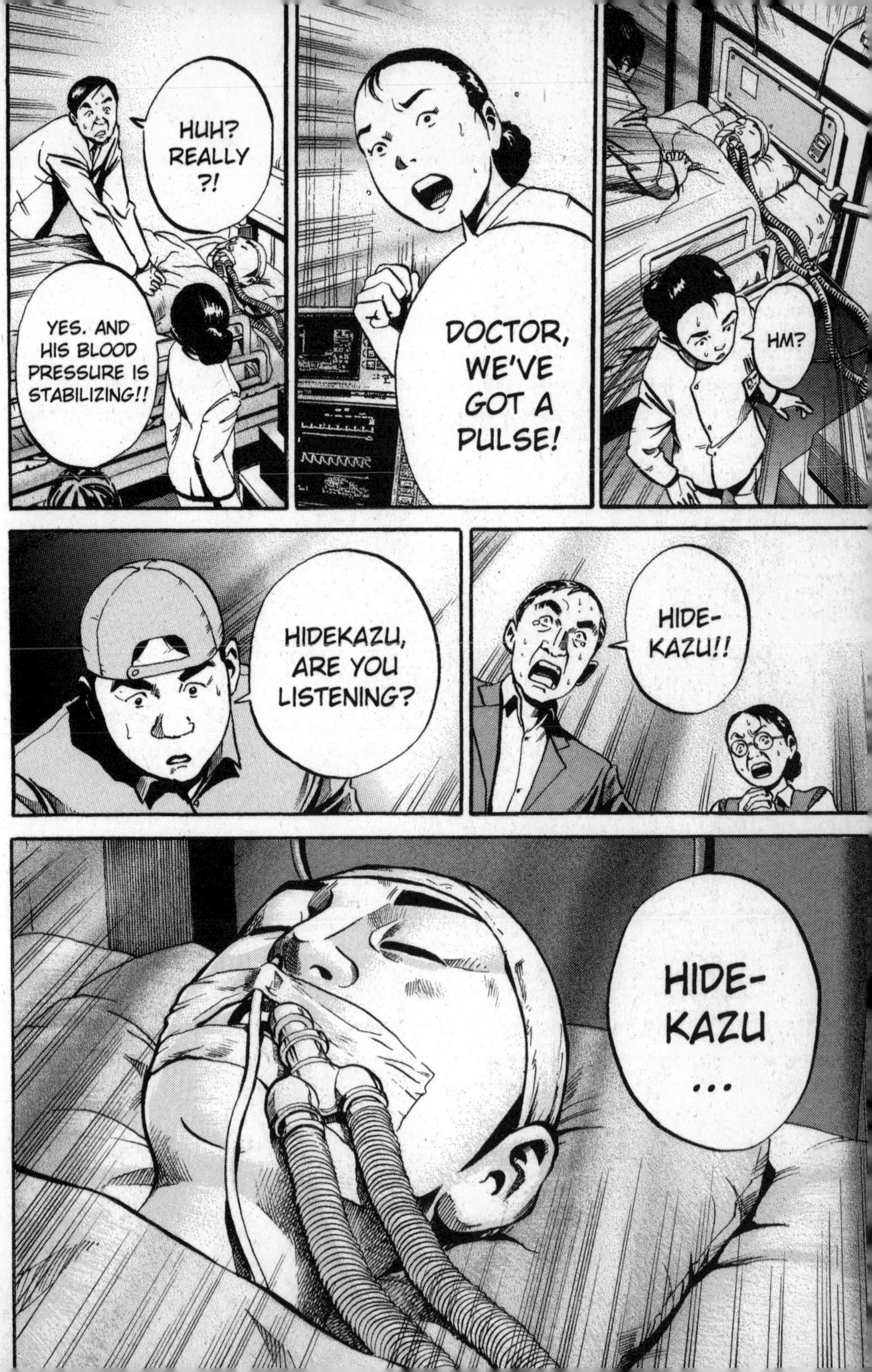
HM?
DOCTOR, WE'VE GOT A PULSE!
HUH? REALLY ?!
YES. AND HIS BLOOD PRESSURE IS STABILIZING!!
HIDE-KAZU!!
HIDEKAZU, ARE YOU LISTENING?
HIDE-KAZU ...

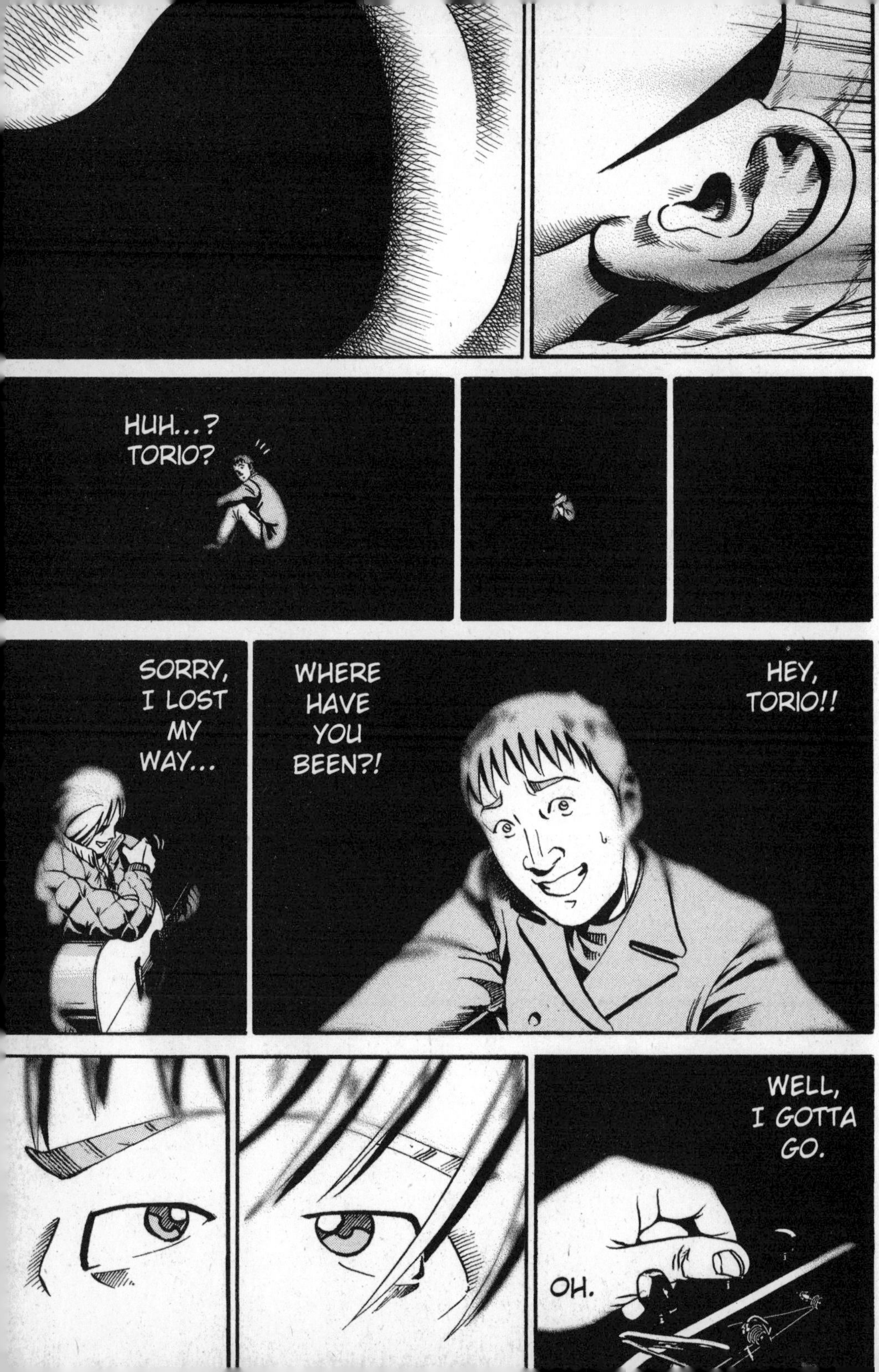
HUH...? TORIO?
HEY, TORIO!!
WHERE HAVE YOU BEEN?!
SORRY, I LOST MY WAY...
WELL, I GOTTA GO.
OH.

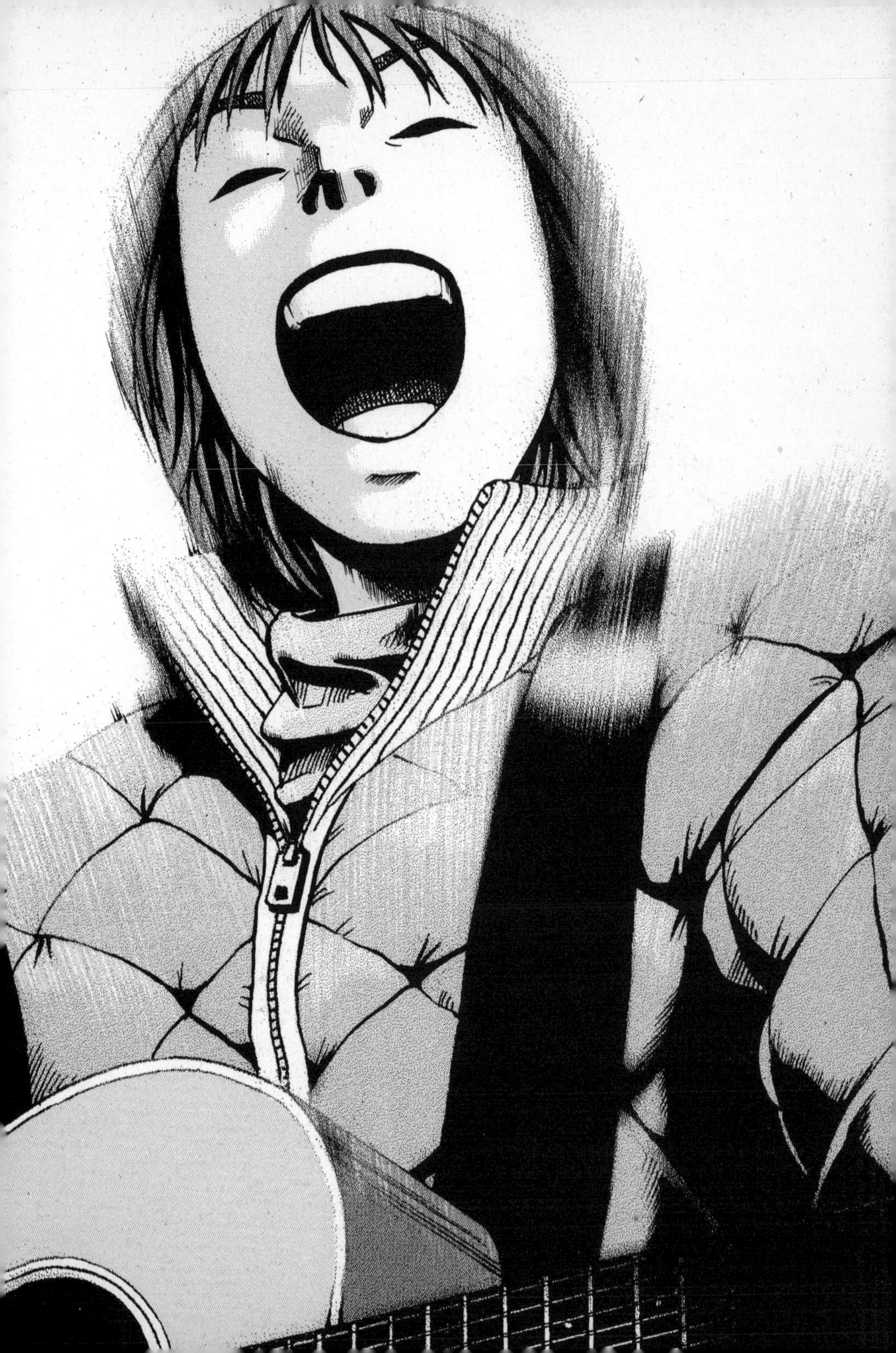

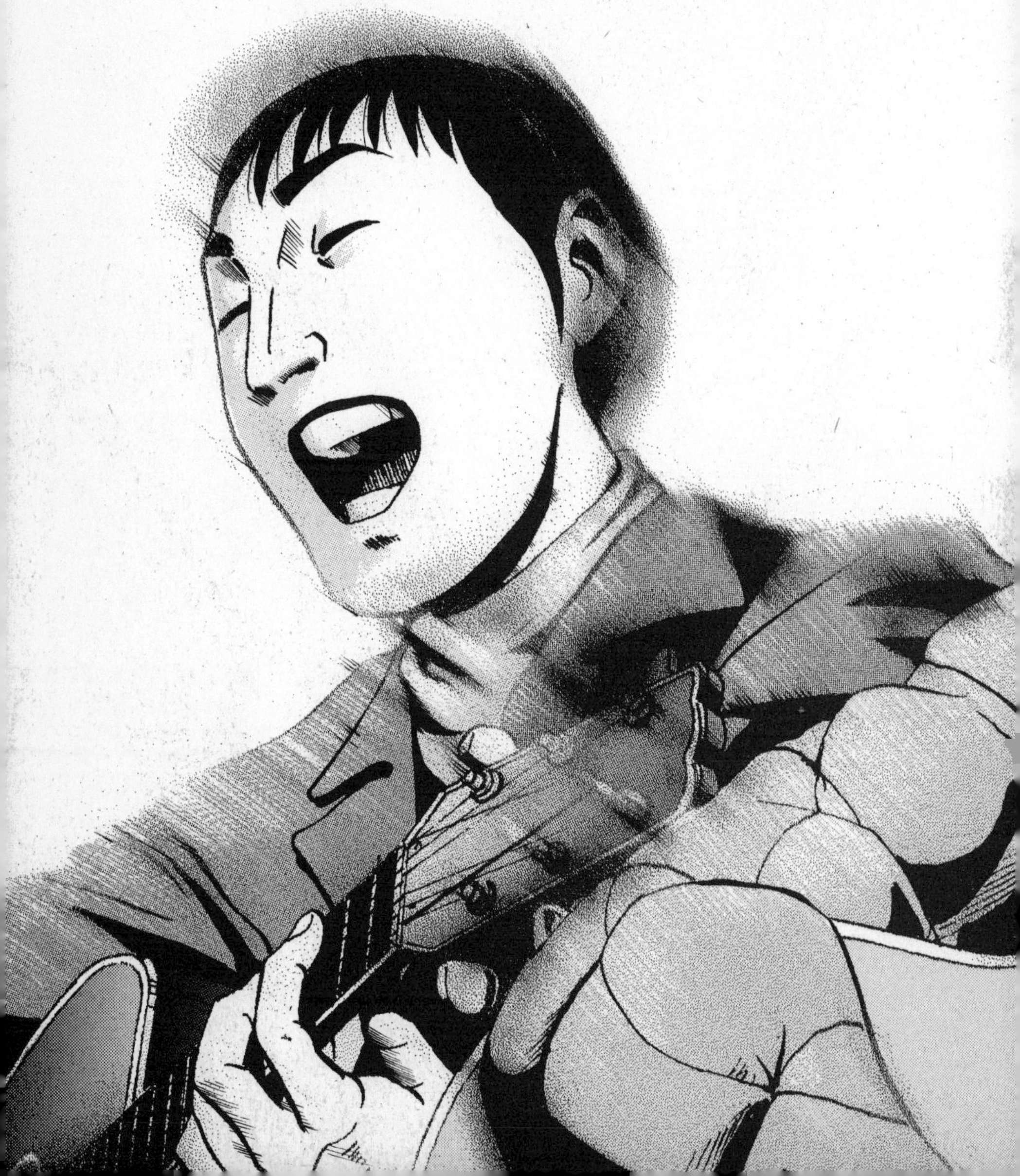

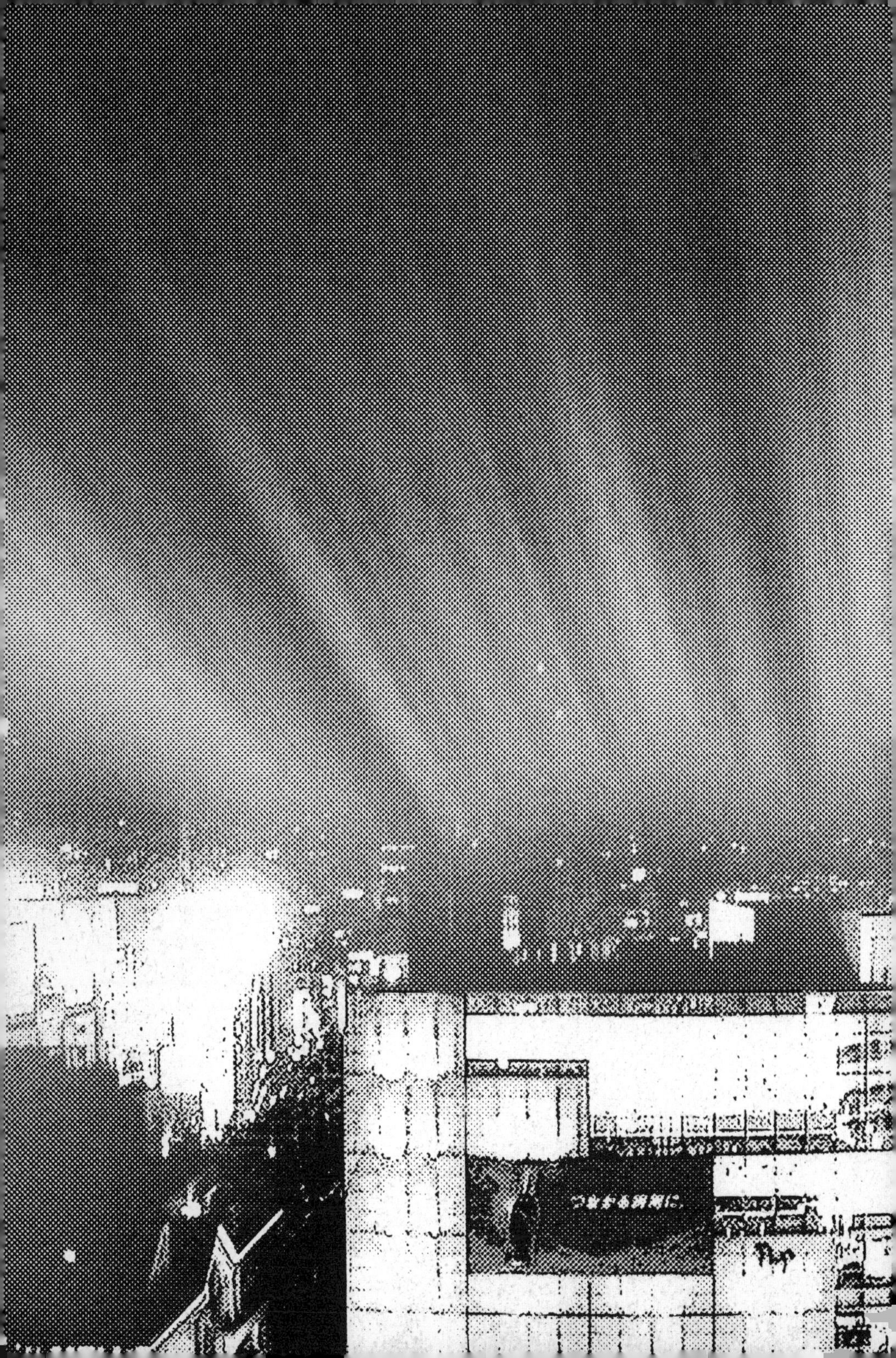

STRUM
STRUM
STRUM
STRUM
TICK

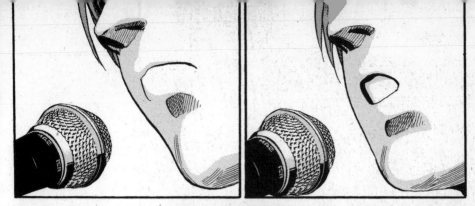

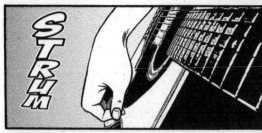

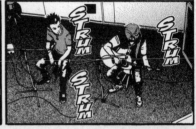

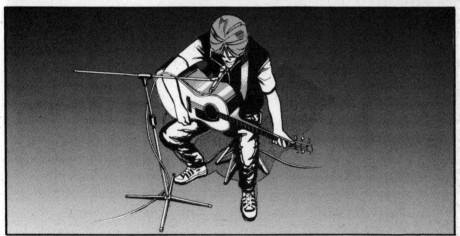

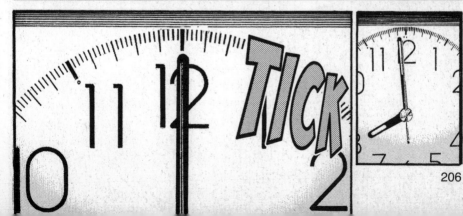

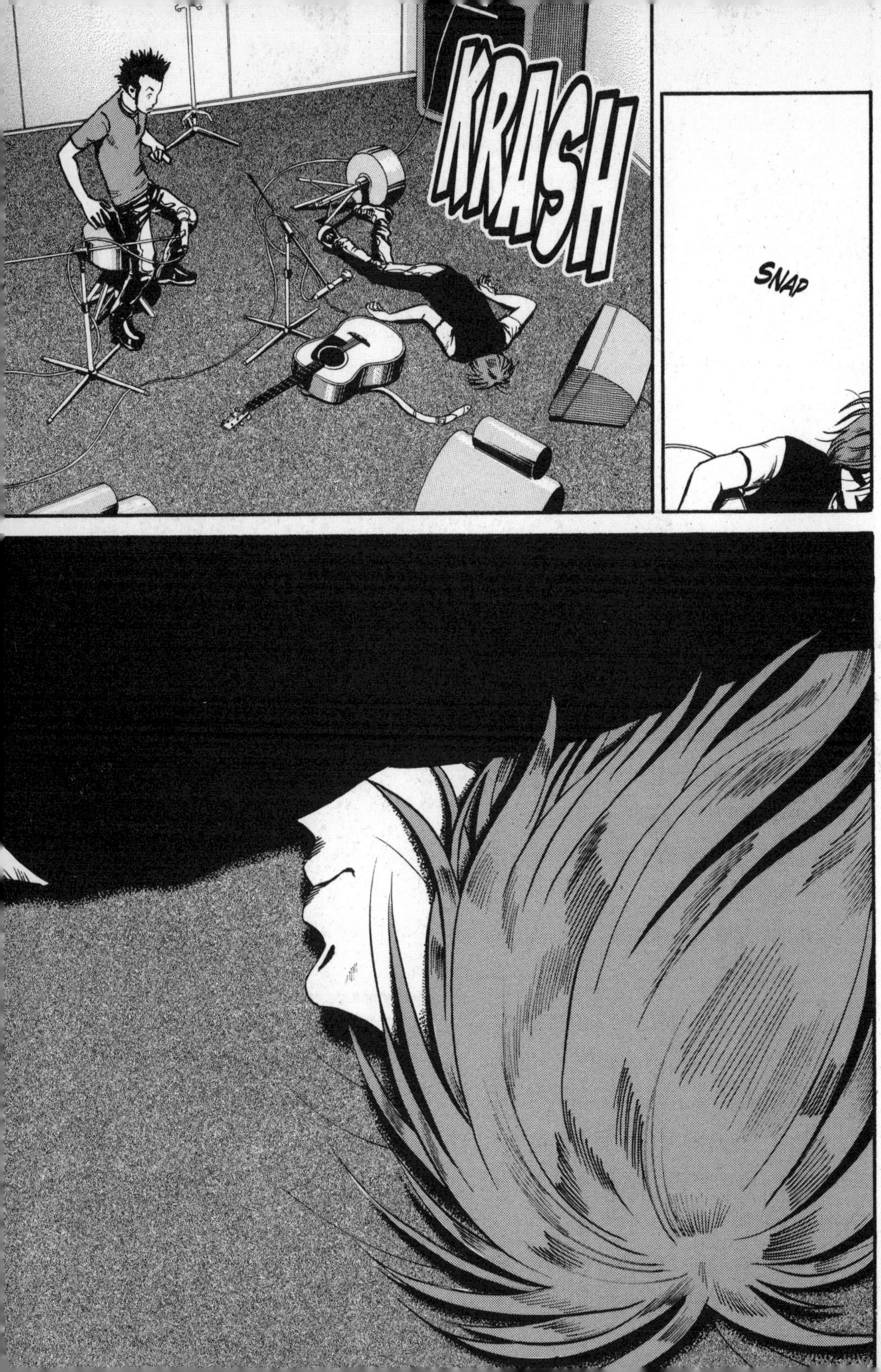
SNAP
KRASH

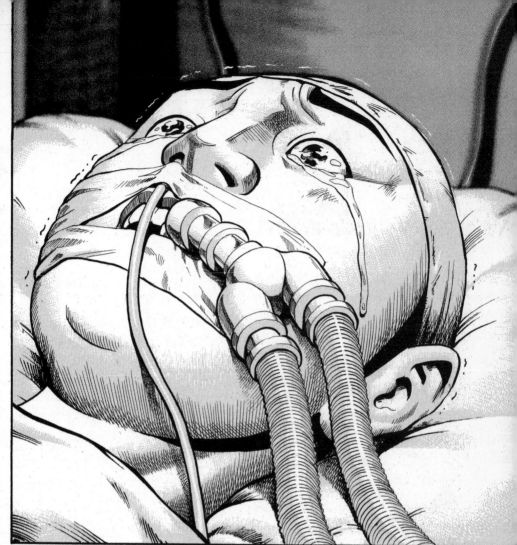

MR. MORIO, CAN YOU HEAR ME?

HIDEKAZU!!

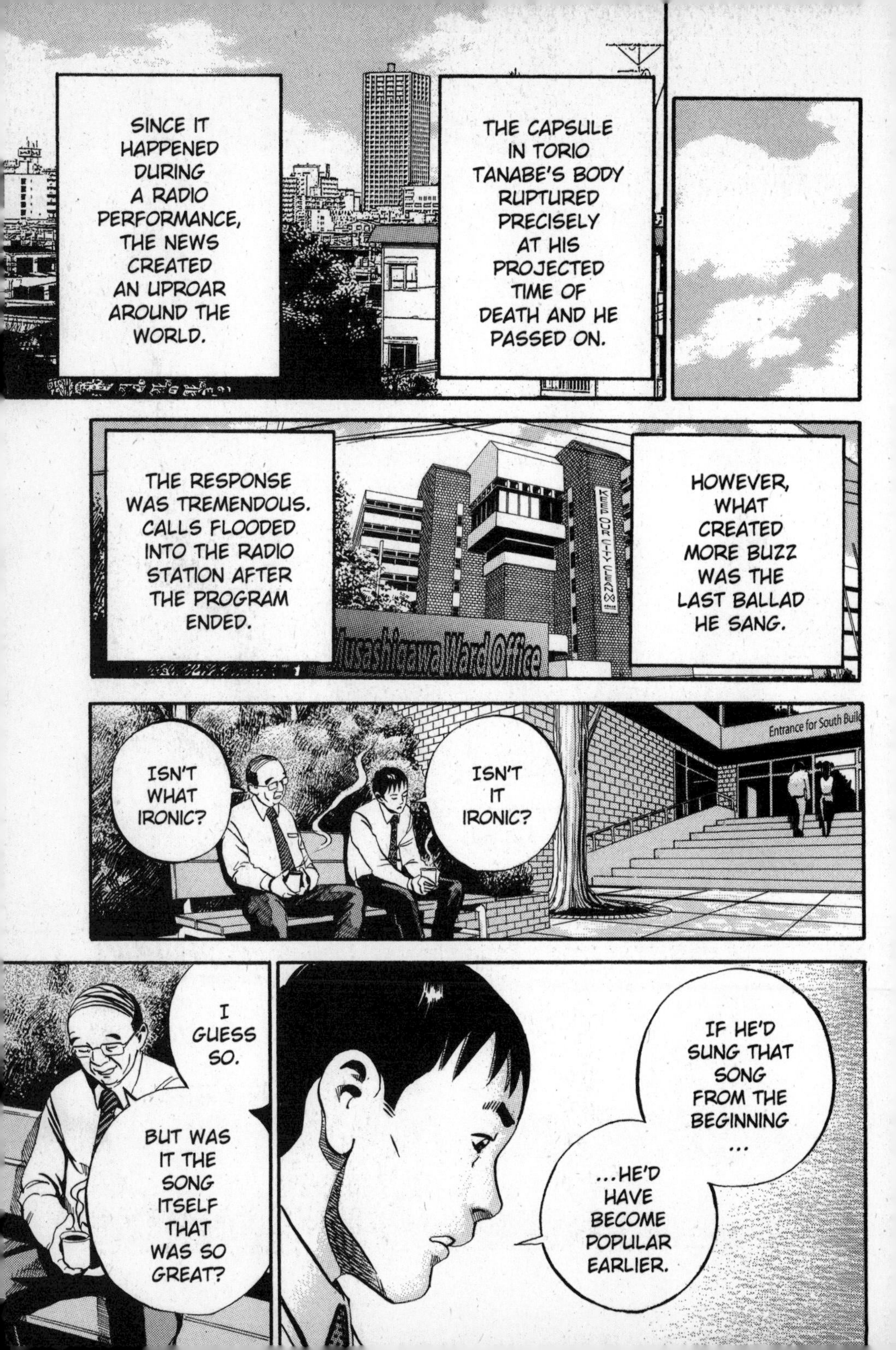
THE CAPSULE IN TORIO TANABE'S BODY RUPTURED PRECISELY AT HIS PROJECTED TIME OF DEATH AND HE PASSED ON.
SINCE IT HAPPENED DURING A RADIO PERFORMANCE, THE NEWS CREATED AN UPROAR AROUND THE WORLD.
HOWEVER, WHAT CREATED MORE BUZZ WAS THE LAST BALLAD HE SANG.
KEEP OUR CITY CLEAN
THE RESPONSE WAS TREMENDOUS. CALLS FLOODED INTO THE RADIO STATION AFTER THE PROGRAM ENDED.
ISN'T IT IRONIC?
ISN'T WHAT IRONIC?
IF HE'D SUNG THAT SONG FROM THE BEGINNING...
...HE'D HAVE BECOME POPULAR EARLIER.
I GUESS SO.
BUT WAS IT THE SONG ITSELF THAT WAS SO GREAT?

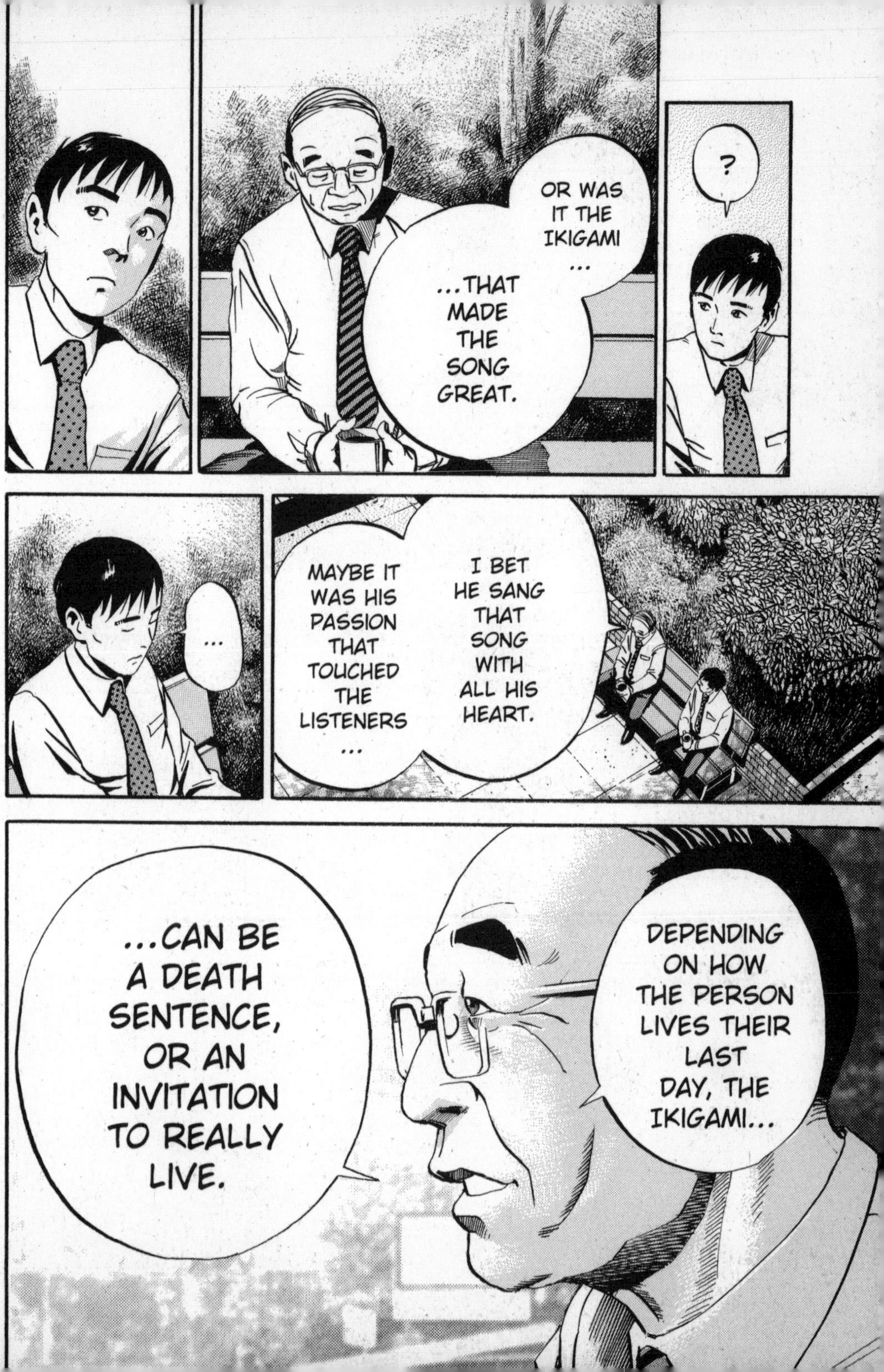
?
OR WAS IT THE IKIGAMI ...
...THAT MADE THE SONG GREAT.
I BET HE SANG THAT SONG WITH ALL HIS HEART.
MAYBE IT WAS HIS PASSION THAT TOUCHED THE LISTENERS ...
...
DEPENDING ON HOW THE PERSON LIVES THEIR LAST DAY, THE IKIGAMI...
...CAN BE A DEATH SENTENCE, OR AN INVITATION TO REALLY LIVE.

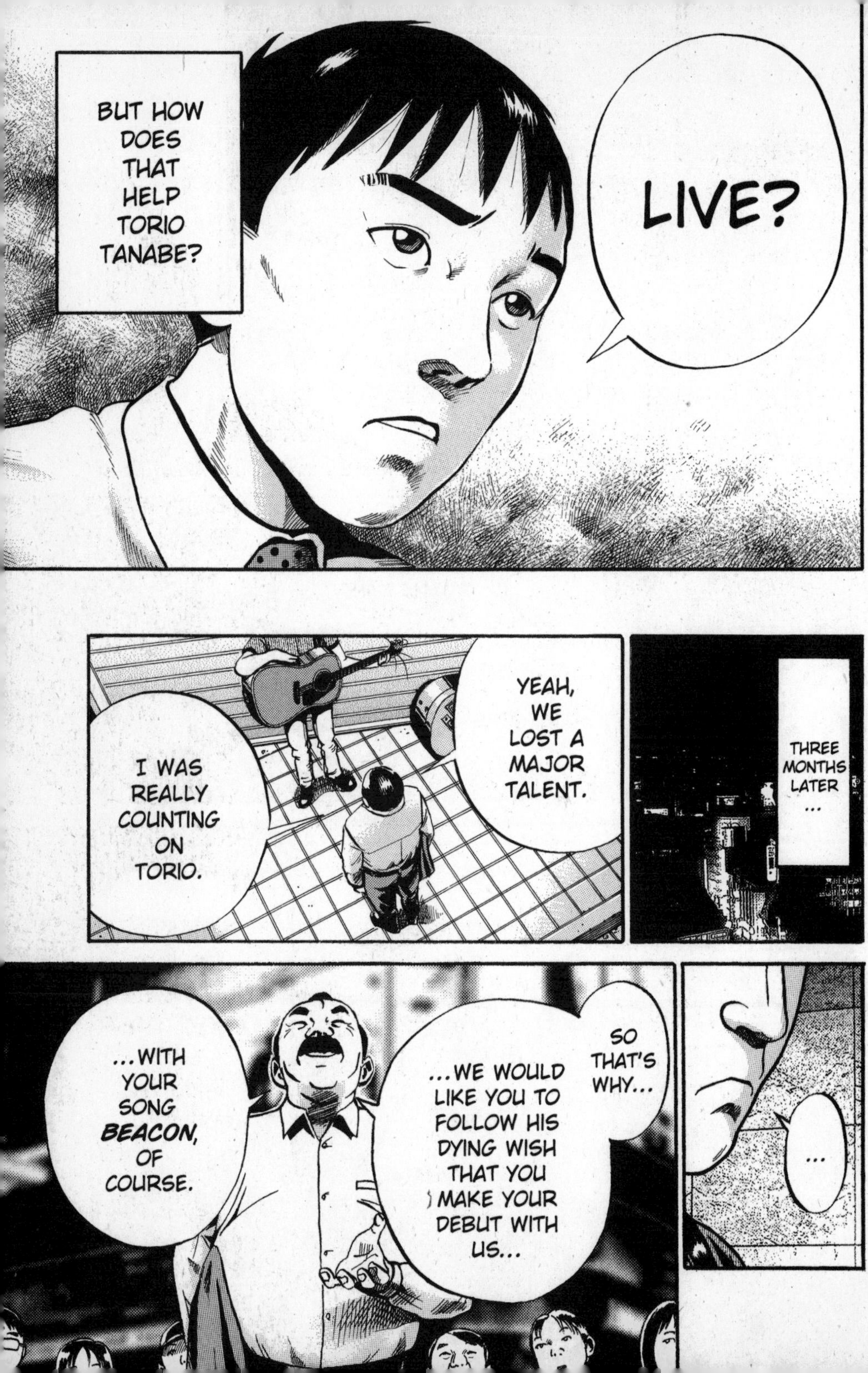
LIVE?
BUT HOW DOES THAT HELP TORIO TANABE?
THREE MONTHS LATER ...
YEAH, WE LOST A MAJOR TALENT.
I WAS REALLY COUNTING ON TORIO.
...
SO THAT'S WHY...
...WE WOULD LIKE YOU TO FOLLOW HIS DYING WISH THAT YOU MAKE YOUR DEBUT WITH US...
...WITH YOUR SONG *BEACON*, OF COURSE.

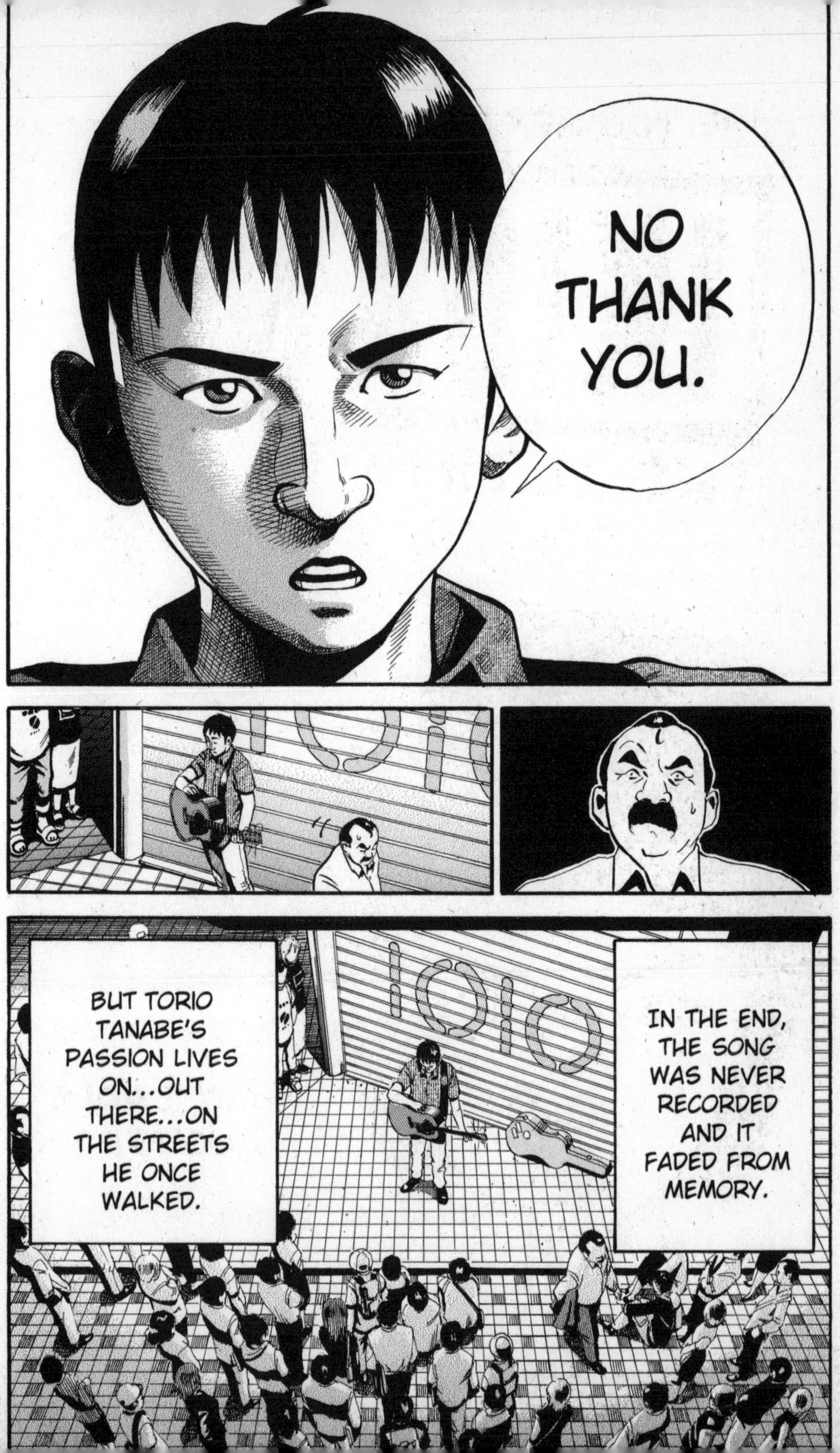
NO THANK YOU.
IN THE END, THE SONG WAS NEVER RECORDED AND IT FADED FROM MEMORY.
BUT TORIO TANABE'S PASSION LIVES ON...OUT THERE...ON THE STREETS HE ONCE WALKED.

ARE YOU NEXT?

IKIGAMI

THE ULTIMATE LIMIT

VOL.**2**

**Featuring
Episodes 3
*The Pure
Love Drug*
& 4 *Leaving
for War!***

**AVAILABLE
AUGUST 2009!**

Motoro Mase was born in Aichi in Japan
in 1969 and is also the artist of *Kyoichi*
and, with Keigo Higashino, *HE∀DS*,
which, like *Ikigami*, was serialized in
Young Sunday. In 1998, Mase's *AREA*
was nominated for Shogakukan's 43rd
grand prize for a comic by a new artist.

LOVE MANGA?
LET US KNOW WHAT YOU THINK!

OUR MANGA SURVEY IS NOW AVAILABLE ONLINE. PLEASE VISIT: VIZ.COM/MANGASURVEY

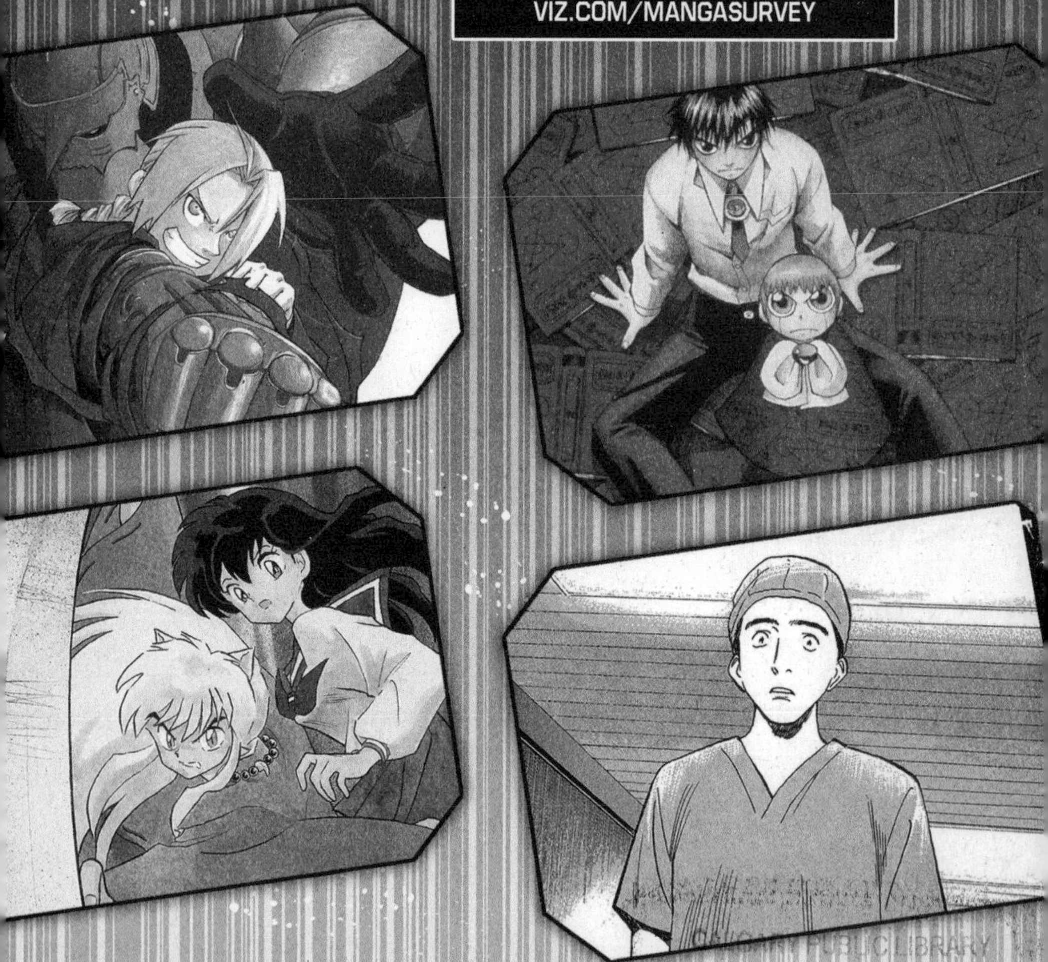

HELP US MAKE THE MANGA YOU LOVE BETTER!

viz media